Topics in Information Systems

Editors:

Michael L. Brodie
John Mylopoulos
Joachim W. Schmidt

Query Processing in Database Systems

Edited by

Won Kim
David S. Reiner
Don S. Batory

With 127 Figures

Springer-Verlag
Berlin Heidelberg New York Tokyo

Series Editors

Dr. Michael L. Brodie
Computer Corporation of America, Four Cambridge Center
Cambridge, MA 02142/USA

Dr. John Mylopoulos
Department of Computer Science, University of Toronto
Toronto, Ontario M5S 1A4/Canada

Dr. Joachim W. Schmidt
Fachbereich Informatik, Johann Wolfgang Goethe-Universität
Dantestraße 9, D-6000 Frankfurt a. M. 11/FRG

Volume Editors

Dr. Won Kim
Microelectronics & Computer Technology Corporation
9430 Research Boulevard, Austin, TX 78759/USA

Dr. David S. Reiner
Computer Corporation of America, Four Cambridge Center
Cambridge, MA 02142/USA

Dr. Don S. Batory
Department of Computer Science, The University of Texas
at Austin, Austin, TX 78712/USA

ISBN-13:978-3-642-82377-0 e-ISBN-13:978-3-642-82375-6
DOI: 10.1007/978-3-642-82375-6

Library of Congress Cataloging in Publication Data. Main entry under title: Query processing in database systems. (Topics in information systems) 1. Data base management–Addresses, essays, lectures. 2. Electronic data processing–Distributed processing–Addresses, essays, lectures. I. Kim, Won. II. Reiner, D. S. (David S.), 1952-. III. Batory, D. S. (Don S.), 1953-. IV. Series. QA76.9.D3Q47. 1984. 001.64. 84-20274
ISBN-13:978-3-642-82377-0 (U.S.)

Softcover reprint of the hardcover 1st edition 1985

2145/3140-543210

Topics in Information Systems

Series Description

Dramatic advances in hardware technology have opened the door to a new generation of computer systems. At the same time, the growing demand for information systems of ever-increasing complexity and precision has stimulated the need in every area of Computer Science for more powerful higher-level concepts, techniques, and tools.

Future information systems will be expected to acquire, maintain, retrieve, manipulate, and present many different kinds of information. These systems will require user-friendly interfaces, powerful reasoning capabilities, and shared access to large information bases. Whereas the needed hardware technology appears to be within reach, the corresponding software technology for building these systems is not. The required dramatic improvements in software productivity will come from advanced application development environments based on powerful new techniques and languages.

The **concepts, techniques**, and **tools** necessary for the design, implementation, and use in future information systems are expected to result from the integration of those being developed and used in currently disjoint areas of Computer Science. Several areas bring their unique viewpoints and technologies to existing information processing practice. One key area is **Artificial Intelligence** (AI) which provides knowledge representation and reasoning capabilities for knowledge bases grounded on semantic theories of information for correct interpretation. An equally important area is **Databases** which provides means for building and maintaining large, shared databases based on computational theories of information for efficient processing. A third important area is **Programming Languages** which provides a powerful tool kit for the construction of large programs based on linguistic and methodological theories to ensure program correctness. To meet evolving information systems requirements, additional research viewpoints and technologies are or will be required from such areas as **Software Engineering, Computer Networks, Machine Architectures,** and **Office Automation.**

Although some integration of research results has already been achieved, a quantum leap in technological integration is needed to meet the demand for future information systems. This integration is one of the major challenges to Computer Science in the 1980s.

Topics in Information Systems is a series intended to report significant contributions on the integration of concepts, techniques, and tools that advance new technologies for information system construction. The series logo symbolizes the scope of topics to be covered and the basic theme of integration.

The logo will appear on each book to indicate the topics addressed.

	Artificial Intelligence	Databases	Programming Languages
concepts			
techniques			
tools			

The first book of the series, "On Conceptual Modelling: Perspectives from Artificial Intelligence, Databases and Programming Languages", Michael L. Brodie, John Mylopoulos, and Joachim W. Schmidt (Eds.), February 1984, which deals with concepts in the three areas, has the logo:

	•	•	•

The second book, "Query Processing in Database Systems", Won Kim, David S. Reiner, and Donald S. Batory (Eds.), March 1985, which deals with Database and Programming Language concepts, AI and Database techniques, and Database system tools, has the logo:

		•	•
	•	•	
		•	

The third book, "Office Automation", Dionysios C. Tsichritzis (Ed.), March 1985, which will deal with the design and implementation of Office Systems, has the logo:

		•	
	•	•	
	•	•	•

Future books in the series will provide timely accounts of ongoing research efforts to reshape technologies intended for information system development.

March, 1985

Michael L. Brodie
John Mylopoulos
Joachim W. Schmidt

Table of Contents

Section IV. Database Updates through Views

Section V. Database Access for Special Applications

Section VI. Techniques for Optimizing the Processing of Multiple Queries

Section VII. Query Processing in Database Machines

Section VIII. Physical Database Design

Introduction

This book is an anthology of the results of research and development in database query processing during the past decade. The relational model of data provided tremendous impetus for research into query processing. Since a relational query does not specify access paths to the stored data, the database management system (DBMS) must provide an intelligent query-processing subsystem which will evaluate a number of potentially efficient strategies for processing the query and select the one that optimizes a given performance measure. The degree of sophistication of this subsystem, often called the optimizer, critically affects the performance of the DBMS.

Research into query processing thus started has taken off in several directions during the past decade. The emergence of research into distributed databases has enormously complicated the tasks of the optimizer. In a distributed environment, the database may be partitioned into horizontal or vertical fragments of relations. Replicas of the fragments may be stored in different sites of a network and even migrate to other sites. The measure of performance of a query in a distributed system must include the communication cost between sites. To minimize communication costs for queries involving multiple relations across multiple sites, optimizers may also have to consider semi-join techniques.

An extra dimension of difficulty arises when the database is distributed over a network of heterogeneous computers running DBMSs which support different data models. Typically, one translates the conceptual models (schemas) of the underlying databases to a common conceptual model and then defines a global conceptual model using the view mechanisms. User queries against this global model are translated into queries against the conceptual models of the underlying systems.

Much effort has been directed toward understanding the problems that arise when updates are issued against views. Many current DBMSs allow users to define views on the physical database and grant query privileges on the views to other users. However, it is often difficult, even impossible, for the effect of an update issued against the view to propagate to the physical database.

Current DBMSs have been designed largely to meet business data processing requirements, such as inventory control, airline reservations, banking, and so forth. However, they do not provide the functions and performance demanded by data management in computer-aided design of VLSI chips, database access by expert systems, and statistical data processing. Research into the query characteristics and storage requirements of these applications is currently of great interest.

Optimizers in current relational systems only attempt to minimize the cost of processing single queries. To significantly improve the performance of these systems, multiple queries which reference the same relations may have to be simultaneously evaluated, or common subexpressions in a set of queries isolated and the results reused. Research along these lines is only beginning.

Recognizing the inherent mismatch between the conventional von Neumann processor architecture and the nonnumeric processing requirements of DBMSs, many researchers have proposed alternative architectures for nonnumeric data processing. They have proposed various algorithms for processing queries under these architectures.

Optimizers find optimal plans for evaluating queries based on available access paths and storage structures. Physical database design addresses the problems of selecting an optimal set of access paths and storage structures to support a class of applications. This was an active area of research even before relational query processing became fashionable. Physical database design must take into account such factors as frequency and types of access, database characteristics (size, distribution of data values, etc.), and query processing techniques. Further, it needs an accurate cost model of the existing access structures.

The book begins with a survey, by Jarke, Koch, and Schmidt, of important research results in query processing. Then it guides the reader through most of the important research topics in query processing, organized around seven sections: query processing in distributed DBMSs, query processing for multiple data models, database update through views, database access for special applications, techniques for optimizing the processing of multiple queries, query processing in database machines, and physical database design.

We have three papers on distributed query processing. Lohman, et al., provide an overview of the architecture of the R* distributed relational DBMS, and discuss the query processing strategy explored for the system. To preserve autonomy among sites, R* compiles a query at each site having a relation referenced in the query. The R* optimizer considers CPU, I/O, and communications costs. Yu analyzes the costs and benefits of various semi-join strategies, and discusses estimation of intermediate result sizes. He also considers tree versus cyclic queries, and multiple copies of relations and relation fragments. Kambayashi summarizes techniques for converting cyclic queries into tree queries, which may then be processed by well-known semi-join based techniques.

There are two papers on multimodel query optimization. Dayal discusses integration of conceptual schemas of existing distributed databases that may be stored under heterogeneous DBMSs, and presents optimization of queries against the integrated schema. Logical integration is achieved through generalization (ISA) hierarchies. He also considers optimization of nonprocedural queries against underlying DBMSs that support procedural interfaces. Rosenthal and Reiner describe an architecture for supporting relational queries to data stored under both network and relational models.

They express intermodel mappings as system-generated relational views, and use view substitution to perform translations automatically.

There is only one paper on view update. Furtado and Casanova discuss two basic approaches to view update problems. One is to treat a view as an abstract data type containing the view definition and the set of allowed view updates. The other is to define general procedures for translating view updates to database updates based on conceptual schema dependencies.

We have three papers which describe data access problems that some important special classes of applications impose. Lorie, et al. discuss extensions to System R to support database organization and access requirements of VLSI CAD applications. These extensions support complex objects, clusters of related records that belong to different relations as single units for purposes of retrieval. Vassiliou, Clifford, and Jarke identify the database access requirements of expert systems, present four architectural strategies for coupling these systems to databases, and investigate criteria for choosing among the strategies. Ozsoyoglu and Ozsoyoglu describe Summary Table by Example (STBE), a QBE-like screen-oriented query language for statistical databases. They also compare expressive powers of the language with SQL and Aggregation by Example, and then outline techniques for evaluating queries expressed in STBE.

To stimulate research in the relatively unexplored area of global optimization, we include three papers. Jarke presents techniques for recognizing and exploiting common subexpressions in different representations (including PROLOG) of relational queries. He also shows that the programming language abstraction "selector" is a useful concept in considering access path support for multiple queries. Kim examines various issues that arise in simultaneously processing a set of SQL queries, and offers a first-cut strategy for grouping queries and sequencing the execution of the query groups. Queries are grouped based on considerations of data dependence and estimated access costs of individual queries. Kambayashi and Ghosh introduce the reader to the notion of the consecutive retrieval (CR) property. A set of queries referencing a common file can be processed in a single scan of the file, if the queries possess the CR property. The authors also discuss techniques for processing a set of N queries that does not have the CR property in n ($1 <= n << N$) scans of the file.

There are two papers on database machines, one on a commercial system and one on an ongoing large-scale research project. Ubell provides an overview of the architecture of Britton-Lee's Intelligent Database Machine (IDM). He outlines the structure of the IDM DBMS software and discusses its performance advantages. Shaw gives a brief description of the organization of the NONVON relational database machine prototype and considers query processing algorithms on the machine.

The book ends with three papers in the section on physical database design. Batory reviews recent advances in the modeling of the storage structures in DBMSs and shows how these advances can lead to a technology that may automate the development of physical database software, software which handles placement and retrieval of data on secondary storage. March and Carlis survey some classical modeling and optimization techniques that have been used for the record structuring and access path design problems. Whang, Wiederhold and Sagalowicz present an overview of the theory of separability, which reduces the problem of assigning access structures to a database to the collective subproblems of optimizing the access structures of individual relations (record types), independently of other relations (record types). They show application of the theory to the physical design of relational and network databases.

March 1985

Won Kim
David Reiner
Don Batory

Section I

Introduction to Query Processing

Introduction to Query Processing

Matthias Jarke, Jürgen Koch, Joachim W. Schmidt

Abstract. Query processing in databases can be divided into two steps: selecting an 'optimal' evaluation strategy, and executing it. We first present elementary nested loop and relational algebra algorithms for query execution and point out some opportunities for improving their performance. A survey of optimization strategies, structured in query transformation techniques and access planning methods, follows. Finally, extensions for special-purpose query systems are briefly addressed.

1 Performance Considerations in Database Systems

Database management systems (DBMS) are now a widely accepted tool for reducing the problem of managing a large collection of shared data for application programmers and end users. The user interacts with the system by submitting requests for data selection (*queries*) or manipulation (*updates*). Both kinds of operations frequently involve access to data described to the system in terms of their properties rather than their location. A sequence of queries or updates which is logically a single unit of interaction with the database is called a *transaction.*

To fulfill its mission, a DBMS must be efficient in the sense that it minimizes the consumption of human and machine resources for processing transactions submitted to it. The costs of *human resources* in utilizing a DBMS are determined, among other factors, by the power and friendliness of the language provided to each type of user (application programmer or end user), and by the system's response time. The goals of language power and fast response time may be in conflict since it is often difficult to implement a powerful language construct efficiently. It is the task of the database implementor to reduce this potential problem.

Machine resources used by the DBMS include the storage space for data and access paths in secondary memory, as well as for main memory buffers, and the time spent by the CPU and channels for data transfer to and from secondary memory and other computers (in distributed databases). The trade-off between these costs components is influenced by the architecture of the database system.

In a geographically distributed DBMS with relatively slow communication lines between the sites where data reside and the sites where requests originate, communication delay dominates the costs while the other factors are only relevant for local suboptimization. In centralized systems, the emphasis is on minimizing secondary storage accesses (transfer channel usage), although for complex queries the CPU costs may also be quite high. Finally, in locally distributed DBMS's, all factors have similar weights resulting in very complex cost functions.

There is also a higher-level trade-off between user and machine cost components [APER83]. An effort to minimize response time is reasonable only under the assumption that user time is the most important bottleneck resource. Otherwise, direct cost minimization of machine resource usage can be attempted. Fortunately, user and machine-oriented goals are largely complementary; where goal conflicts arise, they can often be resolved by assigning limits to the availability of machine resources (e.g., main memory buffer space).

Exact optimization of these cost factors is usually not only computationally infeasible but also prevented by the lack of precise database statistics, i.e., information about the size of data objects and the distribution of data values. Nevertheless, it is customary to use the term *query optimization* for the heuristic selection of strategies to improve the efficiency of executing individual queries. Database management systems can support the achievement of efficiency by providing the following subsystems:

1. a physical design environment which allows the physical structure of the database to be adapted to an expected usage pattern [MARC84];
2. a transaction management mechanism that allows multiple access sequences to be executed concurrently but without mutual interference that would lead to inconsistent data [GRAY81];
3. a query processing subsystem that evaluates queries efficiently within the constraints created by the two previous mechanisms.

This chapter addresses the question of how to construct a query processor for a relational DBMS (other types of database systems will be considered briefly). We first discuss how high-level language queries can be represented in the DBMS (sect. 2). Next, we contrast two elementary algorithms for processing a given query, and present examples and a general framework for improving their efficiency (sect. 3). In sections 4 and 5, two basic strategies within this framework will be investigated: the transformation of a query into a form that can be evaluated more efficiently, and the generation of a good access plan for the fast evaluation of a given representation form. Environments where conventional query processing is not sufficient will be reviewed in sect. 6.

2 Queries and Query Languages

Many user interfaces can be constructed on top of the same database system. This paper will use a *relational framework*. We briefly review relational data structures and integrity constraints before focusing our attention on the representation of relational queries; for more background on the relational model of data, the reader is referred to the literature (e.g., [MAIE83], [ULLM82]). In the relational model, *data* are organized in tables or *relations*. The columns of the tables are called *attributes;* all values appearing in an attribute are elements of a common *domain*. The rows of the tables are called records, *tuples,* or simply relation elements.

In addition to these structural properties, relational databases must often satisfy certain *semantic integrity constraints*. For example, a frequent type of integrity constraint has the format: "if any two tuples of relation R agree in attributes A1, ..., Am, then they must also agree in attributes B1, ..., Bn." In this case, we say that A1, ... Am *functionally determine* B1, ..., Bn. Moreover, if B1, ..., Bn represent all attributes of R, we say that A1, ..., Am form a *key* of R, provided there is no proper subset of A1, ..., Am that functionally determines B1, ..., Bn.

A relational database schema and examples of a query formulated in a number of popular query languages are provided in Fig. 2.1. The database (which will be used throughout this paper) describes EMPLOYEEs, the DEPARTMENTs and managers they work for, and the OFFICEs they are using. One employee can have several offices and each office can be occupied by several employees; the OFFICE-USE relation describes the assignment of employees to offices.

Query interfaces like the ones shown in Fig. 2.1 may cater to different groups of database users (novices or experts, casual or frequent). For query processing purposes, it is useful to map all of these interfaces into a common intermediate language and have the query processor deal only with that language. Such a language should be powerful enough to express a large class of queries. It should also have a well-defined theoretical basis in order to allow the query processor to specify efficiency-oriented query transformations. If very powerful end user interfaces must be supported, it may be necessary to provide full programming capabilities with the intermediate language — a database programming language [SCHM83]. This paper will describe query processing methods in the framework of the (tuple) relational calculus, integrated into the database programming language, Pascal/R [SCHM77]. This language is not meant to be a user-friendly query language for end users but allows for a uniform description of most existing query processing methods.

The *relational calculus* [CODD72] is a non-procedural notation for defining a query result through the description of its properties. The representation of a query in relational calculus consists of two parts: target list and selection expression. The *selection expression* specifies the contents of the relation resulting from the query by means of a first-order predicate (i.e., a generalized Boolean expression possibly containing existential and universal quantifiers). The *target list* defines the free variables occurring in the predicate, and specifies the structure of the resulting relation. The reader can use the following example to relate the relational calculus representation to his or her favorite query language from Fig. 2.1.

```
Relational Database Schema (keys are underlined):

   EMPLOYEE  (eno, ename, marstat, salary, dno)
   DEPARTMENT(dno, dname, mgr)
   OFFICE    (floor, room, capacity)
   OFFICE-USE(eno, floor, room)
```

```
Example Query in English:

   names of single employees in the computer
   department who make less than $40000.-
```

```
SQL:

   SELECT ename
   FROM   EMPLOYEE
   WHERE  salary < 40000 AND marstat = single AND
          dno = (SELECT dno
                 FROM DEPARTMENT
                 WHERE dname = 'computer')
```

```
QUEL:

   RANGE OF e IS EMPLOYEE
   RANGE OF d IS DEPARTMENT
   RETRIEVE (e.ename) WHERE
            e.salary < 40000 AND e.marstat = single AND
            e.dno = d.dno AND d.dname = 'computer'
```

Query by Example:

EMPLOYEE	eno	ename	marstat	salary	dno
		p.	single	<40000	15

DEPARTMENT	dno	dname	mgr
	15	computer	

Fig. 2.1. Examples of end user query languages

Example 2.1:

Names of single employees in the computer department
who make less than $ 40000.

```
[<e.ename> OF EACH e IN EMPLOYEE:
                    e. salary < 40000 AND e.marstat = single
                    AND
                    SOME d IN DEPARTMENT
                         (d.dno = e.dno AND d.dname = 'computer')]
```

In the target list, i.e., in the subexpression preceding the colon, the range of the (free) variable e is restricted to elements of the EMPLOYEE relation. The EMPLOYEE relation is therefore called the *range relation* of e. The term '<e.ename>' indicates that only the names of employees are retained in the result.

The selection expression following the colon defines constraints on the free variable. First, two *restrictive terms* determine that only single employees with a salary of under $ 40000 are of interest. Second, a quantified subexpression must be satisfied (read: "there exists some DEPARTMENT tuple, say d, such that ..."). A *join term*, relating EMPLOYEEs to their DEPARTMENTs, is AND-connected to another restrictive term that restricts attention to computer departments. The comparison operators usually allowed in terms are =, <>, <, >, <=, and >=.

The relational calculus allows variables to be bound to different range relations. For example, variable e is bound to EMPLOYEE and variable d is bound to DEPARTMENT. In addition to the logical operator AND, the operators OR and NOT can also be used in predicates. The following two examples illustrate more complex queries, using universal quantifiers and multiple tuple variables over one relation.

Example 2.2:

Names of departments where all employees earn less than $ 40000.

```
[<d.dname> OF EACH d IN DEPARTMENT:
               ALL e IN EMPLOYEE
                    (e. salary < 40000 OR e.dno < > d.dno)]
```

Example 2.3:

Employees who make less than $ 40000 and have an office on the same floor where their manager has one.

```
[EACH e IN EMPLOYEE: e.salary < 40000 AND
SOME empoff IN OFFICE-USE
     (empoff.eno = e.eno
     AND
     SOME d IN DEPARTMENT
          (d.dno = e.dno
          AND
          SOME mgroff IN OFFICE-USE
               (mgroff.floor = empoff.floor AND mgroff.eno = d.mgr)))]
```

A relational calculus query is said to be in *prenex normal form* if its selection expression is of the form

SOME/ALL r1 IN rel1 ... SOME/ALL rn IN reln (M)

where M is a quantifier-free predicate (i.e., a Boolean expression) called the *matrix*. For instance, queries expressed in QUEL (see Figure 2.1) are always in prenex normal form. If, furthermore, M is of the form

(T11 AND ... AND T1k) OR ... OR (Tm1 AND ... AND Tmk)

(where the Tij are terms) the query is said to be in *disjunctive* prenex normal form (DPNF). The query in Example 2.2 is in DPNF while those in the other two examples are not. The set of all Tij for a given i is called the i-th *conjunction* of the matrix; a query which contains only one conjunction is called a *conjunctive query* [CHAN77].

In [CODD71] the relational calculus was introduced as a yardstick of expressive power. A representation form is said to be *relationally complete* if it allows the definition of any query result definable by a relational calculus expression. Relational completeness has to be considered a minimum requirement. An often-cited example for a conceptually simple query which goes beyond relational completeness is "find the employees reporting to manager Smith at any level." Furthermore, users often request aggregated summary data which cannot be described in pure relational calculus. For example, a query for "offices with free capacity" requires a count function over the relation OFFICE-USE to be computed. However, the extension of relational calculus by aggregate functions is rather straightforward [KLUG82a].

Thus far, we have considered queries in their role as requests by end users. Queries are also used as part of update transactions which change the stored data based on their current value. For example, an update request "raise by 5% the salaries in all departments where nobody earns more than $ 40000.–", would involve answering the query given in Example 2.2. Moreover, query-like expressions are used internally in a DBMS to express integrity constraints or access rights [STON75]. Such a constraint might be: "a manager is entitled to at least one non-shared office." An 'intelligent' DBMS could apply this constraint to rephrase a query for "offices with free capacity" in a way that does not count space in the private offices of managers.

3 Query Processing and a General Optimization Framework

There have been two principal approaches to constructing a general query evaluation algorithm for relational databases: the direct interpretation of calculus expressions as nested loop procedures, and the translation of typical subexpression patterns into operations of a relational algebra. In this section, we review both approaches and then state a general framework, in which improvements to each procedure and hybrids between them can be described. The direction of such improvements is indicated by means of examples.

3.1 Nested Loop Solutions

Any query processing algorithm must state how the target list and the selection expression of a query will be evaluated. The most straightforward algorithm translates the relational calculus query into a nested loop. For describing this procedure, we employ a PASCAL-like database programming language which offers a FOR EACH construct that retrieves single tuples in system-determined sequence, and can evaluate quantifier-free Boolean expressions. The language also provides mechanisms to declare relational variables, to assign values (relations) to them, and to insert new subrelations using the operator, :+.

A query of the form

```
[<f1, ..., fn> OF EACH r IN rel: pred(r)]
```

translates to the program:

```
result : RELATION OF RECORD f1: ...; fn: ... END;
BEGIN
  result := []; (* the empty relation *)
  FOR EACH r IN rel DO
  IF bool(pred(r)) THEN result :+ [<r.f1, ..., r.fn>]
END
```

This extends easily to the case of more than one variable in the target list. The quantifier-free Boolean expression, bool(pred(r)), is derived recursively from the quantified selection predicate, pred(r), by creating Boolean functions for each quantifier in pred(r), as indicated in the following example.

Example 3.1:
The query of Example 2.1 would translate into the program:

```
result : RELATION OF RECORD ename: ... END;

FUNCTION some-d(e) : Boolean;
BEGIN
 some-d := false;
 FOR EACH d IN DEPARTMENT DO
  some-d := some-d OR d.dname = 'computer' AND d.dno = e.eno
END;

BEGIN
 result := [];
 FOR EACH e IN EMPLOYEE DO
  IF e.salary < 40000 AND e.marstat = single AND some-d(e)
  THEN result :+ [<e.ename>]
END.
```

A closer look at this simple procedure reveals a number of efficiency problems which should be solved by query optimization methods. Four points of attack will be mentioned, some of which will be studied in more detail later.

1. The semantics of quantifiers can be taken into account when implementing the functions. For example, the loop in function some-d could stop, after the first DEPARTMENT tuple satisfying both conditions has been retrieved:

```
FUNCTION some-d(e) : Boolean;
BEGIN
 reset(DEPARTMENT);
 REPEAT read(DEPARTMENT)
 UNTIL eor(DEPARTMENT) OR
     DEPARTMENT^. dname = 'computer' AND
     DEPARTMENT^.dno = e.dno;
 some-d := NOT(eor(DEPARTMENT))
END;
```

2. If indexes or other fast access paths are available, the implementation of the function, some-d, can make use of them. For example, if a primary index exists for the DEPARTMENT relation, only one access to the corresponding DEPARTMENT tuple is required for each EMPLOYEE tuple.

3. The method does not fully utilize available buffer space. Modern computer systems retrieve data from secondary storage in blocks rather than tuple-by-tuple, and can often keep more than one block in main memory simultaneously. This can be exploited by executing the algorithm block-wise rather than record-at-a-time [KIM80], possibly in conjunction with buffer management strategies [SACC82].

4. Each call of the function, some-d, retrieves all tuples of the DEPARTMENT relation (until one qualifies, at least). It can be seen from the expression that only DEPARTMENT tuples with dname='computer' can possibly qualify. It may therefore be useful to first extract the corresponding subrelation, and then have the function, some-d, work on that subrelation rather than on the complete DEPARTMENT relation.

Generalizations of these ideas can be found in many query optimization algorithms. For example, the *decomposition* algorithm used in INGRES [WONG76] combines a general nested loop procedure (called 'tuple substitution') with the pre-evaluation of separable subexpressions as in the last strategy mentioned (called 'detachment').

3.2 Algebraic Solutions

Translating a query into a sequence of high-level operations provides a widely used alternative to nested loop algorithms. The *relational algebra* [CODD72] includes general set operations as well as specialized relational operators. The *restriction* operator evaluates a query whose selection expression contains one restrictive term. For example,

RESTRICT (DEPARTMENT, dname='computer') =
[EACH d in DEPARTMENT: d.dname = 'computer']

The *projection* operator constructs a vertical subset of a relation:

PROJECT (EMPLOYEE, [ename]) =
[<e.ename> OF EACH e IN EMPLOYEE: true]

The *join* operator permits two relations with at least one comparable attribute to be combined into one, e.g.,

JOIN (EMPLOYEE, dno = dno, DEPARTMENT) =
[EACH e IN EMPLOYEE, EACH d IN DEPARTMENT: e.eno = d.dno]

If no restriction is placed on the combination of tuples, the join degenerates to a *Cartesian product.*

Example 3.2:

The complete query of Example 2.1 corresponds to

```
PROJECT(RESTRICT(RESTRICT(JOIN(EMPLOYEE,
                                dno = dno,
                                RESTRICT(DEPARTMENT, dname
                                = 'computer')),
                           salary < 40000),
                  marstat = single),
         [ename])
```

Note that the existential quantification of the variable, d, is evaluated by applying a projection operator to the result of the join. Similarly, a more complex operation called *division* can be used for universal quantification.

We give below a general translation algorithm introduced in [CODD72] and refined by [PALE72]. It translates a relational calculus query given in DPNF to a sequence of algebra operations. The query from Example 2.1 serves as an illustration. Note the production and manipulation of major intermediate results that distinguishes algebraic methods from pure nested loop solutions.

1. Evaluate restrictive and join terms applying restriction and join operations to the range relations of the variables involved.

int1 := RESTRICT (DEPARTMENT, dname= 'computer')
int2 := JOIN (EMPLOYEE, dno=dno, DEPARTMENT)
int3 := RESTRICT (EMPLOYEE, salary < 40000)
int4 := RESTRICT (EMPLOYEE, marstat=single)

2. Combine the results of step 1 for all terms appearing in one conjunction by means of join or Cartesian product operations. This step evaluates the AND-connection of terms within each conjunction.

   int5 := JOIN (int1, dno=dno, int2)
   int6 := JOIN (int5, eno=eno, int3)
   int7 := JOIN (int6, eno=eno, int4)

3. Construct the union of the conjunction results computed in step 2. If a particular variable is missing in a certain conjunction, it can be added by another Cartesian product operation between the conjunction's result and the range relation of the missing variable. This step evaluates the OR-connection between conjunctions and thus completes evaluation of the matrix (and is therefore not required in our example).

4. Evaluate the quantifiers from right to left using projection for existentially quantified variables and division for universally quantified variables.

   int8 := PROJECT (int7, [attributes of EMPLOYEE relation])

5. Evaluate the target list
   result := PROJECT (int8, [ename])

The algebraic approach partitions the query optimization problem into two tasks: translating the query into a 'good' sequence of operations, and optimizing the implementation of each operation. Strategies for the former subproblem will be considered in section 4. Here, we briefly address the implementation of algebra operations. In particular, by introducing the join operation we gain the freedom for considering an alternative to the nested loop solution and its derivatives: the *merge join*. In this method, the two relations to be joined are sorted by the same attribute and then scanned concurrently to find all pairs of matching tuples.

The implementation of merge join is slightly more complex than it would seem from this simple description. If neither of the two join attributes is a key to its relation (i. e., the join implements a many-to-many relationship), intermediate relations may have to be built. From the program sketch provided in Fig. 3.1, it is evident that the choice of which is the 'inner' and the 'outer' relation will influence the size of these intermediate results. However, in Example 3.2, where dno is a key to DEPARTMENT, no intermediate relations are needed if DEPARTMENT is chosen as the 'inner' relation. Methods can be devised to compress the intermediate results required in algebraic methods. Attributes not appearing in the query can be removed by an initial projection operation, or a tuple identifier can substitute for a complete relation element [PALE72]. Where Cartesian product operations are required, it is even possible to represent *all* elements of a relation by a special value [JARK82]. However, the advantages of data compression must be traded off against the costs of decompressing the final query output.

```
------------------------------------------------------------------
| (* outer, inner : the two relations to be joined                |
|    outer^, inner^ : buffers for the last read elements          |
|    outer^.f, inner^.g : the join attributes                     |
|    current : a variable indicating the current join value       |
|    joinresult : a relation whose attribute set is the union     |
|                 of the attribute sets of outer and inner *)     |
|-----------------------------------------------------------------|
| BEGIN                                                           |
|  sort(outer by f); sort(inner by g);                            |
|  reset(outer); reset(inner);                                    |
|  read(outer); read(inner);                                      |
|  joinresult := [];                                              |
|  REPEAT                                                         |
|   WHILE NOT (eor(inner) OR eor(outer) OR outer^.f<>inner^.g) DO |
|    IF outer^.f < inner^.g THEN read(outer) ELSE read(inner);    |
|   IF NOT (eor(inner) OR eor(outer))                             |
|   THEN BEGIN (* Cartesian product of joining subrelations *)    |
|         intermediate := []; current := outer^.f;                |
|         WHILE inner^.g = current AND NOT (eor(inner)) DO        |
|         BEGIN                                                   |
|          intermediate :+ [inner^];                              |
|          read(inner)                                            |
|         END;                                                    |
|         WHILE outer^.f = current AND NOT (eor(outer)) DO        |
|         BEGIN                                                   |
|          FOR EACH irec IN intermediate DO                       |
|              joinresult :+ [<outer^, irec>];                    |
|          read(outer)                                            |
|         END                                                     |
|        END                                                      |
|  UNTIL eor(outer) OR eor(inner)                                 |
| END.                                                            |
------------------------------------------------------------------
```

Fig. 3.1. A merge (equi-)join algorithm for m:n relationships

Naive use of the relational algebra has one severe disadvantage: it separates operations which could easily be executed in a parallel or pipelined fashion. For instance, the last two projections in the translation example above could be combined into one projection (as shown in Example 3.2). One way out of this dilemma is the explicit introduction of parallel processing [YAO79]. Alternatively, one can provide more powerful operations. Examples include the semijoin operation (see Sect. 4.4, below), and the graft and prune operations for evaluating quantified queries proposed in [DAYA83].

3.3 Integrated Solutions: A General Optimization Framework

Many query optimization heuristics have emerged from each of the two basic query processing strategies presented in the previous subsections. Such heuristics were often developed as efficiency-enhancing add-ons to implemented DBMS. The two approaches overlap only partially in their coverage of query optimization opportunities. In addition, researchers identified classes of queries for which fast special-purpose algorithms exist. It is the task of a query optimization subsystem to identify and compare the applicable strategies for each query. However, the amount of optimization is restricted by the goal to minimize the overall costs, including the cost of the optimization itself.

There seems to be a need for an integrated framework in which all of the ideas can be brought into play in a structured manner. We utilize such a framework to organize our survey of query optimization techniques:

1. Apply logical transformations to the query representation that standardize, simplify, and ameliorate the query to streamline the evaluation and to detect applicable special-case procedures.
2. Map the transformed query into alternative sequences of operations, i.e., generate a set of candidate 'access plans'.
3. Compute the overall cost for each access plan, select the cheapest one, and execute it.

Transformation strategies are to a large degree independent of the database state at a given time, and thus can be applied mostly at compile time. The richness of the access plans generated and the optimality of the choice, however, are dependent upon the degree of knowledge about current physical database characteristics. Most of the access plan evaluation should therefore be performed at runtime; nevertheless, due to implementation difficulties, access plans are often completely generated at compile time [SELI79]. A meta-database (e.g., an augmented data dictionary) must maintain general information about the database structure and statistical information about the database contents.

4 Transformation of Query Representations

A query can be represented in a number of semantically equivalent relational calculus expressions. Some are better suited for efficient evaluation than others. The strategies presented in this section try to convert a given expression into a better one. They standardize and simplify a query, and assign it (where possible) to a class of queries for which fast algorithms exist. Some of the transformations presented below are *syntactic* in nature; they rely on general equivalence of language expressions whose validity is independent of any particular query or database. In contrast, *semantic* transformation strategies utilize knowledge about a particular database or application, often represented by integrity constraints.

4.1 Specialized Query Representations

While the principle underlying all of these transformations is readily explained in the relational calculus framework, special-purpose representations have been proposed in which certain transformation algorithms are easier to describe. In particular, the so-called tableau representation [AHOS79], [SAGI81] is used in the simplification of a query, whereas object and operator query graphs are mostly applied in detecting special cases of queries.

Figure 4.1 gives a *tableau* representation of Example 2.1. Tableaux are a tabular notation for a subset of relational calculus queries characterized by containing only AND-connected terms and no universal quantifiers. The columns of a tableau correspond to the attributes of the underlying database. The first row of the matrix serves the same purpose as the target list of a relational calculus expression. The other rows describe the predicate.

eno	ename	marstat	salary	dno	dname	mgr	
	a2						
b1	a2	single	<40000	b2			EMPLOYEE
				b2	computer	b3	DEPARTMENT

Fig. 4.1. Tableau representation of Example 2.1

The symbols appearing in a tableau are distinguished variables denoted ai (corresponding to free variables), nondistinguished variables denoted bj (corresponding to existentially quantified variables), constants (corresponding to the constants in restrictive terms), blanks, and tags (indicating the range relation). A join term is indicated by having the same variable appear in different rows. Tableaux serve as a convenient notation for simplifying a large class of queries; an example will be given in section 4.3.

Figure 4.2 shows an object graph for the relational calculus expression in Example 2.1, and Fig. 4.3 gives an operator graph, corresponding to the equivalent relational algebra expression of Example 3.2. Nodes in *object graphs* represent objects, such as (relation) variables and constants. Edges describe terms that these objects are to fulfill [PALE72], [WONG76]. *Operator graphs* describe an operator-controlled data flow. They represent operators as nodes and connect them by edges, indicating the direction of data flow from existing data structures to the desired result [SMIT75], [YAO79].

4.2 Standardization of Query Representations

Most query evaluation algorithms initially transform a given query into some standard representation in order to obtain a uniform starting point from which optimization can be attempted. Most standard forms utilize prenex normal form, as introduced in section 2. For example, standardization of SQL queries [KIM82] removes the distinction between joins and nesting in that language, replacing nested expressions by joins. SDD-1 [BERN81c] and Pascal/R [JARK82] standardize relational calculus queries

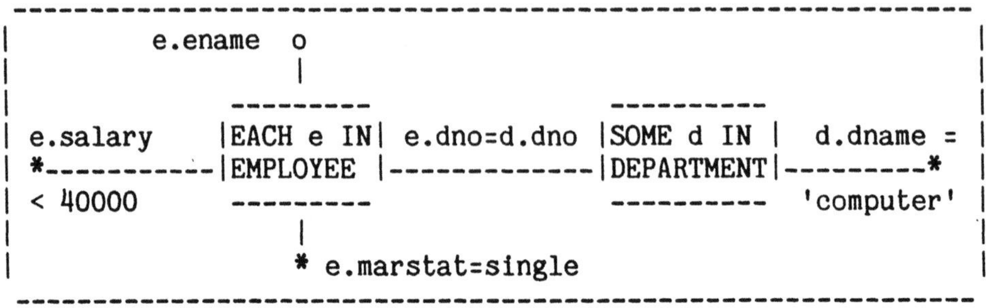

Fig. 4.2. An object graph representing the calculus query

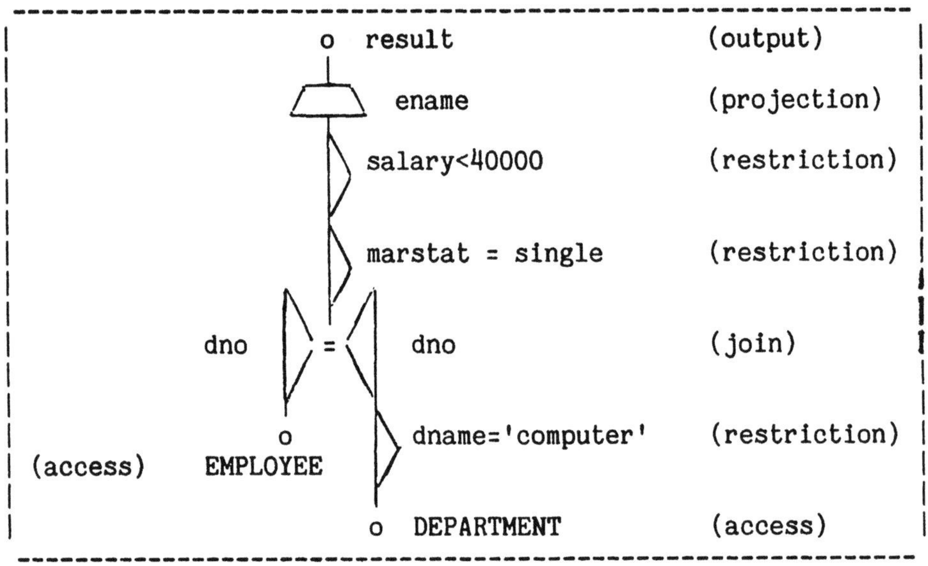

Fig. 4.3. An operator graph representing the algebra query

further into DPNF, in order to facilitate the decomposition of a query into independently evaluable subexpressions. (However, there may be cases where such a decomposition leads to unnecessary operations [GRAN81].) INGRES [WONG76] prefers a conjunctive normal form to achieve fast rejection of tuples which do not satisfy the matrix.

Example 4.1:

The standardization of the expression in Example 2.1 involves the application of a quantifier movement rule:

pred1 AND SOME r IN rel (pred2) = SOME r IN rel (pred1 AND pred2).

The repeated application of this transformation leads to the DPNF:

```
[EACH e IN EMPLOYEE:
  SOME d IN DEPARTMENT
  (e.salary < 40000 AND e.marstat = single AND
  e.dno = d.dno AND d.dname = 'computer')]
```

4.3 Simplification of Query Representations

Even in standard form, a query may be phrased in many ways, in particular, with differing degree of redundancy. The query optimizer should try to avoid unnecessary operations caused by redundant predicates. One might argue that users are unlikely to formulate queries with redundant predicates. However, there is no assurance. Moreover, the query submitted to the DBMS may be a translation from a higher-level end user interface (e.g., a natural [OTTH82] or deductive language [REIT78]), which utilizes views defined on the schema of stored database relations. Queries on views are normally translated into queries on stored relations by substituting the expression defining a view for the view identifier and renaming variables appropriately [STON75]. Such a direct translation, however, can produce unnecessarily complex queries.

Example 4.2:

Consider the following query as a direct translation from the natural language query: "what are the names of single computer people in a tax bracket under 50%?"

```
[<c.ename> OF EACH c IN compemp:
                    c.marstat = single AND SOME t IN tax50 (t.eno = c.eno)]
```

Let the views, compemp and tax50, be defined as:

```
compemp = [EACH e IN EMPLOYEE:
           SOME d IN DEPARTMENT
           (e.dno = d.dno AND d.dname = 'computer')]

tax50 = [EACH e IN EMPLOYEE:
              e.marstat = single AND e.salary < 40000
              OR
              e.marstat = married AND e.salary < 80000]
```

After view subsitation and standardization, the query becomes

```
[<c.ename> OF EACH c IN EMPLOYEE:
 SOME d IN DEPARTMENT SOME t IN EMPLOYEE
 (c.dno = d.dno AND d.dname = 'computer' AND c.marstat = single AND
 t.marstat = single AND t.salary < 40000 AND c.eno = t.eno
 OR
 c.dno = d.dno AND d.dname = 'computer' AND c.marstat = single AND
 t.marstat = married AND t.salary < 80000 AND c.eno = t.eno)]
```

Would the reader recognize our simple standard example in this monster? Yet, this is precisely the task of query simplification. For expressions containing no universal quantifiers, tableau techniques can be used for simplification. Such a query can be broken down into conjunctive subqueries. Thus, two tableaux result from Example 4.2 (Fig.4.4).

eno	ename	marstat	salary	dno	dname	mgr	
	a2						
b1	a2	single	b2	b3			EMPLOYEE
				b3	computer	b4	DEPARTMENT
b1	b5	single	<40000	b6			EMPLOYEE

eno	ename	marstat	salary	dno	dname	mgr	
	a2						
b1	a2	single	b2	b3			EMPLOYEE
				b3	computer	b4	DEPARTMENT
b1	b5	married	<80000	b6			EMPLOYEE

Fig. 4.4. Tableaux for view query

The first tableau produces the same result as the one in Fig. 4.1. To see why, we need to know that eno (as a key of the EMPLOYEE relation) functionally determines ename, marstat, salary, and dno in all rows tagged EMPLOYEE. Since b1 appears in in the eno columns of rows 1 and 3, we can substitute a2 for b5, < 40 000 for b2, and b3 for b6, such that the two rows become equal. Applying a syntactic simplification rule, pred AND pred <==> pred (which holds for any predicate — see Fig. 4.5(a)), one of the duplicate rows can subsequently be dropped; the resulting tableau equals the one in Fig. 4.1, except for renaming of nondistinguished variables. The second tableau represents the empty relation. Using the same reasoning as before, the entries in the marstat column of rows 1 and 3 should be equal — a contradiction with the actual tableau.

The relational calculus basis for syntactic simplification is given by idempotency rules (Fig. 4.5(a)). A sophisticated application of such rules is complicated by the fact that they apply to arbitrary subexpressions which may be at a higher level than individual terms. A prerequisite for high-level simplification is therefore the recognition of *common subexpressions,* to which the rules can be applied. [HALL76] describes heuristics that detect common subexpressions using a bottom-up merge procedure in an operator graph.

For certain classes of queries, efficient algorithms exist that minimize the number of rows in a tableau (and thus the number of join operations in the underlying query) [AHOS79]. As the above example demonstrates, the application of semantic integrity constraints yields further opportunities for simplification [JARK84b], [OTTH82], [REIN84], [SAGI81], based on relational database theory (see, e.g., [MAIE83]). More sophisticated applications of semantic constraints also cover the access planning step (sect. 5), using AI-based heuristic deduction for what has been called *semantic query optimization* [KING81], [HAMM80]. Semantic rules *(guard conditions* [ULLM82]) can finally be used in horizontally distributed databases to locate relevant data, and thus to simplify queries in the sense that only sites are accessed where relevant data actually reside.

Additional opportunities for simplification arise if empty relations (Fig.4.5(b)) or the semantics of the comparison operators are considered. Of particular interest is transitivity [ROSE80]. Joins can be simplified to restrictions by *constant propagation*

r.A op s.B AND s.B=const ==> r.A op const

or an expression can be proven *unsatisfiable* in cases such as

r.A. > s.B AND s.B >= t.C AND t.C >= r.A.

```
-----------------------------------------------------------------
| (a) simplification: some idempotency rules                      |
|                                                                 |
| pred OR pred        <==> pred   pred AND pred        <==> pred  |
| pred OR NOT(pred)   <==> TRUE   pred AND NOT(pred)   <==> FALSE |
| p1 OR (p1 AND p2)   <==> p1     p1 AND (p1 OR p2)    <==> p1    |
| pred OR FALSE       <==> pred   pred AND FALSE       <==> FALSE |
| pred OR TRUE        <==> TRUE   pred AND TRUE        <==> A     |
|-----------------------------------------------------------------|
| (b) simplification: rules for empty relations                   |
|                                                                 |
| [<r.A1,..,r.An> OF EACH r IN []: pred]  <==> []                 |
| SOME r IN [] (pred)                     <==> FALSE              |
| ALL  r IN [] (pred)                     <==> TRUE               |
-----------------------------------------------------------------
```

Fig. 4.5. Simplification rules in relational calculus

4.4 Improvement of Query Representations

For many queries, the choice of differing original formulations or simplification strategies may lead to different evaluation costs. Further transformations try to improve a query representation by detecting special cases, for which fast algorithms exist. In sect. 3.2, we observed that a *sequence of projections* from the same relation can be combined into one. The same holds for *sequences of restriction operations*. Such enhanced operations will tend to be profitable if either none or all of the participating attributes are indexed. If there is a mixture of indexed and nonindexed attributes, the difference in performance will be smaller.

Join operations are more complex than restriction or projection. It is therefore often useful to execute *one-variable operations as early as possible* [SMIT75] in order to reduce the input size of subsequent joins. There may be a conflict between this heuristic and the previous one; the optimal solution depends on file structures and join algorithms used by the query processor.

Example 4.3:
The algebra expression in Example 3.2 can be improved to

```
PROJECT (RESTRICT (JOIN (EMPLOYEE,
                          dno = dno,
                          RESTRICT(DEPARTMENT,
                          dname = 'computer'),
                   salary < 40000 AND marstat = single),
         [ename])
```

and further to

```
PROJECT (JOIN (PROJECT (RESTRICT (EMPLOYEE,
                                  salary < 40000 AND marstat=single),
                        [ename,dno]),
               dno = dno,
               PROJECT (RESTRICT (DEPARTMENT,
                                  dname='computer'),
                        [dno])),
         [ename])
```

In the relational calculus representation, a (partial) order can be imposed on the execution of subexpressions using so-called (range-)nested expressions [JARK83]. The range relation concept of the relational calculus is extended to include relation-valued expressions, rather than just relation names. The following transformation rules may be used to generate a nested expression.

```
[EACH r  IN rel: p1 AND p2]        <==>[EACH r IN [EACH r' IN rel: p1] :p2]
SOME  r  IN rel  (p1 AND p2)       <==>SOME  r IN [EACH r' IN rel: p1] (p2)
ALL   r  IN rel  (NOT(p1) OR p2)<==>ALL    r IN [EACH r' IN rel: p1] (p2)
```

The object graph of a nested query contains the extended range expression in its nodes (Fig. 4.6). If p1 contains only restrictive terms, nested expressions represent the heuristic of evaluating one-variable expressions first.

Example 4.4:

The second version of Example 4.3 corresponds to:

```
[<e.ename> OF EACH se IN [<e.ename, e.dno> OF EACH e IN EMPLOYEE:
                                       e.salary< 40000 AND e.marstat
                                       single]:
     SOME cd IN [<d.dno> OF EACH d IN DEPARTMENT:
                                       d.dname='computer']
           cd.dno = se.eno)]
```

An interesting property of range-nested expressions is that they can be easily generalized beyond restrictive predicates. Let p2 contain a quantified subexpression over a certain variable, say s, the matrix of which (possibly after internal range nesting) consists of only one join term, linking s to r. In this case, the (extended) range expression of s can be evaluated independently and only the result of it must be passed on for processing the join term. For example, in the query of Example 4.4, we can create a (hopefully very small) list of dno's and then test the EMPLOYEE tuples only against this list, rather than against the complete DEPARTMENT relation.

The *stepwise reduction* approach represented by nested expressions was first introduced for non-quantified variables in the INGRES decomposition algorithm [WONG76]: if two subexpressions overlap in a single variable, one of them can be *detached* and evaluated separately. [YOUS79] presents experimental evidence for the advantages of this heuristic in terms of processing time. Subquery detachment has captured wide-spread attention especially in distributed databases since it may reduce considerably the amount of data transfer if the detached subexpression is executed at a different site from the rest of the query. In the algebra representation, a new operator, *semijoin* [BERN81a], was introduced to map the idea:

```
SEMIJOIN (rel1, f = g, rel2) =
          [EACH r1 IN rel1: SOME r2 IN rel2 (r1.f = r2.g)]
```

Thus, a semijoin is 'half of a join', i.e., its result corresponds to that of a join between rel1 and rel2, projected back on the attributes of rel1. The ideas of nested expressions, query detachment, and semijoin are closely related to the object graph representation of queries. As it turns out, a query can be completely resolved by a sequence of semijoins if and only if there exists an equivalent formulation whose object graph is a tree [GOOD82]. Examples 2.1 and 2.2 are such 'tree queries', whereas Example 2.3 is a 'cyclic' query (Fig. 4.6). Techniques for recognizing and processing cyclic queries are treated in [KAMB84].

There are cycles which can be transformed into equivalent acyclic query graphs. Such cycles include those which (a) are introduced by transitivity [YUOZ79], [BERN81a]; (b) contain certain combinations of inequality join term edges [BERN81b]; [OZSO80]; (c) are "closed" by universally quantified variables [JARK83]; (d) contain variables that can be decomposed by use of functional dependencies [KAMB83].

```
---------------------------------------------------------
|   ----------------                 ------------        |
|  |    EACH e IN    |  e.dno = d.dno  | EACH d IN  |    |
|  |    EMPLOYEE:    |-----------------| DEPARTMENT |    |
|  | e.salary<40000  |                 |            |    |
|   ----------------                 ------------        |
|          |                                  |           |
|          | empoff.eno            mgroff.eno |           |
|          | = e.eno                  = d.mgr |           |
|          |                                  |           |
|  ---------------                 ---------------       |
| | EACH empoff    | empoff.floor =  | EACH mgroff    |  |
| | IN OFFICE-USE  |-----------------| IN OFFICE-USE  |  |
|  ---------------   mgroff.floor    ---------------     |
---------------------------------------------------------
```

Fig. 4.6. Cyclic object graph for Example 2.3

5 Access Planning

The transformation step reduces the number of possible evaluation algorithms for a query to those for which efficient execution can be expected. Nevertheless, a large number of possibilities remain. The query optimizer can sequence the operations and it can choose the best implementation for each one. Typically, the optimization of access plans is a three-step process. The steps may be interleaved with each other and sometimes also with the transformation step.

1. Generate reasonable logical access plans, i.e., operator graphs of the improved query representation. Often, monadic operations are removed from the graph to focus on the most expensive tasks: the execution of join operations [ROSE82].

2. Augment the logical access plans by details of the physical representation of data (location of data, sort orders, existence of physical access paths, statistical information).

3. Apply a model of access and processing costs to select the cheapest access plan.

5.1 The Role of Physical Database Structures

The evaluation of access plans depends heavily on the physical database structure. In the simplest case, the database is *centralized*. There may, however, still be a choice between access to base data or some auxiliary direct access structures. Additionally, the sequence of operations has to be determined in a way that minimizes the number of secondary storage accesses.

Evaluating queries over *distributed databases* requires the additional consideration of communication costs; the main goal becomes the reduction of data transfer between sites, even at the expense of more local processing. A typical example is the implementation of a join as a sequence of two semijoins [BERN81a] in a vertically distributed database, in which whole relations or projections thereof reside on one site. If there is also horizontal fragmentation (i.e., restrictions of a relation reside on one site [ULLM82], [GAVI82]), projection and restriction may also become distributed operations.

A general strategy for distributed query processing is the decomposition of a query into subqueries to be executed where the data reside, as contrasted to the collection of all required data at one site, where the whole query is subsequently executed [CERI82]. Subqueries can be processed in parallel on different machines; therefore, the optimizer has a choice of minimizing either response time or resource consumption (e.g., total communication delay [APER83]). If database fragments overlap [MAIE83], there is often a choice of where to retrieve certain data. The answer depends on the relative speed of processors and communication channels: do we have a homogeneous or a heterogeneous network? For example, it may make sense to have complex operations executed at a large computer even if a copy of the data is available on a local personal computer. The topology of the network may also influence the complexity of access planning. In an arbitrary network, queueing delay is a major cost factor [EPST78] which can only be influenced by global decisions.

Finally, a host computer or computer network can delegate the storage management functions of database processing to separate *database machines*. In the *software backend* approach [MARY80], the DBMS is transferred to a stand-by general-purpose computer that executes all database operations. This approach is relatively cheap and permits parallel execution of other tasks on the host computer. However, in very database-intensive applications, the database machine itself, or its communication channels to the host, can become a system bottleneck.

In such a case, a *hardware backend* can be employed [LANG78], [OZKA82] that brings on-board logic close to the stored data in order to implement query optimization strategies, such as early evaluation of restrictions and parallelism. A hardware backend typically consists of a set of cooperating parallel processors. The division of labor between these processors can be determined by partitioning the database into cells [SU79] or by partitioning the query evaluation algorithm into functions [DEWI79]. The introduction of such hardware devices can lead to new algorithms for implementing operations, such as joins or semijoins [VALD84].

5.2 Generation and Selection of Access Plans

Example 5.1:

Suppose our example company plans to concentrate all computer personnel on the fifth floor. Hence, managers of all computer departments with employees assigned to offices outside the fifth floor should be assembled for a meeting. Assume that each database relation resides in a different site, and that sites are connected by slow communication lines so that local processing cost can be neglected in the optimization. After applying all the transformations proposed in sect. 4, the access planning subsystem receives the following query:

```
[c<.mgr> OF EACH cd IN [EACH d IN DEPARTMENT:
                             d.dname = 'computer']:
          SOME e IN EMPLOYEE
                  (e.dno = cd.dno AND
                  SOME not5 IN [<o.eno> OF EACH o IN OFFICE-USE:
                                                    o.floor <> 5]
                        (not5.eno = e.eno))]
```

Obviously, this is a simple chain query (a special case of tree queries) which can be solved from inside out. This solution requires transferring eno's of employees not working on the fifth floor, say 5000, from the OFFICE-USE site to the EMPLOYEE site, and dno's for such employees, say 100, from the EMPLOYEE site to the DEPARTMENT site. The two computer departments among these are located -- at a total cost of 5100 transfers.

Fortunately, there is an alternative strategy which also involves semijoins but does not follow the quantifier sequence directly: (a) transfer the dno's of the, say, 5 computer departments from the site of the DEPARTMENT relation to the site of the EMPLOYEE relation; (b) tranfer the, say, 250 eno's and dno's of the employees working in these five departments to the OFFICE-USE site (cost is 255 if a hierarchical data representation is chosen during the transfer, 500 for a relational representation); (c) check which of these eno's relate to offices outside the fifth floor and send their (two) dno's back to the DEPARTMENT site. The total cost of this strategy is 262 (respectively 507) transfers, about 5% of the above straightforward strategy.

The example illustrates two points. First, the query optimizer must plan its access strategy and cannot rely on universal heuristics; second, to do its job, it needs information about database statistics or at least estimates. (For example, in guessing the 250 eno's above we assumed uniform distribution of employees over departments.) Under these requirements, there are several different ways to proceed.

First, each alternative access plan can be generated and evaluated *completely* before executing the query. This approach can cover parallel or feedback evaluation strategies in a realistic way but the optimization effort is high. Therefore, complete planning has been proposed only for restricted environments: two-variable expressions [YAO79]; monadic operations in horizontally distributed databases [GAVI82]; completely homogeneous networks [HEVN79], [CHUH82]; chain queries [CHIU81] and tree queries [GOUD81], [CHIU80]; and star computer networks [KERS82]. Even some of these have to resort to heuristic methods for reasons of complexity. Other researchers develop heuristic methods from the beginning [CHEU82], [YUCH83]. System R and R* limit the feasible join strategies to permit exhaustive search [SELI79], [SELI80].

Practical systems often plan *hierarchically*, generating an access plan sequentially from subplans at various levels. For example, System R [CHAM81], [SELI79] generates a plan for a nested SQL query by optimizing each query block, and then linking all these subplans. In the distributed systems, SDD-1 [BERN81c] and Multibase [SMIT81], the levels are global access planning, and local query optimization at each site.

The cost of strategies can also be computed *incrementally* concurrently with their generation. This approach allows whole families of strategies with common parts to be evaluated in parallel and thus reduces the costs of optimization considerably. For example, [ROSE82] suggest retaining only the minimal-cost way to each intermediate result while discarding other ways as soon as their non-optimality is detected. A similar approach is followed by the commercial INGRES version [KOOI82].

An extension of the incremental approach is a *dynamic* query optimization procedure. The idea derives from the observation that, at each step in query processing, the optimizer need only select the next operation optimally. To guarantee overall optimality, only the consequences of this decision for the rest of the algorithm must be estimated. A dynamic procedure has actual information about the sizes of all its operands including intermediate results. This information can also be used to update the estimates of the remaining steps. System R re-calculates the full cost of each strategy after each operation; however, it limits the search space by allowing only one intermediate result, essentially making the operator graph look like a list structure. (As noted in sect. 3.3, System R also performs this procedure at compile time and, therefore, cannot make use of information about the size of intermediate results.) INGRES [YOUS79] and SDD-1 [BERN81c] permit multiple intermediate results but employ greedy heuristics with little or no lookahead beyond the next operation.

5.3 Problems of Cost Estimation

We have demonstrated the need for quantitative information about the database. Unfortunately, such information is not very easy to obtain. In particular, the size of intermediate data structures to be retrieved or transfered is difficult to estimate. General estimation methods require detailed database statistics [MUTH83]; where they are missing, simplifying assumptions must subtitute for them. A valid parameter system for estimating the size of intermediate results under such assumptions [RICH81] must have measurable input parameters but its formulas must be general enough to apply to intermediate results at any level. For estimation purposes, the database state at query time is seen as the result of a random process that generates tuples from the Cartesian product of the attribute universes (governed by integrity constraints). A universe is a finite subset of the attribute domain that covers all actual values in the database (e.g., the domain of salary (integer) is restricted to a universe by the salary range in a company). [RICH81] presents a parameter system that computes the result size for any sequence of relational algebra operations, under the assumption that the size of all the universes and of each possible projection are known. Estimates for the size of projections, given the semantic constraints of the database and the sizes of universes and database relations, are derived in [GELE82].

The relationship between the size of intermediate results and the number of actual secondary storage accesses depends on the physical storage structures involved, the size of buffers, and the proportion of relation elements to be accessed. If all elements of an operand of size N have to be accessed to find the desired elements, the optimal number of secondary storage accesses is approximately N/B where B is the blocking factor of the operand. [WHAN83] estimates the number of accessed pages under random placement assumptions. If direct access is used with optimal clustering, the number of secondary storage accesses to retrieve n elements is reduced to n/B.

The traditional uniformity and randomness assumptions about value distributions and tuple placements tend to overestimate costs and thus to bias the query optimizer against the use of direct access structures [CHRI81]. However, the more sophisticated techniques require more statistical information about the database. The question of how to maintain such information with tolerable overhead is not yet fully resolved.

6 Extensions

Additional requirements and opportunities for query optimization arise outside the traditional framework of processing single relational queries. Some query languages permit expressions that are more powerful than those expressible in relationally complete languages [CHAN82]; others work on objects that are more complex than the flat records of the relational model. Other chapters in this book address these problems in depth; in the sequel, we provide a brief overview.

The first extension to be mentioned here is the simultaneous optimization of *multiple* related queries, which can follow two approaches. First, the evaluation of common subexpressions can be *shared* among queries; subexpressions accessing the same physical data page can do so with a single secondary storage access [SHNE76], [JARK84a]. Second, a system for multiple query optimization can *invest* in the creation of physical access paths, such as sorting or temporary indexes, which pay off for the batch as a whole but would not be justifiable for any single query [ROUS82]. Finally, intermediate results of some queries can be stored for later use as partial results of other queries [FINK82]. Little is known about detailed results in this area. [KIM84] and [JARK84a] describe preliminary architectures and language constructs, and a number of ongoing research projects are described in [IEEE82].

Particular needs for query optimization arise when a DBMS is interfaced with *artificial intelligence* systems, such as expert systems or natural language systems [REIT78]. For example, expert systems try to simulate the behavior of a human expert in a specific and usually narrow domain. With the increasing popularity of expert systems in the business world, the need arises for them to obtain information about real-world facts from a corporate database [VASS84]. Instead of duplicating the database for the expert system, coupling existing DBMS with the expert system can be attempted [JARK84c]. Once such a connection exists, it can also be employed in the reverse direction, namely to enhance an existing database system with deductive capabilities [NICO83]. Both directions of interaction, however, do not use stored data directly but require inference procedures to work on them [MINK78].

A reasoning task submitted to the AI system usually translates into a sequence of related database calls. Optimization techniques include: the combination of multiple tuple-oriented database calls into set-oriented operations [KUNI82], [VASS83]; the simplification of such retrieval requests [JARK84b], [OTTH82]; the reorganization of stored knowledge, with the objective of simulating improvement heuristics like the ones discussed in sect. 4.4 [WARR81]; and the use of intermediate results for multiple query optimization [GRAN81], [JARK84a], which is especially useful in executing recursive database calls [HENS84], [MINK83].

Several application areas require specialized data structures for efficient manipulation. *CAD/CAM* and *text processing* focus on modelling objects that are much more complex than flat records [LORI84]. One way to address this problem is to define complex structures on top of a conventional database, allowing multiple views of the structures and substructures [JOHN83]. Another approach is the extension of the traditional relational model by non-first normal form relations [SCHE82], in which attribute values can be complex data structures such as arrays or even relations, making the data model recursive [LAME84]. Query optimization for such extensions is an interesting, little researched area.

In *statistical* databases, data could in principle be stored as standard relations since most statistical data are represented in tables anyway. However, the size and redundancy of such tables [SHOS82], the large number of null entries for attributes that are not applicable to particular relation elements, the difficulty to distinguish between attribute names (category attributes) and attribute values, and the need for computing summary data [KLUG82b] lead to new techniques for user interfaces, data modeling, and query evaluation [EGGE80], [OZSO84], [SHOS82].

Finally, heterogeneous distributed database systems (e.g., [SMIT81]) require the submission of queries to different data models such as *networks* or *hierarchies*. The point here is to go beyond a simple translation and to address optimization issues [DAYA82], [KATZ82]. One problem in these 'navigational' models is the existence of information-bearing access paths, which may have to be used to compute a join. A complementary problem, however, is to avoid following unnecessary access paths by simplifying queries during the translation process. View processing mechanisms similar to those discussed in sect. 4.3 can be used for this purpose [REIN84].

References

[AHOS79, see AHO79] [APER83] [BERN81a] [BERN81b, see BERN81c] [BERN81c, see BERN81d] [CERI82] [CHAM81, see CHAM81a] [CHAN77, see CHAN77a] [CHAN82, see CHAN82a] [CHEU82] [CHIU80, see CHIU80a] [CHIU81] [CHRI81] [CHUH82, see CHU82] [CODD72, see CODD72b] [DAYA82 see DAYA82b] [DAYA83, see DAYA83b] [DEWI79] [EGGE80] [EPST78] [FINK82] [GAVI82] [GELE82] [GOOD82, see GOOD82c] [GOUD81]

This work was supported in part by the Deutsche Forschungsgemeinschaft under grant no. SCHM 450/2–1

[GRAN81] [GRAY81] [HALL76] [HAMM80] [HENS84] [HEVN79] [IEEE82] [JARK82] [JARK83] [JARK84c, see JARK84a] [JARK84a, see JARK84d] [JARK84b] [JOHN83] [KAMB83, see KAMB83a] [KAMB84] [KATZ82, see KATZ82a] [KERS82] [KIM80, see KIM80a] [KIM82] [KIM84, see KIM84b] [KING81] [KLUG82a] [KLUG82b] [KOOI82] [KUNI82] [LAME84] [LANG78] [LORI84] [MARC84] [MAIE83] [MARY80] [MINK78] [MINK83] [MUTH83] [NICO83] [OTTH82, see OTT82] [OZKA82] [OZSO80] [OZSO84, see OZSO84b] [PALE72] [REIN84] [REIT78] [RICH81] [ROSE80] [ROSE82, see ROSE82a] [ROUS82, see ROUS82a] [SACC82] [SAGI81, see SAGI81b] [SCHE82] [SCHM77] [SCHM83] [SELI79] [SELI80] [SHNE76] [SHOS82] [SMIT75] [SMIT81] [STON75] [SU79] [ULLM82] [VALD84] [VASS83] [VASS84, see VASS85] [WARR81] [WHAN83, see WHAN83b] [WONG76] [YAO79] [YOUS79] [YUCH83, see YU83] [YUOZ79, see YU79b]

Section II

Query Processing in Distributed Database Management Systems

Query Processing in R*

Guy M. Lohman, C. Mohan, Laura M. Haas, Dean Daniels,
Bruce G. Lindsay, Patricia G. Selinger, and Paul F. Wilms

ABSTRACT

This chapter describes how statements in the SQL language are processed by the R* distributed relational database management system. R* is an experimental adaptation of System R to the distributed environment. The R* prototype is currently operational on multiple machines running the MVS operating system, and is undergoing evaluation. The R* system is a confederation of autonomous, locally-administered databases that may be geographically dispersed, yet which appear to the user as a single database. Naming conventions permit R* to access tables at remote sites without resorting to a centralized or replicated catalog, and without the user having to specify either the current location of or the communication commands required to access that table. SQL data definition statements affecting remote sites are interpreted through a distributed recursive call mechanism. Tables may be moved physically to other databases without affecting existing SQL statements. SQL data manipulation statements are compiled at each site having a table referenced in the statement, coordinated by the site at which the statement originated. As part of compilation, the distributed optimization process chooses the best place and the best way to access tables and join them together. Optimization uses dynamic programming and careful pruning to minimize total estimated execution cost at all sites, which is a linear combination of CPU, I/O, and communications (both per-message and per-byte) costs.

1. INTRODUCTION

Probably the most extensive and best-known relational query processing and optimization strategy that has been implemented to date is that for System R [SELI 79]. This chapter describes the changes to processing of SQL statements -- including data definition statements, database administration statements, and data manipulation statements (commonly called ***queries***) -- that were required to extend System R to the distributed environment in the R* distributed relational DBMS.

An enterprise may require a distributed DBMS for one or more of the following reasons:

- **Economic.** The databases of larger firms simply exceed the storage capacity and processing power of a single machine. Economies of scale have lowered the cost of smaller machines to be competitive with the large mainframes on which DBMS systems have traditionally relied. Competition has also reduced the cost of communications links between computers.

- **Organizational.** Most enterprises using DBMSs are themselves both geographically and organizationally distributed. Frequently, databases supporting each organizational component have been developed independently but eventually require nondisruptive integration, either due to new requirements or organizational changes (e.g., acquisitions). DBMSs must therefore be distributed, if they are to model effectively the organization that they serve. They must provide each component a degree of local responsibility for, and control over, the data that it "owns".

- **Technical.** Performance and availability are enhanced when data can be situated close to the majority of its users, rather than in a distant center. The impact of the failure of one machine -- or the link to it -- is reduced, particularly when redundant copies of the same data are maintained on other machines. Response time can be reduced when the work to be done can be partitioned among several machines executing in parallel.

Begun in 1979, R* is an experimental adaptation to a distributed environment of System R [BLAS 81].[1] IBM products SQL/DS (for the DOS/VSE operating system) [SQL], SQL/DS Release 2 (for the VM operating system), and DB2 (for the MVS/370 and MVS/XA operating systems) incorporated techniques explored by System R. Most user interfaces and SQL statements for R* are upwardly compatible with those for the centralized systems. There are, however, differences in the data definition and authorization capabilities between SQL/DS and DB2. Where this is the case, R* uses the SQL/DS approach.

In R*, each "***site***" is an independently administered relational database, which is controlled by its own copy of R*. "Sites" need not be geographically dispersed on separate computers, though they often are. Hence a "site" is synonymous with a distinct "logical database". We postulate that the data in each database has both a geographical and functional affinity that defines its contents, its preferred physical location, and its primary users. For example, a company might have a manufacturing database at its plant and an inventory database at its warehouse across town. It is likely that most of the users of the manufacturing database will be at the plant, and those of the inventory database at the warehouse. However, R* enables these sites to be loosely confederated into a network that permits sharing of data among authorized users of those individual databases. For example, the transportation department of our hypothetical company would need to make updates to *both* databases as finished products are taken from the plant to the warehouse. As with System R [CHAM 81a], we also postulate that most database activity originates from pre-defined transactions that are executed repeatedly using the same basic SQL statements but with different parameters. For example, our hypothetical company might have a program to add items to the inventory database each time a shipment is received at the warehouse, a program to delete those in a shipment leaving the warehouse, and another program to summarize the inventory status daily, weekly, quarterly, and annually.

The objectives of R* are:

- **Single-System Image.** The user should be shielded from the added complexity of a multi-database system. Application programs accessing only a local database should run unchanged in the distributed system. An SQL statement accessing tables at multiple sites should have to specify neither the locations of those tables nor the communications commands to move those tables between sites. Physically moving a table to a different site should not necessitate changing the table's name, as that requires changing all SQL statements that access it. An SQL statement updating data at multiple sites should complete at all sites or at none.

- **Site Autonomy.** Each site should be capable of operating independently on its own data, even if communications are lost with *all* other sites, so that availability of the system is not diminished by being part of a network. Hence, there should be no reliance upon any centralized services. Data should be shared between two sites only after the DBAs for both sites mutually agree to do so. The owner of a table should retain responsibility for controlling access to that table by users at all sites. Different sites should even be allowed to run different versions (releases) of R*, so that upgrading R* will not require all sites to change versions simultaneously.

- **Minimal Impact on Performance.** Data should be located close to the site(s) whose users access it the most, so as to minimize the inherent delay of accessing remote data. Users of local data should not be significantly affected by the overhead added by a more complex distributed system. Communication protocols and algorithms should be carefully designed to minimize the cost of remote data access and transfer.

The implementation of R* in fact satisfies all of these goals. Specific design decisions required to meet a goal will be pointed out throughout the chapter.

---

1 Hence the origin of the name: The star in R* (pronounced "R star") comes from the Kleene Star operator of mathematics, defined by R* = [, R, RR, RRR, RRRR, ...]. It denotes zero or more R.

Section 2 will give a brief overview of the architecture and status of R* as a whole, emphasizing SQL statement processing. Section 3 will discuss R* features relevant to data definition and administration. The processing strategy for data manipulation statements will be presented in Section 4, followed by a more detailed description in Section 5 of their optimization. In Section 6 we contrast these mechanisms of R* to other distributed query processing schemes, and conclude with Section 7.

2. BACKGROUND

The architecture of R*, shown in Figure 1, was partly inherited from System R [BLAS 81]. The database language component, RDS*, is based upon the Relational Data System (RDS) component of System R, but required significant changes in order to support distributed databases. The RDS* oversees both pre-compilation and execution of SQL statements, invoking the other components to provide needed services. The RDS* provides SQL language parsing, catalog maintenance, access authorization, query optimization, access structure generation, and interpretive run-time routines. The database storage system, RSS*, provides to the RDS* the lower-level file management system functions of resource management, locking, and transaction management for individual tables at its site. It utilizes IBM's Virtual Sequential Access Method

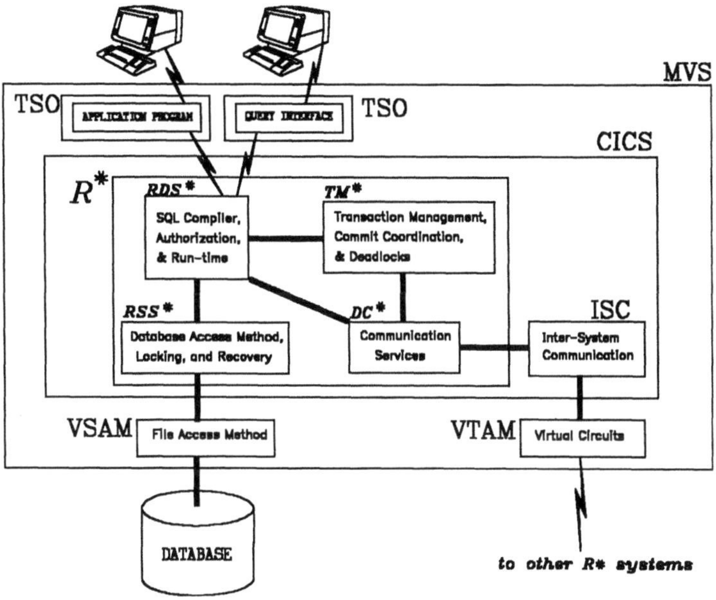

Figure 1: Architecture of R*

(VSAM) [VSAM] for storing all database files. The RSS* is essentially unchanged from the Relational Storage System (RSS) of System R, except that RSS* now supports 2-phase commit, and the deadlock detection and resolution functions of the RSS have been removed and expanded in the distributed Transaction Manager, TM*. TM* also deals with the much more complicated problems of uniquely naming transactions, 2-phase commit protocols, recovery, and both global and local deadlock detection and resolution when a transaction involves more than one site. The Distributed Communications component, DC*, was added to provide an interface between the other R* components and IBM's Customer Information and Control System (CICS) [CICS]. At each site, R* runs as a CICS jobstep within the MVS operating system, and communicates with other R* sites through the standard Inter-Systems Communication (ISC) facilities of CICS, which use the Virtual Telecommunications Access Method (VTAM) of System Network Architecture (SNA).

This chapter will concentrate on the changes to the RDS* to support distributed databases. The design and implementation of the other three components are described in [OBER 79], [MOHA 83], and [LIND 83], among other references.

As of this writing, R* is fully implemented and operational. It has been tested linking over 12 logical databases distributed among three inter-connected IBM 4341 computers in IBM San Jose Research Laboratory's Distributed DB/DC Lab. The size of this installation is limited by the availability of resources, not any limitations of R*. Joint studies with selected IBM customers and internal installations within IBM have been established to evaluate the functionality of R* in real applications. All data definition and data manipulation statements have been implemented except for UNIONs of two or more SQL statements. In addition, the use of VIEWs as an object of authorization is not yet supported. We distinguish these "***protection VIEWs***" from standard "***shorthand VIEWs***", which *have* been implemented [BERT 83a] and which enable a user to name an (unmaterialized) table as the result of an SQL statement, for brevity and convenience of reference. Work is continuing on optimizer validation and sensitivity analysis, interfaces to personal-computer workstations, and added features to support snapshots [ADIB 80a], replicated tables, and vertically and/or horizontally partitioned tables in a manner which is more transparent to users than is currently possible.

3. DATA DEFINITION AND ADMINISTRATION

SQL data definition statements enable an R* user at any site to ACQUIRE and DROP DBSPACEs ("segments" in System R); CREATE and DROP TABLEs, VIEWs, INDEXes, and SYNONYMs; INSERT COMMENTs on tables and columns; DROP PROGRAMS; and to add columns retroactively to existing tables; provided that the user is properly authorized. Database administration statements include the access authorization statements of System R (GRANT/REVOKE <privilege> ON <object> TO/FROM <user>) [SQL], and the new R* statements INTRODUCE DATABASE and MIGRATE TABLE discussed in section 3.4.

Data definition and access authorization in R* differs from System R primarily in the way that objects such as tables and views are named internally, and in the resulting changes to the catalog structure. All of these statements of SQL are compatible with R* and are interpreted, just as was done in System R. However, data definition statements submitted to one site but pertaining to another are simply forwarded to the relevant site. In addition, privileges on tables and programs in R* may now be GRANTed to *groups* of users [WILM 81].

3.1. NAMING CONVENTIONS

In System R, the external (or ***print***) name given to a table, view, or any other database object was internally qualified by the userid of its owner,[2] so that the owner could name a table whatever he wanted without worrying about collisions. The format for internal names of objects was therefore:

```
<object_name> ≡ <owner's_userid>.<owner_given_name>
```

This default qualification could be overriden by a user defining his own shortened synonym for any table or view name:

```
CREATE SYNONYM <print_name> FOR <object_name>;
```

When assigning globally unique internal names in the R* distributed environment, however, our goal of site autonomy dictates that we avoid depending upon a centralized name server or checking with all sites to avoid name collisions of either userid names or database object names. We accomplish uniqueness through the following R* naming conventions [LIND 81]. Each *database* (site) is assigned a unique database name

2 The default ***owner*** of an object is the userid that CREATEd it, but a DBA may also CREATE an object for that owner [SQL].

when it is first created. This name never changes. A locally unique userid is qualified by the name of the database to which that user is attached (and has CONNECT authority), to form a ***two-part userid*** that is unique throughout the network:

```
<R*_userid> ≡ <local_userid>@<database_name>
```

So, for example, there can be two distinct users SMITH@NY and SMITH@LA. A *database object* is qualified not only by this new, two-part userid, but also by the name of the database *at which it is first created* (its ***birth site***).[3] Note that this *need not be the same as* the ***store site***, the database in which the table *is currently stored*. Hence the format for the internal ***system-wide unique name*** of database objects in R* is a four-part name:

```
<R*_object_name>
      ≡ <R*_userid>.<owner_given_name>@<object_birth_database>
      ≡ <owner_userid>@<owner's_database>.<given_name>@<birth_database>
```

Note also that a suitably authorized user can CREATE an object at a birth site that is different from his database. The only purpose of including the object's birth site is to partition the name space, and to incorporate within the object's name a "home" site that always knows where the object is currently stored.

A print name that is not a four-part name is resolved into a system-wide unique name either via an explicit SYNONYM, as in System R, or via implicit defaults: <owner_userid> defaults to the current user and site names default to the current site.

3.2. CATALOG MANAGEMENT

System catalogs are maintained by the RDS* and are used during the pre-compilation of SQL statements to locate database objects by mapping the system-wide unique name of an object referenced in an SQL statement to an RSS*-level object at a given site. They also contain descriptive information and statistics, which constitute a "data dictionary" that is used during query optimization (see section 5). Again, site autonomy considerations preclude us from depending upon a centralized catalog (which would be inaccessible if the machine on which it resides were to fail) or synchronously broadcasting updates to replicas of the system catalog at each site (which would leave the replicas at failed sites inconsistent with those at operational sites, or else be forbidden whenever any one site failed). Instead, each R* site maintains its own catalog [LIND 81].

The catalog for a site consists of separate tables for each type of object (table, view, column, synonym, etc.) that the site "knows about". A site "knows about" a table -- and thus has an entry in its tables catalog, if that table (1) was born at that site, (2) is currently stored there, and/or (3) has been referenced by a statement originating at that site. The last type of entry, called a ***cached*** entry, is a copy of the entry from the store-site's catalog that was made the first time this site referenced that table. It is updated only when a version number stored in it is found to be inconsistent with the version number of the entry for that table at its store site (see section 4.2 below), or when its entry for the current store site proves to be inaccurate [LIND 81, WILM 83]. For reasons of site autonomy, the store site is the primary repository of complete catalog information for an object, including its statistics. Birth-site catalog entries simply contain the current store site of a table.

Storing system catalogs as tables permits them to be accessed using the same query language (SQL) and maintained by the same storage and recovery mechanisms as for users' tables. This recursive technique of storing the system catalogs as self-describing tables also simplifies bootstrapping at database generation time [DANI 82b].

During the processing of any SQL statement, a ***catalog lookup*** must be performed for each table that is referenced in that statement. The catalog entry at the store site for that table must be retrieved by the ***query site***, the site that initially received that statement. First the query site's catalog is searched for an entry on that table. If the table happens to be stored at the query site, as we postulate will happen most often,

3 Recall that we are using "site" and "database" interchangeably.

or if there is a cached entry for the table at the query site, then catalog lookup is complete without having to access any remote sites for catalog lookup. If the query site is the birth site for that table, then it contains a birth-site entry that points to that table's store site, which can be retrieved in one remote site access. If no entry is found in the query site's catalog, then the catalogs of the table's birth site -- specified as part of the table's name -- must be searched for an entry containing the table's store site. This case requires one remote site access; two if the store site is different from the birth site.

The catalog information obtained for any SQL statement is always verified later in its processing by actually accessing the store site of each of its objects. In cases when a query site's catalog had contained a cached entry with a table store site that was made obsolete at catalog lookup time by an earlier table migration, we may mistakenly go to the supposed store site, find no entry, and subsequently have to return to the birth site for the latest, definitive information on the *real* store site. Though this mistake costs us up to three remote site accesses (supposed store site, birth site, and real store site), it is unlikely to occur often because we postulate that tables will be MIGRATEd infrequently and cached entries are corrected by the processing of the first statement that detects the error [LIND 81].

3.3. PROCESSING DATA DEFINITION AND ACCESS AUTHORIZATION STATEMENTS

As in System R, data definition and access authorization statements are interpreted. However, in R*, statements issued at one site may affect objects at other sites. This is implemented in R* by a ***distributed recursive call*** to a single, common routine at the appropriate remote site, rather than having one routine for each possible combination of origin, execution site, and statement type. The call passes only the statement and the userid (for authorization), and returns a completion code. The called site may, as part of its processing, decide in turn to call another site in the same way.[4] Besides providing more unified and verifiable code, this approach also enhances the autonomy of participating sites, since providing the entire SQL statement allows complete checking of incoming recursive calls in context rather than as an isolated request [WILM 83].

Data definition and access authorization statements cause the catalog entries for some database objects to be updated. If that object is a *static* object (e.g., a DBSPACE [SQL]) or a special authorization (DBA, CONNECT, or RESOURCE) on a database, then the site whose catalog should be updated is either explicitly specified in the SQL statement or is the query site (the default). If the object is a *dynamic* object such as a table, then the query site does a catalog lookup as described in the previous section, invokes the store site to update its catalog entry, and caches a correct entry in the query site's catalog if one did not exist or was obsolete. The entries at the birth site are also changed only for MIGRATE, DROP, and CREATE statements. DROP DBSPACE and CREATE and DROP VIEW have the obvious ramifications to catalog entries for their constituent objects.[5] All remote actions are invoked using distributed recursive calls within a single transaction, so that catalog updates for a single SQL statement complete at all sites or at none. The current implementation performs the calls sequentially because simplicity outweighed performance considerations, but nothing in the R* communication mechanisms or the call mechanism precludes some parallel execution at remote sites [WILM 83].

3.4. NEW R* DATABASE ADMINISTRATION STATEMENTS

To achieve the R* goals of site autonomy and system availability, it is important to be able to add a new database site to the network without requiring a synchronized system generation at all sites, and to be able to limit the sites that have access to another site's database. Both objectives are accomplished in R* with the new statement:

4 This would be done, for example, when DROPping a DBSPACE or a VIEW causes a cascade of DROPs of other objects (see section 4.3).

5 Because a view is defined in the form of an SQL SELECT statement, which may reference several tables and/or other views, discussion of view definition is deferred to section 4.

```
INTRODUCE DATABASE <my_database>
          TO       <other_database>
          AT       <other_database_network_address>
          IDENTIFIED BY <my_DB_password>, <other_DB_password>;
```

Only when the DBAs of *both* sites have indicated their willingness to share data with the other by (asynchronously) issuing this statement will any user at <my_database> be able to access tables at <other_database>, and vice versa. Providing <other_DB_password> authenticates the introduction to <other_database>; <my_DB_password> is stored by <other_database> and used to authenticate each new session that <other_database> tries to initiate with <my_database> (see section 4.4). This *site-wide* protection from all access by another site (authorized or not) is *in addition to* the normal data access authorization mechanisms provided by SQL/DS for individual objects [SQL]. Note that this mechanism is a bilateral, independent agreement between two sites and is not transitive, i.e., just because A and B are INTRODUCEd, and B and C are INTRODUCEd, does *not* mean that A and C are automatically INTRODUCEd. This protects a site that has established a relationship with another site from any relationships entered into by that other site.

The owner of a table (or a DBA at all affected sites) may physically relocate that table to another site with the new statement:

`MIGRATE TABLE <table_name> TO <new_store_site>;`[6]

so that it may be stored at the site that uses it the most. Note that: (a) the table's name is unchanged by this move; (b) the current location of the table need not be known by the user issuing the MIGRATE TABLE statement; (c) the table's birth site must be available, since its catalog entry pointing to the current store site *must* be updated; (d) logging of these changes by the RSS* at each site permits each to recover its database to the state prior to the issuance of the MIGRATE TABLE statement, should it fail to complete satisfactorily; and (e) the table is transferred via the query site (rather than directly between the old and new store sites) because we cannot presume that both sites have been INTRODUCEd, but both must have been INTRODUCEd to the query site in order for the statement to be valid.

4. DATA MANIPULATION STATEMENT PROCESSING

Processing of SQL data manipulation statements in R* is changed from that of System R largely in that it may require the coordinated efforts of more than one processor. Thus, the majority of problems that arise relate to the division of work among, and coordination between, the sites that participate in processing that statement. Only the query site and those sites storing one or more tables referenced in the SQL statement ***participate*** in its processing. Henceforth, we will use the term "query" for a single SQL data manipulation statement, such as SELECT... , UPDATE... , INSERT... , or DELETE... . We first review the sequence of steps for processing an SQL query, from the time it is submitted through execution. We then concentrate upon the precompilation step, which compiles the nonprocedural SQL statement that was submitted at a single site into ***access structures***, a sequence of parameters to R* run-time routines, for each participating site. Finally, the coordination of sites during execution is summarized briefly.

4.1. PROCESSING STEPS

The processing sequence for an application program containing one or more "embedded" SQL queries, as well as interactive SQL queries, is the same as that for SQL/DS [SQL, CHAM 81a]. The ***preparation phase***, shown in Figure 2, first performs the ***precompilation step***. This step locates and compiles each SQL

6 Actually, <new_store_site> is specified as the DBSPACE whose name contains the new store site as one part.

query into a sequence of access structures, stored as a ***section*** of an ***access module*** for the application program containing the query, as described in the next section. Each site participating in the compilation of that query stores: (1)in its access module, the access structures to perform *its* portion(s) of the work for the query, called ***subsections***; and (2) catalog entries recording which database objects (tables, views, authorizations, etc.) the access module depends upon for proper execution. Finally, precompilation replaces each EXEC SQL in the application program at the query site with a CALL to an R* linkage routine in the host language, with parameters that identify the access module and section number to execute. This program, now containing only "pure" host language statements, is input to the usual compilation and link steps for that host language, producing executable code with branches to the R* linkage routine.

During the ***execution phase***, shown in Figure 3, the user's object program CALLs the run-time manager of the RDS* via the R* linkage routine, passing it parameters that identify the correct access module and section number. The RDS* run-time manager loads that access module. Then, using the access structures of the correct section, it executes one or more calls to TM* to manage transactions, to the RSS* in order to access the database, and to DC* to move data between sites.

As in System R, R* queries are compiled in this manner rather than interpreted. The access modules produced by query compilation can be optimized and generally run much faster, because the bindings represented in the access module bypass several levels of interpretation and authorization that must be applied to the original query. Users may compile the programs during periods of low system usage, and later execute the access modules any number of times. Because we postulate that the majority of applications will in fact execute the same application programs repeatedly, the cost of *one* compilation of its imbedded SQL queries is amortized over *many* executions. Even for ad hoc queries, compilation consumes relatively few resources and results in a small, efficient routine with "a shorter path-length and smaller working set than a general-purpose SQL interpreter because it is tailored to a specific query" [CHAM 81a].

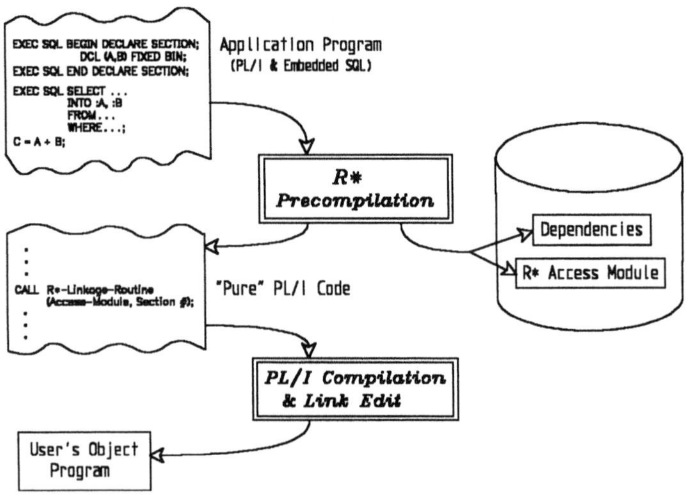

Figure 2: R* Preparation Phase of Processing

4.2. DISTRIBUTED QUERY COMPILATION

Since the tables referenced in a single SQL query may reside in databases at different sites, each site participating in the query will have some work to accomplish, in concert with the other sites, to satisfy the query. The problem is how to divide the work among sites in a manner that balances the goal of site autonomy against the goal of efficient cooperation. Having a single site compile the query into executable code and distributing pieces of that code to each site would ensure efficient and correct coordination among sites, but would preempt all other sites' control over access to their databases and would require that all sites be executing under the same version of the system at any given time. On the other hand, a fully distributed compilation scheme would provide maximal autonomy for each site, but would consume costly overhead negotiating a consensus on coordination among sites and might result in an approach that is locally cheapest for each site but globally suboptimal [DANI 82a].

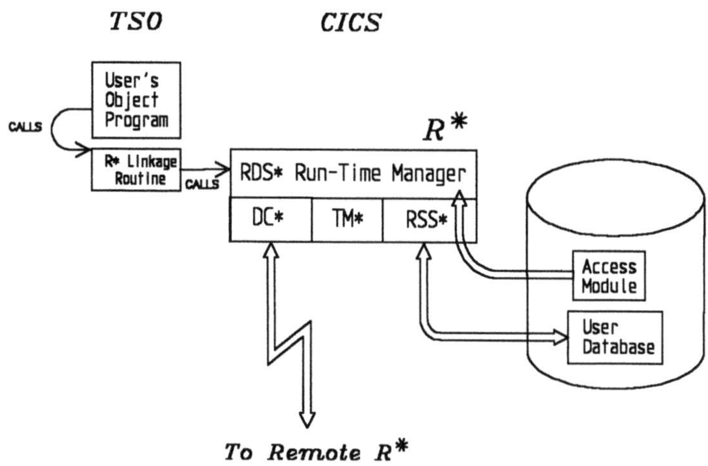

Figure 3: R* Execution Phase of Processing

R* uses a distributed compilation scheme in which a single site -- called the ***master site*** -- coordinates the high-level global aspects of compilation and delegates to all other participating sites -- called ***apprentice sites*** -- the local decisions and local access structure generation. The master site is always the query site, so any participating site may be a master or apprentice for a given query, depending upon which site received the query. However, a site in apprentice mode performs many of the same functions as the site in master mode, so many of the same R* routines can be used in either mode. The master broadcasts its global decisions to the apprentices in the form of a high-level, procedural sequence called the ***distributed plan***. This, along with the original SQL statement modified by name resolution and view composition, is stored in each apprentice's database, then used to locate those portions of the plan that are relevant to it and to compile those portions into its subsection(s) in its access module. Passing global plan information in such a high-level form and having each apprentice compile the SQL query has several advantages. Allowing each site to generate the access structures that *it* knows to be correct preserves that site's autonomy. Secondly, this approach permits each site to utilize any version of R* that is upwardly compatible with the version utilized by the master. Finally, this form of distributed plan is generally more compact than distributing executable code. Storing all information received from the master allows each apprentice to re-compile its portion of the plan independent of the other sites, if necessary. The sequence for each type of site, and how the sites interact, is shown in Figure 4 and detailed below [DANI 82a], [DANI 82b]:

1. **Parsing.** Each site independently re-parses the SQL statement using its own parser, creating its own internal parse tree that is augmented and modified by later steps. Shipping the master's parse tree would save re-parsing by each apprentice, but would require uniform internal representations and manipulations of the parse tree at all sites, effectively limiting all sites to the same version of R*.

2. **Name Resolution.** (Master Only) Print names are resolved to system-wide unique names, using either local SYNONYMs or defaults, and the original SQL query is modified. Name resolution must be performed at the master site, since the correct name-resolution context is not available at other sites.

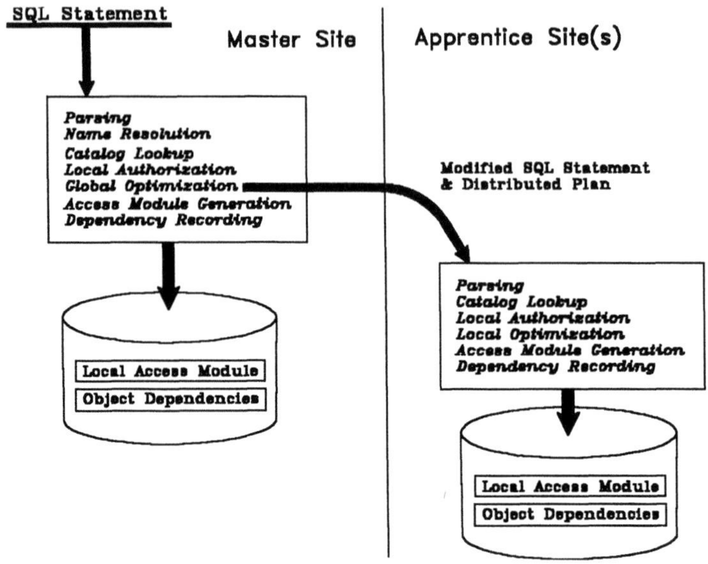

Figure 4: Distributed Query Compilation in R*

3. **Catalog Lookup.** The master performs catalog lookup as described in section 3.2, and adds the catalog information for each table to the distributed plan to save the apprentices from re-executing this step.

   If the catalog lookup reveals that the name is a view, then the parse tree corresponding to that view is merged into the parse tree for the query in lieu of the view name, and the original SQL statement is modified accordingly. If the master is either the site at which the view was originally defined, or a site containing one of the "real" (stored) tables that was referenced either directly in the view or indirectly in one of *its* constituent views, then it will have in its database a parse tree and version number[7] for that view. Otherwise, its catalog lookup will return the SQL definition of the view from the site that originally CREATEd it, and the master will have to re-process it just as is done at view-definition time. This involves re-parsing the composed view-definition statement that was stored during that view's definition (see section 4.3 below). In either case, catalog lookup is performed for all real tables in the view, to verify that they still exist and the user has the necessary authorizations.

   Apprentice catalog lookup is limited to verifying the currency of the catalog entries used by the master for tables or views pertaining to that apprentice, by comparing the apprentice's version number to that in the cached entries used by the master. If the version numbers disagree, the apprentice forces re-initiation of the entire compilation process for that SQL statement by aborting the compilation transaction, since the master's global plan is based upon obsolete data.

4. **Authorization Checking.** For reasons of site autonomy, each participating site checks its own authorization table to determine whether the user on whose behalf the query is being compiled has the appropriate access privileges for any referenced objects that are stored at that site. Since only shorthand views have been implemented, views cannot be an object of authorization.

5. **Optimization.** Here the non-procedural SQL statement is transformed into a procedural sequence (or "plan") of operations -- such as table accesses, joins, projections, inter-site transfers, and sorts -- that minimizes total estimated execution cost over all participating sites. The roles of the master and

---

7 The version number is necessary because a user may have DROPped and re-CREATEd a view having the same name but a different definition.

apprentices in this step are radically different, as described in more detail in Section 5. The master uses its parse tree and the statistics drawn from the catalog entry for each table to devise a ***global plan*** for the query, and to broadcast to the apprentices the ***distributed plan*** that contains:

- the original SQL query, with print names replaced by system-wide unique names and views composed into the query (i.e., with only real tables specified in the FROM list).
- catalog entries for the tables, views, and columns referenced in the query, including version numbers to verify their currency and the statistics used by the master to do global optimization.
- the master site's global plan, in a high-level form that is devoid of internal representations such as its parse tree structure or machine-executable code.

Each participating site then uses its parse tree and the distributed plan to locate the portions of the global plan that are relevant to it, and to optimize its own detailed ***access plan*** for those portions, within the constraints dictated by the distributed plan.

6. **Access Module Generation.** Each participating site compiles the optimized access plan -- for its portion(s) of the work only -- into a low-level access module, and stores it in its database. Whereas System R generated actual machine code for this module, R* stores more flexible and compact ***access structures*** that are analogous to P-codes used in some Pascal implementations, and which are interpreted at execution time. These structures specify sequences of calls to RSS*, moves of data to and from the RSS* interface, evaluation of residual predicates that are not expressible as RSS* search arguments (***SARGs***) [SELI 79], data-type conversions, arithmetic and aggregation operations, and transfer of data to users or other sites.

7. **Dependency Recording.** The access module at each participating site depends upon the continued existence and validity of database objects stored at that site. These ***dependencies*** are stored explicitly in catalogs at that site. The ***usage catalog*** has one entry for each table, index, or view that was used in a distinct piece of work for a query. The ***authorization catalog*** for that object type has one entry for each object referenced by that access module. These catalogs are searched whenever the definition or store site of a table is changed (DROPped, MIGRATEd, but *not* when columns are added with the ALTER statement), an index or view is DROPped, or a privilege is revoked. Access modules dependent upon these changed objects are then invalidated. The next time a program tries to execute an invalidated access module, re-compilation is automatically invoked. In limited cases such as the dropping of an index, it may be sufficient to re-compile only at the affected site, but in most cases global re-compilation will be necessary [NG 82].

Note that *all* steps in this distributed compilation must be treated as a distributed transaction, so that valid access modules and dependencies are successfully stored at *all* participating sites, or at *none* of them. Save points are established after the successful compilation of each SQL statement compiled, to minimize the amount of work that may have to be rolled back.

4.3. VIEW DEFINITION

The definition of views[8] in R* is analogous to query processing, since views are defined in terms of queries on tables and/or other views: only the optimization and access-module generation steps are bypassed, and the "distributed plan" contains somewhat different information. The site at which the view is defined (the ***view definition site***, abbreviated ***VDS***) plays the master role. As with any other data definition statement, the view definition statement is forwarded to the VDS if it is submitted to a site other than the VDS. Each site containing a table that is referenced in the view, either directly or indirectly (i.e., in another view), acts as an apprentice. These sites are called ***"glue" sites*** of that view, because they enable objects that reference the view to locate the sites at which its real tables reside.

8 As noted earlier, only shorthand views have been implemented in R*, and discussion here is limited to them. For a discussion of the problems posed by protection views, see [BERT 83a] and [DANI 82b].

The VDS first performs parsing, syntax checking, and catalog lookup, as in query processing. If the view references another view, however, the VDS retrieves the original SQL definition of the referenced view (possibly from a remote site if the definition has not been cached at the VDS) and performs ***view composition***, merging the parse tree of the referenced view into that of the view being defined. This is done once at view-definition time to avoid view composition at all participating sites every time the view is referenced. The VDS then "un-parses" the composed parse tree into an SQL-like ***composed view-definition statement*** in which only stored tables are referenced. Parse trees are never transmitted between sites because another site may be running a different version of R* with a different parser. The VDS next determines the set of all glue sites for this view. If the view contains only real tables, then the glue sites are all the store sites of those tables. If view V references another view W, the glue sites of V are the union of W's glue sites and the store sites of V's real tables. The VDS then broadcasts to all its glue sites: the composed statement; the catalog entries it used; and, for each view that the VDS used in view composition, (a) its name, (b) its set of glue sites, and (c) a version number. Receipt of this information triggers view-definition processing at the glue sites, which is identical to that of the VDS except that view composition and broadcast of an "un-parsed" statement are of course unnecessary, and each glue site verifies the currency of the catalog entries used by the VDS for local objects.

Instead of an access module, each participating site stores in its database the composed view-definition statement and its parse tree for the view, the view's set of glue sites, and the view's dependencies upon local objects (including other views). This information is needed whenever the view is referenced, in order to notify all the glue sites of the dependency of the query's access module upon the tables in the view, since the view is a virtual object and has no real "store site" that must be a participant to the query's compilation. Suppose for illustration that the dependency of an access module upon a view V were stored only at its definition site S. If site S happened to store none of the real tables referenced in view V, and another view U was defined in terms of view V, then subsequent compilations of queries referencing view U would never detect if view V had been DROPped, because view V would have been composed into view U and hence its definition site S would not need to participate in compilation [BERT 83a]. In order to drop view V, all of its glue sites must be contacted by S to invalidate all programs and views that reference V; if any glue sites are inaccessible, the DROP cannot be performed.

4.4. COORDINATION DURING EXECUTION

An R* execution not only involves distributed processes executing on behalf of a user query, but also may involve multiple users computing in parallel, each with its own set of processes. A user's program may link many such queries into a transaction that may be distributed over several sites and yet can be backed out in the presence of process, processor, and/or communication failures.

An R* user executes initially as a single process at the user's site. The user's application program interacts only with its local R* database manager. When the access structures indicate that data from a remote site is required, the local R* database manager requests the data from the appropriate remote site, which causes the creation of a dependent process at the remote site. All inter-site communication in R* is between R* processes at different sites, and never between R* and a remote application program. The R*s at the two sites work in parallel, transferring buffers of data between sites. Any process may in turn require data at one or more other sites, and so on, leading to a ***tree of processes*** associated with this single query. Since optimization does not require all work at a site to be performed contiguously, more than one process of the tree may be located at the same site [LIND 83, MOHA 83].

R* accomplishes inter-site communication by establishing a ***virtual circuit*** or ***session*** between the two sites. The first time that a process A requests some action at another site on behalf of a given user, R* creates a new process B at the remote site, and retains that process for subsequent use by the same user. This allows R* to amortize the setup costs over multiple requests that access data at the same site, without having to re-transmit the user identity (for authentication) and transaction identifier with each request, and to retain a distributed state that can improve performance. Sessions may span transactions, and are discontinued only when the application program finishes. Asynchronous ***datagrams***, rather than virtual circuits, are used only for distributed deadlock detection and for recovery of uncommitted transactions, since the relative times at which nodes receive and acknowledge these informational messages is not critical [LIND 83].

5. QUERY OPTIMIZATION

We now describe the R* changes to the System R optimizer [SELI 79]. The original ideas on the necessary changes were published in [SELI 80], and later refined in [DANI 82a], [DANI 82b], and [NG 82]. Exact cost formulas, too voluminous to detail here, may be found in those references.

The purpose of query optimization in R* is to decide five major aspects of execution, described below, in a way that will minimize total estimated execution cost at all sites. The total cost is a linear combination of four cost components: CPU, I/O, and inter-site communication costs in terms of the number of messages initiated (an overhead factor) and the number of bytes transmitted (a message-length factor). The linear coefficients are installation-dependent, and reflect the relative weighting of each cost component. We currently assume that each weight is identical for all sites. Whereas System R and earlier versions of R* [DANI 82b] immediately converted all costs to equivalent page I/Os, the R* optimizer now evaluates and retains all costs in terms of the four cost components as well as the weighted total. For a 4341 CPU having a nominal speed of 1.3 MIPS, 3380 disk drives, and 50 kilobit/s communications lines, the weights to convert each component to milliseconds are: CPU = 0.000769 ms/instruction, I/O = 23.48 ms/IO (initiation, seek, latency, and transfer time), and communications = 11.54 ms/message and 0.16 ms/byte.

Many optimization algorithms proposed in the literature ignore the *intra*-site costs of CPU and I/O, arguing that the per-request cost of messages far exceeds the cost of requesting a page from disk (I/O) or of invoking a CPU-intensive module such as the RSS. While this is true in absolute terms, it has been shown that, when multiplied by the frequency with which these operations are requested in a "typical" query that joins two tables at different sites, CPU and I/O costs can *both* dominate message costs [SELI 80]. This observation has many consequences for our approach. First, since the high CPU and I/O costs of sorting cannot be ignored, we should try to exploit the *order* of intermediate and final results. In particular, some very efficient join algorithms such as the merge join require tables to be ordered on the join columns [BLAS 77], and/or the user may have requested the results to be in a specific order (via the ORDER BY or GROUP BY clauses) or without duplicates (using the DISTINCT function). Hence, the R* optimizer keeps track of the order of all partial and final results, and evaluates alternative table access methods (e.g., indexed vs. sequential access) and join methods. Secondly, "greedy" heuristics that do all local processing contiguously and move the least amount of data at each step (e.g., [CHAN 82]) may "lead us down the primrose path", choosing a suboptimal strategy that sends too many little messages or is I/O- or CPU-intensive. In particular, strategies using semi-joins [BERN 81a], [KAMB 82] ignore the cost of storing, retrieving, and possibly having to sort the semi-joins' intermediate results, usually by assuming they fit in main memory [GARD 83]. And typically these intermediate results lack indexes to facilitate ordering and/or applying join predicates. When these costs are included, the number of situations in which semi-joins would be advantageous appear very limited. Therefore, R* optimization does not use semi-joins, does not require all local processing to be done together, models costs in more detail than any other known optimizer, and utilizes a form of dynamic programming (described below) that always chooses the global optimum from among all possible combinations of our decision variables, without having to exhaustively enumerate all of them.

The five major aspects decided by the R* optimizer are discussed here. The first three of these are the same as those for System R, as is the overall approach to the solution.

1. **Order of Join.** All permutations of the order in which tables are joined (and therefore accessed) are considered, adding one table at a time. The impact of associativity is, however, ignored. For example, for a join of four tables, we evaluate the cost of ((A*B)*C)*D, where "*" denotes "join", but *not* (A*B)*(C*D).[9]

2. **Access Method.** If indexes are defined on any join or ordering columns, then the cost of doing an index scan is compared with that of doing a sequential scan of the relation (in physical order), possibly sorting it into an "interesting" order (for a join or ordering clause).

[9] This pruning simplifies the optimizer considerably, and risks a missed optimum *only* when C and D are both large tables at the same site that join on few rows. In that case, however, we are likely to pick ((C*D)*A)*B, shipping the composite C*D to the site(s) of A and/or B, unless A and B have identical characteristics or C and D reside at the query site.

3. **Method of Join.** The merge join method is compared with the nested loop join method. Blasgen and Eswaran have shown that one of these two join methods is always optimal or very close to optimal for single-site join operations [BLAS 77].

4. **Join Site.** For the join of two given tables at different sites, we may wish to (a) move the (possibly composite) outer table to the site of the inner table to join it there, (b) move the inner table to the site of the outer, ***or*** (c) move both the inner *and* outer tables to a third site yet to be specified [SELI 80].

5. **Inner-Table Transfer Strategy.** For options (b) and (c) above, in which the inner table is moved to another site, we consider: (a) re-fetching the inner-table tuples from their store site as needed, incurring additional communication costs; ***or*** (b) fetching the table once and incurring the additional I/O cost of storing it at the join site.

The use of a dynamic programming algorithm and careful pruning of dominated alternatives significantly reduces the number of combinations of possible values for the above decision variables. Dynamic programming may be used because, for each of the join methods used by R*, the cost of joining an additional table to a composite outer table depends only upon the size of the composite, the order of the tuples in the composite, and the location of the composite's results, but *not* on how the composite was formed.

As in System R, the optimization algorithm iterates on the number of tables joined together thus far. In the first iteration, all possible plans for accessing each table individually are generated, using alternative access methods that produce distinctly ordered results for each table. In iteration two, all possible joins of two tables are tried, using alternative join methods, sites, and table transfer strategies. However, the fetch-once-and-store option (option 5b above) is not evaluated for nested-loop joins because the RSS* does not permit indexing temporary tables as they are created, and hence the cost of multiple scans of the temporary relation in the nested-loop join would be prohibitive. Thus, if the two tables are at different sites, 3 alternatives are evaluated for nested loop joins and 5 for merge joins, for each combination of two single-table plans generated in the first iteration, as enumerated in [SELI 80] and [DANI 82b]. This is four times the number that need be evaluated if the tables were at the same site. If two alternatives produce the same result in the same order *and at the same site*, the more expensive alternative is pruned. Joins that would require a Cartesian product are deferred to as late as possible because of the large number of tuples likely to be generated [PALE 74, SELI 79]. The third iteration joins a third table to the minimum-cost plan for each distinct two-table plan, again pruning more expensive plans that are equivalent in results, order, and site. Joining one table at iteration N to the cheapest plans for N-1 tables continues until all tables specified in the FROM clause of the SQL query have been joined. Finally, the best plan to deliver the result to the query site in the order specified by the user is chosen by comparing the costs of (a) sorting a result to achieve the requested order *vs.* using a plan that naturally results in that order, and (b) moving a result to the query site *vs.* using a plan that naturally results at that site.

The predicates specified in the WHERE clause of the SQL query are always evaluated as soon as the required tables have been joined. In relational algebra terms, this is equivalent to saying that projection and restriction operations are always done before joins, whenever possible. This simple heuristic has been known for some time [PALE 74], and is almost universally practiced.

The master planner is responsible for ***global planning***, i.e., for deciding unilaterally all *inter*-site matters. For example, the master decides *for tables at different sites* the order of the tables and the method by which they are joined, the order of tuples in intermediate and final results, all execution sites, and the inner-table transfer strategy. For definiteness in its estimations, the master only *suggests* an order and method of join for tables *joined contiguously within a single site* and an access method for *all* tables. However, these suggestions may be overruled by the responsible apprentice, since these *intra*-site decisions do not affect any other site, so long as these decisions do not contradict the inter-site constraints decided by the master. For example, so long as the master decides tables T1 and T2 at apprentice site A are to be joined without any intervening joins to tables at other sites, optimization at A can join T1 and T2 in any order, using any join method and access methods. If the global plan requires the result of the join to be in a certain order (perhaps for a merge join to a third table at another site or for an ORDER BY clause), the optimizer at A compares the cost of using an indexed access path (if any) for the outer table with the cost of sorting the result.

6. COMPARISON WITH OTHER STRATEGIES

Several distributed query optimization strategies have been proposed by different researchers, and implemented to varying degrees which are difficult to assess. These algorithms can be classified along many dimensions, some of which are summarized in Figure 5. Some of these dimensions are explained in more detail below:

- ***Compilation vs. Interpretation.*** As pointed out earlier, System R introduced the notion of precompiling SQL statements embedded in programs that are expected to be executed repetitively, and we found no reason to alter this approach in R*. The pros and cons of this approach for a centralized data base system are analyzed in [CHAM 81a]. R* interprets only the data definition, authorization, data administration statements, as these statements are expected to be executed infrequently and can profit little from the early bindings available to queries. In any case, very little optimization can be performed for these statements. Other systems, such as Computer Corporation of America's SDD-1 [ROTH 80] and University of California's Distributed INGRES [STON 82], interpret *all* database statements. However, CCA's new DDM [CHAN 83] is following the R* approach of early binding, and centralized INGRES is changing from the interpretation approach to the compilation approach [STON 80]. Early binding, which occurs when statements are compiled, means that there may be a significant hiatus between the times of binding and execution. During this hiatus, the characteristics of the data might have changed, and thus the original execution strategy might have become inefficient. Late binding allows the most up-to-date information to be used in making the optimization decisions, but incurs significant overhead every time the same query is re-executed.

Figure 5: Comparison of Some Major Distributed Query Processing Algorithms.

Papers & *Systems*	Optmiz. Timing	Objective Function	Cost Compo-nents	Network Topology	Use Semi-Joins	Fragment Handling	Run-Time Use of Replicas	Complexity of Algorithm
APER 83	Static	Response Time OR Total Time	Per-Msg, Msg Length	General	Yes	No	No	Polynomial ('Close to Optimal')
BERN 81b *SDD-1*	Static	Total Time	Msg Length	General	Yes	No	No	Polynomial (Local Opti-mum)
CHU 82	Static	Total Time	Msg Length, CPU	General	No	No	Yes	Exponential (Global Optimum)
EPST 78 *Distributed INGRES*	Dynamic	Response Time OR Total Time	Msg Length, CPU	General OR Broad-cast	No	Yes	No	Polynomial (Local Opti-mum)
KERS 83 *UNITY*	Static	Response Time	Msg Length, I/O	Star	Yes	No	No	
NGUY 80 *POLYPHEME*	Dynamic	Total Time	Msg Length	Broadcast	No	No	No	'Dynamic Programming'
SELI 80	Static	Total Time	Per-Msg, Msg Length, CPU, I/O	General	No	Yes	No	Exponential (Global Optimum)
YU 83 *MERMAID*	Dynamic	Total Time	Per-Msg, Msg Length	General	Yes	Yes	Yes	'Simple & Efficient'

- ***Optimization Timing.*** R*'s optimizer, like most others, optimizes the entire query before execution of the query begins: either immediately before execution starts or at compile time. These *static* algorithms rely upon the existence of a good technique for estimating the size of all intermediate results, and errors in those estimations are compounded by their use in later estimations, possibly leading to the selection of a suboptimal plan for executing the query. *Dynamic* algorithms optimize the query as execution proceeds, usually after each table has been joined. The actual size of the intermediate result thus far is used to determine what the next processing step should be and to which site it should be sent. While this reduces the propagation of estimation errors, it precludes compilation, requires more communication of intermediate results statistics for optimization (in the middle of execution), and may not fully exploit all potential parallelism during query execution. Dynamic optimization algorithms are described in [NGUY 80], [EPST 78], and [EPST 80]. The algorithm of [YU 83] is a hybrid strategy: dynamic optimization is invoked if the actual size of an intermediate result turns out to be significantly different from the size estimated by the static optimizer.

- ***Optimization Scope.*** All optimizers to date, including that of R*, have optimized each query independently. The only known exceptions are the algorithms of of [CELL 80] and [ONUE 83], which can optimize more than one statement at a time. The first algorithm optimizes for the mean response time of different users' queries. It takes into account the impact of workload on response times. The second algorithm optimizes multiple queries of the same user to be able to take advantage of intermediate results of one query in processing the following queries.

- ***Objective Function.*** While almost all known algorithms, including R*, use only total time (or resources consumed at all sites) as the optimization criterion, the algorithms of [APER 82], [EPST 78], and [EPST80] permit optimizing either total time *or* response time. The latter criterion takes into consideration parallel execution at all sites.

- ***Cost Components.*** In virtually all optimizers, costs are assessed as a linear combination (weighted sum) of one or more cost components. R*'s optimizer is the most complete of any optimizer, including CPU, I/O, and both per-message overhead and message length communications components. Though the importance of considering local processing costs (CPU and I/O) was demonstrated in [SELI 80], many researchers' algorithms continue to consider only communication costs. Examples of such algorithms are the ones described in [APER 83], [BERN 81a], [BERN 81b], [NGUY 80], and [YU 83], and the ones actually used in CCA's SDD-1 and University of Grenoble's POLYPHEME [ADIB 80b]. More recent approaches, however, have begun to consider local processing costs (e.g., [CHU 82] and the DDM design [CHAN 83]). Among those algorithms that consider communication costs, few researchers model a fixed (overhead) cost associated with sending a message, in addition to a cost which depends on the amount of information to be transmitted. Such set-up costs are generally very high. The algorithms of [BERN 81a], [BERN 81b], [CHU 82], [EPST 78], and [NGUY 80] ignore per-message costs.

- ***Network Topology.*** R* makes no assumptions about the topology of the network linking sites, except that all links have the same rates (weights in the cost function), an assumption made by all other known algorithms. Some algorithms, such as those of [EPST 78] and [NGUY 80], are designed to take advantage of networks supporting a broadcast protocol. In such networks, the same message cost is incurred regardless of the number of sites to which the message is sent. The algorithm of [KERS 82] is limited to star networks.

- ***Operators.*** Some optimization algorithms, such as those of [APER 83], [BERN 81a], [BERN 81b], and [YU 83], consider only the relational algebra operators and the semi-join operator. The R* and Distributed INGRES [EPST 78] algorithms also consider more complex operators such as aggregate functions (e.g., AVG and MAX). While neither of these algorithms support semi-joins, R* has the distinction of supporting nested queries, in which a predicate (WHERE qualification) of an SQL query itself can be a function of another, nested SQL query block (SELECT...FROM...WHERE...). Often nested queries can be converted into joins [KIM 82], but when the predicate uses a set operator such as IN, the semantics are slightly different if the nested query contains duplicates [LOHM 84]. R* does not support explicit UNION, DIVISION, INTERSECTION, and DIFFERENCE operators, whereas [CHU 82] and others do. Many papers on distributed query processing do not discuss precisely how the join operator is implemented or whether alternative methods are evaluated, as does System R and R*.

- ***Fragment Handling.*** Some of the relational systems support the horizontal and vertical fragmentation of relations. A horizontal fragment or partition is specified by a restriction operation. The general requirement is that the partitions should not overlap. A vertical fragment is specified by a projection onto a set of columns, including a *key* column. The algorithms of [EPST 78], [EPST 80], [SELI 80], and [YU 83] deal with fragments. To our knowledge, Distributed INGRES is the only system which has implemented support for (non-overlapping, horizontal) fragmentation [STON 82]. The query processing strategy dealing with fragments has not been designed yet for R*.

- ***Run-Time Exploitation of Replicas.*** Most of the algorithms assume that data is not replicated. The algorithms of [CHU 82] and [YU 83] exploit the run-time use of replicas of relations to reduce message transmissions. The disadvantage of considering replicas is that the optimization decision space becomes larger. In addition, updating replicas poses considerable problems when sites fail. Although it is possible in R* for the same user to CREATE a copy of the same table at multiple (birth) sites, the "replication" is not transparent to the user: the user remains responsible for ensuring the consistency of those tables, and the optimizer is incapable of exploiting the redundancy because it considers the tables to be "different".

7. CONCLUSIONS

The R* prototype has demonstrated the feasibility of adapting a centralized relational DBMS to the distributed environment in a way that meets the three design goals of single-system image, site autonomy, and reasonable performance. Execution performance of both data-definition and data-manipulation statements is surprisingly fast, depending of course upon the type and loading of the host machines and the speed of communication lines. We are still investigating performance anomalies in a few very complex queries. While the optimizer requires much more space to store the increased collection of potential solutions due to the added dimension of execution sites, delay is noticeable to an interactive user only for very large tables (thousands of tuples) and extremely complex queries having multiple nested query blocks [KIM 82, LOHM 84].

In the near future we intend to evaluate and validate the performance of the R* extensions to the System R optimizer, much as was done for System R by [ASTR 80], and in more detail than was done for Distributed INGRES [STON 82]. We also hope to improve the cost formulas to better conform to reality, and to isolate and improve situations for which bad plans are chosen or performance is anomalous. Sensitivity analyses will aid us in deciding where to concentrate improved detail in our modeling, and where the model can be simplified. Perhaps some heuristics or "rules of thumb" can be gleaned from this empirical analysis, which should help us to prune our enumeration tree of alternative plans further, without risking the omission of a truly optimal plan. We are also investigating ways to relax the current constraints that the cost weights be uniform at each site and between all sites. Other on-going R* research topics include the implementation of "snapshots" of tables that are periodically updated [ADIB 80a], protection views [BERT 83a, DANI 82b], replicated and partitioned tables [SELI 80], and interfacing personal databases on workstations with R* databases.

8. ACKNOWLEDGEMENTS

R* is the creation of a synergistic effort of many people, not all of whom are listed as co-authors of this chapter. The authors wish to acknowledge other colleagues whose collective work is reported in part in this chapter. Bob Yost, R*'s current manager, is also responsible for the DC* component for inter-site communication. Ruth Kistler and George Lapis implemented significant portions of the access structures mechanism and systems-level routines. Tony Ng developed automatic detection and re-compilation for distributed queries.

References

(ADIB80a) (ADIB80b) (APER83) (ASTR80) (BERN81a) (BERN81b, see BERN81d) (BERT83a) (BERT83b) (BLAS77) (BLAS81) (CELL80) (CHAM81a) (CHAM81b, see CHAM81) (CHAN82, see CHAN82b) (CHAN83, see CHAN83a) (CHU82) (CICS) (DANI82a) (DANI82b) (EPST78) (EPST80) (ESSL82) (GARD82) (HEVN79) (KAMB82, see KAMB82b) (KIM82) (KERS82) (LIND79) (LIND81) (LIND83) (LOHM84) (LUK83) (MOHA83) (NG82) (NGUY80) (OBER82) (ONUE83) (PALE74, see PALE72) (ROTH80) (SELI79) (SELI80) (SQL, see SQL81) (STON80) (STON82, see STON82a) (VSAM) (WILL82) (WILM81) (WILM83) (WONG76) (YAO79) (YU83)

Distributed Database Query Processing

C.T. Yu

Abstract

In a distributed database environment, it is common that queries access data from different sites. In such situations, it is reasonable to attempt to limit the amount of data transfer across sites. Many algorithms have been suggested. In this chapter we present the problems encountered in distributed query processing and some of the common techniques to estimate sizes of intermediate results, to make use of semi-joins to reduce data transfer, to find improved sequences of semi-joins and to handle multiple copies of relations and fragments of relations.

1. Introduction

In this chapter we present a number of techniques to optimize query processing in distributed databases. The problem of optimizing query processing in a distributed environment is an intrinsically difficult problem, as some of its subproblems have been shown to be NP-hard [GOOD82a, HEVN80, YULA82]. Efforts have been made to solve the problem. For example, techniques making use of dynamic programming [CHHO80, YULO79] have been employed to minimize total transmission cost for certain types of queries known as tree queries where operations are restricted to semi-joins [BERN81]. It is unlikely that an elegant and efficient solution can be found for general queries in a general setting, where relations may be fragmented and have duplicated copies, and where the cost function involves both transmission and local processing costs. In R*[WILL81], various strategies are enumerated and the cheapest among the strategies is taken. For a complicated query the time to enumerate the strategies can be very substantial. It is not clear whether all potentially optimum strategies have been enumerated.

In the above algorithms, methods to estimate the sizes of intermediate results are employed. These methods are based on certain independence assumptions, which are usually not valid in practice [CHRI83, REIN82]. Since the estimated sizes of intermediate results are expected to differ significantly from those of the actual results, it is unlikely that the true optimum is obtained even for restricted environments. Thus, finding optimum or close to optimum solutions for distributed query processing in a general environment is not yet possible. In this chapter we present the problems encountered in distributed query processing and some techniques that are likely to be useful. Some of the existing techniques may not be covered here.

In Section 2 some definitions are given. Some common techniques to estimate intermediate result sizes are given in Section 3. The simple SDD-1 algorithm, which makes extensive use of the semi-join operation [SDDI79, SDDI81], is sketched in Section 4. The significance of semi-joins in query processing is given in Section 5. Improvements to the SDD-1 algorithm in generating better semi-joins are outlined in Section 6. The handling of duplicate copies of relations and fragments is given in Sections 7 and 8, respectively.

2. Definitions

In this chapter a relational data base [CODD70, CODD72, DATE77, ULLM80] with relations distributed at different sites is assumed. The standard operations are join, select, project, union, intersection and quotient. The most commonly used operations are project, select and join. They will be used to answer queries of the following form.

{Target component | qualification component}, where the qualification component identifies the tuples of the relations satisfying the query and is of the form AND (Ri.Ak = Rj.Al), i.e., it is the conjunction of equality clauses where the R's stand for the relations and the A's for the attributes; the target component specifies the attributes of certain relations to be output to the user and is of the form (Rt.As, ..., Rg.An). For example, consider the query {(R1.A1, R3.A3) | (R1.A1 = R2.A1) AND (R1.A2 = R3.A2)}. For each tuple of R1, each tuple of R2 and each tuple of R3 satisfying (R1.A1 = R2.A1) AND (R1.A2 = R3.A2), the tuple of R1 and the tuple of R3 are projected on attributes A1 and A3 respectively to be presented to the user.

If a clause of the form (Ri.Ak = constant) appears in the qualification of the query, this clause can be processed at the local site containing Ri and therefore can be eliminated. If the qualification of a query is a disjunction of equality clauses, then each clause can be treated as the qualification of a subquery. After evaluating the subqueries, the results are merged to provide the answer to the original query. Thus, we shall restrict ourselves to conjunctive queries.

Suppose each relation is not fragmented. When projections and selections are performed, only local processing is involved. However, when joins are executed, communication cost between different sites may be incurred in addition to local processing cost. For example, if R1 and R2 are in different sites, in order to perform their join, either R1 is sent to the site containing R2 or R2 is sent to the site of R1 before the operation can take place.

Usually, local processing costs are evaluated in terms of the number of disk accesses and CPU processing time while communication costs are expressed in terms of the total amount of data transmitted. For geographically dispersed computer networks, communication cost is usually dominant, but for local networks, local processing cost is of significance. In this chapter, we present techniques which are useful for both geographically dispersed and local networks.

We assume that the cost of transferring an amount of data, say X, from one site to another site to be c0 + c1*X, where c0 is the start-up cost of initiating transmission and c1 is a proportionality constant. The cost for answering a query can be made in terms of the total cost measure [HEYA79]. It is the sum of the costs of transferring data. For example, where X amount of data is transferred from site1 to site2 and Y amount of data from site2 to site3 in order to answer a query, the total cost is (c0 + c1*X) + (c0 + c1*Y) = 2c0 + c1(X+Y).

Since the amount of data transferred affects the cost of a strategy, we should attempt to reduce it. A promising approach is to make use of semi-joins [BERN81]. The semi-join from relation R2 to relation R1 on attribute A is denoted by R2-A->R1 where R2 is the sending relation, R1 is the reduced relation and A is the joining attribute. It can be obtained by joining R1 and R2 on attribute A, then projecting the resulting relation on the schema of R1. Consider the semi-join from relation R2[B,C] to relation R1[A,B] on attribute B. Instead of computing the join and then the projection, R2-B->R1 can be obtained by projecting R2 on attribute B, then joining the result of the projection with R1. We can easily see that R2-B->R1 is always no bigger than R1, and is usually much smaller in size. In Figure 2.1(a), the attribute values {b3,b4} of R1 do not appear in

R2. Thus, the corresponding tuples {(a2,b3)}, (a2, b4), (a3,b3)} are eliminated from R1. The semi-join from R2 to R1 consists of the retained tuples {(a1,b1), (a2,b1)}.

Suppose R1 and R2 are at different sites and the join of R1 and R2 is desired at the site containing R1. Suppose each value in each of the attributes A, B and C has unit width. To obtain a join of R1 and R2 at the site containing R1, one method is that we send R2 to R1, then take the join at the site containing R1. This method has communication cost c0 + c1 [7(1+1)] = c0 + 14c1. The second method consists of sending the B-attribute values of R1, i.e., {b1, b3, b4} to the site containing R2. Then eliminate all those tuples of R2 whose B-attribute values do not appear in {b1,b3,b4}, i.e., R1--B->R2 is computed. This yields {(b1,c1)}. Then the reduced R2 is sent back to the site containing R1 to join with R1. In this example, the sending of R1 projected on B costs c0 + c1(3). The sending of the reduced R2 costs c0 + c1(1+1). Thus, the second method is better than the first if 2c0 + 5c1 < c0 + 14c1. For small c0, the use of semi-join in this example is justified. On the other hand, if the number of B-attribute values in common between R1 and R2 is large, as in Figure 2.1(b), the use of semi-join is not profitable. Clearly, it is desirable to have an estimate of the number of attribute values in common between two relations so that a decision to execute certain semi-joins or not to execute them can be made to minimize the cost of processing a query.

(a)

R1

A	B
a1	b1
a2	b1
a2	b3
a2	b4
a3	b3

R2

B	C
b1	c1
b2	c2
b5	c1
b5	c2
b6	c4
b7	c2
b8	c3

R2 --- B ---> R1

A	B
a1	b1
a2	b1

(b)

R1

A	B
a1	b1
a2	b1
a3	b5
a2	b4
a3	b3

R2

B	C
b1	c1
b2	c2
b4	c1
b3	c2
b4	c4
b4	c2
b3	c3

R1 --- B ---> R2

B	C
b1	c1
b4	c1
b3	c2
b4	c4
b4	c2
b3	c3

Figure 2.1: Illustrating semi-joins.

3. Estimation

The performance of a distributed query processing algorithm depends to a significant extent on the estimation algorithm used to evaluate the sizes of intermediate relations. Thus, it is very important to choose a reasonable estimation algorithm. Some commonly used algorithms are as follows.

Suppose relations R1 and R2 are single attribute relations. Suppose further that the values of the common attribute, say A, are uniformly and independently distributed on the relations. We seek the estimated size of R2-A->R1, i.e., $|R2\text{-}A\text{->}R1| * w$, where $|X|$ denotes the cardinality of X and w is the average width of an attribute value in attribute A.

Let pi be the probability that a value in attribute A appears in Ri, i = 1,2. pi is called the <u>selectivity</u> of Ri on attribute A. It is given by $|Ri|/|A|$. Since the values in the two relations are independently distributed, the probability that a given value appears in both relations is p1p2. Thus, the expected number of distinct values in common between the two relations is $|A|p1p2$, where $|A|$ is the cardinality of the domain of the attribute A. The size of the reduced R1 can be estimated to be $|A|p1p2w$. This can be rewritten as $|R1|p2w$.

Suppose R2 is the same as before but R1 is a relation with two attributes A and B. After the semi-join, R2-A->R1, the cardinality of R1 can be estimated as $|R1|p2$ where $|R1|$ is the number of tuples of R1 before the semi-join. Since R1 may be used to reduce some other relation, say R3, by performing a semi-join from R2 to R3 on the B-attribute, it is of interest to estimate the cardinality of R1 projected on B, after the execution of R2-A R1. This estimation problem is related to the following problem: "There are n balls with m different colors. Find the expected number of colors if t balls are randomly selected from the n balls". The correspondences are: n balls being the number of tuples of R1 before the semi-join; m colors being the number of distinct values of R1 projected on the B-attribute before the semi-join; the t selected balls correspond to the number of tuples of R1 after the semi-join. The expected number of colors of the t selected balls is

$$m * \left[1 - \prod_{i=1}^{t} \left(\frac{n((m-1)/m) - i + 1}{n - i + 1}\right)\right].$$

This solution is the same as the solution given by [YAO77] in a different problem, namely, block-access problem. It should be pointed out that while t is a parameter given in the ball-color problem, the number of tuples of R1 after the semi-join needs to be estimated. Some inaccuracy in the estimation is expected. The formula, if evaluated in the present form, is expensive computationally and may cause overflow or underflow for large t. The following function given in [SDD1V1, SDD1V2] is an approximation to the above formula, after t has been estimated.

$$\begin{cases} m & \text{if } t \geq 2m \\ (t+m)/3 & \text{if } 2m > t \geq m/2 \\ t & \text{if } (m/2) > t \end{cases}$$

A semi-join strategy can be viewed as a directed graph, where the vertices are the relations and a directed edge from Ri to Rj, i.e., Ri-->Rj denotes the semi-join from Ri to Rj. The semi-joins which are executed first are those involving nodes with in-degree (the number of edges directed toward a node) = 0. For example, in the semi-join strategy Ri-->Rj-->Rk, Ri has in-degree = 0 and the semi-join Ri-->Rj is executed first. After the execution of the semi-join, the reduced Rj, denoted by Rj', is produced. The strategy becomes Rj'-->Rk. Rj' has in-degree = 0, implying the semi-join Rj'-->Rk will be executed next.

Now, suppose R1 and R2 are the same as above and R3 is a single attribute relation with attribute B. After R1 is reduced by R2 and R3 using the semi-joins R2-A->R1<-B-R3, the number of tuples of the resulting R1 can be estimated as $p2p3|R1|$, where p3 is the selectivity of R3 under attribute B. Thus, the size of R1 can be estimated as $p2p3|R1|w$, where w is the average width of a tuple in R1. Moreover, the expected number of distinct A values and the expected number of distinct B values in R1 can be estimated by using the block-access formula [YAO77] as described above.

Consider three relations R1, R2 and R3, each having the attribute values A and B. In the following strategies, R1-B->R2-A->R3, and R2-A->R1-B->R3, R3 is reduced by the same set of relations on the same attributes. However, it is easy to find examples in which the reduced relations R3 are different in size for the two strategies after the execution of the semi-joins. Thus, in estimating the size of a relation in a semi-join strategy, it is important to recognize the history of the operations. Such estimation algorithms are given [SDDI81, LUBL81, YCTB83].

Estimation can be performed either statically or dynamically. In static estimation, the entire sequence of semi-joins is planned before the execution of the first semi-join. In dynamic estimation, as soon as a semi-join is planned, it is executed, and the number of tuples of the reduced relation is returned to the estimation algorithm. As a result, a better estimation of the costs of later semi-joins is expected, and the semi-join selected next may differ from the static choice. Thus, there is a trade-off between accuracy of estimation and delay in planning future semi-joins.

4. A simple distributed processing algorithm

In this section, it is assumed that one copy of each relation referred to by the query has been selected. Then, the following two phases (the reduction and the assembly phases) are carried out. In the reduction phase, the cost of a semi-join X--A->Y is defined to be the cost of transferring X.A from the site containing X to the site containing Y (if two sites are the same, the cost is zero). The benefit of the semi-join is the size of Y before the operation minus that of Y after the operation. Assuming that relation Y has to be shipped to another site for final processing and the cost to transfer 1 unit of data is 1, the benefit of the semi-join is the cost saving in data transfer cost. A semi-join is beneficial if its cost is less than its benefit.

The SDD-1 algorithm [SDD179, SDD181] identifies all possible semi-joins between any two relations. For each semi-join, its cost and benefit are estimated. A beneficial semi-join having the smallest cost is then executed (in the second version of the paper, the semi-join having the highest (benefit - cost) is selected). After the execution of the semi-join, the cost and the benefit of each affected semi-join are updated and another semi-join is considered. This process is repeated until no more beneficial semi-join can be found. The identification of all possible semi-joins are given as follows.

The qualification of a query can be represented by a join-graph [BERN81]. The vertices of the join-graph are {Ri.Aj | Ri is a relation, Aj is an attribute and Ri.Aj appears in a clause of the qualification}. The edges of the graph represent the equality clauses. As shown in Figure 4.1(a), an equality clause of the form (Ri.Aj = Rk.Al) is represented by an edge between vertices Ri.Aj and Rk.Al. Since equality is a transitive operator, (Ri.Aj = Rk.Al) AND (Rk.Al = Rt.Am) implies (Ri.Aj = Rt.Am). The attributes Aj of Ri, Al of Rk and Am of Rt are said to be transitively related. If there are two or more attributes of a relation that are transitively related, it is sufficient to retain one of them, since the other can be eliminated by local processing on the relation. Thus, we can rename all attributes of different relations that are transitively related to be the same attribute. In Figure 4.1(b), A1, A4 and A5 in one component of the join-graph are all renamed to be A1, while A2 and A5 in another component are renamed to be A2. In other words, all vertices in a connected component refer to the same joining attribute, and the connected component can be uniquely identified by the attribute. If Ri.Ak and Rj.Ak are in the same connected component identified by attribute Ak, then clearly Ri--Ak->Rj and Rj--Ak->Ri are possible semi-joins. On the other hand, Ri.Ak-->Rj.At, for $t \neq k$, is not a possible semi-join because (Ri.Ak = Rj.At) is neither stated nor implied by the qualification. Thus, all possible semi-joins of the qualification are of the form Ri--Ak->Rj or Rj--Ak->Ri for some attribute Ak, after the renaming of the attributes.

The assembly phase consists of selecting among all sites, the site to which the transmission of all the relations referred to by the query incurs the minimum cost. The site is chosen to be the one containing the largest amount of data after the reduction phase, because the sum of the amounts of data transferred from other sites will be minimum.

Query = {(R1.A1, R2.A2) | (R1.A1 = R2.A4)
AND (R1.A2 = R3.A5) AND (R1.A1 = R4.A5) }

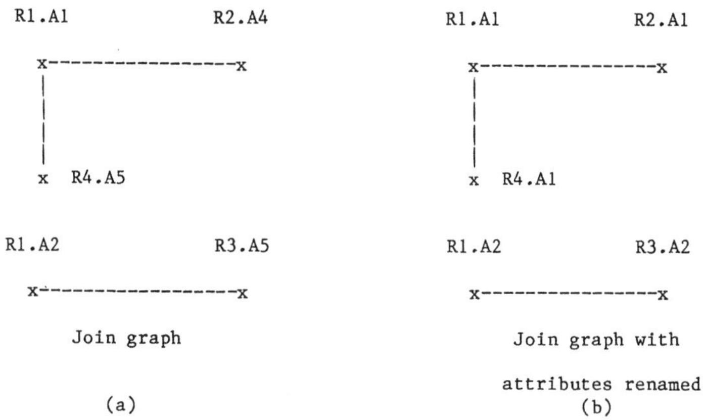

Figure 4.1: Representing a query by its join graph

5. Tree Vs. Cyclic Queries

It is of interest to examine what type of queries can be solved using semi-joins. More precisely, a relation appearing in the qualification of a query is said to be fully reduced if all tuples not satisfying the qualification of the query are eliminated. It is sufficient to process the fully reduced relations instead of the original relations in answering the query. However, it may not be easy to identify all those tuples that do not satisfy the qualification. When a semi-join, say Ri —> Rj is executed, certain tuples of the original relation Rj are eliminated, although the reduced relation Rj need not be fully reduced. After the execution of several semi-joins, the reduced relations can be sent to an assembly site for final processing. Since the reduced relations are not necessarily fully reduced, communication cost in assembling the relations can still be high. Therefore, a precise characterization of the type of queries whose referenced relations can be fully reduced by semi-joins is sought. The characterization is facilitated by defining a query-graph, whose vertices are the relations appearing in the qualifications. An edge (Ri,Rj) with label Ak exists in the query-graph if (Ri.Ak = Rj.Ak) is a clause in the qualification. If (Ri.Al = Rj.Al) also appears in the join-graph, the label of the edge in the query-graph is {Ak,Al}, i.e. the label is to include all attribute names that participate in the clauses involving the relations Ri and Rj. For example, Figure 5.1 gives a join-graph and its corresponding query-graph.

```
        Join-graph                          Query-graph

R1.A2 --------- R3.A2             R2 --A1 -- R1 -- A2 -- R3
                                             |
R1.A1 --------- R4.A1                        A1
  |                                          |
  |                                          R4
  |
R2.A1
```

Figure 5.1:

An example of the join-graph and query-graph for a query.

```
      Join-graph                 Query-graph

R1.A2 ----- R3.A2           R1 --- A2 --- R3
              |             | \            |
              |             |  \           |
            R4.A2           A1  A1         A2
                            |     \        |
                            |      \       |
R1.A1  ---- R4.A1           R2           R4
  |
  |
R2.A1

                      (a)

Equivalent Join-graph         Equivalent Query-graph

R1.A2 ----- R3.A2             R2 -- A1 -- R1 -- A2 -- R3
  |                                       |
  |                                       |
  |                                       |
R4.A2                                    A1A2
                                          |
                                          |
                                          R4
R1.A1 --- R4.A1
  |
  |
  |
R2.A1

                      (b)
```

Figure 5.2:
An example of an equivalent query-graph.

If a query-graph is a tree in the graph-theoretical sense, then it can be shown [BERN81] that a sequence of semi-joins can fully reduce all the relations.

Even if the query-graph of a given qualification is cyclic, an equivalent qualification may have a tree query-graph. For example, in Figure 5.2(a), the qualification has a cyclic query-graph. The qualification is equivalent to that given in Figure 5.2(b) because (R1.A2 = R3.A2) AND (R3.A2 = R4.A2) is equivalent to (R1.A2 = R3.A2) AND (R1.A2 = R4.A2). The latter qualification has a tree query-graph and therefore is solvable by semi-joins. It turns out that a precise characterization of queries solvable by semi-joins is "if a qualification has a tree query-graph or is equivalent to another qualification having a tree query-graph, then the relations referred to by the query can be fully reduced by semi-joins" [BERN81, BERN79]. Such a qualification is a <u>tree query</u>. Any other qualification is a <u>cyclic query</u>. (The characterization is restricted to the qualification. Later on, an algorithm will be given to make use of information specified in the target). In a cyclic query, some of the relations in the qualification may not be fully reduced by semi-joins. Figure 5.3 gives an example of a qualification having a cyclic query-graph. Since there is no other qualification equivalent to it, (except trivial permutations of the clauses), the query is a cyclic query. The relations R1, R2, and R3, referred by the query are given in Figure 5.3(d). If the semi-join R1--B->R3 is used, then R3 remains unchanged because R1.B and R3.B are identical. Similarly, the semi-joins R3--C->R3 and R3--A->R1 have no effect on R3 and R1 respectively. Thus, the original relations R1, R2 and R3 are not affected by semi-joins at all. However, the tuples (0,2) of R1, (2,4) of R2 and (4,1) of R3 do not satisfy the qualification. In fact, no tuples of R1, R2 and R3 satisfies the qualification. In other words, the fully reduced R1, R2 and R3 should be the empty relations.

Qualification

(R1.A=R2.A)AND(R1.B=R3.B)
AND(R2.C=R3.C)

(a)

Join-graph

```
R1.A ------- R2.A
R1.B ------- R3.B
R2.C ------- R3.C
```

(b)

Query-graph

```
R1 --A-- R2
 \       /
  B\    C
    \  /
    R3.C
```

(c)

The relations R1, R2 and R3 cannot be fully reduced by semi-joins

A	B
0	2
1	3

R1

B	C
2	4
3	5

R3

C	A
4	1
5	0

R2

(d)

<u>Figure 5.3</u>: Illustrating that the relations in a query having a cyclic query-graph cannot be fully reduced by semi-joins.

The above discussion illustrates the importance of recognizing qualifications that either have tree query-graphs or are equivalent to other qualifications having tree query-graphs. It turns out that a simple algorithm [YUOZ79, GRAH79] for the recognition of such queries exists. The algorithm has two key steps. Initially, for each relation Rt, the set of attributes of the relation appearing in the qualification, J(Rt), is constructed. Recall that each attribute A of Rt in the qualification denotes a relationship between Rt with the set of relations containing A. In the first step, if there exists a pair of relations Ri and Rj such that J(Ri) C J(Rj), then Ri can be eliminated from consideration. Intuitively, it means that if a cycle incident on Ri exists, then it could be modified to be incident on Rj, since whatever relationship Ri has with any other relation Rk, k≠i, k≠j,is also present between Rj and Rk, due to transitivity of the equality operator. In other words, the cycle need not include Ri and and therefore Ri can be discarded as far as the cyclicity of the query is concerned. In the second step, if any relation is eliminated in step 1, we check if it causes the elimination of an attribute from J(Rt), where Rt is another relation containing the attribute. An attribute is to be eliminated if there is no more than one relation still containing that attribute. (Recall that if a set of relations contain the same attribute, they are related by equality of that attribute. Clearly, no such relationship exists, if there is no more than one relation having that attribute). For example, if Ri.A = Rj.A is the only clause involving attribute A and if Ri is eliminated in step 1, then attribute A will be eliminated from J(Rj) in step 2. The algorithm is simply an iteration of steps 1 and 2. If all relations are eliminated at the end of the algorithm, then the original query is a tree query, because the algorithm does not affect the type of a query (tree or cyclic) and a null query is clearly a tree query. If some relations exist at the end of the algorithm, then it can be shown that [YUOZ79] the original query is a cyclic query. Figure 5.4 illustrates the operation of the algorithm on the query given in Figure 5.2.

```
            J(R1) = {A1, A2}
            J(R2) = {A1}
            J(R3) = {A2}
            J(R4) = {A1,A2}

      Since J(R2) C J(R1), eliminate R2.
            J(R3) C J(R1), eliminate R3.
            J(R4) C J(R1), eliminate R4.

      Since A1 occurs in R1 only, eliminate A1.
            A2 occurs in R1 only, eliminate A2.
            R1 does not have any attribute, eliminate R1.
      All relations are eliminated. Thus this is a tree query.
```

Figure 5.4 Demonstrating that the query in Figure 5.2 is a tree query.

With a minor modification, the above algorithm has an important application in identifying the set of relations that need not participate in the assembly phase. After a sequence of semi-joins has been executed in the reduction phase, the contents of certain relations (with respect to the query) are completely incorporated into other relations through the semi-joins. As a consequence, they need not be sent to the assembly site for further processing. The elimination of such relations lowers both transmission cost and local processing cost.

Example 5.1: Let Q = { R3.E | (R1.C=R2.C) AND (R2.D=R3.D) }.
Suppose the following sequence of semi-joins are executed.

S1: R1-C->R2
S2: R2-D->R3.

After the execution of S1, R1 can be eliminated (as in Step 1 of the algorithm), because its contents are incorporated into the modified R2. After the elimination of R1, attribute C appears in R2 only (and therefore can be removed by Step 2). Similarly, after the execution of S2, R2 can be eliminated. In fact, the answer can be obtained by projecting the modified R3 on E. There is no need to send R1 and R2 to an assembly site. The details of the algorithm to identify such relations are given in [YCTB83].

6. Replacement of Semi-joins by Better Ones

SDD-1 does not eliminate any relations during the reduction phase. As a consequence, it is possible that semi-joins can still be executed on an eliminated relation or from an eliminated relation to another relation. It can be shown [YCTB83] that for networks in which data transfer cost is independent of the sending and the receiving sites, all such semi-joins should either be eliminated or replaced by other semi-joins. In other words, a strategy containing one or more semi-joins involving one or more eliminated relations always has a data transfer cost higher than a corresponding strategy which does not make use of such semi-joins.

As an example, consider the query

Q = {R2.D | (R2.C = R3.C) and (R2.D = R3.D)
and (R2.C = R1.C) and (R1.C = R4.C)}

and the sequence of semi-joins

(1) R1-C->R2 (2) R2-D->R3 (3) R3-C->R4 (4) R4-C->R1 and
(5) R1-C->R3.

After the first semi-join, R1 can be eliminated. Semi-join (2) and (3) do not permit additional relations to be eliminated. Semi-join (4) involves an eliminated relation, namely R1. It can be replaced by (4′) R4-C->R2. Similarly, the eliminated relation R1 in (5) can be replaced by R2 to yield the semi-join (5′) R2-C->R3. It is easy to verify that the cost of executing (4) is the same as that of executing (4′) and the cost of executing (5′) is less than that of executing (5) (because $|R2(C)| \leq |R1(C)|$ after executing (4)). Thus, the cost of executing the sequence of semi-joins (1)-(5) is higher than that of executing the sequence (1)-(3), (4′) and (5′). Furthermore, it can be seen that the size of R2 after executing (4′) is smaller than that of R2 after executing (4) and the size of R3 after executing (5′) is smaller than that of R3 after executing (5). As a result, the cost of assembling the relations after the former sequence of semi-joins is larger than that of assembling the relations after the latter sequence.

Better sequences of semi-joins can be generated efficiently. When a relation, say Ri, is eliminated after the execution of a semi-join, say Ri-A->Rj, the contents of Ri is incorporated into Rj(A). Thus, whenever a semi-join, say S, involving Ri is used, a corresponding semi-join, say S′, with Ri replaced by Rj(A) can be generated. Since the semi-join Ri-A->Rj guarantees Rj(A) to be a subset of Ri, S′ has less cost than S. If Rj is subsequently eliminated by a semi-join of the form Rj->Rk, then any later semi-join involving Ri will be replaced by a corresponding semi-join with Rk substituting for Ri. The details are given in [YCTB83].

The above method generates better semi-joins whenever certain relations can be eliminated. When no relation is eliminated, it is sometimes possible to generate better semi-joins, if some conditions are satisfied.

Consider the substrategy R2--AB->R1<-B--R3. The node R1 has in-degree > 1 and the label in one semi-join is a subset of the label in the other. When these conditions are met, a better strategy can be obtained. For example, R3--B->R2--AB->R1 is such a strategy, because the semi-joins R3-B->R1 and R3-B->R2 are executed with the same cost in both strategies, but the semi-join R2-AB->R1 is executed with a smaller cost in the latter strategy than the former. This process can then be applied to R3, if it satisfies the above conditions. The algorithm given by [LULU80] scans a given strategy and identifies the situations where a node has either in-degree > 1 or out-degree > 1 and checks whether the label in one semi-join involving the node is a subset of that in another semi-join involving the node. When such a situation is detected, the algorithm replaces the substrategy involving the node by a better one. This process is iterated to the preceding nodes satisfying the above conditions.

7. Site and Copy Selection

Unlike earlier algorithms (e.g. [HEYA79], [SDD179] etc.), which select (or assume the existence of) one copy of each relation, it may be desirable to have a primary copy and a number of secondary copies of each relation referenced by the given query. The primary copy of a relation, say Ri, has the characteristics that (1) if Ri is to be reduced (e.g. semi-join of the form Rk-->Ri is to be executed), either the primary copy of Ri is used or the primary copy and all secondary copies of Ri are used.(2) After Ri has been reduced, if no secondary copy of Ri was used, then all secondary copies of Ri should be discarded i.e. they will not be used to reduce other relations. If Ri has not been reduced or all copies of Ri have been reduced, then any copy of Ri can be used to reduce other relations. In other words, in the processing of a query, the primary copy is always active, while some or none of the secondary copies are active. The following example illustrates the usefulness of having more than 1 copy of a relation in a fragmented distributed database environment.

Example 7.1: Let a query be {R1.B|R1.A=R2.A}. R1 has two fragments F11 and F12 with fragment F11 at site S1 and the other fragment F12 at site S2. R2 has two copies, one at site S1 and the other copy at site S2. Existing algorithms (e.g. [CHAN82], [HEYA79], [SDD179], etc.) do not address the issue of using redundant copies but select one copy of R2. A possible semi-join to be executed is of the form R1-A->R2 or R2-A->R1. As a result, F11(A) or F12(A) or R2(A) has to be transmitted across sites. Suppose both copies of R2 are chosen with one copy designated as the primary copy and the other as a secondary copy. Then the semi-join R2-A->R1 can be executed with no data transfer across sites. This saves communication cost. Furthermore, the reduction of the two fragments of R1 by the two copies of R2 can take place in parallel. []

Not all copies of a referenced relation are used as primary and secondary copies. Certain copies of some referenced relations can be eliminated as follows. Site Si is dominated by site Sj if all relations in site Si are also at site Sj. The dominated site Si, together with copies of relations in that site can be eliminated in the processing of the query, because any action involving a copy of a relation in the dominated site can be replaced by a corresponding action involving a copy of the relation in the dominating site Sj. Thus, all dominated sites can be eliminated. After elimination of such sites and the copies of the relations in them, a heuristic method to minimize the total communication cost is to find the minimum number of sites containing the referenced relations. Although the process is exponential in the number of referenced relations, the number of such relations is usually so small that the process is feasible. Details can be found in [YCTL83].

8. Fragment Processing

A horizontal fragment of a relation is a subset of the relation constructed by using the select operation on the relation. A vertical fragment of a relation is constructed by using the projection operation on the relation. In this section, we restrict our discussion to horizontal fragments only.

There are at least 2 ways of handling fragment processing. In the first method, one semi-join is considered at a time. For each semi-join, say Ri-A->Rj, where Ri and Rj may or may not be fragmented, one selects a set of sites where the semi-join can be performed with least data transfer. This can be achieved efficiently as illustrated in Figure 8.1. The sites containing fragments of Rj are sorted in ascending order of the sum of the sizes of fragments of Rj and possibly Ri(A), the projection of Ri on attribute A. In figure 8.1, there are three fragments of Rj and the sites in ascending order are labelled 1,2 and 3.

	Fragments of Ri	Fragments of Rj
site 1		Fj2, size 20
site 2	Fi(A), size 15	Fj1, size 10, total size = 25
site 3		Fj3, size 40
another site	Fi2(A), size 30	

	Amount of data transfer
using site 3 only	20 + 25 + 30 = 75
using sites 2 and 3	15 + 20 + 30 + 30 = 95
using sites 1,2 and 3	15 + 30 + 30 + 15 + 30 = 120

Figure 8.1

The amount of data transfer using site 3 only is compared to that using both sites 2 and 3. If the former amount is less, then using site 3 alone will yield minimum data transfer; otherwise, the amount of data transfer using sites 2 and 3 will be compared to that using all three sites. An efficient procedure to execute the semi-join with least data transfer cost and its details are given in [YCTB83].

Another method to process fragments [EPST78, STON82] is to choose a fragmented relation and to have the other relations referenced by the query replicated at the sites of the chosen fragmented relation. As an example, let a query reference R1 and R2. Suppose R1 contains fragments F11 at site 1 and F12 at site 2 and R2 contains fragments F21 at site 1, F23 at site 3 and F24 at site 4. Then the algorithm may choose R1 to remain fragmented and replicate R2 at sites 1 and 2. The latter operation is performed by sending F21 to site 2, and sending both F23 and F24 to sites 1 and 2. After the transmission of R2 to the sites, R2 is joined with F11 at site 1 and with F12 at site 2. The union of the tuples at the two sites is the final answer. This method allows parallel local processing at multiple sites.

It is clear that the above method of processing fragments may require substantial data transfer. In a realistic environment fragments are not arbitrarily placed and there are placement dependencies between the locations of certain sets of fragmented relations.

The characteristics of fragmented databases are enjoyed in many environments [WONG83, CHAN83, YCTB83].

Definition: Let F1i and F2i be the fragments of R1 and R2 at site i, $1 \le i \le m$. There is a placement dependency between R1 and R2 on attribute A if R1 Join R2 on A = $\cup$ (F1i Join F2i on A). In other words, F1i join F2j on A is null, if $i \neq j$.

Notation: The first subscript refers to relation number, the second subscript refers to site number.

Example 8.1 Consider two relations Student (grade, stid, courseid) and Course (courseid, ...,), representing information about grades of courses taken by students and courses of a university, respectively. The university has a number of campuses. Since a student usually takes courses from his/her campus, the joining of a fragment of the relation Student on a campus and a fragment of the relation Course on a different campus yields null. (If a student takes a course from a different campus or from a different university, the course will be mapped to an equivalent course in his/her campus.) As a result student and course have a placement dependency on the attribute "course id" [].

The following example illustrates how the placement dependency information can help.

Example 8.2 The given query Q is {R1.A|R1.B=R2.B and R2.C=R3.C}. The relations R1, R2, and R3 are fragmented into F11, F12, F21, F22, F31, and F32 respectively. Suppose there is a placement dependency between R1 and R2 on B and another dependency between R2 and R3 on C.

If the two sites containing the fragments are given the subqueries Q1 = {F11.A | F11.B=F21.b and F21.C = F31.C} and Q2 = {F12.A | F12.B = F22.B and F22.C=F32.C},then the answer to Q is the union of the answers to Q1 and Q2. []

In order to recognize those queries that can be processed without data transfer (locally processable queries), the following simple algorithm can be used.

Let Q be a query referencing a set of relations S = {R1, ---, Rj, Rj+1, ---, Rn}. Suppose S1 = {R1, ---, Rj} are fragmented relations and the others are the unfragmented relations. Find two relations in S1 that have a placement dependency between them on certain attributes which are a subset of the joining attributes of the relations in the query. If two such relations cannot be found, then the query is not locally processable, otherwise let LP1 be the set containing these two relations. If there is another relation in S1-LP1 which has a placement dependency with a relation in LP1 on attributes which are subset of the joining attributes of the query, then that relation is added to LP1. This process is repeated until either all relations in S1 are added to LP1, or some relations remain. In the latter situation, the query is not locally processable. In the former situation, if all relations in S-S1 have copies in the sites containing the relations in S1, then the query is locally processable, otherwise not.

A locally processable query can be processed without data transfer in the individual sites. The union of the outputs obtained at the different sites is the final answer. If the query is not locally processable, then the above algorithm partitions the relation in S1 into "fragment groups" such that processing of fragments in each fragment group can be performed without data transfer. After processing such fragment groups, one of the fragment group is chosen and the other relations and fragmented groups are replicated at the sites of the chosen fragmented relations. If databases are designed properly and relations are allocated appropriately, then it is likely that most queries are locally processable queries.

References

(ADIB77) (APER83) (BERN81, see BERN81a) (BERN79) (BLLU82, see BLAC82) (CHAN82, see CHAN82b) (CHAN83, see CHAN83a) (CHAN77, see CHAN77b) (CHEU81) (CHHO80, see CHIU80a) (CHIU80, see CHIU80b) (CHRI83) (CODD70) (CODD72, see CODD72a) (DATE77, see DATE82) (EPST80) (GODA81, see GOUD81) (GOOD82a) (GOOD82b) (GRIF79) (GRAH79) (HEVN80) (HEYA79, see HEVN79) (KAYY82, see KAMB82b) (KETY80, see KERS80) (LUBL81, see LUK81) (LULU80, see LUK80) (REIN82, see REIN82b) (ROGI77, see ROTH77a) (ROG277, see ROTH77b) (SDD179, see GOOD79) (SDD181, see BERN81) (STON82, see STON82a) (ULLM80, see ULLM82) (WILL81) (WONG77, see WONG77b) (WONG81) (WONG83) (WOYO76, see WONG76) (YAO77, see YAO77b) (YCTB83, see YU83) (YULA82, see YU82a) (YULO79, see YU79a) (YUCC82, see YU82b) (YUOZ79, see YU79b)

Processing Cyclic Queries

Yahiko Kambayashi

Abstract

The major purpose of this chapter is to summarize existing methods for query graph modification, to give relationships among them and their applications to cyclic query processing. For processing a cyclic query, we first transform it into a tree query using various methods, and then a tree query processing procedure is applied. The tree query is determined by a spanning tree of the query graph. For processing tree queries, semi-joins can be used instead of joins. Procedures for selecting appropriate spanning trees and application to cyclic query processing procedures for distributed database systems are also discussed.

1. Introduction

Among all relational database operations, the join operation is considered to be the most time-consuming one. Thus in order to process a query which requires more than one relation, it is very important to determine how to perform the join operation. By considering only joins, queries can be divided into two classes: tree and cyclic. There are efficient procedures to handle tree queries. Properties of tree queries and procedures for them have been extensively reported [BERN81a] [BERN81b] [GOOD82a] [GOOD82c] [YU79]. Problems of cyclic processing have been studied by [GOOD82a] [GOOD82b] and useful procedures for cyclic queries have been given in [KAMB82b] [KAMB83].

It has been shown that any procedure for cyclic-query processing contains a process to convert the query into a tree query in some sense [GOOD82a] and there are very good procedures to process tree queries[BERN81a]. We will take the the following approach for processing cyclic queries[KAMB82b] [KAMB83].

(a) Convert a given cyclic query into a proper tree query.

(b) Apply the tree query processing procedure to the resulting tree query .

The major purpose of this chapter is to summarize existing methods for cyclic query processing.

In Section 2, some basic concepts are defined and notations are introduced. Section 3 shows queries and query graphs. Importance of cyclic query processing is also discussed. Section 4 summarizes currently known methods of converting to query graphs, with application to conversion from cyclic queries to tree queries. In Sections 5 and 6, a few of the more important methods are discussed in detail. In Section 7 query processing procedures for distributed database systems are given as applications of these methods.

2. Basic Concepts

A relation scheme is a finite set of **attributes** A_i's ($1 \leq i \leq n$) and it is denoted by $\underline{R}(A_1, A_2, ..., A_n)$ or $\underline{R}$. Each attribute A_i is associated with a value set dom(A_i) which is called a **domain**. A **relation** R on $\underline{R}$ is a finite set of total mappings, called tuples, from the set $\underline{R}$ of attributes to the corresponding domains. A tuple t can be viewed as an n-tuple $(d_1, d_2, ..., d_n)$, where d_i is an element of dom(A_i), by a proper renaming of attributes. Attribute A_i in R_j is denoted by $R_j.A_i$. For simplicity, set union is represented by concatenation; $X \cup Y$ is denoted by XY.

A **projection** of a tuple t on attribute set X is denoted by $t[X]$, which is defined as a part of t corresponding to the attribute set X. The following notations are used for relational operations.

Projection: $R[X] = \{ t[X] \mid t \varepsilon R\}$

θ-selection: $\sigma_{A\theta'c'}R = \{ t \mid t[A] \,\theta\, 'c', t \varepsilon R\}$

θ-restriction: $\sigma_{A\theta B}R = \{ t \mid t[A] \,\theta\, t[B], t \varepsilon R\}$

(Here, θ is a comparison operator such as =, <, >, etc., and c is a constant value. When θ is =, these are called selection and restriction, respectively).

θ-join: $R = R_i\,[R_i.A_k \;\theta\; R_j.A_h]\,R_j = \{t_1t_2 \mid t_1[A_k] \;\theta\; t_2[A_h]\,, t_1 \varepsilon R_i, t_2 \varepsilon R_j\}$

θ-join for more than two relations is expressed by a logical AND of qualification part, such as $[R_{i1}.A_{k1} \;\theta\; R_{j1}.A_{h1}] \wedge [R_{i2}.A_{k2} \;\theta\; R_{j2}.A_{h2}]$. When θ is =, it is called an **equi-join**. Furthermore, if all attributes in $\underline{R}_i \cup \underline{R}_j$ are used as joining attributes, it is called a natural equi-join. In this case, duplication of attributes in $\underline{R}_i \cap \underline{R}_j$ are removed and the resulting relation is defined on $\underline{R}_i \cup \underline{R}_j$.

Natural equi-join : $R = R_i \bowtie R_j = \{ t \mid t \varepsilon R, t[\underline{R}_i] \varepsilon R_i, t[\underline{R}_j] \varepsilon R_j, \underline{R} = \underline{R}_i \cup \underline{R}_j \}$

Since the join operation is associative, the natural equi-join of m relations $R_1, R_2, ..., R_m$ is denoted by $R_1 \bowtie R_2 \bowtie ... \bowtie R_m$.

Fig. 1 (a) shows relation R_1(Professor, Age, Course). Here R_1 is the relation name. Professor, Age and Course are attribute names, and $\underline{R}_1$ ={Professor, Age, Course}. Meaning of each tuple of R_1 is that each Professor whose age is Age teaches a Course. R_1[Professor, Age] and R_1[Professor, Course] are shown in Figs. 1 (b) and (c), respectively. Natural equi-join of the two relations in Figs. 1(b) and (c) is R_1.

R_1(Professor, Age, Course)

Professor	Age	Course
a	30	Database
a	30	Logic Design
b	40	Software

(a)

R_1[Professor, Age]

Professor	Age
a	30
b	40

(b)

R_1[Professor, Course]
= R_2[Professor, Course]

Professor	Course
a	Database
a	Logic Design
b	Software

(c)

Fig. 1 - Decomposition of a relation

R_2(Professor, Project, Course)

Professor	Project	Course
a	p1	Database
a	p1	Logic Design
a	p2	Database
a	p2	Logic Design
b	p2	Software
b	p3	Software

(a)

R_2[Professor, Project]

Professor	Project
a	p1
a	p2
b	p2
b	p3

(b)

Fig. 2 - A multi-valued dependency

Data dependencies are important time-dependent semantic constraints concerned with attribute relationships. A **functional dependency** (FD) : X -> Y is satisfied in relation R if and only if for any pair of tuples t and t', t [X] = t' [X] implies t [Y] = t' [Y]. Thruoghout this paper, we assume $X \cap Y = \emptyset$ for an FD : X ->Y. In Fig. 1 (a), an FD : Professor -> Age is satisfied, since each professor has only one value for Age. As a professor can teach more than one course, Professor -> Course is not satisfied.

A **multi-valued dependency** (MVD) : X ->>Y | Z is satisfied in R (where R = XYZ and $Y \cap Z = \emptyset$) if and only if R = R[XY] ⋈ R[XZ]. As R_2(Professor, Project, Course) in Fig. 2 (a) satisfies R_2 = R_2[Professor, Project] ⋈ R_2[Professor, Course] (see Fig. 2 (b) and Fig. 1 (c)), Professor ->> Project | Course holds in R_2.

If FD : X -> Y is satisfied in R(XYZ), R = R[XY] ⋈ R[XZ] holds. Thus FDs are special cases of MVDs. Fig. 1 (a) satisfies Professor ->> Age | Course.

A **degenerated MVD** (DMVD) (introduced independently in [ARMS80] [SAGI81][TANA78]) : X =>> Y | Z is satisfied in relation R if and only if R = $R_1 \cup R_2$ such that FD : X -> Y is satisfied in R_1 and FD : X -> Z is satisfied in R_2, and $R_1[X] \cap R_2[X] = \emptyset$. If such a DMVD is satisfied, MVD : X ->>Y | Z holds in both R_1 and R_2 because of the existence of the FDs. Since $R_1[X] \cap R_2[X] = \emptyset$, this MVD is also satisfied in R. Thus the DMVD is a special case of MVD : X ->>Y | Z. In Fig. 3 (a), we assume that each professor must have at least one project and must teach at least one course. Furthermore, there are the following constraints: (1) He teaches exactly one course if he has more than one projects. (2) If he has exactly one project, he may teach more than one course. R_3 in Fig. 3 (a) is divided into two relations R_{31} and R_{32} shown in Figs. 3 (b) and (c), where Professor -> Course holds in R_{31} and Professor -> Project holds in R_{32}. Thus MVD : Professor ->> Project | Course holds in both R_{31} and R_{32}. As R_{31}[Professor] ∩ R_{32}[Professor] = ∅, R_3 also

R_3(Professor, Project, Course)

Professor	Project	Course
a	p1	Database
a	p1	Logic Design
b	p2	Software
b	p3	Software
c	P3	Graphics

(a)

R_{31}

Professor	Project	Course
b	p2	Software
b	p3	Software
c	p3	Graphics

(b)

R_{32}

Professor	Project	Course
a	p1	Database
a	p1	Logic Design

(c)

R_3[Professor, Project]

	Professor	Project
*	a	p1
#	b	p2
#	b	p3
	c	p3

(d)

*R_{32}[Professor, Project]

#R_{31}[Professor, Project]

R_3[Professor, Course]

	Professor	Course
*	a	Database
*	a	Logic Design
#	b	Software
#	c	Graphics

(e)

*R_{32}[Professor, Course]

#R_{31}[Professor, Course]

Fig. 3 - A degenerated MVD

satisfies the MVD and it can be decomposed into two relations shown in Figs. 3 (d) and (e).

A **join dependency** (JD) is defined as a constraint such that relation R is always represented by a natural equi-join of n relations obtained by projections of R. An MVD corresponds to the case n = 2. Since a practical subclass of JDs, called acyclic JDs, can be represented by MVDs [BEER81] [FAGI83], we will not use JDs in this paper. Since a relation formed by joining n relations satisfies a JD, there are correspondences between tree queries and acyclic JDs, and between cyclic queries and cyclic JDs. Differences of these problems are not discussed in this paper.

3. Queries and Query Graphs

As among relational operations, joins are most expensive and natural equi-joins are common among θ-joins, we will consider the following query in this chapter.

$$(R_1 \bowtie R_2 \bowtie \dots \bowtie R_m)[T]$$

Here, T is called the object attribute set. Especially when $T=\underline{R_i}$, it is called a **partial result** for R_i. A natural equi-join query with multiple object attribute sets is denoted as follows.

$$(R_1 \bowtie R_2 \bowtie \dots \bowtie R_m)[T_1, T_2, \dots, T_k]$$

A **query graph** Gq = (V, E, L) corresponding to an equi-join query q is a labeled undirected graph. V is a set of vertices, where v_i in V corresponds to relation R_i. Two vertices v_i and v_j corresponding to R_i and R_j are connected by an edge iff there is a clause $R_i.A = R_j.A$ in q. The label of the edge is the union of all such A. E is the set of edges and L is the set of all possible labels for E. L is the family of all non-empty subsets of the attribute set.

Although we will handle only natural equi-join queries, equi-join queries are required for equivalent transformations of natural equi-join queries. Note that any equi-join query can be converted into a natural equi-join query by proper renaming of attributes.

Selection operations on each relation can be represented by an arrow showing the operation. Fig. 4 (b) shows an example. In the following we use R_i and v_i interchangablly if there is no confusion.

Example 1 : Consider the following three relations.

R_1(Professor, Department, Research-Project)
R_2(Author, Title, Keyword)
R_3(Course, Professor, Text, Department)

R_1 denotes that each Professor belongs to Departments and he is engaged in Research-Projects. R_2 shows that each book is written by Authors, and whose title is Title and which has Keywords. R_3 represents that each Course is taught by Professors using Texts, and the Course is offered in Departments. Consider the following query.

"Find all possible combinations of (*p*, *d*, *s*, *t*, *c*) such that professor *p* who belongs to department *d* and whose research subjects contain *s*, teaches course *c* offered in department *d*, using text *t* written by *p* where *t* covers the subject *s*."

This query can be converted into a natural equi-join query by the following renaming.

R_1(Professor, Department, Subject)
R_2(Professor, Text, Subject)
R_3(Course, Professor, Text, Department)

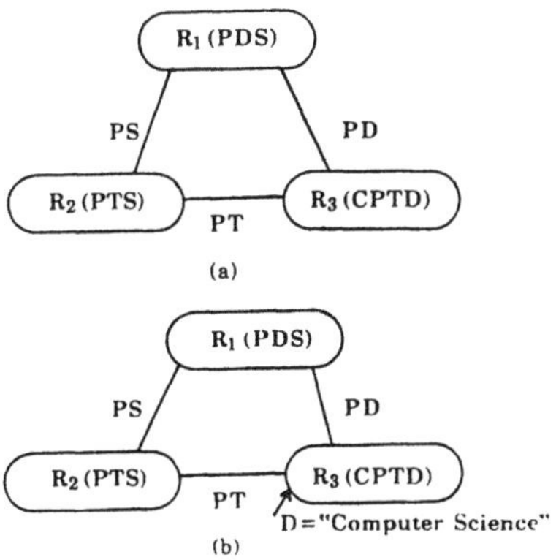

Fig. 4 - Examples of query graphs

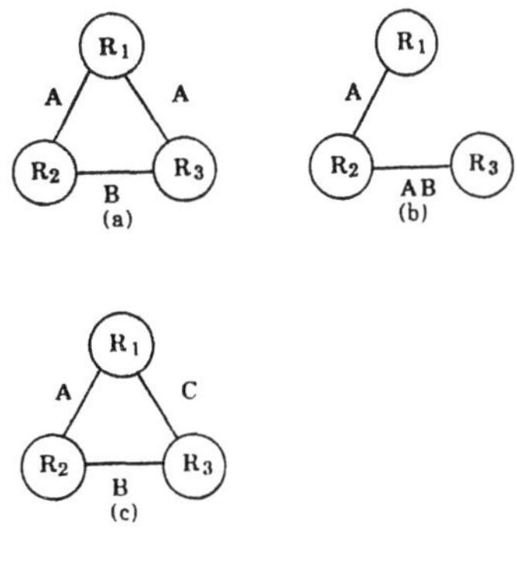

Fig. 5 - Tree and cyclic queries

The query graph corresponding to this query is shown in Fig. 4 (a), where attribute names are shown by their first characters. If there is a selection operation Department = 'Computer Science', we can use the query graph shown in Fig. 4 (b).

Two queries are said to be equivalent if both will produce the same result for any instances of the underlying database schemes. Two query graphs are equivalent if the two corresponding queries are equivalent.

A query is called a **tree query** if it is equivalent to a query whose query graph is circuit-free, otherwise it is called a **cyclic query** [BERN81b]. There exists an efficient procedure to test whether or not a given query is a tree query [YU79] [BEER81]. A special case is treated in [BERN81a].

Example 2 : The query graphs for the following three equi-join queries q_1, q_2, q_3 on relations R_1, R_2 and R_3 are shown in Fig. 5 (a), (b) and (c), respectively.

$q_1 : [R_1.A = R_2.A] \wedge [R_2.B = R_3.B] \wedge [R_3.A = R_1.A]$
$q_2 : [R_1.A = R_2.A] \wedge [R_2.A = R_3.A] \wedge [R_2.B = R_3.B]$
$q_3 : [R_1.A = R_2.A] \wedge [R_2.B = R_3.B] \wedge [R_3.C = R_1.C]$

Although the graph corresponding to q_1 has a cycle, it is equivalent to q_2 whose query graph is acyclic, because equi-join of R_1 and R_3 by A is expressed as equi-join of R_1 and R_2 by A, and equi-join of R_2 and R_3 by A. q_3 is, however, a cyclic query.

The followings are equivalence transformations for queries [BERN81].

Procedure 1 : Elementary Equivalence Transformations of Query Graphs

We assume that there are three vertices v_i, v_j and v_h. Let labels of e_{ij}, e_{jh} and e_{ih} be Y_1, Y_2 and Y_3, respectively. If there is no edge between v_i and v_h, Y_3 is assumed to be $\emptyset$. We can change the label of e_{ih} to any Y_4 satisfying the following condition, where $Z = Y_1 \cap Y_2 \neq \emptyset$.

$Y_3 - Z \subseteq Y_4 \subseteq Y_3 \cup Z$. Here, we assume $Y_1 \neq \emptyset$ and $Y_2 \neq \emptyset$.

If $Y_3 - Z$ is $\emptyset$, Y_4 can be $\emptyset$. In such a case, the edge is removed. If Y_3 is originally $\emptyset$(that is, there is no edge between v_i and v_j), we can add edge e_{ih} whose label is a subset of Z.

Equivalent graphs are obtained by repeated applications of Procedure 1. For example, we apply Procedure 1 to Fig. 5 (a) by regarding i, j and h to be 2, 1 and 3, respectively (Y_1 = A, Y_2 = A, Y_3 = B). As Z = A, A can be added to the label of e_{23}. After the addition. we apply Procedure 1 again by regarding i, j and h to be 1, 2 and 3, respectively (Y_1 = A, Y_2 = AB, Y_3 = A). As Z = A, the label of e_{13} can be $\emptyset$ and the edge is removed. The result is shown in Fig. 5 (b).

A query q is called a tree query if and only if there exists a circuit-free query graph obtained from the query graph for q using the equivalence transformation shown in Procedure 1. The query in Example 1 is shown to be a cyclic query.

A **semi-join** of R_i by R_j is denoted by $R_i \ltimes R_j$ and defined as

$R_i \ltimes R_j = R_i \bowtie R_j[\underline{R_i}] = R_i \bowtie R_j[\underline{R_i} \cap \underline{R_j}]$.

For any tree query all the partial results can be obtained using semi-joins only (see Procedure 2 and Example 3), but there exists a cyclic query whose partial results cannot be obtained by semi-joins [BERN81a].

Procedure 2 : Tree Query Processing Using Semi-Joins

(1) Let Gq be a query graph corresponding to a given tree query q. The graph is a connected tree. Select one vertex as the root of the tree. The level of each vertex is the length of the path from the root to the vertex.

(2)[UP-PHASE] Starting from the leaves of the tree, apply semi-joins as follows.

(2-1) Select v_i satisfying that (a) it was not selected before, (b) all the vertices connected to v_i, whose levels are larger than the level of v_i, were selected already.

(2-2) If v_i is not the root, there exists only one vertex v_j whose level is smaller than the level of v_i and which is connected to v_i. Apply semi-join $R_j \ltimes R_i$ and replace R_j by the result.

(2-3) Repeat the above steps until all the vertices except the root are selected. The partial result for the root is obtained after the UP-PHASE.

(3)[DOWN-PHASE] Starting from the root vertex, apply semi-joins as follows.

(3-1) Select any v_j such that it is connected to v_i whose partial result is already known. The partial result of v_j is given by semi-join $R_j \ltimes R_i$.
(3-2) Repeat the above step until all the partial results have been obtained.

R_1

A	B
1	a
1	b
2	b

(a)

R_2

B	C
b	α
c	β
d	α

(b)

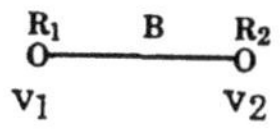

(c)

$R_1' = R_1 \ltimes R_2$

A	B
1	b
2	b

(d)

$R_2' = R_2 \ltimes R_1'$

B	C
b	α

(e)

Fig. 6 - An example of tree query processing using semi-joins

Example 3 : Consider the join of two relations shown in Figs. 6 (a) and (b). The query graph is shown in Fig. 6 (c). Let v_1 be the root of the tree. The above procedure goes as follows.
[UP-PHASE] Apply semi-join $R_1' = R_1 \ltimes R_2$ and replace R_1 by R_1'. In a distributed system, values {b, c, d} are transmitted from the site of R_1 to the site of R_2 to realize the semi-join. R_1' becomes a partial result of the query.
[DOWN-PHASE] Apply semi-join $R_2 \ltimes R_1'$ and replace R_2 by the result (Fig. 6 (e)). In distributed systems {b} is transmitted from the site of R_1 to the site of R_2. R_2' becomes the partial result of the query. Thus the partial results of both relations can be computed using semi-joins.

Adventages of semi-join based procedures are as follows.
(1) In centralized systems, no real joins are required. Join operations usually produce large intermediate relations. Thus space savings are acheived as well as computation time.
(2) In distributed systems, data-transmission cost can be also reduced.

Although it is claimed that most practical queries are tree queries, cyclic-query processing is important for the following reasons.
(1) Cyclic queries do occur as shown in Fig. 4 (a) and Fig. 5 (c). In general, when there is more than one relationship among attribute set X and it is required to obtain X-values satisfying more than one relationship, that query is cyclic. This is illustrated in Example 4.
(2) When the object attribute set of a given query is not contained in any relation scheme used in the query, a procedure to handle a cyclic query is needed. Example 5 shows this case.

Example 4 : Consider the query graph shown in Fig. 7, which corresponds to the following query.

"Find all possible combinations of Professors and Students who belong to the same Department and live in the same City."

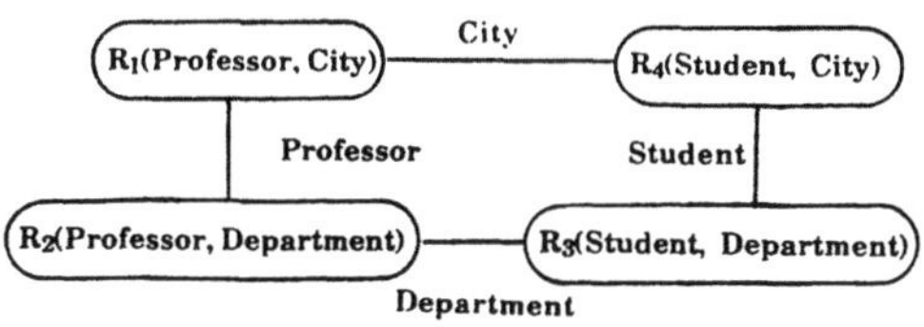

Fig. 7 - A cyclic query

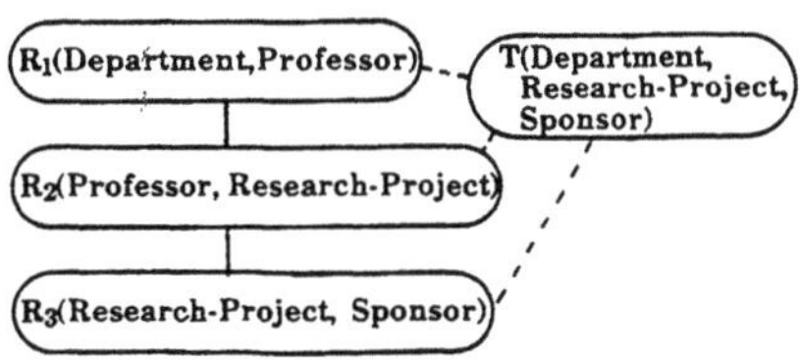

Fig. 8 - A tree query with an object attribute set

There are two relationships between Professor and Student, "belonging to the same department" (represented by R_2 and R_3) and "living in the same city" (represented by R_1 and R_4). The query is cyclic, since it requires Professors and Students satisfying the two relationships.

Example 5 : Consider the following three relations.

R_1(Department, Professor)

R_2(Professor, Research-Project)

R_3(Research-Project, Sponsor)

The natural equi-joins of these relations forms a tree query, but it becomes cyclic if the following object attribute set is given.

T = {Department, Research-Project, Sponsor}

The query graph considering T is shown in Fig. 8, which is cyclic. We have to distinguish edges between relations, and edges between relations and the object attribute set, since in the later case values for the object relation are nulls before the query is evaluated.

We have the following proposition for queries with object attribute sets.

Proposition 1 : A natural equi-join query with object attribute sets is cyclic if and only if there are at least two relations R_i, R_j and an object attribute set T such that $R_i \cap T \neq \emptyset$, $R_j \cap T \neq \emptyset$, $T - R_i \neq \emptyset$ and $T - R_j \neq \emptyset$, when the query graph without the object attributer sets is connected.

Thus except when partial results are to be obtained, we need a procedure for cyclic queries, even if the query without the object attribute sets is a tree.

4. Methods of Converting Query Graphs

In this section we will summarize several methods of converting query graphs together with examples of transformation from cyclic queries to tree queries. Details of the more important methods will be given in the succeeding sections.

Method 1 : Join of relations

If two relations R_i and R_j are joined, the corresponding transformation of the query graph is to merge vertices v_i and v_j such that the resulting vertex is connected to every vertex which is connected to v_i or v_j.

The method is very simple, so it is often used to remove cyclic components of a query graph by joining all relations contained in each cyclic component. Fig. 9 shows a very simple example. By merging relations R_1, R_2 and R_3 in the cyclic query shown in Fig. 9 (a), a tree in Fig. 9 (b) is obtained. Merging of n relations requires n-1 joins. We can reduce the number of joins for conversion from a cyclic query to a tree query.

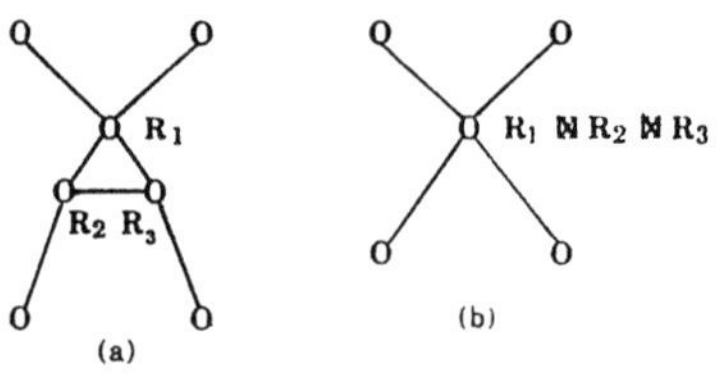

Fig. 9 - Join of relations

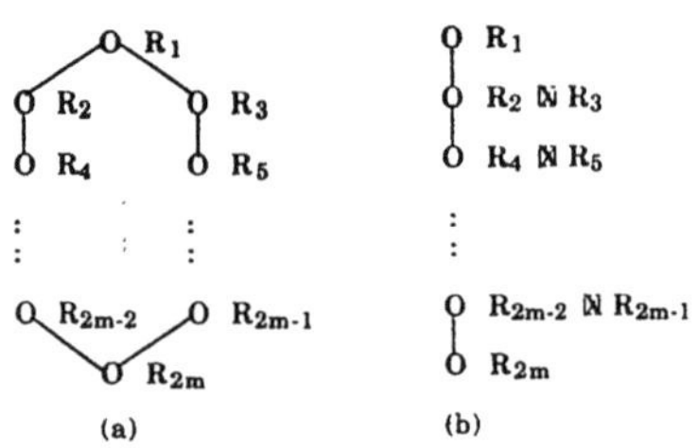

Fig. 10 - Conversion of a cycle into a tree by joins

Example 6 : Consider the query represented by Fig. 10 (a) which consists of 2m (even) vertices. By merging R_{2i-2} and R_{2i-1} for i = 2,3,...,m, we get a tree query shown in Fig. 10 (b) using m-1 joins.

In general we have the following proposition.

Proposition 2: In a query graph, a cyclic component containing a cycle including n vertices can be eliminated by $\lceil n/2 \rceil -1$ joins, where $\lceil i \rceil$ denotes the smallest integer not less than i.

Although the number of joins becomes about half by this method, actual cost for processing the query may not be reduced, since merging of R_{2i-2} and R_{2i-1} may be a direct product operation, which requires all possible combinations of tuples in these relations.

Method 2 : Decomposition of a relation into tuples

The method is known as the query decomposition method developed by for INGRES [WONG76]. If a relation consists of one tuple, a join operation involving the relation can be replaced by a set of selection operations.

For example, suppose R_1 and R_2 are joined on attribute A, and R_1 has just one tuple and its A-value is *a*. The join can be replaced by the selection operation

$R_2[A = 'a']$.

If a relation consists of more than one tuple, we can repeat the above process for each tuple. By this decomposition process, all the edges connected to the vertex corresponding to the relation which is decomposed into tuples, are removed. Thus the process of converting a cyclic query into a tree query using Method 2 is as follows.

(1) Find a set of vertices such that all cycles in the query graph disappears by eliminating these vertices.

(2) Apply the tuple-wise processing method to all relations corresponding to the vertices.

Minimization of the number of vertices selected in step (1) correponds to the problem of finding a minimum set of vertices on an undirected graph such that elimination of these vertices removes all cycles in the graph, which is unfourtunately an NP-complete problem [GARE79]. Parallel processing of tuples is possible by adding tuple identifiers as shown in the following example.

Example 7 : In Fig. 4 if we select R_2 as the relation to be decomposed into tuples for Method 2, the query graph shown in Fig. 11 (a) is obtained, in which the selected tuple is

(Professor= 'p_i', Text= 't_i', Subject= 's_i').

Instead of repeating this process for all tuples in R_2, a combined process can be realized by adding tuple identifieds (TIDs) to indicate the correspondence.

Figs. 12 (a), (b) and (c) show example relations for the query shown in Fig. 4. Since the query is processed for each tuple of R_2, we add TIDs to R_2. TID is also added to the selection operations as shown in Fig. 11 (b). After the selection operations, R_1 and R_3 contains values for TIDs besides values for PDS and CPTD, respectively. This process is realized by generalized semi-joins to be discussed in Section 5. Parallel processingof tuple is realized by joining these relations by PD and TID.

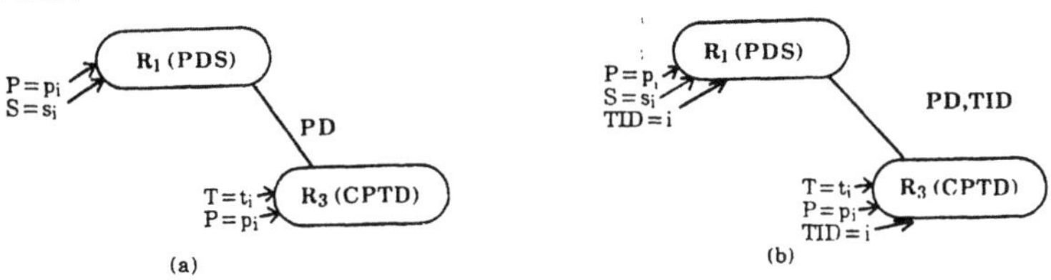

Fig. 11 - Decomposition of a relation into tuples

R_1

Professor	Department	Subject
p1	d1	s1
p2	d2	s1
p3	d2	s2

(a)

R_2

Professor	Text	Subject	TID
p1	t1	s2	1
p2	t2	s1	2
p3	t1	s2	3

(b)

R_3

Course	Professor	Text	Department
c1	p1	t1	d1
c2	p2	t2	d2
c3	p3	t3	d2

(c)

$(R_2 \bowtie R_3)$[Professor, Text]

Professor	Text	TID
p1	t1	1
p2	t2	2

(d)

Fig. 12 - Example relations for the query shown in Fig. 4

Method 3 : Addition of extra attributes

Instead of eliminating vertices, we can eliminate edges. For example, if R_1 and R_2 are joined on attribute A, and a is one of the values common to R_1.A and R_2.A, then the join on this value can be replaced by the two selection operations $R_1[A=a]$ and $R_2[A=a]$. By repeating this convertion for all A-values in both R_1 and R_2, the edge between v_1 and v_2 is removed.

This method has the following advantages over Method 2.

(1) In Method 2 the number of repetition is determined by the number of tuples in the relation selected for tuple-wise processing. The number of repetition required for Method 3 is determined by the number of values which are common to the join attributes in both relations connected to the selected edge. This number is usually smaller than the number required by Method 2. If two relations have m and n tuples, respectively, the number of possible combinations of the join attribute values for these relations is at most min{m, n}. For example, in Fig. 12 both R_2 and R_3 have three tuples, while the number of possible combinations of PT in R_2 and R_3 is two as shown in Fig. 12 (d).

(2) In Method 2 the problem of of minimizing the number of vertices to convert a cyclic query into a tree query is known to be not easy, but the minimum number of edges to remove cycles in a graph is determined by the total number of vertices and that of edges in the graph. Thus the minimization problem is easy for Method 3.

In this method we can also realize parallel processing by sending TIDs of values common to the join attributes. Since the TIDs may be regarded as compressed values for the join attributes, this method is also interpreted as follows.

(1) Add imaginary attribute set X to all edges which require the TID corresponding to X.

(2) Apply the elementary equivalence tansformation (Procedure 1) to the result.

Example 8: Consider the query shown in Fig. 4. We select the edge between R_2 and R_3. This edge is replaced by selection operations as shown in Fig. 13(a). Instead of this conversion we can add attribute set PT to all edges in the graph, and obtain the graph shown in Fig. 13 (b). Since PT is contained in the path from R_2 to R_3 through R_1, the edge between R_2 and R_3 becomes redundant (Procedure 1). The resulting tree query is shown in Fig. 13 (c). For each combination of PT-values realized at the edge between R_2 and R_3, we use a TID as shown in Fig. 12 (d).

Application of this method to processing complicated cyclic queries will be discussed in the next section.

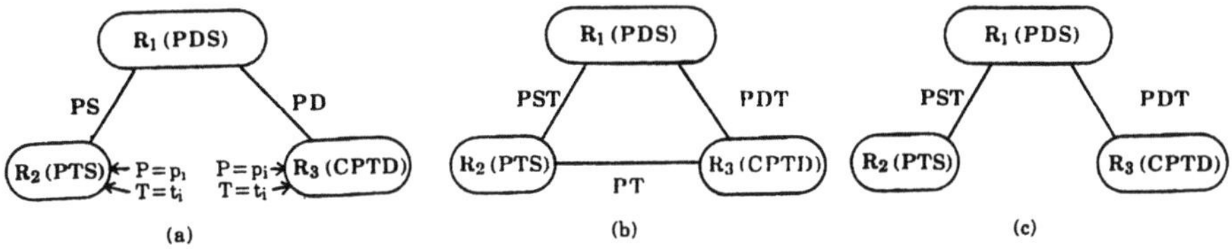

Fig. 13 - Addition of extra attributes

Method 4 : Addition of extra relations

Instead of adding attributes we can convert queries by adding extra relations.
(1) Add vertices corresponding to the extra relations to the query graph. Add appropriate edges.
(2) Apply the elementary equivalent transformation (Procedure 1) to the resulting graph.
(3) Apply operations to compute the instances of the extra relations.

It turns out that the method is not much different from Method 1. The only difference is that attributes not contained in any of the join attribute sets are not required in the extra relation.

Example 9 : Consider the query shown in Fig. 4. We can add the following relation to the query.

R_4(Professor, Subject, Text, Department)

Since this relation contains all the attributes contained in more than one relation, the resulting query is a tree query, as shown in Fig. 14. To compute this relation, we have to join R_1, R_2 and R_3[Professor, Text, Department]. Although Method 1 requires the join of all relations, costs for the two methods are similar.

Method 5 : Horizontal decomposition of relations

Instead of the tuple-wise decomposition (Method 2), we can use other types of horizontal decompositions.
(1) Decompose a relation into subrelations $R_1, R_2, \ldots, R_m$, such that $R = R_1 \cup R_2 \cup \ldots \cup R_m$ and each R_i satisfies some given condition.
(2) For each subrelation apply a query processing procedure.
This method is a generalization of Method 2. Method 7 uses dependencies for the condition of (1). We can use non-disjoint decomposition (i.e., $R_i \cap R_j \neq \emptyset$ for some i, j) for step (1).

Method 6 : Vertical decomposition of relations

If a relation satisfies a functional or multivalued dependency, it can be decomposed into two relations. In many cases, such a decomposition increases the number of cycles in a query graph (consider the conversion from Fig. 10 (b) to Fig. 10 (a) when m=2), but dependencies satisfying some coditions will contribute to reduce the number of cycles. For such dependencies we can use temporary dependencies satisfied by snapshot data as well as one given as database constraints. Conditions for such dependencies together with detailed discussion will be given in Section 6.

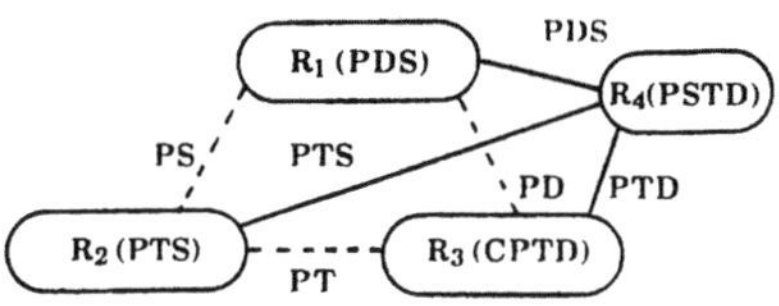

Fig.14 - Addition of an extra relation

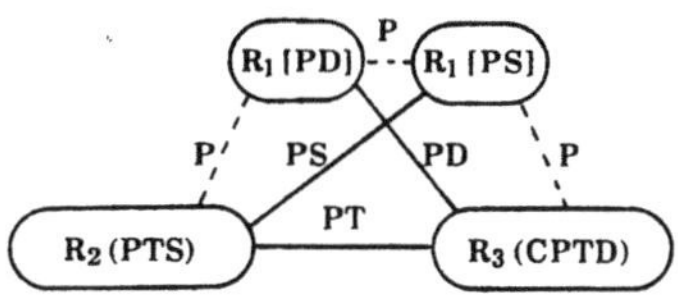

Fig. 15 - Vertical decomposition of R_1

Example 10 : Assume that there is an MVD: P ->> D | S in R_1 of Fig. 4, then R_1 can be decomposed into two relations $R_1[PD]$ and $R_1[PS]$. The query graph obtained after the decomposition of R_1 is shown in Fig. 15. Redundant edges are denoted by dotted lines, and the query is a tree. We can use the following FDs as special cases of the MVD.
(i) P -> D (each Professor belongs to exactly one Department).
(ii) P -> S (each Professor has only one Research-Subject).

Method 7 : Horizontal and vertical decomposition of a relation
Although Method 6 is interesting, in many cases realtions may not satisfy the dependencies to allow removal of cycles. We can use Method 5 so that each subrelation R_i satisfies the given dependency. It is always possible, since a single-tuple relation R_i satisfies any functional and multivalued dependency defined on $\underline{R_i}$.

Example 11 : We assume that FD : A -> B is required in relation R shown in Fig. 16 (a), in order to apply Method 6(vertical decomposition). Although R does not satisfy the FD, each of relations R_1 and R_2 (Figs. 16 (b) and (c), respectively) obtained by horizontal decomposition of R satisfies the FD.

R

A	B	C
1	1	1
1	2	2
2	1	3
2	3	2

(a)

R_1

A	B	C
1	1	1
2	1	3

(b)

R_2

A	B	C
1	2	2
2	3	2

(c)

Fig. 16 - Horizontal decomposition of a relation

In summary, we can classify the above methods into the following four categories.
Addition of vertices: Method 4
Elimination of vertices: Method 1, Method 2
Decomposition of vertices: Method 5, Method 6, Method 7
Elimination of edges: Method 3
Capabilities of these methods may be compared as follows, where A<B means A is a special case of B.
Method 1 < Method 4
Method 2 <Method 5 <Method 7
Method 6 < Method 7
Method 3
Since Methods 1, 2 and 4 are very simple, we will discuss Method 3 in Section 5 and Methods 5, 6 and 7 in Section 6. Details of these methods are given in [KAMB82b] and [KAMB83], respectively.

5. Attribute Addition

In this section a procedure for handling cyclic queries by the attribute-addition approach is discussed. The procedure consists of two steps.

A. First add a proper set of attributes to each relation scheme in order to convert a given query to a tree query. Note that these additional attributes have null values at the beginning of the step B.
B. For the resulting tree query, a procedure similar to the conventional tree-query processing procedure is applied.

If a query graph consists of only one simple cycle as shown in Example 8, the procedure for A is very simple.
(1) Select one edge in the cycle. Let X be the label of the edge.

(2) X is added to all relation schemes in the cycle.
(3) Add X to all labels of the edges in the cycle. Then the edge selected on step (1) becomes redundant.

If there is an interaction of more than one cycle, we can use a spanning tree of a graph. A **spanning tree** for a graph G is defined to be a subgraph of G, which contains all vertices of G, is connected and cycle-free. There exist efficient procedures to compute a spanning tree of a graph. It is known that for egde e not included in the spanning tree, only one simple cycle is formed by adding e to the spanning tree.

Procedure 3 : Conversion of a Cyclic Query into a Tree Query by Attribute Addition
(1) Find a spanning tree of the given query graph.
(2) Edges not included in the spanning tree are removed by this procedure. For each egde e not included in the spanning tree, add the label of e to all edges in the cycle which consists of e and only edges in the spanning tree, so that e becomes redundant (Procedure 1).
(3) Repeat the above step for every edge not in the spanning tree.
(4) Additional attributes for each relation scheme can be determined as follows. Add attributes contained in the labels of edges incident to vertex v to the relation scheme corresponding to vertex v.

Example 12 : Consider the query graph shown in Fig. 17 (a). The spanning tree required on step (1) of Procedure 3 is shown in bold lines. There are two edges e_1 and e_2 not in the tree. Addition of attributes to remove e_1 is shown in Fig. 17 (b). Fig. 17 (c) shows the result of edge labels after step (3) of Procedure 3. Underlined attributes denote extras. If the root relation is $R_1(ADG)$, by the attribute addition it is replaced by $R_1'(ADGH)$, where values for H are nulls.

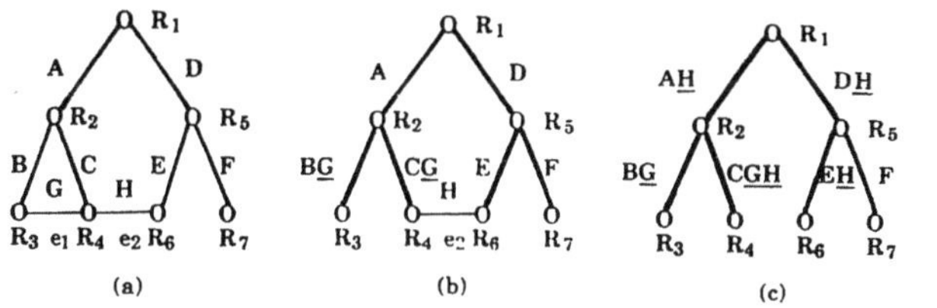

Fig. 17 - Conversion of a cyclic query into a tree query by the attribute-addition approach

After obtaining a tree with additional attributes, a procedure similar to the tree query processing procedure (Procedure 2) is applied. In practice, instead of adding attributes with null values, relations are actually modified dynamically during the process.

To handle relations with additional attributes whose values are nulls, generalized semi-join is defined.

Generalized semi-join : Generalized semi-join $R_i(X\#Y)$ by $R_j(Z)$ is denoted by $R_i(X\#Y) \ltimes R_j(Z)$ and is defined as follows, where $R_i(X\#Y)$ is a relation formed by adding a set Y of attributes whose values are nulls to $R_i(X)$.

$$R_i(X\#Y) \ltimes R_j(Z) = R'(X\cup(XY\cap Z)\#(Y\text{-}Z)),$$
$$\text{where} \quad R'(X\cup(XY\cap Z)) = R_i(X) \ltimes R_j(XY\cap Z)$$

$R'(X\cup(XY\cap Z))$ is the relation obtained by a projection on $XY\cap Z$ of the result of a semi-join of $R_i(X)$ by $R_j(Z)$. In $R_i(X\#Y)$, values for Y are nulls. In R', values of $Y\cap Z$ are not nulls, since these values are determined by R_j. As we need a relation on XY, values for Y-Z are still nulls in the result, which is represented by $R'(X\cup(XY\cap Z)\#(Y\text{-}Z))$. Intuitively, a generalized semi-join is a semi-join in which each null value is assumed to be all possible values in the domain of the corresponding attribute.

Example 13 : We will apply a procedure to the tree obtained by Example 12. We must modify the procedure because values for the extra attributes are nulls. For the extra attributes, real values are not transmitted. Encoded values are used instead for effeciency. The encoded values correspond to the TIDs of the attribute

values at the edge.
(1) Encode G-values contained in both R_3 and R_4. Encode H-values contained in both R_3 and R_6. G- and H-values are replaced by integers, 1, 2, ...
(2) Replace G- and H-values in R_3, R_4 and R_6 by the integers. Note that, for example, tuples in R_3 whose G-values are not contained in the set of G-values of R_4 are not required. Thus tuples which cannot be encoded are not necessary.
(3) Perform [UP-PHASE] of Procedure 2, using generalized semi-joins instead of semi-joins. The partial result for R_1 is obtained after this step.
(4) Perform [DOWN-PHASE] of Procedure 2 using semi-joins.

Procedure 4: Cyclic Query Processing Using Generalized Semi-Joins
This is almost identical to Procedure 2.
(1) Apply Procedure 3 to get a tree query from the given cyclic query.
(2) [UP-PHASE] Apply [UP-PHASE] of Procedure 2. Generalized semi-joins are used instead of semi-joins. The partial result of the root relation R is obtained after the UP-PHASE by projecting the result to the attribute set $\underline{R}$.
(3) [DOWN-PHASE] Same as [DOWN-PHASE] of Procedure 2.

6. Utilizing Dependencies

In this section we will discuss query processing procedures utlizing FDs, DMVDs, MVDs and horizontal decompositions. The following proposition shows a sufficient condition for eliminating a cycle by a decomposition of a relation.

Proposition 3 : Consider the cycle shown in Fig. 18 (a). R_0 is the relation to be decomposed. Let X be the intersection of all the labels of the edges in the cycle. If an MVD: $X' \to\to Y \mid Z$ holds on R_0, where $\underline{R_0} = X'YZ$ and $X' \subseteq X$, then the cycle is removed by decomposing R_0 into two relations $R_0^1(X'Y)$ and $R_0^2(X'Z)$ as shown in Fig. 18 (b).

There are the following special cases.
1. Dependency
   1-1. The MVD: $X' \to\to Y \mid Z$ is actually an FD : $X' \to Y$ or $X' \to Z$.
   1-2. The MVD: $X' \to\to Y \mid Z$ is an DMVD : $X' \Rightarrow\Rightarrow Y \mid Z$.
2. Left-side set
   $X' = \emptyset$. Since X is an intersection of all the labels of the edges in the cycle, it is often to be $\emptyset$.

Because of 2, use of $\emptyset \to Y$, $\emptyset \to Z$, $\emptyset \Rightarrow\Rightarrow Y \mid Z$ and $\emptyset \to\to Y \mid Z$ is very important. It should be noted that if we apply a procedure for tree query processing to the query shown in Fig. 18 (b), all the partial results for the relations in Fig. 18 (b) can be obtained; that is, the partial results for $R_0^1(X'Y)$ and $R_0^2(X'Z)$ are obtained instead of that for $R_0(X'YX)$. If 1-1 or 1-2 is satisfied, the partial result for R_0 can be obtained by joining these for $R_0^1(X'Y)$ and $R_0^2(X'Z)$. It is not generally

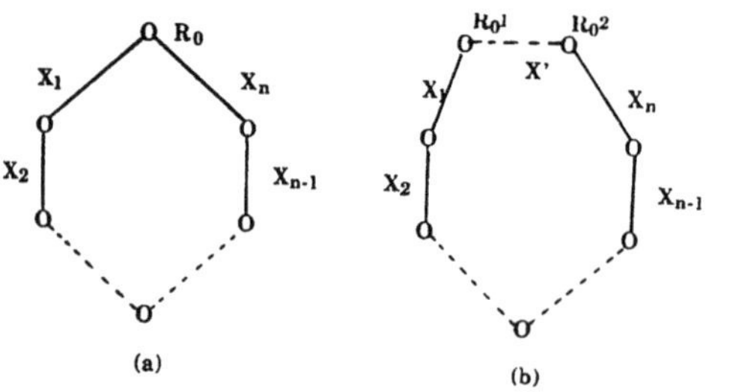

Fig. 18 - Removal of a cycle by an MVD-based decomposition

A	B	D
1	1	2
1	2	3
2	1	2

Fig. 19 - Use of an FD in the intersection of two relations

true for MVDs. If 1-1 or 1-2 is not satisfied, there is a case when the join of the partial results for $R_0^1(X'Y)$ and $R_0^2(X'Z)$ is not the partial result R for R_0, although R[X'Y] and R[X'Z] are given by these partial results (an example is shown in [KAMB83]).

For the dependency to be used, we can use one satisfied by the intersection of two relations. For example, consider R in Fig. 16 (a) and R' in Fig. 19. If two relations are joined, the result satisfies the FD : A -> B although both relations do not satisfy the FD. In general, the following dependencies can be used for Proposition 3.

(1) FDs and MVDs in the set of databse integrity constraints.
(2) FDs produced by relational operations.
  (2-1) If there is a selection operation $\sigma_{A='a'}$ R, then there is an FD : Ø -> A, where a is a constant value.
  (2-2) If there is a restriction operation $\sigma_{A=B}$ R, then there is an FD : A -> B and an FD : B -> A.
(3) FDs and MVDs produced by an intersection of the two relations to be joined, as shown in the above example.
(4) Temporary FDs and MVDs produced during the query processing.

If a snapshot relation satisfies the condition of an FD (MVD), we call it a **temporary** FD (**temporary** MVD). As we do for attribute addition, we can use a spanning tree for the selection of relations to be decomposed, when there is more than one cycle.

Procedure 5 : Conversion of a Cyclic Query into a Tree Query Utilizing FDs, DMVDs and MVDs.
(1) Select a spanning tree in a given query graph..
(2) For each edge not contained in the spanning tree, select one of the two relations corresponding to the two vertices incident to the edge.
(3) Determine the MVD which should be held on the relation selected on (2), in order to remove the cycle.
(4) Decompose the relation using the MVD.

The following problems arise in applying Procedure 5.
(1) The selected relation may not satisfy the required MVD. Thus for the selection of the spanning tree, we must consider the dependencies held in the relations. Selection of a best possible spanning tree is very complicated.
(2) There are cases when Procedure 5 fails to convert a query to a tree, since proper dependencies are not satisfied.
(3) In this procedure we count the number of binary decompositions which corresponds the number of edges not on the spanning tree, as the complexity mesure of the conversion. If the complexity measure is the number of relations to be decomposed as in the case with Method 2, the optimum result cannot be obtained easily.

Horizontal decomposition of a relation is a good solution to handle problems (1) and (2). If we horizontally decompose a relation into single-tuple relations, any FDs and MVDs defined on the scheme of the relation are satisfied. Thus the problem is how to minimize the number of relations satisfying the given dependency. As discussed previously, a pure MVD(which is not an FD or a DMVD) can be used to decompose relation R if the partial result for R is not required. In many cases the left-side set is Ø. We will give procedures for two important cases.

Procedure 6 : Horizontal Decomposition of a Relation into Subrelations Satisfying an FD : X->Y.
(1) For each value x of X, find the set of corresponding values S(x) of Y. Let m be the maximum number of the elements in S(x).
(2) Prepare relations R_1, R_2, ...R_m such that each relation contains at most one tuple t satisfying t[X]=x for each x.

We can use sorting or hashing to find tuples required in (1). Implemention details are omitted here [KAMB83].

Procedure 7 : Horizontal Decomposition of a Relation into Subrelations Satisfying a DMVD Whose Left Set is ∅.
(1) Let ∅=>>Y|Z be a DMVD to be satisfied by relation R. k=0.
(2) Let n(x) (n(y)) denote the number of tuples satisfying X='x' (or Y='y', respectively) in R. Let x_i (y_j) be the value which has the largest n(x_i) (or n(y_j)) among all n(x)'s and n(y)'s. R_k=R[X=x_i] (or R[Y=y_j]) is separated as one decomposed relation. R is replaced by R-R_k.
(4) k=k+1. Repeat step (3) until R becomes empty.

To find the MVD with left set ∅ which will produce the minimum number of relations by horizontal decomposition is NP-complete [GARE79].

7. Query Processing for Distributed Databases

As described in Section 3, for tree queries we need not perform real joins to obtain partial results. Using semi-joins only, the result is represented by a set of relations (i.e., partial results). Thus we can avoid large intermediate results produced by joins, and save memory space as well as computation time. For distributed systems, reduction of the communication cost is also achieved. Since these factors are mainly determined by the selection of spanning trees for the methods given in Sections 5 and 6, this section deals with the spanning-tree selection problem for distributed dartabases.

For expository simplicity, we will make the following assumptions.
(1) Each site has exactly one relation.
(2) Duplication of relations is not considered.
(3) Data-transmission cost is determined by the data size, independent of the distance between the sites.
(4) Direct communication is supported between any two sites.

Consider the query shown in Fig. 20 (a). If the spanning tree shown in Fig. 20 (b) is used where R_5 is selected to be the root, the response time for the query is short, since the tree height is short. On the other hand, if the spanning tree in Fig. 20 (c) is selected, the response time is long. By accumulation of the effect of semi-joins, however, the total amount of data transmitted is usually less than the previous case. In general we have the following criteria for selecting spanning trees.

(1) Reduction of the response time.
(2) Reduction of the total amount of data transmitted.

For (1) we need a tree with a small height, and for (2) a tree having a long path is preferred.

Let d(v_i, v_j) be the length of the shortest path between v_i and v_j. v_o which has the minimum value for $\max_j$ d(v_o, v_j) (=d(v_o,v_i) where v_i is the vertex which maximizes d(v_o, v_i)) is called a center of the graph. There may be more than one

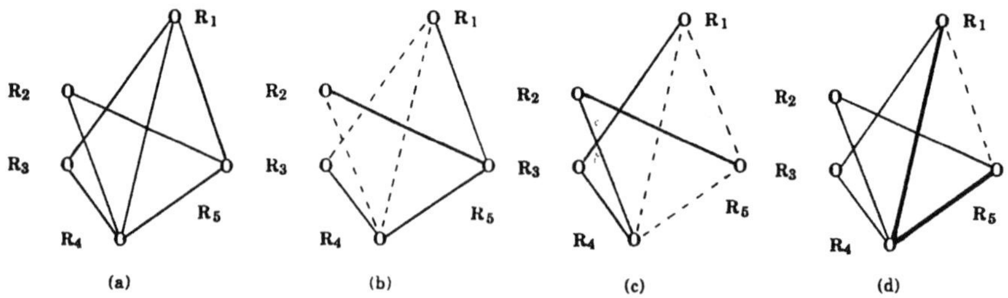

Fig. 20 - Selection of spanning trees

center in a graph. A **mimimum distance tree** rooted at v_o is a tree containing exactly one shortest path between v_o and v_i for any v_i. It is known that such a tree exists for any connected undirected graph. The spanning tree T of the least height is obtained by the following steps.
(1) Find a center v_o of a given query graph.
(2) Compute a minimum-distance tree T rooted at v_o.

Further reduction of the tree height is possible by use of the attribute-addition method.

Example 14: Suppose that the graph in Fig. 21 (a) shows a part of the minimum distance tree, and R_1 is the root of the tree. Since there exists a path R_1-R_2-R_3-R_4 which is assumed to be the longest path in the tree, the response time is determined by this path. We can generate a tree with less height using the attribute-addition method. Connect R_1 and R_4 and form a cycle. By adding attribute B to all edges in the cycle, we can remove the edge between R_2 and R_3. The resulting graph is shown in Fig. 21 (b), whose height is smaller than that of Fig. 21 (a).

By applying this method repeatedly we can always obtain a tree whose height is 1. Processing of a tree of height 1 is almost identical to joining all relations at the root site, except our procedure uses compressed data. When using the attribute-addition method, there is a trade-off problem between the tree height and the computation time.

For reduction of the total amount of data transmitted, we have to find a tree which is as high as possible. If a graph has a Hamiltonian path (a path which contains all vertices) as shown in Fig. 20 (c), the best possible result may be obtained. We can use the following techniques for graphs which do not contain Hamiltonian paths.
(1) Generation of a semi-join process corresponding to a long path: Consider the graph shown in Fig. 22. Instead of starting semi-joins in parall from R_1 and R_6, we first transmit data along R_1-R_2-R_3-R_4. The result of compressed values for attribute set X (the join attribute set between R_1 and R_6) are transmitted to the site of R_6. By applying a semi-join, some unnecessary tuples in R_6 are removed. Thus processing along R_6-R_5-R_4 after this process is cheaper than without the reduction of R_6.
(2) Hierarchical processing of a query[KAMB82b]: In Fig. 20 (c), edges not contained in the spanning tree forms a cycle. We can reduce the size of the relations contained in this cycle, if preprocessing of the cycle is done. For this purpose, we can use the tree shown in Fig. 20 (d).
(3) The attribute-addition method can be also used to increase the height of a tree.

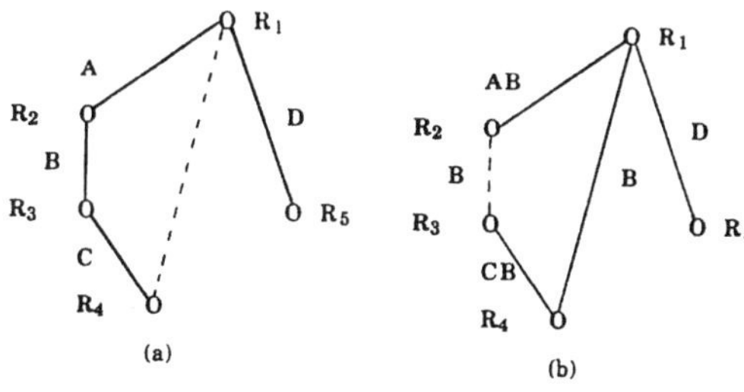

Fig. 21 - Reduction of a tree height using the attribute-addition approach

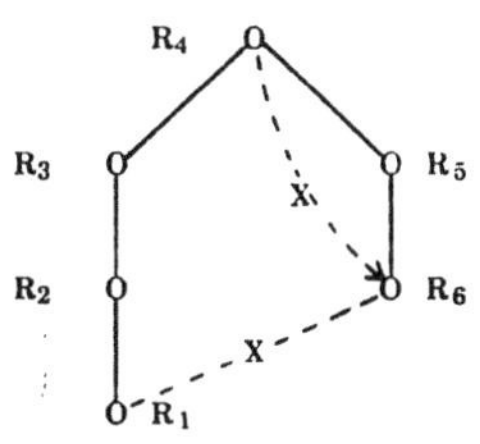

Fig. 22 - Generation of a semi-join process corresponding to a long path

8. Summary

This chapter gives extensive survey of the existing methods for query graph modification. Important combinations among the following possible combinations are discussed.

Addition Deletion	of	Relations Edges Attributes in relations

Horizontal Vertical	decomposition composition	of	Relations Relations realized at edges

One possible extension of the methods is to use other kinds of dependencies. The author believes, however, it is not easy to find completely new methods, since most important relational operations such as projection, selection, joins are used in the query-graph modification methods discussed in this chapter.

Use of horizontal decomposition is counter-intuitive, since it usually increases the complexity of queries. This method is a good example of the application of the dependency theory other than relational database design.

Some papers for tree query processing claim that most important queries are trees. Examples 4 and 5 show the importance of the cyclic query processing. For the conversion from a cyclic query to a tree query, a spanning tree of the given query graph is used. Methods of selecting appropriate spanning trees for distributed databases are discussed in Section 7. Since there is a trade-off problem between data transmission cost and computation time, selection of the best spanning tree is very difficult.

Generalizations for the following cases are also important. Some of them are current research topics.

(1) Query processing strategy considering the size of relations, selectivity etc. [APER83].
(2) Distributed databases with copies and fragement of relations.
(3) Use of broadcast capability of local area networks.
(4) Queries with general θ-joins[BERN79].
(5) Processing of multiple queries.

Acknowledgements : The author is grateful to Professor Shuzo Yajima and Mr. Masatoshi Yoshikawa of Kyoto University who are coauthors of [KAMB82b] and [KAMB83] for their cooperations and discussions. He wishes to express sincere appreciation to Dr. Won Kim and Dr. Don Batory for detailed comments on the first version of this chapter.

References

(APER83) (ARMS80) (BEER81) (BERN79, see BERN79a) (BERN81a) (BERN81b) (FAGI83) (GARE79) (GOOD82a) (GOOD82b) (GOOD82c) (KAMB82a) (KAMB82b) (KAMB83, see KAMB83a) (SAGI81, see SAGI81a) (TANA78) (WONG76) (YU79, see YU79b)

Section III

Query Processing for Multiple Data Models

Query Processing in a Multidatabase System*

Umeshwar Dayal

ABSTRACT

A multidatabase system provides a logically integrated view of existing, distributed, possibly inconsistent, databases that may be stored under heterogeneous database systems. Query processing in a multidatabase system consists of four tasks. First, queries over the user's integrated view must be modified into equivalent queries over the local schemas of the existing databases. Second, the modified queries must be globally optimized to produce an efficient global execution plan, which specifies local processing steps at individual sites, communication steps in which data is moved between sites, postprocessing steps in which the results of local processing steps are combined, and the order in which these steps must be performed. Third, the single-site queries to be executed in the local processing steps must be locally optimized to select efficient access paths. Finally, the optimized single-site queries must be translated into the data languages of the host database management systems. This paper address the first three of these problems.

Logical database integration is achieved primarily through the use of generalization, which is modelled algebraically as a sequence of outerjoins and aggregation operations. Conventional query modification and distributed query processing techniques are inadequate for such views. Previous research on distributed query processing techniques has focused on joins, ignoring selections and projections because they are easy and inexpensive to process in a conventional distributed database system. However, even selection and projection queries over views defined by outerjoins and aggregates can be expensive to process. We develop solutions to this problem. We also solve the problem of local query optimization for navigational database systems such as CODASYL. The main problem here is to compile queries in a high-level query-language into programs that use efficient navigational access paths for evaluating the queries.

-----

* This research was jointly supported by the Defense Advanced Research Projects Agency of the Department of Defense and the Naval Electronic Systems Command and was monitored by the Naval Electronic Systems Command under Contract No. N00039-82-C-0226. The views and conclusions contained in this document are those of the author and should not be interpreted as necessarily representing the official policies, either expressed or implied, of the DARPA, the NAVELEX, or the U.S. Government.

1. Introduction

A multidatabase management system such as MULTIBASE [SMIT81, LAND82] is a system that provides uniform, integrated access to a heterogeneous distributed collection of databases. It differs from a conventional distributed database management system (e.g., SDD-1 [ROTH80], System R* [WILL82], Distributed INGRES [STON77], DDM [CHAN83]) in two significant respects. First, the databases are heterogeneous, i.e., stored under different local database management systems, each with its own data model and language. Second, the databases are preexisting, i.e., have been designed and maintained independently of one another, and hence may be inconsistent.

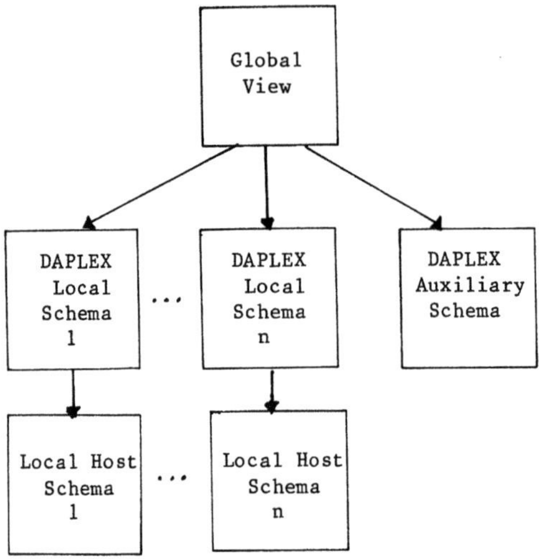

The auxiliary database stores additional data needed for database integration.

Figure 1. Schema Architecture of MULTIBASE

Figure 1 shows how MULTIBASE shields users from these problems of heterogeneity and inconsistency. The local databases are first ´homogenized´ by describing their local host schemas in a common data model, DAPLEX [SHIP81]. Database integration is then achieved by defining a global view tailored to the user´s application over these DAPLEX local schemas; the view definition incorporates directives for resolving differences between the local databases.

A DAPLEX schema is a directed graph, whose nodes are entity types and whose edges are function types (Figure 2). A DAPLEX database consists of entities and functions. The value of a function on an entity may be a single entity or a set of entities. Entities may be scalar (e.g., Real, Integer, String, Boolean) or user-defined. Functions (e.g., Weight) whose values are scalar entities correspond to "attributes" in traditional data models. Functions (e.g., Weapons) whose values are user-defined entities correspond to "relationships".

The homogenization step is quite straightforward, since local host schemas in record-oriented (relational, network, hierarchical, entity-relationship, etc.) data models are easily expressed in terms of DAPLEX entity types and functions. We shall ignore this issue henceforth in this paper.

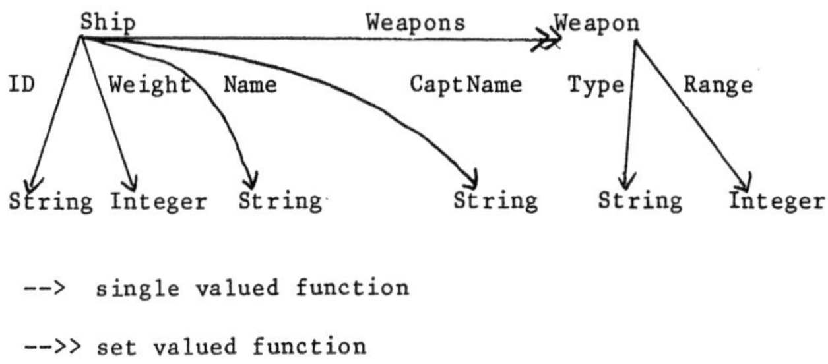

Figure 2. Daplex Schema

Database integration is tricker. The principal mechanism that has been proposed for database integration is generalization [SMIT77, KATZ81, DAYA82c, MOTR81]. Let entity types Ship1 and Ship2 model ship entities in two databases. Suppose that different function types have been defined for Ship1 and Ship2. Then, in the global view, we define a generalization hierarchy consisting of the subtypes Ship1 and Ship2, and a supertype Ship that includes all the function types common to the subtypes.

In addition to declaring which entity types and function types are visible in the global view, we must also specify how to populate the view, i.e., how to derive the entities and function values in the view from those in the underlying databases. The derivation of Ship1 and Ship2 entities is trivial; they are in one-to-one correspondence with the Ship1 and Ship2 entities in the local databases. The derivation of Ship is more complicated. First we have to specify a merge condition

(s1 in Ship1 = s2 in Ship2 iff ID(s1) = ID(s2))

under which an entity of one subtype is to be considered the same as an entity of the other subtype. Then, Ship is the union of Ship1 and Ship2 followed by the identification of pairs of entities that satisfy the merge condition; i.e., for each unique ID value of Ship1 and Ship2, there is a unique Ship entity.

If Ship1 and Ship2 are disjoint, i.e., have no common ID values, then each function on Ship is merely the union of the corresponding functions on Ship1 and Ship2.

The more interesting case occurs when Ship1 and Ship2 overlap, i.e., have some common ID values, and especially when they disagree on the function values of some entity. For example, Ship1 may contain the value 50 for the weight of the ship with ID 1234, while Ship2 contains the value 60. Such inconsistencies are resolved by defining the functions of Ship by aggregation over the corresponding functions of Ship1 and Ship2. For example, first rename the Weight functions of Ship1 and Ship2 to Weight1 and Weight2, respectively; then the Weight value of each Ship entity may be defined as the average of the Weight1 and Weight2 values of Ship1 and Ship2 entities with the same ID values.

Once a global view has been defined for a user, he can then formulate queries in DAPLEX over this view. The processing of a global query consists of four tasks:

1. Query modification. The global DAPLEX query is modified into a DAPLEX query over the DAPLEX local schemas.

2. Global query optimization. A global execution plan is constructed for the modified query. The plan is composed of single-site queries (each posed against exactly one local schema), move operations that ship results of the single-site queries between sites, and postprocessing queries that integrate the results of the single-site queries.

3. Local query optimization. The single-site queries sent to each local site are subjected to local access path optimization.

4. Translation. The optimized queries at each site are translated into equivalent queries or programs over the local host schema in the data language of the host DBMS.

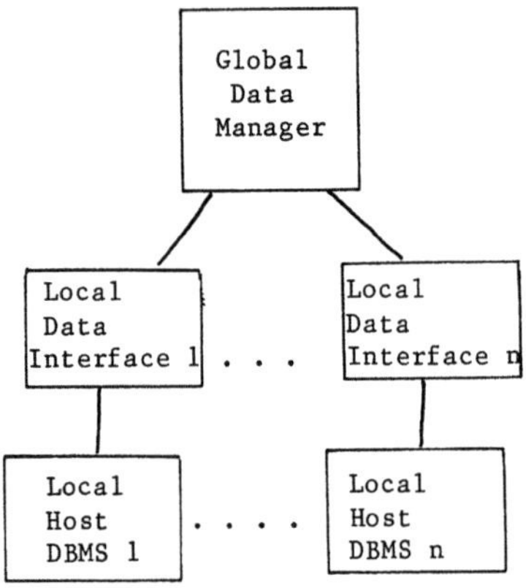

Figure 3. Component Architecture of MULTIBASE

In the MULTIBASE architecture (Figure 3), users submit queries to the Global Data Manager (GDM), which runs at a special global site. The GDM performs query modification and global query optimization; sends single-site queries to the local sites and receives their results; and executes the postprocessing queries. Each local site is equipped with a Local Data Interface (LDI), which performs local query optimization and translation, and returns results to the GDM. The main advantage of this architecture is that the GDM can be largely isolated from the idiosyncrasies of the heterogeneous host DBMSs. The challenge in the design of the GDM is to support the requirement of database integration.

Database integration, especially in the presence of aggregates in view definitions, has a profound impact on query processing in a multidatabase system. Consider, for instance, a query that selects all Ships whose Weight exceeds 55. If the local databases are disjoint, the selection can be performed independently at Ship1's site and at Ship2's site, and the results merged via union. This is no different from the processing required in a conventional distributed database system where some files may be horizontally partitioned [BERN81b, SELI80]. If the local databases overlap, however, more complicated processing is required. For Ships that are common to both databases, the Weight function must be computed as the average of Weight1 and Weight2. This requires that Ship1 and Ship2 entities for these common ships be collected at a common site at which the aggregation can be performed before the selection.

Thus, in general, even selections and projections are expensive to process in multidatabase systems. Because selections and projections are easy to process in conventional distributed database systems, they have been ignored in the query optimization literature (the focus has been on optimizing joins [BERN81b, EPST78, HEVN79, SELI80, YU79]). New techniques for query optimization are needed to deal with the problem of aggregation. This paper describes the techniques developed for MULTIBASE.

Sections 2 and 3 discuss the problems of query modification and global query optimization in multidatabase systems. The reader is referred to [KATZ81, LAND82, DAYA82a, DAYA82c, DAYA83a] for details. In this paper we shall only explain and illustrate the principles underlying our solutions to these problems.

Section 4 discusses the problem of local query optimization for navigational database systems. MULTIBASE has to interface with a wide variety of host DBMSs. Essentially, each LDI presents a DAPLEX interface to a local host DBMS. Since DAPLEX is a high-level query language, queries written in it specify merely which data is to be retrieved, not how to retrieve the data. In general, numerous access paths may be available for evaluating a given query. The selection of an efficient sequence of these access paths is the goal of local query optimization. Some DBMSs, such as INGRES [HELD75], System R [ASTR76], and the ADAPLEX LDM [CHAN82], that support high level query languages, are equipped with their own local optimizers. Other DBMSs, such as IMS and CODASYL, have low-level navigational interfaces. LDIs for these latter systems must perform access path optimization. We describe a simple optimizer for such systems. The reader is referred to [DAYA81, DAYA82b] for details.

The second principal task of an LDI is the generation of a host language query program to implement the local execution plan constructed by the local optimizer. This task requires attention to detail, but otherwise poses no new interesting problems, and will not be discussed further in this paper.

2. View Definition and Query Modification

The integration of existing databases requires powerful view definition capabilities (described in [KATZ81, DAYA82c]). The precise DAPLEX syntax for view definition and queries is irrelevant here; we shall use a stylized, self-explanatory syntax for illustrative purposes.

Some of the view definition capabilities of DAPLEX have direct counterparts in extant relational database management systems [HELD75, ASTR76]: renaming of entity types and function types (e.g., the Weight function on Ship1 is renamed to Weight1); selection of entities based on specified function values (e.g., only Ship1 entities that fly the U.S. flag are included in the view); projection of entities on specified functions (e.g., only the ID, Weight, and Name functions are included for Ship1 entities in the view); and the construction of new entity types in the view by "joining" entity types in the underlying databases (e.g., in Figure 4, the Assignment entity type with functions Assigned-Ship and Assigned-Person is constructed by joining Ship entities and Person entities via the Crew function). In working with an entity-based data model, some care must be exercised to ensure that the view is "closed", i.e., functions do not have dangling references to entity types outside the view. In the example in Figure 4, the definition of the Assignment entity type presupposes that the Ship and Person entity types are also included in the view.

The relational query modification algorithm of [STON75] is easily adapted to work with these DAPLEX views. Essentially, the idea is to substitute for each entity type and function in the view its definition in terms of the underlying entity types and functions. This algorithm is illustrated in Figure 5.

Local Schema

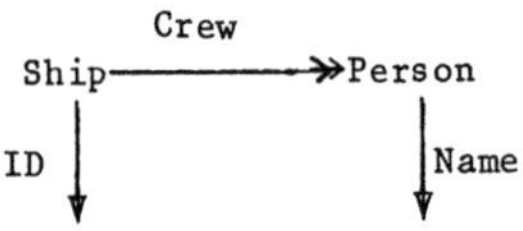

View

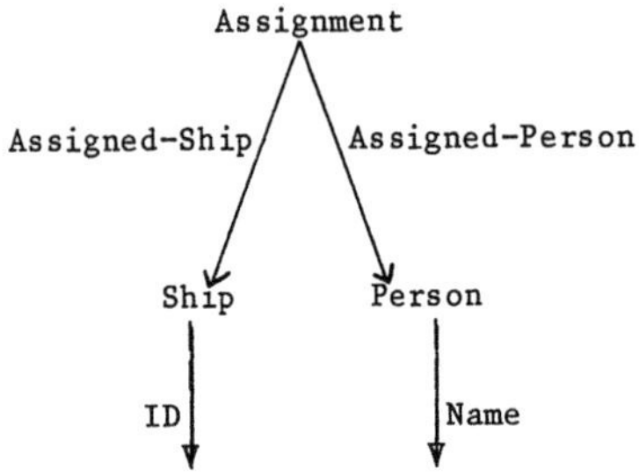


```
derive Assignment from
    for s in Ship
        for p in Person where p isin Crew(s)
             Assigned Ship := s
             Assigned Person := p
        endfor
    endfor
end
```

Figure 4. View Definition by Joining

The most important capability needed for database integration that is missing from relational systems is the definition of generalization hierarchies. A generalized entity type in a view is defined in two steps (see Figure 6). The first step is the outerjoin of the subtypes on a merge condition. (We have borrowed the term "outerjoin" from the extended relational algebra of [CODD79]. The reason for this will become apparent in Section 3.) This step specifies that there is one Ship entity for every distinct member of Ship1 U Ship2 after identifying members on the basis of the merge condition.

The second step specifies how the functions on the generalized entity type are computed from the subtypes' functions. When n subtypes are generalized, the derivation has (2**n)-1 cases. For the cases where the generalized entity is in more than one subtype, its functions are computed by aggregation. Arbitrary aggregates can be specified. A few interesting ones whose properties have been studied are listed in Figure 7. In the view of Figure 7, the ID function is defined using the chooseany aggregate, the Weight function using average, and the Name function using choose-biased.

Modification of queries over generalized entity types is quite complicated. One algorithm, proposed in [DAYA82c], seeks to eliminate all vestiges of the outerjoin operation from the modified query. This algorithm produces a large number of subqueries (see Figure 8a). Separately optimizing each subquery will result in an

Query:
```
for a in Assignment
   for as in Ship where as = Assigned-Ship(a)
     for ap in Person where ap = Assigned-Person(a)
                      and Name(ap) = Bligh
          retrieve ID(as)
     endfor
   endfor
endfor
```

Modified query:
```
for s in Ship
  for p in Person where p isin Crew(s)
    for as in Ship where as = s
      for ap in Person where ap = p and Name(ap) = Bligh
         retrieve ID(as)
      endfor
    endfor
  endfor
endfor
```

After simplification:
```
for s in Ship
  for p in Person where p isin Crew(s) and Name(p) = Bligh
     retrieve ID(s)
  endfor
endfor
```

Figure 5. Query Modification without Generalization

inefficient global execution plan.

The opposite approach of materializing all the entities in the view before evaluating the query can also be inefficient, because it does not apply any selections or projections until the entire view has been materialized.

We adopt a third, hybrid, alternative in which we "carry along" with the query the outerjoin-aggregate derivation of each generalized entity type occurring in the query [GOLD84]. Figure 8b gives an example. This approach permits the global query optimizer to determine whether it is more efficient to process the (2**n)-1 subqueries (as in Figure 8a) or to first materialize the view. (Indeed, as we shall see in the next section, a variety of other options are available to the global query optimizer.)

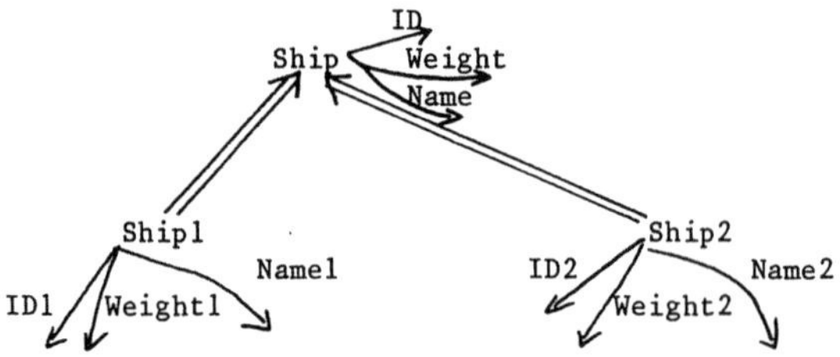


```
derive Ship from
    for s in outerjoin of (s1 in Ship1, s2 in Ship2)
          on merge condition ID1(s1) = ID2(s2)
        case s isin Ship1 and not in Ship2
            ID := ID1(s1)
            Weight := Weight1(s1)
            Name := Name1(s1)
        case s isin Ship2 and not in Ship1
            ID := ID2(s2)
            Weight := Weight2(s2)
            Name := Name2(s2)
        case s isin Ship1 and in Ship2
            ID := chooseany(ID1(s1), ID2(s2))
            Weight := average(Weight1(s1), Weight2(s2))
            Name := Name1(s1)
    endfor
end
```

Figure 6. View Definition by Generalization

To define a function f on an entity type X, in terms of functions f1, f2, ... , fn on subtypes X1, X2, ... ,Xn, respectively:
Let x be an entity of type X, x1 an entity of type X1, etc.

- chooseany(f1(x1), ..., fn(xn)) = { f1(x1), if x isin X1; f2(x2), if x isin X2; fn(xn), if x isin Xn }

  (this requires that the fi´s agree on entities common to their domains)

- chooseall(f1(x1), ..., fn(xn)) = {fi(xi) | x isin Xi}

- choosebiased(f1(x1), ..., fn(xn)) = { f1(x1), if x isin X1; f2(x2), if x is not in X1 but in X2; . . . ; fn(xn), if x is not in x1, ...,, not in xn-1, but in xn }

- average, max, min, count, sum, median

- union, intersection, difference (for set valued functions)

Figure 7. Some Special Aggregate Functions

Query:
```
 for s in Ship where Weight(s) > 55
      retrieve ID(s), Name(s)
 endfor
```

Modified query:
```
  for sl in Shipl where
        (for no s2 in Ship2)(IDl(sl) = ID2(s2))
        and Weightl(sl) > 55
     retrieve IDl(sl), Namel(sl)
  endfor
  for s2 in Ship2 where
        (for no sl in Shipl)(IDl(sl) = ID2(s2))
        and Weight2(s2) > 55
     retrieve ID2(s2), Name2(s2)
  endfor
  for sl in Shipl
     for s2 in Ship2 where IDl(sl)= ID2(s2)
           and average(Weightl(sl), Weight2(s2)) > 55
        retrieve chooseany(IDl(sl), ID2(s2)), Namel(sl)
     endfor
  endfor
```

Figure 8a. Query Modification Over Generalized Entity Types

Modified query:
```
    for s in outerjoin of (sl in Shipl, s2 in Ship2)
          on merge condition (IDl(sl) = ID2(s2))
          with functions

           (case s isin Shipl and not in Ship2
                ID := IDl(sl)
                Weight := Weightl(sl)
                Name := Namel(sl)
            case s isin Ship2 and not in Shipl
                ID := ID2(s2)
                Weight := Weight2(s2)
                Name := Name2(s2)
            case s isin Shipl and in Ship2
                ID := chooseany(IDl(sl), ID2(s2))
                Weight := average(Weightl(sl), Weight2(s2))
                Name := Namel(sl)                          )

          where Weight(s) > 55
        retrieve ID(s), Name(s)
    endfor
```

Figure 8b. Hybrid Approach to Query Modification

3. Global Query Optimization

Any discussion of query optimization must address the following four points:

- what class of queries is considered
- what class of query processing tactics is considered in constructing execution plans

- what cost model is used to estimate the costs of execution plans
- what heuristics are used to enumerate execution plans

We discuss these points in turn in this section.

3.1 Conjunctive Queries

In this paper, we shall restrict discussion to <u>conjunctive</u> DAPLEX queries of the form:

```
for x1 in X1 where Q1(x1)
    for x2 in X2 where Q2(x1,x2)
        . . .
        for xn in Xn where Qn(x1,x2,...,xn)
            retrieve target-list
        endfor
      . . .
    endfor
endfor
```

Each x_i is an iteration variable; each X_i is an entity type and is called the range of x_i; each Q_i is a qualification that can include references to only the variables $x_1,x_2,\ldots,x_i$. Each qualification is a pure conjunction of atomic formulas of the following types:

- one-variable selection clauses: (f(x) op c), (f(x) op g(x)), (c isin h(x))
- value-based join clauses: (f(x) op g(y))
- linked join clauses: (x = f(y)), (x isin h(y))

where x,y are iteration variables; c is a constant; f,g are single-valued functions; h is a set-valued function; and op is a comparison operator. The target-list is a list of single valued functions f(x) whose ranges are scalar entity types (e.g., Real, Integer, String, Boolean).

After query modification, some of the X_i may be replaced by outerjoin-aggregation expressions (as illustrated in Figure 8b). We insist that the qualifications of the modified query also be pure conjunctions.

Conjunctive queries are best depicted graphically. A query graph has one node for each variable in the query; attached to the node is the range of the variable, and any one-variable selection clauses and target-list functions on that variable. For each set of join clauses involving variables x and y, there is an edge between the corresponding nodes. Figure 9 shows the query graph for the queries of Figures 5 and 8b.

Query graphs of DAPLEX queries bear a striking resemblance to relational query graphs [BERN81b]. Indeed, DAPLEX queries have equivalents in an extended relational algebra [DAYA82a, DAYA82d, DAYA83a]. These algebraic equivalents are a convenient vehicle for describing query processing tactics. The range entity type of each variable can be modelled as a relation whose attributes are the functions on the entity type: the relation is populated by one tuple per entity with the attribute values of the tuple being the function values of the entity*. Note that because of set-valued functions, the relations may not be normalized.

Every generalized entity type is modelled by a sequence of outerjoins and aggregation steps. For the example in Figure 6, first construct the outerjoin of Ship1 and Ship2. Then compute the attribute values of Ship tuples by aggregation over the attribute values of the outerjoin, as illustrated in Figure 10.

s in Ship
retrieve ID(s)

p isin Crew(s)

p in Person
Name(p) = 'Bligh'

Figure 9a. Query Graph for the Simplified Query of Figure 5

s in outerjoin ( )
with functions ( )
Weight(s) > 55
retrieve ID(s), Name(s)

Figure 9b. Query Graph for the Query of Figure 8b

Finally, the one-variable selection conditions and target list functions attached to each node of the query graph correspond to selections and projections of the corresponding relations. Figure 12 gives the algebraic equivalents of the DAPLEX queries of Figure 9**. In the rest of this Section, we use the succinct algebraic notation in preference to the more cumbersome DAPLEX syntax.

3.2 Query Processing Tactics

Conventional distributed database management systems use a variety of tactics for reducing the cost of processing queries. One commonly used tactic is to perform selections and projections at individual sites before executing any inter-site joins [SELI80, BERN81b].

---

* Actually, when the function values are non-scalar entities, the corresponding attribute values are surrogates (identifiers or keys) of these entities.

**We have glossed over two important aspects of DAPLEX semantics. First, because of the presence of set valued functions, the extended algebra must deal with unnormalized relations. Specifically, "fancier" predicates are needed to model selections and linked joins of the forms (c isin h(x)) and (x isin h(y)). Second, DAPLEX queries do not normally remove duplicates. For the class of queries considered in this paper, this means only that projection should not remove duplicates [DAYA82d].

Ship1

ID1	Name1	Weight1
1	JFKennedy	50
2	Leningrad	40

Ship2

ID2	Name2	Weight2
1	JohnKennedy	60
3	Bounty	0

Step 1:
Compute the outerjoin Temp := Ship1(ID1=ID2)Ship2

ID1	Name1	Weight1	ID2	Name2	Weight2
1	JFKennedy	50	1	JohnKennedy	60
2	Leningrad	40	-	-	-
-	-	-	3	Bounty	0

Step 2:
Aggregate
Ship(ID,Name,Weight) := chooseany(ID1,ID2)
choosebiased(Name1,Name2)
average(Weight1,Weight2) Temp

Ship

ID	Name	Weight
1	JFKennedy	55
2	Leningrad	40
3	Bounty	0

Figure 10. Outerjoin-Aggregation Sequence for Defining Generalized Entity Types

$\text{Project}_{\text{ID}}(\text{Select}_{\text{Name=Bligh}}\text{Person[Surrogate isin Crew]Ship})$

Figure 11a. Algebraic Equivalent of DAPLEX Query of Figure 9a

$\text{Project}_{\text{ID}}(\text{Select}_{\text{Weight>55}}\text{chooseany(ID1,ID2)}$

choosebiased(Name1,Name2) average(Weight1,Weight2)

(Ship1(ID1=ID2)Ship2)

Figure 11b. Algebraic Equivalent of DAPLEX Query of Figure 9b

A second common tactic is to distribute selections, projections, and joins over unions. Consider, for example, the relational query

$\text{Project}_{\text{Name}}\text{Select}_{\text{Weight>55}}\text{Ship}.$

Suppose that the Ship relation is horizontally partitioned into two fragments, USShip and ForeignShip, which are stored at different sites. Then, the tactic is to replace the original query with the query

$Project_{Name}Select_{Weight>55}USShip \cup Project_{Name}Select_{Weight>55}ForeignShip.$

The two subqueries are then separately optimized. Similarly, suppose that the Person relation is partitioned into the fragments Admiral and Other. Then, the join query

Ship [CaptName = Name] Person.

is replaced by the union of four subqueries, which are separately optimized.

A third distributed query processing tactic that has received considerable attention is the semijoin reduction [BERN81a, BERN81b, YU79]. Consider the join query

USShip [CaptName = Name] Admiral.

Suppose that USShip and Admiral are stored at two different sites, and that the result must be produced at a third site. The cost of moving the relations to the result site can be reduced if we first eliminate tuples that will not participate in the join. For instance, if we move the Name projection of Admiral to USShip's site, we can eliminate all the tuples of USShip that do not join with any tuple of Admiral. This operation is called the semijoin and is denoted

USShip <CaptName = Name] Admiral.

The benefit of this tactic is the reduction in the cost of moving USShip. Against this benefit must be offset the cost of retrieving $Project_{Name}Admiral$, moving it to USShip's site, and executing the semijoin.

These tactics are of limited applicability in a multidatabase system where queries can include outerjoins and aggregates. As we saw in Section 1, it is no longer always possible to distribute selections and joins; e.g., the queries in Figures 8 and 12 are not equivalent.

However, it is still desirable whenever possible to perform local selections (and projections) before moving data to the global site in order to conpute the outerjoin and aggregate. It is desirable because it usually reduces both the local processing cost and the communication cost, since a smaller amount of data is retrieved and moved.

In [DAYA82a, DAYA83a] we worked out for special aggregates and special selection clauses the conditions under which local selection is possible. For example, any selection on a function defined using the chooseall, chooseany, or union aggregate can be performed locally (see Figure 13a). As another example, suppose that in the view of Figure 6, the Weight function on Ship is defined as max(Weight1(s1)), Weight2(s2)), instead of as the average. Then, the selection Weight>55 can be performed locally (see Figure 13b). Finally, in some cases it is possible to do a partial selection locally before moving data to the global site where the outerjoin and aggregate is computed, and then subjected to the full selection. This is illustrated in Figure 14, for the query

$Select_{Weight=55}Ship,$

where the Weight function is defined using the max aggregate. The table in Figure 15 summarizes the cases in which partial or complete local selection is possible.

Another approach to making local selection possible is to use the *semiouterjoin* tactic, introduced in [DAYA82a, DAYA83a, HWAN82]. This tactic works in all cases, no matter what the aggregation and selection conditions are. For the example in Figure 10, the semiouterjoin of Ship1 by Ship2 on the merge condition partitions Ship1 into two subsets: its *private portion* consisting of all those Ship1 entities that have no matching Ship2 entities, and its *overlap portion* consisting of the

```
for s1 in Ship1 where Weight1(s1)>55
   retrieve ID1(s1), Name1(s1) into Result1
endfor

for s2 in Ship2 where Weight2(s2)>55
   retrieve ID2(s2), Name2(s2) into Result2
endfor

for s in outerjoin of (r1 in Result1, r2 in Result2)
     on merge condition ID1(r1)=ID2(r2)
       with functions
         (case s isin Result1 and not in Result2
            ID := ID1(r1)
            Name := Name1(r1)
          case s isin Result2 and not in Result1
            ID := ID2(r2)
            Name := Name2(r2)
          case s isin Result1 and in Result2
            ID := chooseany(ID1(r1),ID2(r2))
            Name := Name1(r1)
     retrieve ID(s), Name(s)
endfor
```

Algebraic Equivalent:

$$\text{Project}_{\text{ID1,Name}}\ \text{chooseany(ID1,ID2)}\ \ \text{choosebiased(Name1,Name2)}$$

$$(\text{Project}_{\text{ID,Name1}}\text{Select}_{\text{Weight1>55}}\text{Ship1})\ (\text{ID1=ID2})$$

$$(\text{Project}_{\text{ID1,Name2}}\text{Select}_{\text{Weight2>55}}\text{Ship2})$$

Figure 12. Incorrect Distribution of Selection

<u>Query</u>:

$$\text{Project}_{\text{ID,Name}}\text{Select}_{\text{ID=1234}}\text{chooseany(ID1,ID2)}$$

$$\text{choosebiased(Name1,Name2) average(Weight1,Weight2)}$$

$$\text{(Ship1(ID1=ID2)Ship2)}$$

<u>After distribution of selection</u>:

$$\text{Project}_{\text{ID,Name}}\text{chooseany(ID1,ID2) choosebiased(Name1,Name2)}$$

$$((\text{Project}_{\text{ID1,Name1}}\text{Select}_{\text{ID1=12343}}\text{Ship1})\ (\text{ID1=ID2})$$

$$(\text{Project}_{\text{ID2,Name2}}\text{Select}_{\text{ID2=1234}}\text{Ship2}))$$

Figure 13a. Correct Distribution of Selection

<u>Query</u>: As in Figure 11b, except that the aggregate for the Weight function is max(Weight1, Weight2)

After distribution of selection:

$Project_{ID,Name}$chooseany(ID1,ID2) choosebiased(Name1,Name2)

$(Project_{ID1,Name1}(Select_{Weight1>55}Ship1)$(ID1=ID2)

$(Project_{ID2,Name2}(Select_{Weight2>55}Ship2)$

Figure 13b. Correct Distribution of Selection

<u>Query</u>: As in figure 13b, except that the selection is changed to

$Select_{Weight=55}$

After distribution of selection:

$Project_{ID,Name}Select_{Weight=55}$chooseany(ID1,ID2)

choosebiased(Name1,Name2) max(Weight1,Weight2)

$((Select_{Weight\geq 55}Ship1)$ (ID1=ID2) $(Select_{Weight2\geq 55}Ship2))$

Note that at the local sites, we can perform partial selections on the conditions $Weight1\geq 55$ and $Weight2\geq 55$, respectively.

Figure 14. Partial Local Selection

complement. (Actually, the overlap portion is the semijoin of Ship1 by Ship2 on the merge condition.) This semiouterjoin is denoted Ship1 < ID1=ID2) Ship2.

Of course, it is equally possible to perform the semiouterjoin of Ship2 by Ship1. In general, if an entity type is the generalization of n subtypes, then any of the n semiouterjoins are possible. (Each semiouterjoin reduces one of the subtypes by the union of all the others.)

The utility of the semiouterjoin tactic is that local selections can now be performed on the private portion. This is illustrated in Figure 16. (For the overlap portion, we can still use the table of Figure 15 to determine if, given the particular aggregate and particular selection condition, partial or complete local selection is possible.)

A semiouterjoin can be implemented in much the same way as a semijoin, since the overlap and private portions can be computed simultaneously. Observe that by itself the semiouterjoin is useless. Its utility as a tactic is that it can reduce the cost of a subsequent selection (or semijoin, as we will see shortly). Thus, a semiouterjoin R1 <) R2 is beneficial if the cost of computing it is offset by the reduction in the size of R1 produced by a selection (or semijoin) that can be performed locally on R1's private portions.

<u>Query:</u> $\text{Select}_{A \text{ op } a}$ agg(A1,A2) (R1(merge condition)R2)

where attribute A is computed by the aggregate agg(A1,A2)

<u>Goal:</u> for different agg and different op, determine if full local selection is possible, i.e., if the above query is equivalent to

agg(A1,A2)(($\text{Select}_{A1 \text{ op } a}$R1)

(merge condition)($\text{Select}_{A2 \text{ op } a}$R2))

If full local selection is not possible, then determine if a partial selection can be performed on R1 and R2, with a final selection after outerjoin and aggregation i.e., if the above query is equivalent to

$\text{Select}_{A \text{ op } a}$agg(A1,A2)($\text{Select}_{A1 \text{ op } a}$R1)(merge condition)($\text{Select}_{A2 \text{ op2 } a}$R2))

for some partial selection conditions (A1 op1 a) and (A2 op2 a), respectively.

agg	op: <	op: =	op: >
chooseany	Full	Full	Full
chooseall	Full	Full	Full
union	Full	Full	Full
max	No	Partial(Use $\geq$)	Full
min	Full	Partial(Use $\leq$)	No
count	No	No	No
sum	No	No	No
average	No	No	No
choosebiased	No	No	No for R1
	Full	Full	Full for R2

A No entry indicates that no local selection is possible.

Figure 15. Distribution of Selection

Next, consider a query containing a join (Figure 17a and b). The aggregates union and chooseany used to define the joining functions, Weapons and WeaponsID, are "well behaved". Hence, the join can be distributed. However, it might not always be beneficial to do so. Sometimes it might be cheaper to construct Ship and Weapon by outerjoin and aggregation before computing the join. Unlike the query processors described in [BERN81b, SELI80], which always distribute joins, we employ this tactic only if it is applicable and beneficial.

If the join is not distributed, it is computed at the global site because that is where the outerjoins and aggregates necessary for constructing Ship and Weapon are computed. Hence, it would be useless to consider performing a semijoin to reduce the cost of the join (since the join is now a local operation).

On the other hand, if the join is distributed, then a semijoin might be beneficial. For instance, consider the query Weapon [Range < Range] Weapon. Again, it is possible to distirbute the join, i.e., to replace the join by four joins involving Weapon1 and Weapone2. Then, we can consider reducing the cost of the inter-site join Weapon1 [Range1 < Range2] Weapon2 by a semijoin.

Given the data of Figure 10

private portion Ship1:

2	Leningrad	40

overlap portion Ship1:

1	JFKennedy	50

Query of Figure 11b is equivalent to:

Project$_{ID1,Name1}$Select$_{Weight1>55}$private portion Ship1

U Project$_{ID,Name}$Select$_{Weight>55}$chooseany(ID1,ID2)

choosebiased(Name1,Name2) average(Weight1,Weight2)

((overlap portion Ship1) (ID=ID) Ship2)

Figure 16. Semiouterjoin Tactic

Finally, as for selections, the use of the semiouterjoin tactic can make it possible to distribute joins or to perform semijoin reductions. In our last example, if we change the definition of Range from chooseall to min, then the join can no longer be directly distributed. However, by first performing the semiouterjoin reduction of Weapon1 by Weapon2, we can accomplish two things:

(a) we can perform the local join of the private portion of Weapon1 with itself;

(b) we can consider using a semijoin to reduce the cost of the inter-site join between the overlap portion of Weapon1 and Weapon2.

To summarize, we consider the following tactics:

- always distribute selections (and projections) whenever possible
- distribute joins only if possible and beneficial
- if beneficial, use semiouterjoins to distribute selections and joins
- if beneficial, use semijoins, but only if the corresponding joins are distributed.

3.3 Cost Estimation

Some previous research in distributed query optimization [BERN81b, HEVN79, HWAN84, YU79] assumed that the critical factor in query processing cost is the cost of data movement, and that local processing costs are negligible by comparison. Thus, the objective of SDD-1's optimizer is to minimize the total amount of data moved [BERN81b]. However, practical experience has shown that local processing costs cannot be ignored. Hence, for MULTIBASE, we use the total cost of data movement and local processing as our objective function. (System R* [SELI80, DANI82]

Expanded View:

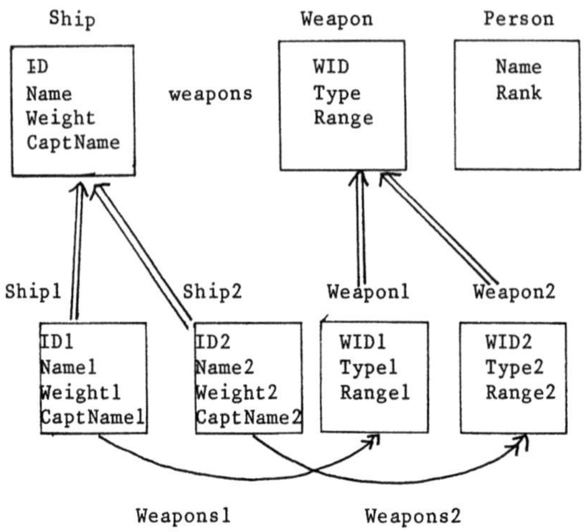

To simplify the graph, we have not drawn the scalar functions as separate edges.

Assume that Weapon's functions are defined by the aggregates

chooseany(WD1,WID2), choosebiased(Type2,Type1), chooseall(Range1,Range2)

Assume that the CaptName and weapons functions are defined by choosebiased(CaptName1,CaptName2) and union (weapons1,weapons2).

Figure 17a. Expanded View to Illustrate a Join Query

and the DDM [CHAN83] use the same objective function.)

Recall that the GDM constructs a global execution plan, which is a graph consisting of nodes describing local processing steps at various sites, postprocessing steps (actually, local processing at the global site), and data movement steps; and of arcs indicating the partial ordering of operations.

Given a global execution plan, its cost is the sum of the costs of all its nodes. The cost of a data movement step is a function of the amount of data moved. The cost of a local processing step depends upon various factors: the relative speed of the site; the operations executed in this step; the sizes of the operands and how they are stored; the available access paths; the local execution plan (i.e., sequence of access paths) chosen by the local optimizer; and the size of the result file. However, the global optimizer at the GDM cannot predict the local execution plan that will be chosen by the local optimizer. Also, in the interests of local autonomy and modularity, it is not desirable to make the GDM aware of all the access paths available at all the sites. (This is the motivation for the two-stage "distributed query compilation" used in System R* [DANI82].)

In practice, we are interested only in the relative speeds of the various sites, and in the tradeoff between data movement cost and local processing costs. Hence, accurate estimates of local processing costs are not essential. In our cost estimation, we shall assume that the cost, C, of a local processing step is a function of the operations to be performed (joins, semijoins, projections, selections, etc.), the sizes of the operands, and the size of the result; that is, $C = w_i(q, n,$

Query over the view of Figure 17a:

$Project_{ID,WID,Type}$Weapon[WID isin Weapons]Ship

After modification:

$Project_{ID,WID,Type}$(aggW (Weapons1 (WID1=WID2) Weapon2))

[WID isin Weapons]

(aggS (Ship1(ID1=ID2)Ship2))

aggW and aggS are long aggregate expressions defining Weapon's and Ship's functions, respectively.

After distribution of the join, this query becomes the equivalent query:

$Project_{ID,WID,Type}$aggW aggS

outerjoin (Weaponi [WIDi isin Weaponj] Shipj)
i=1,2
j=1,2

The outerjoin is on the condition [WID1=WID2 and ID1=ID2].

Figure 17b. Join Query

Dopd, ..., Dopn, Dresult), where w_i is a weighting function for site i, q is the query, n the number of operands in q, Dopj is the size of operand j, and Dresult is the size of the result. If q includes joins, semijoins, and set operations and if site i is capable of implementing these operations by sorting and merging, then we can assume that w_i is proportional to the sum of Dresult and Dopj log Dopj for $1 \le j \le n$. In the worst case, if site i cannot perform these operations by sorting, then we can assume that w_i is proportional to the sum of the result size and the product of the operand sizes. In either case, the weighting function w_i is site-dependent.

The above discussion suggests that we need to derive formulas only for estimating the result size of any local processing step. Formulas for the conventional operations, selection, projection, join, semijoin, are available in the literature (e.g., see [BERN81b, SELI80, SELI79, YAO79]). Formulas for the new operations, semiouterjoin, outerjoin and aggregation, are easily derived. The semiouterjoin produces two results: a semijoin and its complement. The sizes of these results can, hence, be estimated using the formulas for semijoin. The outerjoin and aggregate operations do not change the number of records (entities, tuples); the average size of a record may be affected in the case of the chooseall and set operation aggregates, but it is easily computed. We do not elaborate the cost model any further here.

3.4 Heuristics for Query Optimization

In general, there are many global execution plans for solving a given query. Hence, we need some heuristic for enumerating plans. A variety of heuristic algorithms have been developed for conventional distributed query optimization [BERN81b, SELI80, DANI82, EPST78, HEVN79, YU79]. Any of these can be used as a starting point for our purpose.

For instance, [HWAN82] describes an adaptation of SDD-1's algorithm [BERN81a]: the basic idea is to use local selections and projections, semijoins and semiouterjoins to reduce the volume of data that must be moved to the global site. All joins, outerjoins, and aggregates are computed in a final postprocessing phase at the global site. The tactics of distributing selections and of computing semijoins and semiouterjoins are applied greedily.

Query graph:

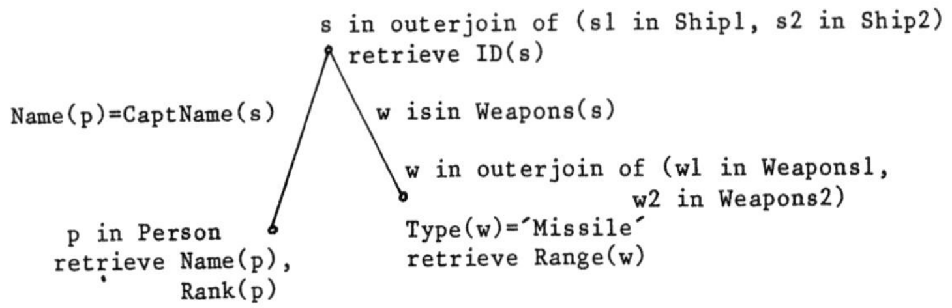

Optimization:

1. Consider the join between s and p.
   The join cannot be distributed to Ship1 and Ship2. Consider the semiouterjoins of Ship1 by Ship2 and vice versa, the semijoin of private portion Ship1 by Person, the semiouterjoin of private portion Ship2 by Person, and the semijoin of Person by the private portions. Select those tactics that reduce the cost of the join.

2. Consider the join between s and w.
   The join can be distributed. Compare the cost of distributing the join to Ship1 and Ship2, the cost of distributing the join to Weapon1 and Weapon2, and the cost of both distributions. For each of these distribution cases, consider the appropriate semijoins. Consider the semiouterjoins of Ship1 by Ship2 and vice versa, and the semiouterjoins of Weapon1 by Weapon2 and vice versa; for each semiouterjoin consider the appropriate semijoin (and for the semiouterjoin of Weapon2 by Weapon1 also consider the benefit of the local selection). Select those tactics that yield the greatest reduction in cost.

3. Select the cheaper of 1 and 2 to perform first.

4. For the join that is to be performed second, re-evaluate the costs and benefits of the various tactics described in step 1 or 2. Select the tactics that yield greatest reduction in cost.

Figure 18. An Example of Query Optimization

A different approach (the one we advocate for MULTIBASE) is based on the enumeration of join orders (as in System R* [SELI80, DANI82] and the DDM [CHAN83]. For the query in Figure 18, there are two join orders to consider. If the number of joins in the query is large, there can be a large number of join orders to consider. Even dynamic programming may be inefficient. A parametric hill climbing heuristic may be used instead. (If the parameter is k, then this heuristic is to examine join sequences of length k at a time, and to select the cheapest of these. When k=1, this heuristic reduces to the greedy heuristic. When k is the number of joins in the query, this heuristic corresponds to exhaustive enumeration.)

As a join is added to the join sequence currently under consideration, the tactics of distributing selections, distributing joins, performing semijoin reductions, and performing semiouterjoin reductions are applied greedily. Figure 18 illustrates the algorithm when joins are enumerated greedily and the tactics are chosen greedily.

One aspect of global query optimization in a multidatabase system has not been emphasized so far: the effect of heterogeneity of the local host DBMSs. Conventional homogeneous distributed database management systems do not have to contend with this problem. Heterogeneity is manifested in two ways: different relative processing speeds of the sites, and different expressive powers of the host languages. The former are easily accommodated; the weighting factors w_i used to estimate costs are adjusted accordingly. The latter is more serious. Some sites may not be capable of computing joins, semijoins, or semiouterjoins, of evaluating inequality comparisons, of storing temporary results, etc. These deficiencies are described to the GDM (the global query optimizer is table-driven), which filters execution plans to ensure that every local processing step can, in fact, be executed at the site to which it is bound. This can be accomplished in one of two ways: by decomposing a single operation into multiple operations (e.g., decomposing a semijoin into a set of selections); or by removing operations (e.g., joins) that cannot be executed at the local site, and adding compensatory postprocessing steps to the plan. The class of plans considered can be severely limited by the inability of sites to store temporary results (e.g., the result of a join, semijoin, or selection) for use in subsequent local processing steps at that site. For example, suppose that in Figure 18, the first join chosen is that between Ship and Person. Then, in Step 4 it may only be possible to use the result of this first join in reducing Weapon; the opposite semijoin of the first join's result by Weapon may not be possible.

4. Local Query Optimization for CODASYL Systems

This section addresses the problem of designing a Local Database Interface (LDI) for host database management systems with procedural, record-at-a-time navigational (i.e., pointer-based access) data manipulation languages. Classic examples of such systems are those based on the CODASYL model.

Conceptually, a CODASYL schema is a directed multigraph, whose nodes are record types, and whose edges are owner-coupled set (abbreviated ocset) types directed from owner to member. A CODASYL database contains many access paths for locating records: CALC keys, indices, pointer chains connecting owners and members of ocsets, pointer chains connecting members of singular ocsets, and (when no other access paths are available) area scans. A CODASYL DML program specifies a sequence of access path traversals from record to record, until all the records needed to process a query have been located.

The LDI must translate single-site DAPLEX queries (sent to it by the GDM) into efficient CODASYL DML programs. First note that the single-site DAPLEX queries are expressed over the DAPLEX Local Schema, whereas the DML programs must be expressed over the CODASYL Local Host Schema. However, there is a close correspondence between these two schemas. The record types of the CODASYL schema are entity types of the DAPLEX schema; the non-repeating fields are single-valued scalar functions; the repeating fields are set-valued scalar functions; and the ocsets are set-valued non-scalar functions*. Given this close (one-to-one) correspondence, we can pretend

* Note that we are ignoring the problem of enforcing integrity under update. An ocset imposes the additional constraint that each member record is connected to exactly one owner record. To enforce this constraint in DAPLEX, we would have to insist that the "inverse" of every set-valued function corresponding to an ocset be single-valued and total.

that the input DAPLEX query is expressed over the CODASYL schema.

We shall ignore the translation problem of generating syntactically legal DML programs. Instead, we focus on the optimization problem of selecting an inexpensive sequence of access paths.

As in Section 3, we describe the class of queries considered for optimization, the class of local execution plans considered, the cost model, and the heuristics used to enumerate candidate execution plans. We illustrate the basic principles here. The interested reader is referred to [DAYA81, DAYA82b] for details.

4.1 CODASYL Tree Queries

Given a CODASYL schema graph, a tree query is a conjunctive DAPLEX query satisfying the following properties:

1. no two variables in the query range over the same record type (and so each node in the query graph can be identified with a record type instead of with a variable);

2. the query graph contains no value-based joins;

3. the query graph is a tree that is a subgraph of (the undirected version of) the schema graph.

Note that because of condition 3, a tree query cannot contain outerjoin-aggregation expressions. Figure 19 shows a tree query.

For queries other than tree queries, the program synthesized by the interface would have to save and compare database keys (record identifiers) and/or to manipulate multiple currency indicators for some record or ocset type, a nontrivial task! Tree queries, on the other hand, can be completely solved by following available CODASYL access paths alone. Hence, in the interests of simplicity, we consider only tree queries*.

4.2 Execution Plans for Tree Queries

Given a tree query, a plan for processing it prescribes an order in which the nodes of the tree are visited. The first node in this sequence is called the entry point of the plan. Every node of the tree appears exactly once in the plan, and, with the exception of the entry point, no node can be visited unless an adjacent node has already been visited. Since the tree is a subgraph of the CODASYL schema graph, this implies that the plan specifies (a) an access path for entry into the database, and (b) a sequence of owner-to-member or member-to-owner traversals.

---

* This restricts only the class of queries that are optimized by the LDI. It does not restrict the DAPLEX queries that can be processed by MULTIBASE as a whole. Arbitrary DAPLEX queries can be decomposed into tree queries, followed, if necessary, by some compensatory postprocessing steps in the GDM.

a. Schema

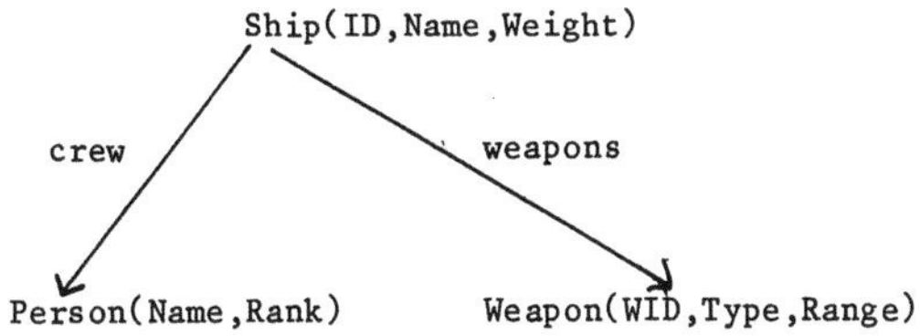

b. Query Graph

```
    s in Ship
    | Weight(s)>55
    | retrieve ID(s)
    |
    | w isin weapons(s)
    |
    w in Weapon
     Type(w)='Missile'
     retrieve Range(w)
```

Figure 19. CODASYL Schema and Tree Query

Access Paths
Ship is a member of a singular ocset
Weapon has a CALC key, Type
The ocset weapons is implemented using member pointers and owner pointers.

Figure 20a. Access Paths

Two execution plans are possible for the query of Figure 19, given the access paths of Figure 20a. These plans are shown in Figure 20b. From each plan, it is fairly straightforward to construct a program. Note that when the owner type of an ocset occurs before the member type in the node order, then occurrences of the ocset are traversed along member pointer chains. If the member type occurs before the owner type, then occurrences of the ocset are traversed "in the opposite direction" using owner pointers, if available, or by traversing the entire length of a member pointer chain (since the last member of every ocset occurrence points back to the owner). The point here is that ocsets can be traversed in either direction. (Of course, the costs of the traversals may be very different.)

In general, all the legal node orders for a query graph can be enumerated by breadth first search. For the query of Figure 21, there are four legal node orders.

4.3 Cost Estimation

The cost of a local execution plan is determined by the number of disc page accesses incurred by the program that implements the plan. The formulas for estimating the number of pages accessed depend upon various parameters listed in Table 1.

Plan 1:

```
Order of visiting nodes: Ship, Weapon
Program:
  use member pointers of singular ocset to
  find next Ship record
  for each Ship record found
    if Weight>55 then
      use member pointers of ocset weapons to
      find Weapon records
      for each Weapon record found
        if Type='Missile' then
          retrieve ID of Ship, Range of Weapon
      endfor
  endfor
```

Plan 2:

```
Order of visiting nodes: Weapon, Ship
Program:
  use CALC key Type to
  find next Weapon record with Type='Missile'
  for each Weapon record found
      use owner pointer of ocset weapons to find Ship record
      for each Ship record found
        if Weight>55 then
          retrieve ID of Ship, Range of Weapon
      endfor
  endfor
```

Figure 20b. Execution Plans for the query of Figure 19

Query graph:

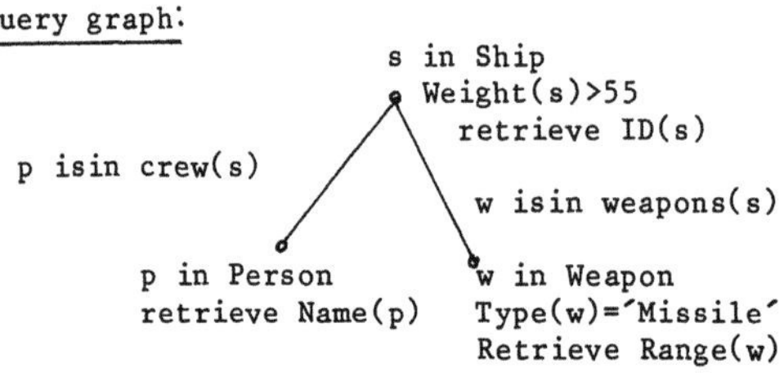

Legal Node Orders:

Ship,	Person,	Weapon
Ship,	Weapon,	Person
Person,	Ship,	Weapon
Weapon,	Ship,	Person

The program for each node order has 3 nested loops.

Figure 21. Legal Node Orders for a More Complicated Query

- $|R|$ = the number of occurrences of record type R
- $|S/R|$ = the average number of members per owner of each occurrence of ocset type L (whose owner type is R and member type is S)
- $|R/S|$ = the fraction of records of the member type of ocset L that have owners (i.e., that are members in an occurrence of the ocset)
- SelR = the combined selectivity of all the one-variable selection conditions on record type R, i.e., the expected fraction of occurrences of R that satisfy the selection conditions
- WidthR = the average width of an occurrence of record type R
- PagesR = the number of pages that must be accessed to find all occurrences of record type R
- PagesS/R = the number of additional pages that must be accessed to find all members of a given occurrence of ocset type L (whose owner type is R and member type is S)
- N_f = the number of pages that must be accessed to find all duplicates of record type R with CALC key f after the first hashed entry into the database. If DUPLICATES ARE NOT ALLOWED for f, then $N_f = 0$.
- K_H = the expected cost in disc page accesses, of hashing;
- K_I = the expected cost of accessing index I.

Table 1. Parameters of the Cost Model

Given these parameters, we can compute the cost of using various access paths to locate all the occurrences of a single record type that are needed at some stage of execution (i.e., the cost of executing a single "use..." statement in Figure 20). There are three costs:

1) SelPagesR = cost of locating all occurrences of record type R that satisfy all the one-variable selection conditions on R

2) SelPagesR/S = cost of locating the owner of a given member record in an occurrence of ocset L (whose owner type is R and member type is S)

3) SelPagesS/R = cost of locating all members that satisfy the one-variable selection conditions, from a given owner record in an occurrence of ocset L

Formulas for estimating these basic record access costs are given in Table 2.

Now we can illustrate the cost estimation of a local execution plan (see Figure 22). Consider the first plan of Figure 20. The cost of accessing the Ship records is SelPagesShip = PagesShip
The number of Ship records that satisfy the selection condition is
$|SelShip| = SelShip * |Ship|$
For each of these Ship records, the cost of accessing the desired Weapon records is
SelPagesWeapon/Ship = PagesWeapon/Ship
The estimated total cost of the plan is SelPagesShip + $|SelShip|$ * SelPagesWeapon/Ship
Figure 22a shows the computation for both plans of Figure 20.

If a CALC key f is used, then SelPagesR = $K_H + N_f$

If a singular ocset with an index I is used, then

SelPagesR = SelPagesR * PagesR + K_I, if I is a clustering index

Y(PagesR, |R|, SelR * |R|) + K_I, if I is not a clustering index

where Y(n,p,r) is the expected number of pages accessed to retrieve r records from a file of n records stored on p pages [YAO77, BERN81b, WHAN81].

If a singular ocset is used, then SelPagesR = PagesR.

If an area scan is used the SelPagesR = size of area in pages.

a. Estimation of SelPagesR

If all member records are clustered on the same page as the owner, then SelPagesR/S = 0

if owner pointers are available, then SelPagesR/S = 1

if the entire ocset occurrence has to be scanned, then SelPagesR/S = (PagesS/R + 1)/2

b. Estimation of SelPagesR/S

If an index I is used, then

SelPagesR = SelS * PagesS/R + K_I, if I is a clustering index

Y(PagesS/R, |S/R|, SelS * |S/R|) + K_I otherwise

If the members have to be scanned in sequence, then SelPagesS/R = PagesS/R

c. Estimation of SelPagesS/R

Table 2. Estimates of Record Access Costs

In general, then, suppose a plan prescribes the node order R0,R1,R2,...,Rk. Suppose that records of type Ri, $1 \le i \le k$, are reached by traversing occurrences of ocset Li (in either direction) from records of type Si. (Obviously, from the definition of a legal node order, Si is one of the Rj's preceding Ri in the node order. Then, estimated cost of the whole plan =

$$\text{SelPagesR0} + \sum_{i=1}^{k} \Big(\prod_{j=0}^{i-1} |\text{SelRj/Sj}| \Big) * \text{SelPagesRi/Si}$$

The expression in parentheses is the product of the expected number of records of R0,R1,...Ri-1 that are selected, and hence the number of times that the statement "use Si to locate records of Ri..." is executed.

Figure 22b shows the calculation for one of the plans of Figure 21. The calculation for the other plans is left as an exercise for the reader.

4.4 Heuristics for Optimization

The optimal plan for a given query can be found by enumerating node orders using dynamic programming. However, since the number of plans is equal to K! where K is the number of nodes in the query graph, dynamic programming can rapidly become infeasible. The parametric hill climbing heuristic described in Section 3.4 can be used instead.

Given the access paths of Figure 20 and the following parameters.

|Ship| = 100	|Weapon| = 2000	|Weapon/Ship| = 20
SelShip = 0.8	SelWeapon = 0.05	|Ship/Weapon| = 1
PagesShip = 100	PagesWeapon = 100	PagesWeapon/Ship = 2
$K_H = 1$	$N_{Type} = 9$	
|Person| = 10000	|Person/Ship| = 100	|Ship/Person| = 0.5
PagesPerson = 100	PagesPerson/Ship = 1	

Plan1:
SelPagesShip = 100   SelPagesWeapon/Ship = 2
|SelShip| = 0.8 * 100
         = 80

    Cost = SelPagesShip + |SelShip| * SelPagesWeapon/Ship
         = 100 + 80 * 2
         = 260

Plan2:
SelPagesWeapon = 10   SelPagesShip/Weapons = 1
|SelWeapon| = 100

    Cost = SelPagesWeapon + |SelWeapon| * SelPagesShip/Weapon
         = 10 + 100 * 1
         = 110

Figure 22a. Cost Estimation for the Plans in Figure 20

Consider the node order Ship, Weapon, Person
SelPagesShip = 100   SelPagesWeapon/Ship = 2
SelPagesPerson/Ship = 1
|SelShip| = 80 |SelWeapon/Ship| = 0.05 * 20 = 1

Cost = 100 + 80 * 2 + 80 * 1 * 1
= 340

Figure 22b. Cost Estimation for a Plan in Figure 21

5. Conclusion

This paper described techniques for global and local query optimization in a multidatabase system. The discussion was restricted to conjunctive DAPLEX queries, which involve selections, projections, and joins, expressed over views whose definitions may include outerjoins and aggregates. Full DAPLEX is a powerful language. Queries can include disjunctions, existential and universal quantifiers, arbitrarily nested "for loops" with retrieve statements embedded in any of these loops, and specified iteration orders. Extending the techniques described here to full DAPLEX requires augmenting our algebraic framework to include unions, operations on trees, and unidirectional outerjoins. The reader is referred to [DAYA81, DAYA82a, DAYA83d, RIES83] for details.

ACKNOWLEDGEMENT

I am grateful to the MULTIBASE and ADAPLEX groups at CCA for their contributions to the ideas presented in this paper; to the text processing group at CCA for their assistance in producing this paper; and to the editors of this book for inviting me to contribute a paper, and for their patience.

References

(ASTR76) (BERN81a) (BERN81b, see BERN81d) (CHAN83, see CHAN83a)
(CODD79) (DANI82, see DANI82b) (DAYA81) (DAYA82a) (DAYA82b) (DAYA82c)
(DAYA82d) (DAYA83a) (DAYA83b) (EPST78) (GOLD84) (HELD75, see HELD75a)
(HEVN79) (HWAN82) (HWAN84) (KATZ81, see KATZ81b) (LAND82) (MOTR81)
(ROTH80) (RIES82) (SELI80) (SHIP81) (SMIT81) (SMIT77) (STON77) (WHAN81)
(WILL82) (YAO77, see YAO77b) (YU79, see YU79b)

Querying Relational Views of Networks

Arnon Rosenthal and David S. Reiner

ABSTRACT

An organization that uses a relational Database Management System (DBMS) also may have a substantial investment in data created under a network (Codasyl) DBMS. We describe an architecture for supporting relational queries to data stored under both network and relational models.

The relational schema that captures the semantics of the Codasyl database is expressed as a collection of relational views with integrity constraints. A SQL query against this system-generated relational schema is translated to a SQL query against "access relations" that are essentially Codasyl records. Set links are represented by join predicates. A modified relational query processor translates queries into calls to the network and relational access routines.

We also suggest a number of source language query simplifications to improve the performance of complex queries generated through view substitution. These can benefit users in relational systems as well as those in our multi-model environment.

1. Introduction

An organization that uses a relational Database Management System (DBMS) to store and access some data may also have a substantial investment in data created under a network (Codasyl) DBMS. We describe an architecture for supporting relational queries and updates to data stored under both network and relational models.

The user will see a relational view of all data, with no distinction between <u>base relations</u>, stored as (possibly indexed) flat files of records, and <u>access relations</u>, obtained from network record types and sets. Queries are issued in a relational language such as SQL. Update translation involves a different set of issues, and is discussed only briefly in this chapter.

Query processing is the task of mapping from physically stored data to the data requested by the user. We believe it desirable to maximize the amount of mapping done in a single well-defined high-level language. With a clean, uniform mapping language, only one routine for composition of mappings (i.e., view substitution) is needed. The query optimizer will be able to work on almost the entire mapping. Finally, the mapping semantics will be far clearer than if they were expressed in a traditional programming language.

Our approach to supporting relational queries against network data has several parts. (Figure 1 shows the different levels of information in our architecture.)

1. Define a schema consisting of <u>access relations</u> that directly model the network structures (Section 2).

2. Produce a <u>relational interface schema</u> above the access relations (Section 2). This schema captures the logical information in the network schema. It also can include base relations directly supported as part of a purely relational system. (The network and relational storage systems are assumed to be under the same concurrency control system.) A user query may reference both the relational interface schema and the views defined above it.

3. Map user queries down to the access and base relation schemas (Section 3).

4. Optimize the resulting query against access and base relations (Section 4).

5. Execute the access strategy produced by the optimizer. The relational system's access strategy interpreter (or compiler) supplies routines for operators like Sort and Join, as well as scans on base relations. For access relations, scan routines must be supplied (Section 4).

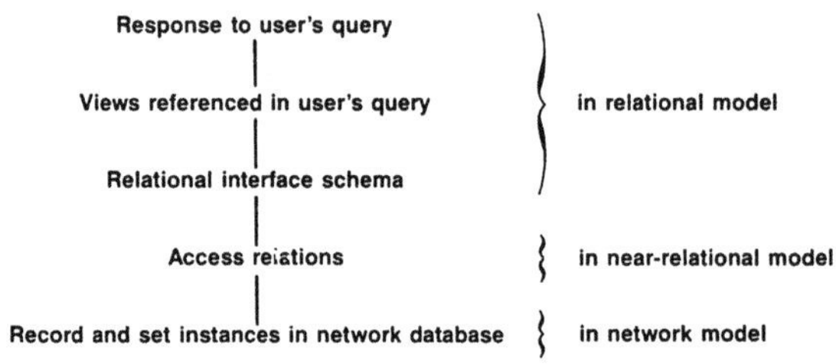

Figure 1. Data Objects in the Processing of a Query

The user's query, the views referenced in a particular query, and the relational interface schema are in the relational model. Our crucial step is to provide the <u>access relation schema</u>, which is close to the level of the network information but is expressed in a slightly extended relational model. This new level has one <u>access relation</u> for each network record type, and one for each set type.

The data model for the access-relation schema consists of the relational model, augmented by link predicates on tuple ids. The extension to the relational model is minor: SQL syntax can handle new predicates, and the relational view substitutor can map user queries down to the access relation level. The only required new facility is in the query optimizer. When the optimizer encounters a link predicate, it must use the underlying network set type as a direct access structure which supplies pointers to the desired tuples. This usage is similar to the use of a hash table or B-tree to identify tuples satisfying an equijoin predicate.

Our architecture (shown in Figure 2) has further practical benefits.

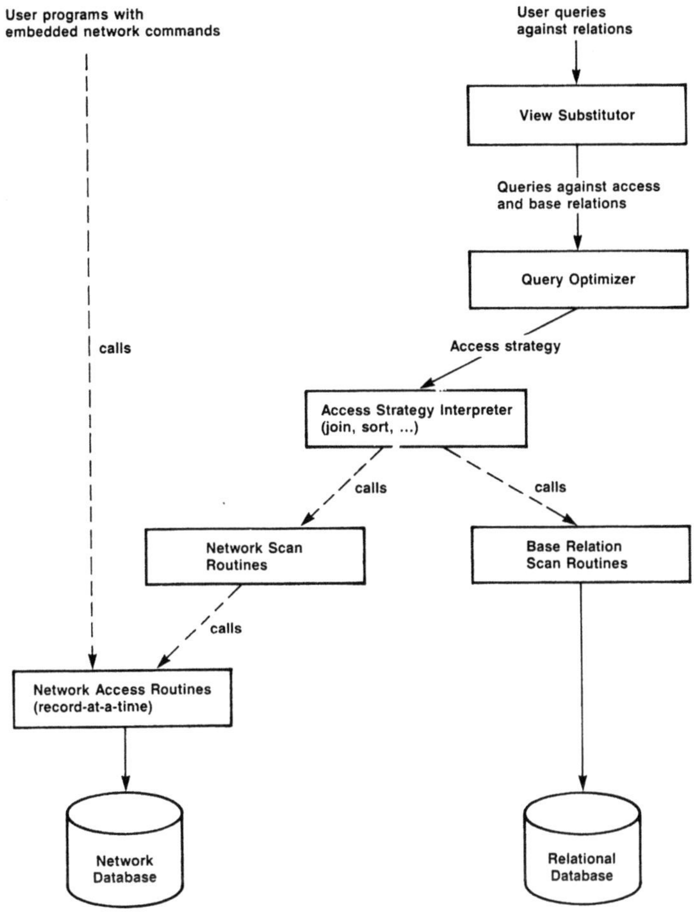

Figure 2. System Overview

- A query or update can reference several relations and views, including some stored as flat files and others supported by network structures.

- A single query optimizer handles the entire mapping from the query to both access and base relations. This ensures uniform treatment for gray areas such as duplicate elimination and update semantics.

- Some capabilities that are useful for network queries are likely to be absent from the original relational system. In our architecture, these facilities would be added to the relational system (benefitting all users) instead of being isolated in software used only for intermodel translations. Examples are query simplifications, support for duplicates and ordered sets, and limited view update (described below). Adding the facilities to the relational system appears no harder than doing an equally good job as part of intermodel translation.

- Correct mappings for relational updates over network data have been described in [ZANI79], [VASS80], and [HWAN81]. These rules map updates against the relational interface schema to updates on the underlying access relations. They solve a special case of the view update problem, updating views defined by a join over a foreign key. Such mappings are an essential part of providing an interface to network data. By implementing them within the relational system, we provide all users with a facility for handling these view updates.

2. Generating a Relational Schema for a Network Database

2.1 Definitions and Conditions

This section contains a necessary but somewhat dry discussion of data model characteristics. Where specific properties of the network model are discussed, we refer to the Codasyl standard [DATE81]. The discussion applies with minor alterations to the Entity-Relationship (E-R) model.

A collection of fields in a network record type is a <u>key</u> if no two record instances can have identical nonnull values in those fields. Let record type R be member type of set type S. A collection of fields of R is a <u>set key</u> of S if no two members that have the same owner record can have identical nonnull values over these fields. The owner's key plus the member's set-key (if both nonnull) uniquely identify member instances. We refer only to keys and set-keys that are minimal collections of fields and that have the properties described. A set type S is called <u>mandatory</u> if every instance of the member type must be a member of some set instance. Any attribute (field) may be labelled "Nulls Not Allowed" (<u>NNA</u>) or "Duplicates Not Allowed" (<u>DNA</u>).

Information in a network database can be represented in a relational schema if:

a. The sequence of members within a set is not significant.

b. Every record type possesses either a NNA key or (for some automatic mandatory set) a NNA set-key [ZANI79].

These conditions are required to accommodate two of the fundamental properties of the relational data model [DATE81]:

i. Any ordering of tuples within a relation is system-defined and is not controlled by the user.

ii. Since a relation is a set, each tuple within it is unique and must contain a combination of attribute values that identify it uniquely.

There exists a set of fields that uniquely identifies instances of each record type if assumption (b) holds and if (as required in Codasyl implementations) automatic mandatory sets do not form a cycle. Instances of each record type REC are uniquely identified within some set, and a chain of automatic mandatory set owners from REC eventually leads to a record type that possesses a NNA key. Instances of REC are identified by the REC key and the chain of set-keys.

In practice, programmers use information-bearing orderings and they allow duplicate records. To capture this information, the relational system must be extended to allow duplicates and ordering. [STON82] discusses the well known technique of adding system-maintained sequence fields to relations. The cost of such remedies does not seem to depend on the architecture used to support relational queries over the network data.

2.2 Treating Record and Set Types as Relations

We consider network record instances to include a system-generated tuple identifier field (tid) which uniquely identifies the record instance. We assume no particular implementation of tids, though physical address will usually suffice. Since the record type has no repeating groups and has the tid field as a key, it is a relation. Tids are treated as ordinary data fields, except that they are not displayed. The tid field of relation R is denoted R.@.

Because tuples are available directly from the network storage system, we call the relation corresponding to a record type an access relation. We also define a relation Link(S) for each set type S in the network schema. For each owner-member pair of record instances linked by the set, Link(S) has a tuple consisting of the owner and member tids.

The access relation schema consists of access relations and link relations, plus appropriate integrity information.

2.3 The Relational Interface Schema

The schema translator will next generate view-relations over the access relation schema. One view is generated for each record type, and one for each set type not used in defining the relation for a record type. These view relations are shown to the user as the relational interface schema.

A relation always can be considered as a predicate over its arguments. We find it useful to treat each Link relation in the access relation schema as a join predicate that connects instances of owner and member types. The fact that (R0.@, R1.@) is a member of Link(S) is denoted (R0.@--link(S)--R1.@). [LORI83, MANO82] use similar constructs as an easy way of extending a relational language to handle network information.

Thus, set types from the network (i.e., Link relations in the access relation schema) are expressed as predicates in the view definitions that constitute the relational interface schema. The optimizer will treat Link as a predicate supported by a special access structure.

Our derived schema is similar to the schemas produced in [HWAN81, KATZ81, VASS80]. [DAYA78] and [HWAN81] formalize the notion of equivalent schemas. The translations in [ZANI79] are not presented here because they would require our system to handle outer-joins [ROSE84], and we wish to introduce view-based translations as simply as possible. However, relations in Zaniolo's schemas have more attributes. Thus, more queries can be written without joins, and more integrity information can be captured by key constraints on single relations.

2.4 A View-Based Schema Translation Algorithm

We first extract all the logical information from the network schema, namely, record and set definitions, and integrity information. An equivalent schema consisting of view-relations is defined by invoking the three rules below, until each record type and each set type has been used once in defining a view. To keep the reader's interest from flagging, detailed rules for deriving integrity constraints are isolated in the next section.

By making different choices of which rule to apply next, more than one relational interface schema could be generated. User intervention or heuristics could guide the choice.

<u>Notation in View-Relation Definitions</u>

- R.* denotes the set of all fields of R, including the tid field. R may be a view-relation or an access relation. The tid field is not user-visible.
- R.Key (NNA) denotes the attributes in one key of R. All attributes of R.Key are NNA. R.Key may not be a tid.
- R.Set-key(S) denotes the attributes of a set-key, all of whose fields are NNA, where R is the member type of S.
- View-relation names are distinguished by the suffix _R. The view-relation that represents a record type REC (and perhaps migrated keys) is denoted REC_R, and the view-relation that represents a set S is denoted S_R.
- Field names of access relations and view relations are the same as the corresponding field names in the underlying network records.
- "|" denotes concatenation of fields (e.g., to form a multiattribute key).

Rules (a)-(c) below guide the derivation of the view-relation schemas, and they also identify a user-visible NNA key of each view relation. The rules for deriving other integrity constraints are in the next section.

a. <u>Independent entities</u>: If network record type R1 contains a user-visible NNA key (denoted R1.Key), then view-relation R1_R is identical to the access relation R1.

   Note that R1_R.Key = R1.Key.

b. <u>Dependent entities</u>: Suppose S is an automatic mandatory set linking owner type R0 to member type R1, and S has a NNA set-key. If view-relation R0_R has already been defined, then:

```
VIEW R1_R IS
  SELECT R0_R.Key,R1.*
    FROM R0_R, R1
    WHERE R0_R.@--link(S)--R1.@
  Key: R1_R.Key IS
         R0_R.Key | R1.Set-key(S)  (NNA, DNA);
```

Note that R1_R.@=R1.@.

c. Relationships: If R0_R and R1_R have been defined, if S links owner type R0 to member type R1 and S was not previously used in applying rule (b), then:

```
VIEW S_R IS
  SELECT R0_R.Key, R1_R.key,
         R1_R.(all fields in set-keys of S)
    FROM R0_R, R1_R
    WHERE R0_R.@--link(S)--R1_R.@
  Key: S_R.Key IS R1_R.Key  (NNA,DNA);
```

Note that S_R.@ = R1_R.@.

The above rules yield a view for record types that possess keys, or for which keys can be obtained from set-keys and the keys of owners of automatic mandatory sets. If no key can be obtained, the record type cannot be converted without duplicates in the relational schema.

Figure 3 shows a sample network schema diagram. It is followed by the network schema itself and the equivalent relational schema. For brevity, we omit data type definitions from the schema.

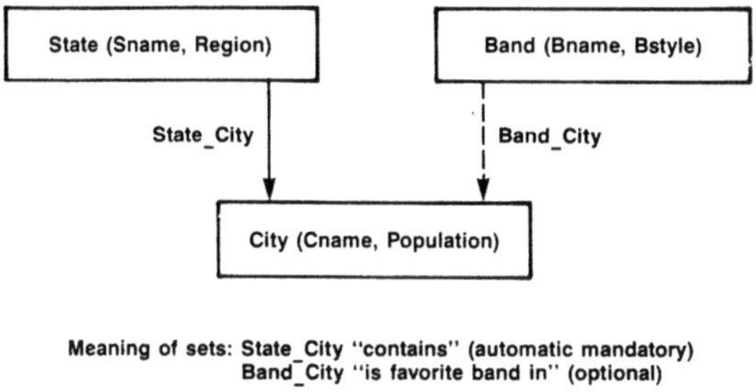

Figure 3. Network Schema Diagram

Network Schema

```
RECORD State
    Sname (NNA, DNA), Region
RECORD City
    Cname (NNA), Population
SET NAME IS State_City    (* State "contains" City *)
    OWNER IS State, MEMBER IS City
    SET-KEY IS Cname
    MEMBERSHIP IS AUTOMATIC MANDATORY
RECORD Band
    Bname (NNA, DNA), nBstyle
SET NAME IS Band_City (* Band "is favorite band in" City *)
    OWNER IS Band, MEMBER IS City
    MEMBERSHIP IS OPTIONAL
```

Equivalent Relational Schema

The derived view-relations are:

```
VIEW State_R IS
    SELECT State.* FROM State
    Key: State_R.Key IS Sname  (NNA, DNA);

VIEW Band_R IS
    SELECT Band.* FROM Band
    Key: Band_R.Key IS Bname  (NNA, DNA);

VIEW City_R IS
    SELECT State_R.Sname, City.*
        FROM State_R, City
        WHERE State_R.@--link(State_City)--City.@
    Key: City_R.Key = (Sname, Cname)  (NNA, DNA)
    Other integrity information:
        City_R[Sname] C+  State_R[Sname];
```

The above three views represent entities. The view below captures the semantics of a relationship.

```
VIEW Band_City_R IS
    SELECT Band_R.Bname, City_R.(Sname, Cname)
        FROM Band_R, City_R
        WHERE Band_R.@--link(Band_City)--City_R.@
    Key: Band_City_R.Key IS (Sname, Cname)
                                              (NNA, DNA)
    Other integrity information:
        Band_City_R[(Sname, Cname)] C+
                                  City_R[(Sname, Cname)]
        Band_City_R[Bname] C+ Band_R[Bname];
```

2.5 Integrity Constraints

Integrity constraints are an essential part of any schema. To protect the user from needing to understand the network model, all integrity information must be included in the relational schema.

The relational constructs that express integrity information are key declarations (DNA and NNA), and inclusion constraints. An inclusion constraint on attributes says that every nonnull value of an attribute R.A must appear as a value of some other attribute R′.B. This is denoted R[A] C+ R′[B] (where [ ] stands for projection and C+ is set inclusion applied to nonnull values). Inclusion constraints may also be defined when A and B are collections of attributes.

Our relational interface schema expresses all the integrity information in Codasyl schemas (as identified and captured differently by [ZANI79]).

- A Codasyl set-key declaration will be captured by declaring (owner-key, set-key) to be DNA in the view-relation that captures the set. This declaration is possible because we include all set-key attributes in the generated view relation. Thus we improve on similar translation algorithms [HWAN81, KATZ81, VASS80] that do not capture set-keys.

- The declaration that a set is "mandatory" is captured by declaring the key migrated from the owner to be NNA in the view relation.

- NNA and DNA constraints on record types translate directly into constraints on access relations.

We now give more details about this translation process. These detailed comments are added to the rules that generate view-relation definitions.

Rule (a) DNA and NNA attributes of a record type become DNA and NNA attributes of the access relation which directly models that record type.

Rules (b) and (c):

1. Keys: Let R1 be in the From-list of view-relation V_R in rule (b) or (c). R1 may be an access relation (in rule (b)) or a view-relation (in rule (c)). Let A denote a collection of attributes of R1 that appears in the target list of V_R. Then:
   If A is a key of R1, then A is a key of V_R.
   If A is a set-key in the set S used in defining V_R
   then R1.A | R0_R.Key is a key of V_R.

2. Inclusions: Let Ri_R be a view relation, and let B = {all attributes of Ri_R that appear in V_R}. (Ri_R may be R0_R in rule (b), or either relation in rule (c).)

   a. Every value for B in V_R came from Ri_R, so declare: V_R[B] $\underline{C}$+ Ri_R[B]. (Ri_R must be a view-relation because the user's schema cannot include constraints on access relations invisible to the user.)

   b. If S is mandatory and Ri_R is R1_R of rule (c), then every tuple of Ri_R must yield a tuple of V_R, so declare: Ri_R[B] $\underline{C}$+ V_R[B].

3. NNA: Whenever a rule transfers a NNA attribute into a view relation, the NNA constraint on the attribute is placed on the view relation.

As it stands, the access relation schema does not capture set-key constraints. The translation algorithm is aware of sets anyway, so we took integrity information directly from the network schema. For formal purposes, or if integrity constraint migration seemed more generally useful, we could have captured set-keys in the access relation schema. First, access relations would be extended so that for each set S, the set owner's tid would appear in each member tuple. The constraint that R.A was a set-key of S would then be expressed by a key constraint on A|(owner's tid).

[HWAN81] points out that the schema they derived (which is similar to ours) also can support a relational interface to an E-R system with m:n relationships. To build a relational interface over such a system, we just change rule (c) of schema generation so that the key is R1_R.Key | R0_R.Key if S is m:n.

3. Query Translation

3.1 Translation by View Substitution

Query translation requires no additional implementation effort. We need not interpret a special data structure that maps the relational schema to the network underneath; we simply perform ordinary relational view substitution.

[HWAN81] presents and proves rules for translating queries against a relational schema supported over an entity-relationship database. Our query translations yield essentially the same result, and can be justified by the same proofs.

The definition of an SQL view V consists of a target list "Target-list(V)", a list of relations "From-list(V)" and a restriction "Where-clause(V)". View substitution modifies a query Q by replacing references to view V with references to relations in From-list(V) [STON75]. The process is repeated until it yields a query in which all references are to access relations. We substitute for a view only after the views derived from it have been eliminated. The view processor need not know the semantics of link, but only that link is a predicate on attributes R.@ and R′.@.

Algorithm to eliminate a view V from a query Q:

(VS1) Delete V from From-list(Q) and append From-list(V) to From-list(Q). (Relations in Q and V must have distinct names. In case of conflict, relation R from V is given a new name R′ during substitution. That is, R′ is a new tuple variable over R.)

(VS2) Replace each attribute V.A in Q by its corresponding entry in Target-list(V). (If V.A corresponds to R.A and R′ was created at step 1, V.A is replaced by R′.A.)

(VS3) Replace Where-clause(Q) by (Where-clause(V) AND Where-clause(Q)).

Example: Consider the relational query Q1:

```
SELECT * FROM City_R
    WHERE Sname = ´Minnesota´ AND
        Cname ≠ ´Frostbite Falls´
```

Application of rules VS1-VS3 yields the following query:

```
SELECT State.Sname, City.Cname, City.Population
    FROM State, City
    WHERE Sname = ´Minnesota´ AND
        Cname ≠ ´Frostbite Falls´ AND
        State.@--link(State_City)--City.@
```

3.2 Query Simplification Rules

Complex collections of views can arise from several sources:

- View-relations above a network database
- Reorganization of a relational database: the old schema is supported as a view, to continue support for existing applications.
- Complicated outerjoins: Outerjoins can be used to specify hierarchical objects with one relation at each level. These hierarchical definitions may use many views.

When substituting for a complex collection of views, the view processor may generate an unnecessarily complicated query. We now show some rules that are applied after each substitution to simplify those queries.

QS1: Elementary algebraic simplifications to the Where-clause

a. Remove unnecessary joins by replacing "T1.A=T2.B and T2.B=constant" by "T1.A=constant and T2.B=constant")

b. Delete redundant predicates (e.g., one of "T1.A=T2.B" and "T2.B=T1.A")

c. Delete identity predicates (e.g., "T.A=T.A")

QS2: Remove unnecessary tuple variables

When a relation appears both in the outer query and in the view, view substitution was forced to create another tuple variable over that relation. Suppose T and T′ are tuple variables over relation T, and the Where-clause is expressed as a conjunction of predicates (called conjuncts). If one of those predicates is T.K=T′.K for some key K of T, then delete T′ from the From list, and replace all appearances of T′ by T.

Simplify the resulting query by applying QS1 to terms that involve T.

Justification: Since K is a key and T.K=T′.K, T and T′ must always reference the same tuple.

As an application of QS2, consider the user query:

```
SELECT State_R.Region, City_R.Sname, City_R.Cname
    FROM State_R, City_R
    WHERE State_R.Sname=City_R.Sname
```

The result of eliminating City_R by rules VS1-VS3 is:

```
SELECT State_R.Region, State_R′.Sname, City.Cname
    FROM State_R, State_R′, City
    WHERE State_R.Sname=State_R′.Sname AND
        State_R′.@--link(State_City)--City.@
```

QS2 eliminates State_R′ and replaces surviving references to it (e.g., in the Target-list) by State_R. The simplified query is:

```
SELECT State_R.Region, State_R.Sname, City.Cname
    FROM State_R, City
    WHERE State_R.@--link(State_City)--City.@
```

One then substitutes straightforwardly for State_R.

QS3: Remove deletable tables

A conjunct in Q of the form "R0.A=R.B" or "R0.@--link(S)--R.@" semi-joins R0 with R if R0 appears in no other conjunct, and R0 has no attributes in Target-list(Q). R0 is called deletable if R0 semijoins with some R, and every R record has exactly one corresponding R0 record.

To remove a deletable table R0, delete R0 from From-list(Q) and delete the conjunct involving R0 from Where-clause(Q). Note that deletion of R0 may cause R to become deletable.

Justification: The contents of a deletable table cannot affect the result of the query. If the number of R0 tuples corresponding to an R tuple is exactly one, the semijoin predicate will be satisfied and would not have created duplicate tuples of R.

QS3 removes a major inefficiency when a query does not need all the record types underlying a view-relation. For example, in query: "SELECT Cname FROM City_R", the cost of accessing State unnecessarily would be quite large.

The "exactly one" condition in QS3 holds if there is an inclusion dependency between R0 and a key of R1. If the user is unconcerned about duplicates (or a Unique operator is later to be applied), then "exactly one" can be replaced by "at least one."

3.3 Preprocessing to Speed View Substitution

Substituting through a large collection of views might slow query translation. Therefore, when a view V is defined over some other view V′, we can apply VS1-VS3 and QS1-QS3 to get a definition of V in terms of From-list(V′). The process continues till all views have been replaced.

The original definition of V can be helpful when semantic information about V′ is helpful in processing the query. After V′ is substituted, it will probably be impossible to use constraint information (e.g., key declarations) on V′ in applying QS2 and QS3. Therefore if the query processor detects the presence of some conditions for simplification (tuple variables created by view substitution, or semijoins with a foreign key), it might perform view substitution from the original definitions, with all the semantic information available.

A similar phenomenon can arise with updates. Constraints might be defined on updates to V′, and in certain cases when an error message cannot be expressed in terms of V, we want to express it using V′ rather than levels farther away from the user.

4. Physical Processing: the Optimizer′s Model of Network Data

Query translation yields an SQL query against access relations. The language is SQL augmented by link predicates. This section describes how scans on access relations are interpreted against network data, and how the query optimizer models the cost of this interpretation.

Relational systems generally access a relation using a sequential or direct access "scan" operator that returns all tuples of a relation that satisfy a predicate [SELI79, ROSE82a, REIN82]. The same scan operations are implemented over all storage structures, whether from a purely relational system (e.g., hash tables and B-trees), or from networks (e.g., ISAM files with set access via linked lists). Because each tuple of an access relation represents a single Codasyl record instance, a scan of an access relation translates very easily to a loop containing calls to the network access routines.

We now discuss how the query optimizer models the cost of scanning via sets. To simplify the presentation below, we assume the query includes just one link predicate.

For access from member to owner, we consider each member record to include the tid of the owner of its set (denoted owner-tid). Access from each member to its owner is a join with the member as the outer loop, owner as inner. The join operator requires no modification, it simply invokes a scan to get tuples of the relation in the inner loop.

The model of access from owner to member has one additional complication. For each owner record, one gets tids for many member records. We conceive of the owner record instance as being augmented by a repeating group of tids.

The optimizer's cost models are extended to deal with link predicates. The cost of getting an owner-tid, or list of member tids, is treated much like the cost of getting pointers from an index. The cost of accessing linked lists and pointer arrays must be modelled, just as the relational system models the cost of accessing B-trees. Fortunately, the optimizer's model of clustered data applies to tuples clustered by member's tid just as it would apply to tuples clustered by an ordinary field value.

Considerable power is derived from our formulation of access via set as a form of direct access to support a join. A relational optimizer considers many different join strategies, more than a network programmer would be able to consider. Some of the factors considered in choosing a join option (i.e., set traversal strategy) are:

- Choosing the outer operand of the join (i.e., whether to visit first the owner or the member). In addition to minimizing join cost, we want an outer operand that results in a desirable sort order for the join's result.

- Sorting the outer relation on the tid field for the inner relation, to make access more sequential.

- Intersecting tid lists (equivalent to intersecting indexes, a strategy supported in some optimizers).

- Performing semijoins (sometimes the query merely wants to test whether the record belongs to a set instance, without needing to see the other records in that set instance).

[ROSE82b] contains detailed models of strategies for accessing tuple id's that support sets. Set implementations are classified based on whether the link information is embedded in the target records (e.g., pointer chain), or is independent of it (e.g., pointer array, direct member pointers). We do not sort or intersect tid lists to speed access to records with embedded tids, since the tids are available only after the records are accessed.

Extending SQL to non-first normal form relations [SCHE82] would allow high-level processing of some hierarchical structures. It would also confer some benefits for processing ordinary queries, because some access structures are most naturally modelled using repeating groups. Index structures of the form (value, ptrl, ptr2, ...) would be modelled directly. An owner record could be given a repeating group of member tids for each set type that it owns.

The optimizer for non-first normal form queries would decide when tuples with repeating groups need to be normalized (e.g., for sort on ptr fields), and would calculate the cost of such normalization.

5. Comparisons with Previous Work

5.1 Features of the Schema Generation Algorithm

1. Each new view-relation is defined from (at most) two relations and one set. This allows simple mapping rules for updates, integrity constraints, triggers, and keys. Some other proposals handle many relations at once, or manipulate foreign keys as lists of fields from several record types.

2. Our schema generation rules can be applied to new record and set types without disturbing existing view-relations. Many decisions in schema generation are arbitrary, dependent on order of presentation or lexical ordering. By making choices slightly differently, an algorithm that ran again from scratch might produce a relational schema very different from the previous run.

3. When record and set types are deleted, it is easy to identify views that need to be dropped. When a view-relation is created, the translator must associate that view relation with the access relations or sets used in its construction. When a record or set type is deleted, the system finds the view-relation to delete. The view manager associated with the original relational system will then delete all views defined over the deleted view.

4. We did not need to extend the relational model to include "null patterns" (collections of attributes where all or none are null) [ZANI79].

5.2 Alternatives to Query Translation

Database conversion: Converting a network database to relational storage is usually impractical since application programs also require conversion. The conversion will lose information unless the relational system can entirely capture duplicate and ordering information currently in the network system. If ordered relations and duplicates are supported, it may be difficult to identify sets whose order was significant.

Data extraction: Data can be extracted from the network system into a relational database. The network database remains the master copy. The problems with the extraction approach are cost and difficulty of update.

Extraction is costly because it must be performed before each session (unless one uses older information), and because during the session, two copies of the data must be stored. The problem with update is that the master copy can be updated only by using a low level, navigational update language. Hence most users and application programmers can perform database maintenance only through transaction programs written by experts.

5.3 Forms of Query Translation

In any query translation approach, queries against lowest level relations must be translated to commands for the network system. Two approaches have been used:

Interpretation: One can interpretively execute each query against a lowest level relation by invoking commands in the network system. The interpreter must be resident in main memory during execution. [CONN79] describes one prototype interpreter.

Compilation to database calls embedded in a host language: The translator produces a program that may then be compiled and executed. This requires less intimate connection with the network system, though one is committed to the particular host language. It appears more difficult to write than an interpreter. [GRAY79] and [ESSL82] describe an early implementation that used this FORTRAN as the host. [VASS80] describes a similar design.

The Multibase system [DAYA84] uses a combination of compilation and interpretation. It is meant to integrate DBMSs with differing properties. Its compiler produces an access strategy that makes use of the primitives available on each underlying system. Any primitives not available there (such as join, or set-at-a-time access) are implemented by the Multibase interpreter.

Unlike all the systems mentioned, we would use relational facilities to translate down to access relations. If one has the facilities of a relational system available, then our architecture makes implementation much easier, and optimization more effective.

In our architecture, scans on access relations are implemented by a simple routine that accesses a single record type. The tuples returned are manipulated using join, sort, and similar facilities of the relational system. Optimization is very effective because the query optimizer works on almost the entire mapping from stored records to the user's result. The full power of the relational query optimizer is available in generating alternative strategies, and in considering the cost of one step when making decisions about other steps.

If the relational facilities stop at the level of the relational interface schema, the translator must map each of those relations to the several network record and set types that implement it. Several kinds of work are needed:

- A traversal strategy must be chosen. Access to a relation in the relational interface schema can require a traversal of several record and set types. Since it is not obvious which traversal path is best, the interpreter needs some optimization capability. Furthermore, this capability must be integrated with the optimization performed at the relational level.

- The traversal must be controlled and executed. Iteration must be properly handled, and result tuples built from extracted fields. Again, this duplicates capabilities present in a relational system. [GRAY79] describes a system built from scratch where these tasks required many thousands of lines of code.

The work closest to our approach was [HWAN81]. This work had a wider scope than ours. Update translation rules were provided and all translation rules were proved correct. We were more concerned with profitably sharing facilities with a preexisting relational system. [ROSE82b] contains a more detailed comparison.

Link predicates do not significantly extend the relational model. Languages for richer supersets of the relational and network models can produce structures that are much more complex than the single relation produced by a query in a conventional language [MANO83], [DATE81]. However, the development effort for the language, user interface, and query optimizer will be formidable.

6. Concluding Remarks

We described an approach to extending an existing relational system in order to provide relational access to data stored as network files. Noteworthy features are:

- The nearly-relational access relation schema directly models network record types.

- The relational schema which captures the semantics of a network database is expressed as a collection of relational views with integrity constraints, defined over the access relation schema.

- Existing view-handling facilities are used to translate relational queries to the base objects, namely access relations and base relations supported directly under the relational model.

- A properly structured optimizer in a relational system can be extended to compile relational queries to any access relations, including network records. Network set traversals are encoded as joins, thus allowing the optimizer to cost-out a very wide range of join strategies, including traversal in either direction.

- Because the optimizer maps all the way down to access relations, it can optimize thoroughly.

- Facilities used to support relational access to network databases (query simplifications, updates to simple views, duplicates and ordered sets) reside in the relational query processor, and hence are available to all users.

- The storage structures are transparent to the user. A query or update can reference information stored under both models.

Query translation produces a mapping from the data format requested by the user (a query against views) to the data formats available from the DBMS. Part of this mapping is expressed in a high level language, and part is implemented in procedural code (the physical database access routines). For relational schemas over network data, we showed that much of the mapping could be expressed in a SQL-like language.

The benefits of the higher level mapping language are that mappings can be unambiguously composed (permitting optimization of several steps simultaneously) and more clearly specified. For example, the problem of updating relational views is far better specified than the problem of updating a relational schema that is related to the underlying network by PL/1 code. The effect is to increase the amount of translation that can be done in a well specified data model.

Acknowledgement

This work was begun while the authors were at the Sperry Research Center. It has benefitted from suggestions made by Won Kim and Murray Edelberg.

References

(CONN79) (DATE81, see DATE82) (DAYA78) (DAYA84, see DAYA85) (ESSL82) (GRAY79) (HWAN81) (KATZ81, see KATZ81a) (LORI83) (MANO82) (MANO83) (REIN82, see REIN82a) (ROSE82a) (ROSE82b) (ROSE84) (SCHE82) (STON75) (STON82, see STON82b) (VASS80) (ZANI79)

Section IV

Database Updates through Views

Updating Relational Views

Anthony L. Furtado and Marco A. Casanova

ABSTRACT

A view is a logical subset of the data base conceptual schema. Providing a facility for supporting views simplifies the user interface, but creates the problem of translating updates on views into equivalent updates on the data base. The translation of a view update may not be unique, it may not even exist or be ill-defined, and it may create inconsistencies in the data base or have side effects on the view. This paper surveys the two basic approaches proposed to solve the view update problem. The first approach suggests treating views as abstract data types so that the definition of a view includes all permissible view updates, together with their translations. The second approach leads to general view update translators and is based either on an analysis of the conceptual schema dependencies or on the concept of view complement to disambiguate view update translations.

1. INTRODUCTION

The complete logical structure of a data base is described by a *conceptual schema* listing the data structures and the integrity constraints of the data base [TSIC77,DATE81]. To delimit or focus on just those aspects of the data base relevant to each group of users, most systems also support the concept of an *external schema* or a *view*. Views simplify the user interface by allowing a user to ignore data that are not relevant to his application. They also provide a degree of protection by shielding data that should not be accessible by a class of users. Furthermore, views also help achieve a degree of logical data independence since it is often possible to alter the conceptual schema without changing the view.

We shall adopt in this paper the relational model of data [DATE81]. In this context a view is sometimes limited to a single-relation external schema and it can be described just like a query (as in System R [DATE81]). However, we shall not make this simplification here when dealing with the general theory of views. The view definition is stored by the system and can be used to materialize *derived relations* from the *stored relations* of the data base. A view definition facility is part of many relational data base systems [BROD82] such as SQL/DS [IBM], QBE [ZLOO77] and INGRES [STON76].

Users interact with a view by issuing queries and update requests. Queries present no particular problem. A query on a view is processed by composing the user query with the view definition, thus obtaining an equivalent query on the stored relations [STON75]. Conceptually, this process is equivalent to creating the derived relations first and then issuing the (view) query on these relations.

Processing view updates poses a difficult problem, though. To translate a view update u, we must find a data base update t such that t maps the current data base state s into a new state s' iff u maps the current view state v (generated from s) into a new view state v', which is generated from s'. Now, t may not be unique, it may not even exist or be ill-defined, and it may create inconsistencies in the data base or have side effects on the view. It should be no surprise then that most data base management systems severely restrict the types of updates allowed on views. The *view update problem* refers to the question of choosing or defining correct view update translations.

This paper surveys several solutions proposed to the view update problem and briefly indicates how they could be used to enhance the view update facilities currently offered by data base management systems.

There are two basic approaches to the view update problem. One approach suggests to treat a view as an abstract data type [BROD81]. That is, the view definition should contain not only a description of how to derive view data from the underlying data base, but also a description of the set of allowed view updates together with their translations into updates over the conceptual schema [CLEM78,ROWE79,SEVC78,TUCH83]. This approach requires the design of an extended view definition language and methods of verifying that update translations are indeed correct (according to some clearly defined correctness criteria). This approach is addressed in Section 3 of the paper.

The second approach is to define general translation procedures. These procedures input a view definition, a view update, possibly with some extra information, and the current data base state and produce, if possible, a data base update that satisfies some desired properties [BANC81,CARL79,COSM83,KELL81,DAYA78,DAYA82,FURT79]. This solution is discussed in Section 4.

Both approaches need a theory characterizing precisely when a data base update is a correct translation of a view update [BANC81,CASA83,DAYA82]. An introduction to this theory, together with basic definitions and notation, is presented in the next section.

A word should be said about the style of presentation. The view update problem has some delicate aspects that cannot be covered without a certain amount of formalization. We have tried to keep the formalism to a minimum, however, and complement it with examples when the notation became too heavy. The space limitations also forced us to give a superficial treatment to some interesting approaches to the problem. The reader is thus urged to consult the references that generated each section.

2. AN INTRODUCTION TO THE VIEW UPDATE PROBLEM

2.1 Basic Definitions and Notation

This section gives general definitions for the notions of conceptual schema and view. Examples will be presented in Section 2.2.

A *relation scheme* is a statement of the form R[A1,...,An], where R is the *name* of the scheme and A1,...,An are the *attributes* of the scheme; if the number of attributes is n, the scheme is said to be *n-ary.*

A *relational schema* is a pair S = (RS,IC) where RS is a set of relation schemes and IC is a set of sentences, the *integrity constraints of the schema.* A *data base state,* or simply a *state,* of S is a function s assigning to each n-ary relation scheme in RS an n-ary relation over a given domain. A *data base update* of S is a mapping t from the set of states of RS onto itself. A state of S is said to be *consistent* iff it satisfies all integrity constraints of S. If an update t of S maps consistent states into consistent states, then we say that t *preserves consistency.*

An *external schema* or *view* over a data base schema S is a triple V=(RV,CV,f) where SV=(RV,CV) is a relational schema as above and f is a mapping from states of S into states of SV (over the same domain as the states of S). We also say that f is the *view definition mapping,* and we will be flexible about the way f is defined. A *view state* of V is simply a state of SV and a *view update* of V is just an update of SV.

This general definition of view will be used in sections 3 and 4.2. However, in sections 2.2, 4.1 and in parts of section 4.2, we will use a simplified concept of view.

When the view V=(RV,CV,f) has a single relation scheme R[A1,...,An], no constraints, and the mapping is defined using a relational algebra or relational calculus expression, we will use the notation R = f as an abbreviation for V=(RV,CV,f) (the attributes of R are inherited from the expression).

Throughout this paper, S=(RS,IC) will denote a data base schema, V=(RV,CV,f) and V'=(RV',CV',f') views over S; s and s' will also be used to denote consistent states of S, v consistent states of V, u an update of V and t an update of S.

In this paper we will be mostly concerned with three questions [BANC81]:

Q1. Given a view update u on V, when does a data base update t translate u?

Q2. What sets of view updates do we want to translate, that is, what sets of updates users are to be allowed on the view?

Q3. How do we associate with each view update a data base update that translates it?

Answers to Q2 and Q3 reflect the view update strategy adopted and are dealt with in sections 3 and 4. Thus, we address only Q1 here.

In order for t to be considered a translation of u at all, t must take any s into some s' such that u takes the view state f(s) into the view state f(s'). In addition, t must preserve consistency with respect to the integrity constraints of S. If t satisfies both conditions, we say that t is an *exact translation* of u [DAYA82]. But we might have exact translations that unnecessarily modify the data base, as exemplified in Section 2.2 below. So, we consider that t is (minimally) *acceptable* [BANC81] iff it leaves the data base state unchanged if u made no change on the view. That is, for any s, if u(f(s))=f(s) then t(s)=s.

To summarize, any translation of a view update must be exact and acceptable. Broadly speaking, *the view update problem* is concerned with finding or defining such translations.

2.2. What are the Problems with the Execution of View Updates?

Consider a data base schema whose relation schemes are E[EMP,DEP], M[DEP,MGR] and E'[EMP,DEP], noting that E and E' are defined on the same attributes (and so are trivially union-compatible [DATE81]). Assume that the constraints of the schema are two functional dependencies E:EMP→DEP and M:DEP→MGR as well as the inclusion dependency E[DEP] ⊆ M[DEP]. (That is, every EMP is assigned to a unique DEP in E, every DEP has a unique MGR in M, and every DEP in E must also occur in M). For simplicity, we shall consider that E' is not subjected to any constraint. Consider now a set of single-relation views whose mappings are defined through relational algebra operations on the stored relations. Using the simplified notation introduced in Section 2.1, the views are:

V1 = E[DEP='Sales'] (E restricted to DEP = 'Sales')
V2 = M[DEP='Sales'] (M restricted to DEP = 'Sales')
V3 = E[EMP] (E projected on EMP)
V4 = E[DEP] (E projected on DEP)
V5 = E*M (the natural join of E and M)
V6 = E grouped by DEP and
restricted to count(EMP) > 2
V7 = E U E' (E union E')
V8 = (E[DEP=DEP]M)[EMP,MGR] (E joined to M on DEP
and projected on EMP,MGR)

Note: V6 is obtained by grouping (or partitioning, see [FURT77]) the tuples of E, so that employees of the same department are in the same group, and retaining only the groups of more than two tuples.

Consider now the following data base state:

E

EMP	DEP
John	Sales
Peter	Finance
Alice	Sales

M

DEP	MGR
Sales	Mary
Finance	Jane

E'

EMP	DEP
Joan	Toys

together with the corresponding view states:

V1 EMP	DEP
John	Sales
Alice	Sales

V2 DEP	MGR
Sales	Mary

V3 EMP
John
Peter
Alice

V4 DEP
Sales
Finance

V5 EMP	DEP	MGR
John	Sales	Mary
Peter	Finance	Jane
Alice	Sales	Mary

V6 EMP	DEP

V7 EMP	DEP
John	Sales
Peter	Finance
Alice	Sales
Joan	Toys

V8 EMP	MGR
John	Mary
Peter	Jane
Alice	Mary

We shall use these views and the example data base state to illustrate several problems arising from the translation of view updates consisting of one-tuple insertions, deletions or replacements (following [FURT79]). Although more than one problem may be found in some examples, only one will be stressed in each case. We first state the general problem to be illustrated and then list one or more view updates, together with a brief discussion of what might happen when one tried to translate them. The data base state is assumed to be the one just described.

1) A constraint may be violated.

- insert (Peter,Sales) into V1:
  The natural translation of this update, a simple insertion of (Peter,Sales) into E, violates the FD E:EMP→DEP since E contains (Peter, Finance) in the example data base state;

- delete (Sales, Mary) from V2:
  Again, translating the update as a simple deletion of (Sales,Mary) from M violates E[DEP] ⊆ M[DEP] since E contains (John,Sales) in the example data base state.

2) A result which does not conform with the view definition may be produced.

- insert (Mark,Finance) into V1:
  V1 contains only employees in the Sales Department.

3) A result conforming with the view definition may be produced, but tuples lying outside the view may be involved.

- replace (Peter,Finance) by (Peter,Sales) in V1:
  The straighforward translation of this view update as a replacement of (Peter,Finance) by (Peter,Sales) in E creates a tuple in V1 by modifying a tuple in E that originally generated no tuple in V1.

- delete (Peter,Finance) from V1:
  As before, even if the tuple exists in E, it may not generate a tuple of V1.

4) An effect different from that expected from the nature of the operation may be produced.

- replace (John,Sales) by (John,Finance) in V1:
  A straighforward translation as a replacement in E may be perceived as a deletion from V1; the modified tuple however remains in E.

5) It may be necessary to include undefined values (nulls).

- insert (Roger) into V3:
  The only reasonable translation is to insert (Roger,-) into E (where '-' stands for an undefined value).

6) Attributes outside the view may be affected.

- delete (Sales) from V4:
  if this view update is translated as a deletion of all tuples of the form (x,Sales) from E, the names of the employees denoted by x are lost.

7) Multiple effects on the stored relations may be produced.

- replace (Sales) by (Marketing) in V4:
  To translate this single-tuple update on V4, all tuples (x,Sales) in E must be changed to (x,Marketing).

8) A multiple effect on the view may be visible.

- replace (John,Sales,Mary) by (John,Sales,Jane) in V5:
  The natural translation, a single replacement of (Sales,Mary) by (Sales,Jane) in M, changes all tuples (x,Sales,Mary) in V5 to (x,Sales,Jane), instead of only the intended tuple.

9) An entire group of tuples, or none at all, may be changed.

- insert (Roger,Sales) into V6:
  Consider the translation that inserts the tuple into E. If there exists only two tuples, like (John,Sales) and (Alice,Sales) in E, then none may belong to V6 before the update; the translation may then result in the insertion of the entire group of three tuples into V6.

10) More than one translation may exist.

- insert (Roger,Sales) into V7.
  The translation can insert the tuple either into E or into E' or into both.

- replace (John,Mary) by (John,Jane) in V8.
  Assuming that (John,x) is in E, and (x,Mary) and (y,Jane) are in M, the translation can either replace (John,x) by (John,y) in E or (x,Mary) by (x,Jane) in M.

Observing these examples, we remark that they have anomalous aspects and, hence, we would be unsure about how to translate them or if they should even be allowed.

Case (1), for instance, does not lead to an exact translation. Case (2) does not meet our requirement for an acceptable translation, since, if allowed, it would modify the stored relation E without actually changing the view V1.

Although we could point out non-exact or non-acceptable translations in the other cases, we shall instead examine other related problems. In the first example of case (3), if no user's view includes both departments involved in the attempted transfer of the employee, we could think of a "cooperative" execution of the update by two authorized users, which mimics a common real-world practice. In fact, this is but one example of the phenomenon of mutual *interference* (or influence) among views. Cases (4) and (6) also show updates having effects outside the view being directly updated.

Interference is really a much broader issue in data bases, since views need not be mutually disjoint. Thus, even if the effects of an update are apparently confined to one view, they may affect other views sharing part of the same stored relations. For instance, the update on V4 in case (7) also affects V1.

Case (5) is another example where cooperation is needed. It suggests that introducing an employee and assigning him to a department are separate actions, possibly by different users. Note that the relational model requirement that keys cannot have undefined values prevents us from inverting the order of the two actions: a tuple like (-,Sales) could not be inserted into E.

In general, introducing additional constraints can help disambiguate translations of view updates. In case (10), the first example dealing with the union of E and E' is ambiguous because there is nothing in their definition to distinguish them. We might suppose instead that E is constrained to record only full-time employees and E' only part-time employees, thereby introducing a distinguishing implicit attribute.

Similarly, the ambiguity of the second example of case (10) could be removed with an additional functional dependency M:MGR→DEP; this would exclude the insertion of (x,Jane) into M if (y,Jane) is already in M.

The anomaly in case (4) is that the effect is incongruous with the nature of the intended operation. In cases (8) and (9) the expected effect is produced, but other effects also take place. This situation is not very different from interference among views; here the unsolicited side effects result from an operation on the same view but would appear to its user as unrelated to his action.

Combining multiple updates triggered by a single update and effects outside the view, we may envision a way to perform the update of the second example of case (1) that preserves the inclusion dependency. The deletion of (Sales, Mary) from M would be followed by the deletion of all tuples of the form (x,Sales) from E. However, this is again an ambiguous situation: how do we decide if the constraint must be enforced either by forbidding the offending update or by triggering other compensating updates? As before, the answer is to introduce further constraints, in this case on the relationship between employees and departments. Using CODASYL 78 [DATE81] terminology, we would decide for the former solution if employees are *mandatory* members and for the latter, if they are *fixed* members. So, an open-ended number of constraints, other than just dependencies, may be used to reduce the degree of arbitrariness when allowing or forbidding updates on views and choosing how to translate them.

3. THE ABSTRACT DATA TYPES APPROACH

The abstract data types approach characterizes the objects of a type by the operations performed on them and hides from the programmers details about how such objects are represented [BROD81].

A trivial example that will help understand how the approach can be applied to view updates is that of stacks. Suppose that stacks are represented by PASCAL arrays and that the stack operations CREATE, ISEMPTY, TOP, PUSH, POP are implemented (translated) by functions or procedures in whose bodies assignment and subscripting operations on arrays are used. Thus, inside a procedure for the PUSH operation we might have:

```
...
t := t + 1;
A[t] := v;
...
```

where t indicates the top element of the stack represented by array A, and v is the value being pushed.

We would be grossly mistaken if we interpreted in terms of arrays what the procedure above does. As an array operation what we have is simply that an array element is assigned a value, whereas after the PUSH operation all elements of A with subscripts less than the incremented value of t are invisible. More precisely, this is a consequence of the combined behavior of the stack operations, which allows only the top element to be seen. Conversely, the POP operation, which does not even change the array (it only decrements t), not only removes the current top element but also restores the previous one.

The analogy with views is immediate. Stacks are comparable to derived relations, permitting us to see a limited part of the stored relations, which in turn are comparable to the arrays used to represent stacks. It follows that, analogous to stack operations (translated into one or more array operations), we should introduce *application-oriented operations* [SEVC78] to handle views of specific data bases (an example will be given at the end of this section). The view definition would specify, for each application-oriented operation, an exact translation on the underlying stored relations. Since the designer has complete control of the translations, they may possibly have multiple effects, all of which may not necessarily be visible through the view.

Some application-oriented operations pertinent to our running example are to hire, fire, assign and transfer employees, to create, rename and extinguish departments, to raise a department to the status of "major department" (more than two employees), to attach an employee to a manager, etc.

Some of the benefits of this approach are:

1) Certain updates are no longer anomalous when we cease to consider them as unconditional applications of single tuple insertion, deletion or replacement operations.

2) Ambiguity is avoided since, when explicitly translating the application-oriented operations, arbitrary decisions can be made in the absence of pertinent constraints.

3) The application-oriented operations will often provide a more user-friendly interface to non-professionals in data processing who are knowledgeable in their application areas.

4) Constraints are automatically enforced if view updating is restricted to the defined application-oriented operations. (Note that this strategy also enforces constraints more efficiently than most other automatic enforcement strategies). This decision corresponds to the *encapsulation* strategy, which is inherent in the abstract data types approach.

An unusual feature of data bases, as compared to the well-known cases of abstract data types in the programming languages literature, is that data bases are shared objects. However this does not make the approach inapplicable, even though it requires a careful analysis to ensure that the entire set of operations effectively excludes all undue interferences among the views (see [CASA83]).

A disadvantage of the approach is the work required to define the operations and the need to possibly redefine them during the lifetime of the data base. Yet, this seems preferable to the prevailing practice in many organizations of forbidding users to perform updates in real-time, out of fear of constraint violation. The problem is especially serious due to the fact that most data base management systems neither permit the declaration nor enforce constraints, except for the most trivial classes.

On the other hand, the abstract data type approach is compatible with existing data base management systems, as demonstrated in [TUCH83] for SQL/DS, although the introduction of additional language features seems desirable. To give the flavor of such features, we show an example of a module through which a user can attach an employee to a manager. (A module is understood here as a set of data base data structures plus a set of operations on these structures).

Example 3.1: Definition of a Module.

```
module SUBORDINATION extends PERSONNEL_DB
       schemes
               B[EMP,MGR]
       constraints
               ∀e∀m∀n(B(e,m)  ∧ B(e,n) => m=n)
       operations
               ATTACH(e,m):
                  insert (e,m) into B;
    using
       view definitions
               B[EMP,MGR]: {(e,m) / ∃d(E(e,d)  ∧ M(d,m))}
       operations translations
               ATTACH(e,m):
                  if ∃d M(d,m)  ∧  ~∃d' E(e,d')
                     then insert (e,d) into E;
end-module
```

We assumed the existence of a previous module, PERSONNEL_DB, defining two relation schemes, E[EMP,DEP] and M[DEP,MGR], subjected to the integrity constraints $E{:}EMP \rightarrow DEP$, $M{:}DEP \rightarrow MGR$, $M{:}MGR \rightarrow DEP$ and $E[DEP] \subseteq M[DEP]$.

The module SUBORDINATION is then defined over PERSONNEL_DB. It contains a relation scheme, corresponding to a derived relation, and an integrity constraint, which is a consequence of the FDs of the PERSONNEL_DB module. The only operation is ATTACH. Users of the module need know only these three parts of the module definition: the relation schemes, integrity constraints and operations. The definitions under the 'using' clause should not be visible since they correspond to an implementation of the module objects in terms of the objects of the underlying module. Finally, note that the constraints of PERSONNEL_DB are preserved by the translation of the ATTACH operation, since it produces no effects if m does not manage a department or if e is already assigned to some department. Since the module constraint is a consequence of those of PERSONNEL_DB, the translation also indirectly preserves consistency with respect to the module constraints.

As an example of the effects of ATTACH, assume that the current data base state is

E	EMP	DEP
	John	Sales
	Peter	Finance
	Alice	Sales

M	DEP	MGR
	Sales	Mary
	Finance	Jane

and the view state is

B	EMP	MGR
	John	Mary
	Peter	Jane
	Alice	Mary

Then, we will have

- ATTACH(John,Jane) fails since John has already been assigned to Sales.
- ATTACH(Robert,Laura) fails since Laura does not manage a department.
- ATTACH(Robert,Jane) succeeds since Jane manages a department and the tuple (Robert,Finance) is inserted into E. □

The module concept illustrated above is fully discussed in [TUCH83], where the combination of views as an encapsulation device with the modular design of data base schémas is investigated.

4. THE AUTOMATIC TRANSLATION APPROACH

The broad goal of the automatic translation approach to the view update problem is to define, for each view V and each *complete* set U of updates on V, a *translator* T for U.

A class U of updates users are allowed to make on a view V is said to be *complete* if it satisfies the following minimum requirements [BANC81,SEVC78]:

1) If u and v are in U then the composition of u and v is also in U.

2) If the view is updated, using an update in U, then there is an update in the set that brings the view back to the original state (thus users may cancel the effect of any previous update).

A mapping from view updates in U to data base updates is in turn said to be a *translator* for U iff [BANC81]

1) for any u in U, T(u) must be an exact, acceptable translation of u (see Section 2.1), and

2) the translation of the composition of two view updates in U must be the composition of the translations.

Example 4.1:

Let S be a data base schema whose relation schemes are E[EMP,DEP] and M[DEP,MGR], and whose constraints are E:EMP→DEP, M:DEP→MGR. Let V be a view over S whose only scheme is EN[EMP], defined by projecting E onto EMP.

Let U be the set of all single tuple insertions and deletions in V and their composition. Then one can easily prove that U is complete.

Let T be the translator that associates to each u in U a translation T(u) defined as follows:

1) An insertion of a tuple (e) in EN is translated as an insertion of a tuple (e,-) in E, provided that e does not occur in EN;

2) A deletion of a tuple (e) from EN is translated as a deletion of a tuple (e,d) from E, for some department d.

3) The translation of a sequence of insertions and deletions in EN is translated as the sequence of translations of the insertions and deletions.

Then one can also easily prove that T is a translator for U. □

The basic problems one must face when defining a translator is that the view definition alone may not provide sufficient information on the relationship between view updates and data base updates. A way out of this dilemma is to explore the data dependencies pertaining to the conceptual schema, together with the view definition, to detect conditions under which view updates can always be unique and correctly translated [CARL79,KELL81,DAYA78,DAYA82,FURT79]. This solution is discussed in Section 4.1. A second solution uses the concept of view complement to disambiguate the semantics of view updates and is addressed in Section 4.2.

4.1 The View Dependency Graph Approach

The first strategy to design general translators for view updates we consider explores the structure of the dependencies of the underlying conceptual schema to disambiguate view updates. We present a brief summary of this approach, following [DAYA78,DAYA82].

In this section we will work under the following assumptions:

1) The constraints of the conceptual schema are restricted to be single-attribute functional dependencies and keys, that is, FDs of the form R:A→B, where A and B are attributes of R, and keys consisting of just one attribute. (This assumption is stronger than the one found in [DAYA82], but it simplifies the presentation of the basic ideas of the method). Moreover, every relation scheme must have a primary key.

2) Views are restricted to contain just one relation scheme and no constraints; moreover, the view mapping must be defined using just restrictions, selections and joins involving only equalities.

3) The view updates are restricted to be single- and multi-tuple deletions and replacements and single tuple insertions.

Due to the nature of the results, it is convenient to adopt a language called SQL [DATE81,IBM] to express view definition mappings, and also to express view updates. A single-relation view, with no constraints, will then be defined as follows:

```
(1)   DEFINE VIEW R (B1,...,Bn)
        AS SELECT ti1.Aij1,...,tin.Aijn
             FROM R1 t1,...,Rm tm
            WHERE <qual>
```

where <qual> contains only clauses of the form "t.A = c" or "t.A = u.B" (t and u may be the same). We say that the attribute Aijk of Rik *generates* the view attribute Bk, for each k in [1,n].

We shall also assume for simplicity that no two tuple variables range over the same scheme and that, if the qualification implies an equality of the form t.A=u.B, then this equality is explicitly included in the qualification.

The structure of the view definition is captured by defining a labeled directed graph G(V)=(N,E) constructed as follows:

1) for each attribute A of each relation name Ri occurring in the FROM clause, there is a node in N labeled "Ri.A";

2) for each view attribute Bj, there is a node labeled "R.Bj";

3) for each constant c occurring in the qualification, there is a node labeled "c" in N;

4) for each view attribute Bk, there are arcs (R.Bk,Rik.Aijk) and (Rik.Aijk,R.Bk), if Aijk generates Bk;

5) for each equality R'.A'=R".A" in the qualification, there are arcs (R'.A',R".A") and (R".A",R'.A');

6) for each restriction R'.A'=c in the qualification, there are arcs (R'.A',c) and (c,R'.A').

The *view dependency graph* is obtained by incorporating in G(V) the information provided by the FDs of the underlying schema. This is done as follows:

1) for each FD Ri:A→B, add the arc (Ri.A,Ri.B) to G(V);

2) if the qualification implies R'.A'=c, which can be detected by a path from R'.A' to c in G(V), add arcs (R".A",R'.A') to G(V), for each node R".A" of G(V) such that R" occurs in the FROM clause.

Note that the view dependency graph depends only on the view definition and on the dependencies of the conceptual schema. Hence it can be constructed and stored together with the view definition.

Example 4.2:

Let S and V be defined as follows:

a) S is a data base schema whose relation schemes are E[EMP,DEP] and M[DEP,MGR], and whose constraints are E:EMP→DEP, M:DEP→MGR.

b) V is a view over S defined as:

```
DEFINE VIEW EDm(EMP,DEP)
  AS SELECT E.EMP, E.DEP
       FROM E, M
      WHERE E.DEP=M.DEP AND M.MGR=m
```

Then, the view dependency graph of V is:

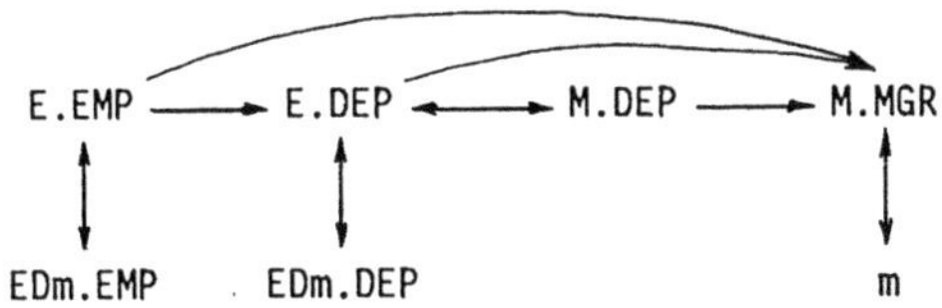

□

We shall now state how the view dependency graph can be used to derive conditions on the translatability of deletions. Similar conditions can be found in [DAYA82] for insertions and replacements.

Let V be a view defined as in (1) above. Again using the syntax of SQL, a *simple deletion* on V is a deletion of the form:

```
(2)     DELETE R
         WHERE Bk1=c1 AND ... AND Bkp=cp
```

Consider the following translation procedure for deletions of this form:

step 1:
Choose one relation name Ri occurring in the FROM clause of V.

step 2:
The translation of the deletion will be

```
DELETE Ri
 WHERE Ri.Ki IN
     ( SELECT ti.Ki
       FROM R1 t1,...,Rm tm
       WHERE <qual>
         AND SOURCE(Bk1)=c1 AND ... AND SOURCE(Bkp)=cp )
```

where Ki is the primary key of Ri (which exists by assumption), and SOURCE(Bj) denotes the expression Rq.Aiq, if Aiq generates Bj.

It is obvious that the proposed translation, call it t, preserves consistency since deletions cannot violate keys and FDs. Moreover, t is clearly acceptable since, if the view deletion qualification fails, so does the the qualification of t. Hence, if the view deletion does not modify the view, t also does not modify the data base. It can also be easily shown that t performs the desired deletions, that is, the tuples of V that should be deleted indeed are. However, t may have side effects and, hence, may not be an exact translation. The view dependency graph then comes in our help. It is proved in [DAYA82] that t is an exact translation of u iff, for each attribute B of V, there is an attribute A of the relation scheme Ri chosen in the first step of the procedure such that there is a path from A to B in the view dependency graph.

The following example illustrates a successful application of this result.

Example 4.3:

Let S and V be as in Example 4.2. Let u be the following simple deletion on V

```
DELETE EDm
 WHERE DEP=d
```

A possible translation t of u is:

```
DELETE E
 WHERE E.EMP IN
     ( SELECT E.EMP
       FROM E, M
       WHERE E.DEP=M.DEP AND M.MGR=m
         AND E.DEP=d ).
```

Since there is a path from E.EMP to EDm.EMP and a path from E.DEP to EDm.DEP, t is an exact translation of u.

As a concrete scenario, assume that m='Mary' and d='Sales' and let the current data base state and the current view state for ED-Mary be

```
E  EMP     DEP          M  DEP      MGR     ED-Mary EMP     DEP

   John    Sales           Sales    Mary            John    Sales
   Peter   Finance         Finance  Jane            Alice   Sales
   Alice   Sales           Toys     Mary            Albert  Toys
   Albert  Toys
```

Then, the translation of the previous view deletion (for m='Mary' and d='Sales') will correctly delete tuples (John,Sales) and (Alice,Sales) from E. Furthermore, note that if we change d to be 'Finance', the translation will not delete (Peter,Finance) from E since (Finance,Mary) is not in M (hence the qualification of the translation fails). □

The next example illustrates an unsuccessful translation.

Example 4.4:

Let S, V and u be as in Example 4.3. Consider the following translation t' for u

```
DELETE M
 WHERE M.DEP IN
     ( SELECT M.DEP
       FROM E, M
       WHERE E.DEP=M.DEP AND M.MGR=m
         AND E.DEP=d )
```

This time we cannot deduce that t' is an exact translation of u since there is no path from an attribute of M to EDm.EMP.

Indeed, assuming the same concrete scenario as in Example 4.3, the translation t' will delete (Sales,Mary) from M. As a consequence we have:

- (John,Sales) and (Alice,Sales) vanish from the view ED-Mary, but remain in E.
- (Sales,Mary) is deleted from M, which is by itself undesirable since the intention of the view update was to delete all employees of the Sales department, not its manager.
- If (Sales,Mary) is reinserted into M, the two tuples (John,Sales) and (Alice,Sales) will reappear in ED-Mary. Moreover, if (Sales,Jane), say, is inserted into M, these two tuples will appear in ED-Jane. □

The procedure described above for translating simple deletions is not deterministic since there might be more than one Ri satisfying the above conditions. The view definition should then include additional information to completely disambiguate the translation (see the following Section).

To conclude, we observe that similar, but somewhat more complex conditions, are obtained in [DAYA82] for insertions and replacements. The net result is a translator for a large class of (sequences of) insertions, deletions and replacements, which can be used to relax the very stringent conditions imposed on view updates by some currently existing systems (such as System R [DATE81]).

4.2 The View Complement Approach

A second strategy to completely specify the translation of view updates is to tell the system which parts of the data base should not be affected by the view updates. We will present a brief summary of the theory behind this approach, taken from [BANC81], and some suggestions to transform it into a practical tool [CHAN83,COSM83].

Let us begin with the key definition of view complement. Let S=(RS,IC), V=(RV,CV,f) and V'=(RV',CV',f') be as in Section 2.1. Intuitively, V' is the complement of V iff V', together with V, suffices to reconstruct the original data base. That is, any information not contained in V should be present in V'. More precisely, let f X f' denote the function f" such that f"(s)=(f(s),f'(s)). Then, V' is the *complement* of V iff the mapping f"=f X f' is one-to-one when restricted to the consistent states of S. This implies that we can move from a consistent state s of S to a pair of states (v,v')=f"(s) of V and V', and then return to s (via the inverse of f") without losing information.

Example 4.5 [BANC81]:

If s denotes a state and E a relational expression, let s(E) denote the value of E in s. Let S, V and V' be as follows:

a) S is a data base schema whose relation schemes are E[EMP,DEP] and M[DEP,MGR], and whose constraints are E:EMP→DEP, M:DEP→MGR, M:MGR→DEP, and E[DEP]⊆M[DEP] and M[DEP]⊆E[DEP].

b) V is a view over S whose only relation scheme is EM[EMP,MGR], with EM:EMP→MGR as constraint, and whose view mapping is f = (E*M)[EMP,MGR] (the natural join of E to M, followed by the projection on EMP and MGR). That is, f(s)=v iff v(EM)=s((E*M)[EMP,MGR])

c) V' is another view whose only relation scheme is M'[DEP,MGR], with M':DEP→MGR and M':MGR→DEP as constraints, and whose view mapping is f' = M (that is, M' coincides with the manager table M itself). Hence, we have f'(s)=v' iff v'(M)=s(M).

Then V' is the complement of V. Indeed, let f"=f X f'. Recall that f" maps a state of S into a pair of states of V and V'. Recall that a state of S is a function assigning to E and M binary relations, a state of V is a function assigning to EM a binary relation, and a state of V' is a function assigning to M' another binary relation. To prove that V' is the complement of V, we have to show that f" is one-to-one when restricted to the consistent states of S. We proceed as follows

(1) for any state s of S, f"(s) = (v,v') iff
v(EM) = s((E*M)[EMP,MGR]) and
v'(M') = s(M)

Now, using the dependencies of S, we can show that

(2) for any consistent state s of S,
s((((E*M)[EMP,MGR])*M)[EMP,DEP]) = s(E)

Let s' and s" be two consistent states of S and suppose that f"(s')=f"(s"). That is, using (1), we have

(3) s'((E*M)[EMP,MGR]) = s"((E*M)[EMP,MGR])

(4) s'(M) = s"(M)

Using (2), (3) and (4) above, it follows that

(5) s'(E) = s'((((E*M)[EMP,MGR])*M)[EMP,DEP])
= s"((((E*M)[EMP,MGR])*M)[EMP,DEP])
= s"(E)

Thus, from (4) and (5) it follows that s'=s", which establishes that f" is one-to-one on the consistent states of S. □

The above example illustrates that it is difficult to prove that two views are complementary. However, it is relatively straightforward to convince oneself that (see [BANC81])

1) A view always has a complement (the underlying schema is always a complement of any view);

2) a view can have many complements, even if only minimal complements are considered (under a precise notion of minimality); and

3) the complement of a view describes the information not visible within the view.

It is a remarkable result of the theory that if u is at all translatable, then its translation can be easily computed.

More precisely, we say that u is *V'-translatable* iff

1) for any consistent state s of S there is a consistent state s' of S such that f(s')=u(f(s)) (i.e., s' reflects the update u on V); and

2) f'(s')=f'(s) (the value of the complement V' is the same in s and s').

If g and h are functions, let $g^\circ h$ denote the composition of g and h, that is, $(g^\circ h)(x)=g(h(x))$. Let I denote the identity function on the set of states of V'. If u is V'-translatable, then the translation of u is achieved by the update t on S defined by (see Figure 1)

$$t = g \circ h \circ f''$$

where

- f'' = f X f',
- g is the inverse of f''
- h = u X I.

We call the mapping T associating each update u with the translation t as defined above the *translator induced by V'*.

The theory of view complement then suggests the following strategy to cope with view updates. The data base administrator, together with the definition of each view V, must also fix a complement V' of V indicating which parts of the data base should not be affected by updates on V. A translation procedure must then be found such that each update u on V is either rejected as untranslatable or mapped to a data base update t that maintains the data in V' invariant. If U is a set of updates on V such that each update in U is V'-translatable, then it follows that the translator T induced by V' is exactly the desired procedure.

But the converse also holds. If T is a translator for a given complete class U of updates on V, then there is a complement V' of V such that (i) any u in U is V'-translatable; and (ii) T is the translator induced by V' [BANC81].

To render the above strategy usable in practice, we must find

1) a method of checking if V' is the complement of V;

2) a method of deciding if each update in U is V'-translatable; and

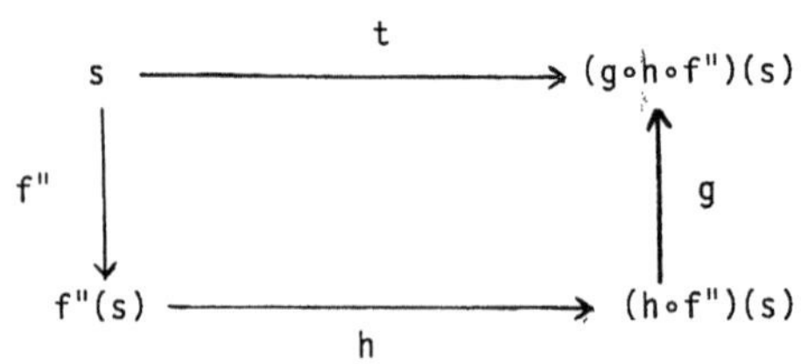

Figure 1: Translation of View Update u

3) a method of computing the inverse of f X f', which is necessary to completely describe the translator.

Further work is still required in these directions, but some results already exist.

These three questions have been investigated in [COSM83] for the simple case where S contains a single relation scheme R[A1,...,An], and a set F of functional and join dependencies, and where all views are single-relation and are defined by projections of R.

Let ATTR={A1,...,An}. Using our simplified notation, let V=R[X] and V'=R[X'] be two views obtained by projecting R on X and on X', respectively.

It is shown that V' is a complement of V iff ATTR=X $\cup$ X' and F implies the MVD $R{:}X\cap X' \rightarrow\rightarrow X'-X$. In one direction, this result is obvious, since if F implies the MVD $R{:}X\cap X' \rightarrow\rightarrow X'-X$, then the decomposition of R into R[X] and R[X'] is lossless. Therefore, if s and s' are two consistent states of S such that s(R[X])=s'(R[X]) and s(R[X'])=s'(R[X']), we have s(R)=s(R[X]*R[X'])=s'(R[X]*R[X'])=s'(R), which suffices to establish that V and V' are complementary.

Necessary and sufficient conditions for the translatability of single-tuple insertions, deletions and replacements, with emphasis on the complexity of the tests involved, are also presented. As an example of the kind of results obtained, suppose now that all constraints are FDs. The insertion of a single tuple u into V is translatable as the insertion of a tuple t such that t[X]=u and t[X'] iff

1) F implies $R{:}X\cap X' \rightarrow X'$, but not $R{:}X\cap X' \rightarrow X$;

2) $u[X\cap X']$ is in $R[X\cap X']$; and

3) the insertion of T into R does not violate any of the dependencies in F.

Note that, since F implies $R{:}X\cap X' \rightarrow X'$, t is uniquely defined.

Example 4.6:

Let S be a conceptual schema whose only relation scheme is E[EMP,DEP,PROJ] and whose only constraint is E:EMP$\rightarrow$DEP. Let V be the view defined by projecting E onto EMP and PROJ. Then the view V' obtained by projecting E onto EMP and DEP is a complement of V by the above result. Moreover, the insertion of <e,p> into V can be translated as the insertion into E of a tuple of the form <e,d,p> such that <e,d> is in E[EMP,DEP], provided conditions (2) and (3) are also satisfied (both depend on the current state of S). Note that condition (1) is trivially satisfied.

For example, consider the following data base state

R	EMP	DEP	PROJ
	John	Sales	P1
	Peter	Finance	P1
	Albert	Sales	P2

Then, the insertion of u=(John,P2) is correctly translated by t=(John,Sales,P2) since none of the conditions are violated. But the insertion u=(Robert,P2) fails since condition 2 is not met.

An interesting suggestion to render the idea of view complement usable in practice, which we now briefly describe, can be found in [CHAN83]. We will work under the following assumptions:

1) Updates are restricted to be single- or multi-tuple insertions, deletions and replacements.

2) Only *simple* views are considered, that is, views consisting of a single relation scheme, with no constraints, whose view mapping is defined by using a single relational operator. Thus, a view can de defined using the simplified notation V=e, where e is a relational expression with a single relational operator.

Since views over views are allowed, this last restriction can be circumvented by breaking the definition of a complex view into a sequence of definitions of simple views. On the other hand, this restriction induces a taxonomy of views according to which relational algebra operator was used in the view mapping (an approach also taken in [FURT79]).

The general idea is to construct an interpreter that takes a given view update u, the view definition and the current data base state and produces a unique exact, acceptable translation of u. One of the problems again is ambiguity. Instead of using view complements directly, a *relational invariant* is defined for each type of update on each view. A relational invariant is a relational expression indicating that no update of the type in question must neither alter any tuple in the relation denoted by the invariant nor insert or delete any tuple that satisfies the invariant.

For example, let V=A U B be a single-relation view obtained by the union of the base relations A and B. Consider an insertion u on V. Then, we can translate u either as an insertion on A or an insertion on B or both. If, however, we declare A (understood as an atomic relational expression) as an invariant under insertions on V, the ambiguity disappears.

Now, given an update u on a view V, the interpreter constructs all possible translations for u. This is accomplished with the help of *update templates* indicating all possible choices for each view update. The interpretation is a recursive process since V may be defined over other views. Those candidate translations that violate consistency or violate an invariant are discarded. If only equivalent translations result from the interpretation process, the view update is accepted as translatable and the operations resulting from the translation process are executed (see [CHAN83] for details).

It is feasible to implement such translation strategy, provided that violations of invariants or integrity constraints can be detected with reasonable efficiency. A way to achieve this goal would be to restrict the type of invariants or constraints allowed by the system.

5. CONCLUSIONS

A common tendency is to define views only for query and authorization purposes, and afterwards try to solve the problems created by view updates. We feel that the update requirements should be considered from the start.

From the point of view of the data base designer, the automatic translation approach is on a first thought much more comfortable. However, if additional information is not included in the view definition, the class of view updates that can be correctly translated by the system is extremely limited. Moreover, this additional information, for example in the form of adequate view complements, is not always easy to define since it involves several checks to guarantee that indeed view update translations can be correctly performed.

The abstract data types approach, on the other hand, places the burden of implementing view updates on the data base designer right from the beginning. He must define a set of application-oriented operations that represent the desired updates, together with translations that perform the operations and preserve consistency of the data base.

As our last remark, future data base systems should include better view definition facilities that take into consideration the view update problem. As a humble start, a view definition language following the abstract data types approach could be added to existing systems. Using results from the automatic translation approach, view update translators could also be designed to handle a richer class of view updates than that processed by currently existing systems. Furthermore, such results can be combined with the abstract data type approach to create comprehensive view definition software tools that alleviate the burden of the data base designer. Also relevant in this regard are efforts towards the synthesis of update transactions with the help of theorem provers [SANT81].

References

(BANC81) (BROD81) (BROD82) (CARL79) (CASA83) (CHAN83, see CHAN83b)
(CLEM78) (COSM83) (DATE81, see DATE82) (DAYA78) (DAYA82, see DAYA82e)
(FURT77) (FURT79) (IBM) (KELL81) (ROWE79) (SEVC78) (SANT81) (STON75)
(STON76) (TUCH83) (TSIC77, see TSIC77a) (ZLOO77)

Section V

Database Access for Special Applications

Supporting Complex Objects in a Relational System for Engineering Databases

Raymond Lorie, Won Kim, Dan McNabb, Wil Plouffe, and Andreas Meier*

Abstract: Relational databases are of increasing interest for applications outside the traditional business data-processing environment. We have introduced the notion of complex objects as one extension to a relational database system (System R) to better support these non-business applications, in particular, engineering design. In this chapter, we discuss five aspects of complex objects: concepts and semantics, implementation, query optimization, efficient use within application programs, and user interface.

1. INTRODUCTION

After a decade of research and development activity, relational database systems are now commonly available as products. This fact clearly shows that these systems represent a major new approach to data management, at least for a certain range of applications. In fact it is the business environment that provided the paradigms for data structuring and data usage in those systems. It is not surprising therefore that the first and most obvious applications are from that environment.

But there are many other computer users who have come to realize that the management of data is a most important and difficult problem. In particular engineers, who have extensively used computers for their numerical analysis needs, now recognize that new ways of managing the design data are essential to handle the increased complexity of artifacts being designed. The aerospace industry and the VLSI industry provide rather striking examples of complex development projects that involve a huge amount of interrelated data produced by many cooperating designers.

Until now engineering and design data have been handled by specially designed, ad-hoc systems or by simple file systems. Ad-hoc systems have not been able to take advantage of the recent advances in the database field and are becoming obsolete. They also tend to force a strict separation between engineering data and non-engineering data that is often difficult and artificial. On the other hand, file systems suffer from severe inherent drawbacks. When the number of files becomes very large, the management of the file names, owners, and other attributes becomes a problem in itself. Also the way the data is physically organized within the file must be known to the programs that access the data, providing no data independence at all; that is, any change in the data organization requires changing the programs. Sharing data between files is also hard. Design objects, such as a VLSI chip, consist of vari-

*Present Address: Institut fur Informatik, ETH, Zurich

ous well-defined components (and each component consists of subcomponents, etc.), but it is difficult for different design objects to share these components. Rather, each subcomponent must be copied into the component at a higher-level of abstraction, causing integrity problems.

Several authors [HASK82, HAYN81, KATZ82] have expressed the view that relational systems should help close the gap between business and engineering applications. Advantages claimed for the relational model in the classical data processing domain include ease of use, data independence, increased productivity, and multi-file correlation. These advantages should also hold for design applications. In addition, the relational model should help manage the complexity of design applications and still provide the required flexibility in data management.

A closer analysis shows however that engineering applications exhibit characteristics that impose specific requirements on the database system and that enhancements could be made to relational systems to improve support, not only for these applications, but for a wider class of non-business applications. In this chapter we analyze one particular requirement and discuss a particular proposal to meet such a requirement. The proposal extends the relational model by introducing the notion of complex object. The concept and semantics are discussed first. Then it is shown how the implementation can take advantage of the existence of complex objects for improving the performance of the system and application programs. Finally, language extensions are discussed.

2. LOGICAL VIEW OF A COMPLEX OBJECT

The notion of complex object has been introduced in [HASK82, LORI83]. A complex object is a group of tuples consisting of a single root tuple that defines the object, and one or more dependent tuples that describe the object. Typically, these dependent tuples reside in one or more relations distinct from the relation containing the root tuple. The complex object can be seen as a cluster of tuples that are most likely to be used together. As shown below, in many applications such a cluster is inherently hierarchical. The complex object concept implements such hierarchies in a relational framework.

Consider, as an example, a design application (loosely inspired by a VLSI data structure) where artifacts are designed in a hierarchical way, building higher level cells from lower level cells that can just be "called" (instantiated) several times. Figure 1 represents a cell A and a higher level cell B that calls for four instances of A. In addition to instances of lower level cells, a cell can also contain one or more paths made from rectangles. Cell A does not have any such path, while Cell B has one such path comprising three rectangles. A reasonable relational schema for such an application is shown in Figure 2.

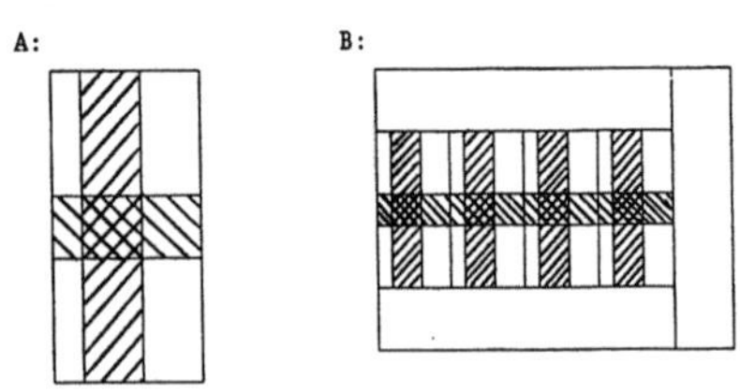

Figure 1. Two Cells.

In the relation CELL, CELLKEY is the unique key of a cell. In INSTANCES, INSTKEY is the key of an instance (or ICELL.INSTKEY could be used as a 'concatenated key'). Also, ICELLTYPE contains the CELLKEY of the cell of which it is an instantiation. The same pattern is used in PATHS and RECTANGLES; note that since concatenated keys are not used, CELLKEY need not be specified in RECTANGLES.

CELL	CELLKEY	unique identifier (name)
	CDATA	other data for CELL
INSTANCES	INSTKEY	unique identifier (name)
	ICELL	parent identifier, matches CELLKEY
	ICELLTYPE	CELL identifier of subcell
	IDATA	other data for INSTANCES
PATHS	PATHKEY	unique identifier (name)
	PCELL	parent identifier, matches CELLKEY
	PDATA	other data for PATHS
RECTANGLES	RECTKEY	unique identifier (name)
	RPATH	parent identifier, matches PATHKEY
	RDATA	other data for RECTANGLES

Figure 2. Simple Relational Schema.

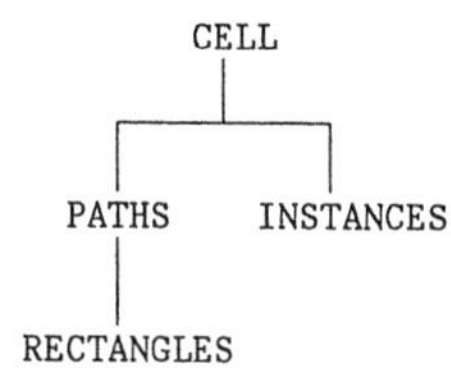

Figure 3. CELL Complex Object.

We now introduce the corresponding complex object. Figure 3 represents the structure of the object CELL. The relation CELL is the root. The structure of a complex object is specified using two new column types: IDENTIFIER and COMPONENT OF. A column of type IDENTIFIER is the primary key of the relation; the IDENTIFIER value of a tuple is generated by the system when the tuple is created, and saved as the value in the IDENTIFIER column. Component relations are distinguished by the presence of a COMPONENT OF column that specifies the parent relation. The value in a COMPONENT OF column is the IDENTIFIER value of the parent tuple in the parent relation.

Since the structure is specified by introducing new column types, extensions to the SQL language [CHAM76] are minimal. For the example, the SQL definition of the relations is given in Figure 4, and the database contents for Figure 1 are represented in Figure 5.

CELL	CID	type = IDENTIFIER
	CDATA	other data for CELL
INSTANCES	IID	type = IDENTIFIER
	ICELL	type = COMPONENT_OF(CELL)
	ICELLTYPE	type = REFERENCE(CELL)
	IDATA	other data for INSTANCES
PATHS	PID	type = IDENTIFIER
	PCELL	type = COMPONENT_OF(CELL)
	PDATA	other data for PATHS
RECTANGLES	RID	type = IDENTIFIER
	RPATH	type = COMPONENT_OF(PATHS)
	RDATA	other data for RECTANGLES

Figure 4. Schema Using a Complex Object.

The definition of ICELLTYPE is of interest. As before, this field must identify the type of cell that is instantiated and must therefore contain a data element that refers to a CELL. Since one has already introduced unique identifiers, one can also introduce a new type called REFERENCE. A reference value is the identifier of the referenced record in the same or a different complex object.

CELL:

CID	CDATA
$123000100	this is cell A
$123000200	this is cell B

INSTANCES:

IID	ICELL	ICELLTYPE	IDATA
$123000202	$123000200	$123000100	1st inst of A in B
$123000203	$123000200	$123000100	2nd inst of A in B
$123000204	$123000200	$123000100	3rd inst of A in B
$123000205	$123000200	$123000100	4th inst of A in B

PATHS:

PID	PCELL	PDATA
$123000206	$123000200	data for path

RECTANGLES:

RID	RPATH	RDATA
$123000207	$123000206	first horizontal rectangle
$123000208	$123000206	vertical rectangle
$123000209	$123000206	second horizontal rectangle

Figure 5. Database Tuples for the Cells A and B.

Since the system knows the definition of the structure, it can enforce various semantic integrity constraints. A tuple cannot be inserted into a non-root relation without specifying the identifier of a valid parent; thus one can not have orphans. The deletion of a tuple will trigger the deletion of all children, children of the deleted children, etc., recursively. Identifiers of root tuples are not reused, so references to wrong objects are not possible. Also, since the system knows about the existence of complex objects, it can allow users to invoke such global functions as copying an object, moving an object, and fetching an object with single requests. This last function is extremely useful and is explained in detail in Section 5.

3. PHYSICAL STRUCTURE OF A COMPLEX OBJECT

We now turn our attention to the implementation of complex objects. The parent-child structure is implemented using links to connect two tuples that belong to the same object. Each tuple contains two parts: the first part contains the fields seen by the user; the second part (called the appendix) contains the fields that are used for implementation and not seen by the user. The appendix of a parent tuple has a column containing a link to the first child. The child tuple has a column that contains the link to the parent. The appendix in the child tuple has also two columns that are used to store the forward and backward links between siblings. This structure is repeated as many times as there are child relations.

A common implementation of a link consists in storing the identifier of the to-tuple within the from-tuple. If the identifier corresponds to a physical location, any reorganization requires the reconstruction of all links. Our scheme for assigning identifiers avoids this problem and also provides new and useful access paths for retrieval involving identifiers. This is summarized below; a more detailed description can be found in [LORI83].

A root tuple is assigned a 10-byte identifier obtained by concatenating an 8-byte unique identifier with two null bytes. There is an index on the root identifiers to allow direct access.

A non-root tuple is assigned a logical 10-byte identifier obtained by combining the 8 significant bytes of the root identifier with a unique 2-byte number identifying the tuple in the complex object. The 2-byte identifiers are used to implement the links between tuples of the same object. The appendix of a non-root tuple always contains the 8-byte identifier of the root; it is therefore easy to return the full 10-byte identifier of a non-root tuple to the user. (The user sees only the logical 10-byte identifier values.) To control the allocation of 2-byte identifiers, one uses a map associated with a root tuple as part of its appendix.

The map is logically a vector of entries. The i-th position in the vector contains the location (the TID in System R [ASTR76]) of the tuple having i as its 2-byte identifier and the RID (relation identifier) of the component relation to which it belongs. Given the 2-byte identifier, the TID is obtained by direct access into the map. The 2-byte identifiers are allocated in sequential order; when a tuple is deleted, the position in the map corresponding to its identifier is marked 'available' and will be reused the next time an identifier is generated.

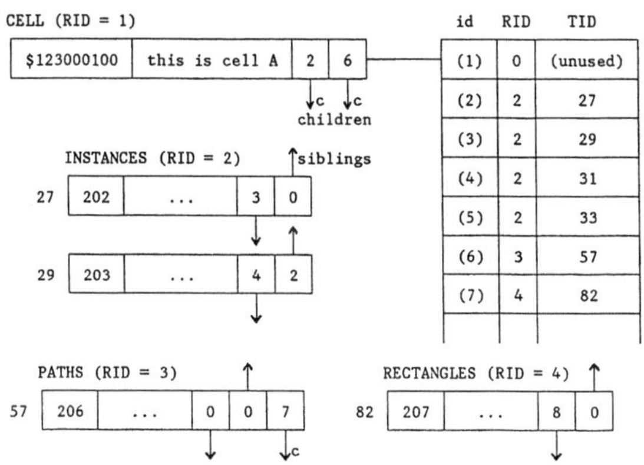

Figure 6. Example of Complex Object with Partial Map.

Figure 6 shows our implementation of complex objects using a map. The map introduces a level of indirection that has the following advantages:

- It implements stable identifiers that are not affected by database reorganization; therefore these values can be used in one relation to refer to tuples in another relation.
- It permits the use of small 2-byte identifiers, without losing a direct mapping to the physical addresses.
- It permits copying a complex object without any relocation other than adjusting the physical addresses in the map.
- It actually implements an index on non-root identifiers in a very compact way. Given an identifier, one can fetch the root, access the map, get the corresponding entry and find the physical address of the tuple. Thus the map implements a compact cross-relation index for all tuples within a single object.
- It permits getting all the tuples in an object without traversing any lists. This is very useful to return all the tuples of a complex object to the user in a single call to the database system, as explained in Section 5.

4. OTHER ACCESS PATHS FOR COMPLEX OBJECTS

The System R optimizer is the subsystem that generates potentially viable plans for executing a given SQL query or data manipulation statement (update, insert, delete) and selects the one with the lowest expected cost. A complete description of the way it arrives at an optimal plan for executing any arbitrary SQL query or data manipulation statement is given in [SELI79]. Briefly, the optimizer first examines various characteristics of a given statement, such as the predicates in the WHERE clause, whether the statement involves joining two or more relations, whether the result of the query should be in some user-specified order, whether duplicates should be removed from the query result, and so on. The optimizer then determines possible access paths that may be used to evaluate the statement and generates a plan for each of the reasonable access paths and computes the expected cost for the plan. It then selects a plan which results in the minimal expected cost. The cost the optimizer uses is a weighted sum of the page I/Os and the CPU processing time.

The System R optimizer considers only two types of access paths for the generation of plans and computation of expected costs of the plans: SEGMENT SCAN and INDEX SCAN. A segment is a logical block of pages that contains one or more relations and associated indexes. A SEGMENT SCAN is a sequential scan of all the pages in the segment. An index is a tree structure that provides quick associative access on a key and also access by sorted order of the key. An index may be clustered or unclustered. A clustered index places tuples of a relation in a physical order close to the logical order of the key values. There can be several indexes on a single relation (one clustered and the remainder unclustered).

A map contains the tuple identifiers of all the tuples within a complex object. As such, the map associated with a complex object offers an opportunity to expedite the execution of queries involving the complex object. We recognized three types of predicates that may be evaluated using the map and thus extended the optimizer to consider the map as an additional access path when generating a plan for a statement involving a complex object. That is, the optimizer still generates a query-processing plan using conventional access paths such as a SEGMENT SCAN or an INDEX SCAN, if it decides that they are cheaper than the map even when complex objects are involved.

One way in which the map can be effective is in evaluating predicates of the form "W = value" where W is the name of a column with type IDENTIFIER. The value consists of a 10-byte identifier. To locate a tuple that satisfies this type of predicate, the system first retrieves the map identified by the 8-byte identifier of the complex object and then finds the desired map entry using the 2-byte internal identifier. The map entry provides the tuple identifier of the desired tuple.

Suppose, for example, that a query contains the predicate "IID = $123000205". That is, a tuple which contains '$123000205' is to be found. The system first retrieves the map for the complex object identified by '$1230002'. It then reads the tuple identifier (TID) in the 5th entry of the map. The TID thus found is the logical address of the desired tuple.

A second way to use the map is for the predicates of the form "X = value" where X is the name of a column of type COMPONENT OF. The system first locates the map associated with the complex object, and then, using the 2-byte internal identifier in the value as the index into the map, finds the tuple identifier of the parent tuple. It fetches the parent tuple, which in turn contains the internal identifier of the first child tuple that satisfies the "X = value" predicate. The first child tuple in turn contains the internal identifier of its sibling tuple, and so on. That is, once the parent tuple is retrieved, all its component tuples can be fetched using the map repeatedly.

For example, suppose a query contains the predicate "RPATH = $123000206". All tuples that contain '$123000206' in the COMPONENT OF column are to be found. The system first locates the map corresponding to the complex object whose identifier is '$1230002'. It then reads the TID in the 6th entry in the map. The tuple identified by the TID is the parent of all tuples that satisfy the predicate. The system fetches this parent tuple and reads the 2-byte internal identifier of the first child tuple. Suppose the 2-byte identifier is 7. The system then reads the TID in the 7th entry of the map to locate the first child tuple. The first child tuple in turn contains a 2-byte identifier, say 8, which indexes into the map for the next sibling tuple. By repeatedly looking up the map in this way, all children tuples are fetched.

A third way of using the map is for predicates of the form "Y = value" where Y is the name of a column of type INTERNAL REFERENCE (all references must be to tuples in the same object, otherwise the (EXTERNAL) REFERENCE column type should be used). The system first locates the map. It then sequentially scans all map entries. For all entries corresponding to the relation of interest, it fetches the tuples to see if their INTERNAL REFERENCE column contains the value shown in the predicate.

Suppose a query contains the predicate "PATHREF = $123000206". The system finds the map for the complex object '$1230002'. For each entry in the map which identifies the relation of interest, the system fetches the tuple using the TID found in the map entry. If the value in the INTERNAL REFERENCE column is 6, the tuple satisfies the predicate.

The reader may find it instructive that the range of tuples scanned by each of the above three types of MAP SCANs is restricted to a single complex object. In particular, the extended optimizer does not provide any MAP SCAN support for a predicate of the form "Z = value" where Z is the name of a column of type (EXTERNAL) REFERENCE. The reason is that tuples which satisfy this query, that is, tuples which contain the indicated value in their EXTERNAL REFERENCE column, range over the entire relation rather than being restricted to the portion of the relation that are part of a single complex object. The use of the map makes no sense for this type of predicate.

When a query or data manipulation statement requires joining of N relations (N > 1), the System R optimizer generates plans for executing the statement by first generating the plans for the first K relations (for K=1, 2, ... N-1) and successively combining them with the scan methods for the (K+1)st relation. The three types of MAP SCANs augment the SEGMENT SCAN and the INDEX SCAN, as methods of scanning a single relation to retrieve all tuples which satisfy predicates involving columns of the relation. In other words, the extended optimizer considers the MAP SCANs for processing not only single-relation queries (queries involving only one relation which is part of a complex object structure), but also N-relation queries involving N of the relations in a complex object structure.

5. FETCHING COMPLEX OBJECTS

In applications that use all or some of the data which makes up one instance of an object, the usual way to fetch a complex object is to code several nested loops that fetch the root tuple, each of its children, each of their children, and so on, one tuple at a time until the necessary data have been retrieved. In SQL, a cursor [ASTR76] must be defined for each relation in the complex object, and a procedure must be written to retrieve all tuples (see Figures 7 and 8). (Note: The example procedure ignores the problems associated with allocating and controlling buffer space for the returned tuples, or handling any abnormal return codes.)

Clearly, many requests are being made from the application program to the database system with only a small portion of the object data being returned each time. Yet, engineering applications tend to require a large volume of data to be moved from the database into the application's data areas for use in design and analysis work.

Since the system knows the structure of a complex object, the application should be able to declare which data it wants from an object. Then the system can return all the desired data in one request, which in turn can considerably simplify data area management in the application program. This is accomplished using the complex fetch.

```
EXEC SQL DECLARE CELLC CURSOR FOR
  SELECT CELLKEY,CDATA INTO :CELLKEY,:CDATA
         FROM CELL;
EXEC SQL DECLARE INSTC CURSOR FOR
  SELECT INSTKEY,ICELL,ICELLTYPE,IDATA
         INTO :INSTKEY,:ICELL,:ICELLTYPE,:IDATA
         FROM INSTANCES
         WHERE ICELL= :CELLKEY;
EXEC SQL DECLARE PATHC CURSOR FOR
  SELECT PATHKEY,PCELL,PDATA
         INTO :PATHKEY,:PCELL,:PDATA
         FROM PATHS
         WHERE PCELL= :CELLKEY;
EXEC SQL DECLARE RECTC CURSOR FOR
  SELECT RECTKEY,RPATH,RDATA
         INTO :RECTKEY,:RPATH,:RDATA
         FROM RECTANGLES
         WHERE RECTKEY= :PATHKEY;
```

Figure 7. Cursor Definitions without Complex Object.

```
EXEC SQL OPEN CELLC;
IF SQLCODE = 0 THEN DO;
  EXEC SQL FETCH CELLC;
  IF SQLCODE = 0 THEN DO;
    /* Move CELL tuple data */

    EXEC SQL OPEN PATHC;
    DO WHILE (SQLCODE = 0);
      EXEC SQL FETCH PATHC;
      IF SQLCODE = 0 THEN DO;
        /* Move PATHS tuple data */

        EXEC SQL OPEN RECTC;
        DO WHILE (SQLCODE = 0);
          EXEC SQL FETCH RECTC;
          /* Move RECTANGLES tuple data */
        END;
        EXEC SQL CLOSE RECTC;

      END; /* FETCH on PATHC */
    END; /* OPEN  and DO WHILE on PATHC  */
    EXEC SQL CLOSE PATHC;

    EXEC SQL OPEN INSTC;
    DO WHILE (SQLCODE = 0);
      EXEC SQL FETCH INSTC;
      /* Move INSTANCES tuple data */
    END;
    EXEC SQL CLOSE INSTC;

  END; /* FETCH on CELLC */
END; /* OPEN on CELLC */
EXEC SQL CLOSE CELLC;
```

Figure 8. Fetch of CELL without Complex Object.

Figure 9 illustrates an application program which uses the complex fetch; it is functionally equivalent to what Figures 7 and 8 accomplish. The first SELECT statement declared for the complex fetch is the root of the subtree of a complex object to be fetched, and the remaining SELECTs must refer to children of the first relation, or each other, in any order. The entire complex object can be fetched by specifying all of the relations in the object definition, and by not specifying any WHERE clauses in the SELECT statements. Or, any subset of the object may be specified by adding WHERE clauses to the SELECT statements, and by specifying SELECT statements for only a subset of the relations which constitutes a connected subtree of the complex object structure.

The new special column names ->FIRST(relation), ->NEXT, ->PREVIOUS, and ->PARENT are used to indicate connecting indexes between the tuples of fetched data. FIRST points to the first child tuple of a component relation. NEXT points to the next sibling in the same relation, and PREVIOUS points to the previous sibling. PARENT points from a child tuple to its parent. The pointer in each case is an index into a

```
EXEC SQL DECLARE CC COMPLEX CURSOR FOR
  SELECT CID, CDATA, ->FIRST(INSTANCES), ->FIRST(PATHS)
         FROM CELL;
  SELECT ICELLTYPE, IDATA, ->NEXT, ->PREVIOUS
         FROM INSTANCES;
  SELECT PDATA, ->NEXT, ->FIRST(RECTANGLES)
         FROM PATHS;
  SELECT RDATA, ->NEXT
         FROM RECTANGLES;
EXEC SQL END COMPLEX;

EXEC SQL BEGIN DECLARE SECTION;

  DCL 1 CELLSTR BASED(CELLPTR),
        2 CELLID  CHAR(10),       /* IDENTIFIER               */
        2 CDATA   ...,
        2 IFIRST  FIXED BIN(15), /* Index FIRST INSTANCES  */
        2 PFIRST  FIXED BIN(15); /* Index FIRST PATHS      */
  DCL 1 INSTSTR BASED(INSTPTR),
        2 ICELLTYPE CHAR(10),     /* Ref id of another CELL */
        2 IDATA   ...,
        2 INEXT   FIXED BIN(15), /* Index NEXT INSTANCES   */
        2 IPREV   FIXED BIN(15); /* Index PREV INSTANCES   */
  DCL 1 PATHSTR BASED(PATHPTR),
        2 PDATA   ...,
        2 RFIRST  FIXED BIN(15), /* Index FIRST RECTANGLES */
        2 PNEXT   FIXED BIN(15); /* Index NEXT PATHS       */
  DCL 1 RECTSTR BASED(RECTPTR),
        2 RDATA   ...,
        2 RNEXT   FIXED BIN(15); /* Index NEXT RECTANGLES  */

  DCL CHAR_VAR CHAR(32760) VARYING; /* Data Buffer         */

EXEC SQL END DECLARE SECTION;

EXEC SQL OPEN CC
         TEMPLATES CELLSTR,INSTSTR,PATHSTR,RECTSTR;
IF SQLCODE = 0 THEN DO;
  EXEC SQL FETCH CC INTO :CHAR_VAR;
  IF SQLCODE ¬= 0 THEN CALL HANDLE_ERROR;
END;
EXEC SQL CLOSE CC;
```

Figure 9. Complex Fetch Example, Declarations and Code.

directory which contains offset pointers into the data areas provided in the FETCH statements.

The OPEN statement specifies the TEMPLATES list of structure names that define each tuple type. As many structures must be named as there are SELECT statements in the complex-cursor declaration, and they must be in the same order. These structures define the data mappings as they are moved into the output buffer specified on FETCH.

At FETCH time, the complex object tuples are placed into the data area CHAR_VAR. Subsequent fetches pass any remaining data. After all the tuples have been returned, a directory is returned which contains a complete list of tuple offsets within blocks that were returned earlier. Once in memory the tuples are accessed by overlaying the CHAR_VAR buffer with the declared structures (CELLSTR, INSTSTR, PATHSTR, RECTSTR) based on pointers that can be set using the index data.

If another FETCH is executed after a complete object with its directory has been returned, another FETCH on the 'root' SELECT is initiated and another object begins. This allows many objects to be fetched based on the search criteria of the first SELECT statement.

6. HIGHER - LEVEL USER INTERFACE FOR COMPLEX OBJECTS.

To retrieve data from a component relation, the user often has to join component tuples with a parent or ancestor tuple. The user is therefore concerned with the internal structure of the complex objects and has to define several join predicates along particular branches which involve IDENTIFIER and COMPONENT OF columns. Consider the query:

```
SELECT RDATA, PDATA, CDATA
FROM   RECTANGLES, PATHS, CELL
WHERE  RPATH = PID AND
       PCELL = CID
```

The query is a three-way join between relations in a single complex object definition and will only involve tuples that are within the same object. This type of join is very common and expressing it requires a join predicate for each pair of relations in the hierarchy.

An operator is introduced that simplifies the specification of such joins. Let us denote a join of two relations A and B on columns A.$A and B.$A by the new notion A-B which is called 'implicit join from A to B':

```
A-B := JOIN(A,B|A.$A=B.$A)
```

This join is an equi-join between the column of type IDENTIFIER in the parent relation and the column of type COMPONENT OF in the child relation. Therefore, A-B is equivalent to B-A. One can simplify the denotation of these joins by assuming the join predicates rather than specifying them explicitly. We use the notation A-B in the FROM clause instead of A,B to that effect.

The notation for implicit join generalizes to a linear sequence of relations in a straightforward manner. The last query can be written in a simpler and more intuitive way:

```
SELECT RDATA, PDATA, CDATA
FROM   CELL-PATHS-RECTANGLES
```

In [MEIE83] the notion of implicit join is generalized to subtrees of the complex object hierarchy. This greatly simplifies the user interface when manipulating data within a complex object.

Besides system-generated identifiers (column type IDENTIFIER), a relation may have a column containing user keys (usual column types are INTEGER, CHARACTER, etc.). A user key value may or may not exist and may sometimes be changed. To support access to an individual tuple of a relation based on the user key, we define a new index called KEY INDEX that specifies a unique binding of the user key to the corresponding IDENTIFIER.

Let us suppose the CELL relation is given a new column CELLKEY to contain user keys. The special index is defined by

```
CREATE KEY INDEX ON CELL (CELLKEY)
```

The KEY INDEX allows the user to retrieve data by user keys rather than identifiers.

The concept of a key index is accompanied by two built-in functions: the KEY function and the ID function.

The built-in function KEY can be used in the SELECT list or the WHERE clause to find the user key corresponding to an identifier.

For example, the query

```
SELECT ICELLTYPE
FROM   INSTANCES
WHERE  ICELL = xxx
```

would return the identifiers of the cells instantiated for ICELL=xxx. If the user is interested in the user keys rather than the identifiers of these cells, the way the query must be written in SQL is as follows:

```
SELECT CELLKEY
FROM   INSTANCES, CELL
WHERE  ICELL = xxx AND
       CID = ICELLTYPE
```

The KEY function simplifies the notation since one can write

```
SELECT KEY(ICELLTYPE)
FROM   INSTANCES
WHERE  ICELL = xxx
```

Now consider the insertion of a tuple into INSTANCES. Since the tuple to be inserted contains a COMPONENT OF or REFERENCE type column (in fact it contains both), one needs to know the identifier of the component or referenced tuple. Often, this identifier will have been created in the same program and is therefore known. However, if it is unknown, then a query is needed to retrieve this identifier from the database. To simplify the task, the built-in function ID is introduced: it returns the value of the identifier corresponding to the supplied user key. For example, to create an instance of a cell X in a cell Y (where X and Y are user keys), one can write

```
INSERT INTO INSTANCES VALUES ( any, ID(Y), ID(X), data )
```

The built-in function ID can be evaluated to yield the desired identifiers if there is a user key index for the referenced relation and if the submitted key exists.

7. SUMMARY

This chapter has discussed several aspects of complex objects as an extension to a relational database system, one which enforces semantic constraints among a group of heterogeneous but related tuples. Two new column types, IDENTIFIER and COMPONENT OF, were defined to express the hierarchical relationships between tuples which are to be enforced. In addition, the REFERENCE column types were defined to express weaker, non-hierarchical relationships between tuples. The implementation of the IDENTIFIER, COMPONENT OF, and INTERNAL REFERENCE column types uses a map that is associated with the root tuple of a complex object, and that can be used to optimize queries involving the object. Then an additional function, complex fetch, that is available from within an application program was discussed; and finally, two additions to the user interface, implicit join and key index, were presented. We believe that these extensions increase the usability and functionality of System R for non-traditional applications which deal with large amounts of structured, but heterogeneous data items.

References

(ASTR76) (CHAM76) (HASK82) (HAYN81) (KATZ82) (LORI83) (MEIE83) (SELI79)

Database Access Requirements of Knowledge-Based Systems

Yannis Vassiliou, Jim Clifford, and Matthias Jarke

Abstract

Knowledge bases constitute the core of those Artificial Intelligence programs which have come to be known as Expert Systems. An examination of the most dominant knowledge representation schemes used in these systems reveals that a knowledge base can, and possibly should, be described at several levels using different schemes, including those traditionally used in operational databases. This chapter provides evidence that solutions to the organization and access problem for very large knowledge bases require the employment of appropriate database management methods, at least for the lowest level of description -- the facts or data. We identify the database access requirements of knowledge-based or expert systems and then present four general architectural strategies for the design of expert systems that interact with databases, together with specific recommendations for their suitability in particular situations. An implementation of the most advanced and ambitious of these strategies is then discussed in some detail.

1.0 INTRODUCTION

Evidence for the successful application of Artificial Intelligence (AI) research is nowhere stronger than in the area of Knowledge-Based or Expert Systems (ES) [CLIF83]. In addition to being among the first AI systems which are finding their place in the commercial world, Expert Systems seem to lessen the controversies between differing AI research approaches, and even contribute to wider overlaps of AI with sciences like Philosophy or Cognitive Science.

Although a formal theory of Expert Systems is yet to be developed, there are some key common features that can be identified. As a computer system attempting to act like a human expert in a limited application domain, an ES shares similar goals with other, more traditional, computer application systems. What differentiates an ES from these traditional systems are its overall architecture, and, usually, its method of development. Expert Systems are typically developed in an incremental way. A small group of about three people, filling the three roles of application domain expert, programmer, and knowledge engineer, successively refines the ES to approximate the behavior of the expert.

This work was carried out as part of a joint study with the IBM Corporation.

It may be argued, however, that this approach is very similar to that taken in Information Systems Analysis and Design, especially when the technique of "prototyping" is used. The interested reader will find more information on this aspect of ES construction in [HAYE83] or other introductory articles on Expert Systems -- we shall not be concerned with the incremental nature of ES development in this chapter.

Overall architecture seems to be the most unusual aspect of Expert Systems. An often-quoted motto of ES researchers is that "in the knowledge lies the power." In consequence, an ES is based on two principles: the appropriate representation of the application domain knowledge, and the control of this knowledge. These two principles are embodied in the two top-level components of the ES architecture: a knowledge base and an inference engine. The application domain knowledge is represented in a knowledge base, which is further divided into two subcomponents: the data level (ground, specific facts), and the knowledge level (rules, general principles, or problem heuristics). This division of the ES knowledge base brings together two research threads in AI: declarative and procedural representation schemes.

The other architectural component of an ES, the control mechanism, is often termed an inference engine. The inference engine matches a problem description to the stored knowledge. This match can be done either to analyze a certain situation (e.g., in medical diagnosis) or to synthesize a solution for a specific problem (e.g., a computer configuration). Such an inference engine can be a pattern matcher, theorem prover, or network search mechanism customized for a particular expert system, or it may exist already in the compiler of a corresponding knowledge representation language such as OPS-5 [FORG80], Prolog [KOWA79], or EMYCIN [VANM79]). Even in the latter case, some additional control mechanism may be required to cut down the number of inferences to be made. Typical of the control techniques employed are state-space search, propagation of constraints, and problem reduction [GEVA82].

It is with respect to knowledge representation that strong parallels between AI and Database Management research can be drawn. Knowledge representation schemes in AI share the same objective with the data models which have been developed for Database Systems, namely, to represent data for an enterprise or "slice of reality." However, AI-based knowledge representations emphasize the richness, flexibility, and faithfulness of the representation, while the data models are limited from their realizations as Database Management Systems (DBMS), which emphasize efficient access and manipulation of a more permanently structured, stored representation of reality [1]. This difference is largely the result of the motivations in these two fields: modelling human reasoning processes on the one hand, and information management on the other.

After several years of parallel developments in AI and Database Management, it is now generally recognized that the two fields can benefit from exchanges of accumulated expertise in representation topics. This chapter considers the possible uses of Database Management principles and techniques for AI, and specifically for Expert Systems.

Following a brief introduction to AI knowledge-representation schemes and their use in current Expert Systems, the data-access requirements of an ES are identified. An analysis of four Expert System architectures for efficient access and storage of at least part of their knowledge base is then presented. These possible architectures are contrasted with a number of different data access requirements to present a set of specific recommendations for the

----

[1] [TSIC82] gives a detailed description of several data models, while [MYLO84] presents a comprehensive introduction to knowledge representation. Furthermore, both [WONG77] and [BROD84] examine the relationships between AI and DBMS representation schemes.

implementation of the data access component in an Expert System. Finally, some important research issues for the realization of these architectures are examined. Throughout the chapter we will illustrate various concepts and issues with examples taken from a life-insurance expert system currently under development at New York University.

2.0 KNOWLEDGE REPRESENTATION - AI AND DBMS

In this section, we examine AI knowledge representation strategies and relate them to their counterparts in Database Management Systems. A major conclusion that can be drawn is that it is possible to have multiple representations for the knowledge base of an ES. Furthermore, at least part of the knowledge base of an ES can be represented as a database under the control of a DBMS. Therefore, the designer of an ES has to consider the tradeoff between the choice of a specialized representation which allows for efficient access and storage of data, and the cost of providing translations between it and other representations more suitable for inference purposes.

According to the classification scheme in [NAU82], the ES's application domain knowledge can be described at two levels: data and knowledge. Generally, at the data level, the object types, their properties and relationships, together with the object instances are represented. This, in DBMS terms, corresponds to a database. At the knowledge level, rules and/or procedures and actions on the objects, together with meta-knowledge about the scope, limits, relevance, and importance of what is known are represented. There is no direct correspondence with DBMS concepts. Yet, some parallels can be drawn between representation at the knowledge level and data dictionary entries, coupled with externally written application programs for a database.

The separation of the knowledge base in data and knowledge levels should not be confused with the often-made distinction between declarative and procedural knowledge representation schemes [MYLO84]. In declarative representations, the knowledge base is a collection of declarative statements, while in the latter, a set of procedures constitute the knowledge base. But, a declarative representation scheme (e.g. first-order logic) can be used for the representation of the application domain both at the data and knowledge levels.

2.1 Knowledge: Domain Rules, Principles, And Heuristics

A knowledge base can be regarded as a collection of procedures expressed in some language (in AI systems, this has typically meant LISP). It is generally believed that the pattern-directed procedures of PLANNER [HEWI71] had a major influence in procedural knowledge representations [MYLO84]. Such procedures are not "called", as in ordinary programming languages, but are "activated" by the inference engine whenever the knowledge base is searched or modified.

Production Rules [WATE79] have become the most popular schemes among pattern-directed procedures. Each rule is a simple program with the format:

IF <condition> THEN <action>

where the condition is typically a conjunction of predicates, and the action activates other procedures which potentially change the state of the knowledge base. Production rules can be used to represent a variety of different types of inference, as illustrated in the following examples:

1. From SITUATION to APPROPRIATE ACTION:

    IF evidence of diabetes is found
        THEN request a doctor's statement from applicant

2. From PREMISE to CONCLUSION:

IF thiazide is present in the blood
THEN applicant is taking high blood pressure medication

3. PROPERTY INHERITANCE

IF applicant is female
THEN applicant has a greater life-expectancy than a male

Production rules are typically used as description tools for problem-solving heuristics, replacing a more formal analysis of the problem into a deterministic algorithm. In this sense, the rules are thought of as "rules of thumb," incomplete but very useful guides to making decisions that cut down the size of the problem space being explored. These rules must be provided as input to an expert system by the human expert. This is usually done iteratively, perhaps by means of an interactive program that guides and prompts the expert to make this task easier, and which might also do some limited consistency checking. Rules have been proposed in some sense as a simulation of the cognitive behavior of human experts. Viewed in this light, rules can be seen not just as a neat formalism to represent expert knowledge in a computer but rather as a model of actual human behavior.

In combination with pattern-directed procedures, conditional probabilities and static descriptions of phenomena have been used in Expert Systems for the representation of knowledge (e.g., in Internist [POPL77]).

Given a suitable interpretation of logical formulas, first-order logic can also be used to represent procedural knowledge for the application domain. For example, assuming that P, Q, R are formulas, then the formula P AND Q -> R can be interpreted procedurally as: to show that R is true, first show that P and Q are true. For example, the logical formula:

applicant (X) AND age(X,Y) AND greater(Y,50) AND
visited-doctor(X,Date) AND difference-in-days(Date,Today,Z) AND
less(Z,90) --> needs-physical(X) OR needs-doctor-statement(X)

asserts that an applicant over 50 years old who has seen a doctor within the last three month must either submit a doctor's statement or submit to a physical examination.

A major problem with general first-order logic for knowledge representation is the difficulty in expressing control structures that efficiently guide the use of a large knowledge base. In the hope of reducing such problems, practical tools such as the logic programming language Prolog do not use full first-order logic, but only the subset known as definite (Horn) clauses. Furthermore, Horn clauses are interpreted in a procedural way reminiscent of the backward chaining of production rules, leading to a more efficient search process. However, the power of representation is reduced since only a subset of first-logic order is used. For instance, the example presented above is not a Horn clause.

2.2 <u>Data: The Declarative Representation Of Facts</u>

2.2.1 <u>First-Order Logic</u>. - Precise knowledge can be stated as assertions over objects that take the form of first-order predicates with functions and equality [KOWA79]. For example, unary predicates such as "male(X)" or "disease(X)" might be used to classify which of a set of objects were, respectively, males and diseases. Predicates of binary and higher degrees ("doctor-of(X,Y)", "premium(X,Y,Z)", etc.), and functions of arbitrary degrees (e.g. "age(X)") can also be defined. Simple facts are represented as instantiations of predicates, i.e., with actual values instead of variables (e.g. male(John), doctor-of(John, Elizabeth). Since logic is purely declarative it allows multiple uses of the same piece of knowledge, but, as mentioned above, it has been criticized for lack of organizational principles. There is a simple and direct correspondence between first-order logic and the relational model; [GALL78] provides a comprehensive view of this correspondence.

2.2.2 Networks. - Semantic networks [BRAC79] seem to be more popular in other AI applications (e.g., natural language processing) than in expert systems. Nevertheless, a number of expert systems rely on network formalisms, among them very large systems such as Internist [POPL77], Prospector [HART78], and Sophie [BROW81]. A portion of the knowledge about an insurance application and some of its related entities is represented in Figure 1. Networks are a natural and efficient way to organize knowledge: nodes describe objects, concepts, or situations whereas arcs define the relevant relationships. "Reasoning" in a network-based system corresponds to traversing the network along the arcs, or to pattern matching of problem descriptions with subnets; a large number of exact and heuristic mechanisms exist for these tasks. One advantage of semantic networks over logic (often referred to as "chunking") is that all knowledge about the object being described can be explicitly represented around the object, thus allowing for associative access to related knowledge. The disadvantages of the network approach stem from the lack of formal semantics for the structures, which makes verification of the correctness of reasoning very difficult. NETL [FAHL79] and KLONE [BRAC79] are examples of computer languages that have been developed for the access and manipulation of semantic networks. It is interesting to note that the networks of the CODASYL model of data can be viewed as a very simple form of semantic network.

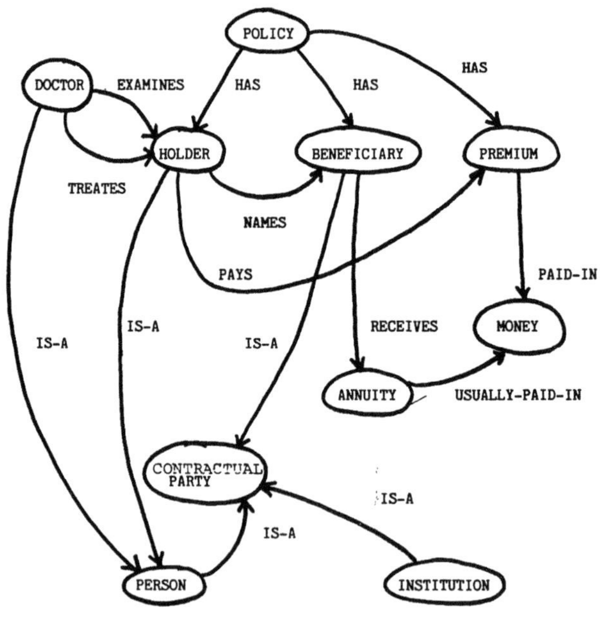

FIGURE 1: SEMANTIC NETWORK EXAMPLE

2.2.3 Frames. - Much knowledge is based upon experience, the expectations aroused from previous situations and the application of general concepts to a specific problem. Frames [MINS75, BOBR77] are a very general and powerful knowledge-structuring device that takes these psychological phenomena into account. They are templates for stereotypical situations, and provide a structure to such experiential knowledge by offering so-called slots which can be filled with type descriptions, default values, attached procedures, etc. The notion of attached procedures, in particular, allows for the development of general-purpose strategies for maintaining a frame-based knowledge representation. Figure 2a shows a simple instantiated frame representing information about a particular insurance policy. This particular frame might be expanded as in Figure 2b with slots to attach procedures that would

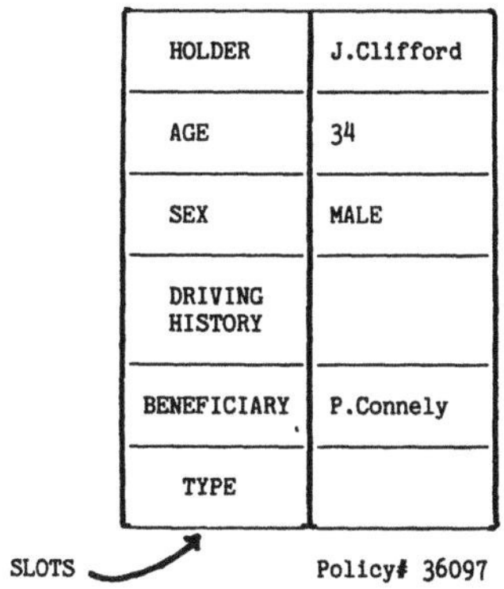

FIGURE 2a: FRAME EXAMPLE

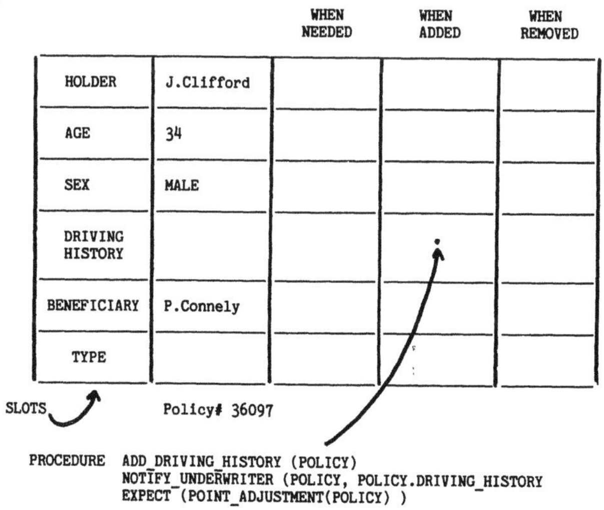

FIGURE 2b: FRAME EXAMPLE WITH PROCEDURAL ATTACHMENT

automatically be invoked when the knowledge base is modified by, e.g., addition or deletion of values in any of the slots of a frame. Like semantic networks, frames offer organizational principles for representing knowledge which are superior than the ones offered by logic formalisms. Several computer systems have been developed for the manipulation of these complex data structures. Among these, we mention KRL [BOBR77], STROBE [SMIT83], and FRL [GOLD77].

2.2.4 Multiple Knowledge Representations. - It has been argued [DAVI81] that no one of the knowledge representation methods is ideally suited for all tasks. In very complex systems requiring many sources of knowledge simultaneously (e.g., for speech recognition [ERMA80]), the elegance of uniformity may have to be sacrificed in favor of exploiting the benefits of multiple knowledge representations each tailored to a different subtask.

It is worth noting that it may often be difficult to distinguish between the data and knowledge levels in an Expert System. The same situation can be represented either at the data level, or at the knowledge level. Using the logic formalism of PROLOG, which combines procedural and declarative knowledge, we present an example of this phenomenon.

Consider the definitions of rating classifications given to prospective customers of an insurance company. The parameters for determining the rating are the customer's age, and the number of debit points accumulated from an analysis of other personal information. (For instance, a person gets "x" debit points if he or she smokes.) For example, a customer whose age is between 15 and 29, with an accumulated 20 points or fewer, is rated "preferred". With increasing age, the number of points that will disqualify a customer from getting a "preferred" rating decreases. Similar definitions exist for other classifications, such as "standard", "bad risk", "terrible risk", etc.

Procedurally, one can represent these classifications as production rules or logic clauses:

```
preferred  IF
     ((age between 15 and 29) AND (points between 0 and 200)) OR
     ((age between 30 and 39) AND (points between 0 and 150)) OR
     ((age between 40 and 49) AND (points between 0 and 100)) OR
     ((age between 50 and 99) AND (points between 0 and 50)).
```

with similar clauses for the other ratings.

Alternatively, these classifications can be given in a declarative way, by using logic assertions (unit clauses) with the general format: [2]

```
rating(Min_Age,Max_Age,Min_Points,Max_Points,Rate_Class).
```

The "meaning" of such an assertion would reside in its interaction with the other predicates and rules in the knowledge base. These would have to be structured to give this assertion its interpretation as:

> A person between the ages of Min_Age and Max_Age, with a number of points between Min_Points and Max_Points, is classified in the specified Rate_Class.

For instance, the assertions:

----

[2] In this Prolog notation, predicates and constant values are represented in lower case, and variable names always start with an upper-case character.

```
rating(15,29,0,200,'preferred').
rating(30,39,0,150,'preferred').
rating(40,49,0,100,'preferred').
rating(50,99,0,50,'preferred').
```

and the clause:

```
preferred IF
  rating(Min_Age,Max_Age,Min_Points,Max_Points,'preferred').
```

define "preferred" customers. It can be seen that the above combines descriptions at the data and knowledge levels.

Notice the strong similarity between the above representation scheme with the relational model, where the last clause is similar to a relational "view" defined on the stored table RATING, as a selection where the Rate_Class attribute has value 'preferred'. This latter, declarative, representation is more flexible than the one that uses only procedural rules, in that it allows for multiple ways of viewing the ratings classifications. For instance, the question "what is the maximum number of points that a 50 year old customer may accumulate and still get a preferred rating" can be answered directly, given the declarative representation. Of course, depending on the application, this flexibility may not be necessary.

2.3 Remarks

It is fair to say that, in general, AI knowledge representation schemes are more powerful than their counterparts in database management, and in particular, the three popular data models: relational, hierarchical, and network. For instance, AI representation schemes embed inferencing capabilities. Using fixed inference rules, it is possible to deduce new facts from old ones.

However, the computer systems that have been developed for the manipulation of the basic objects (frames, semantic networks, etc.) in AI representation schemes lack most of the secondary storage management facilities, which are commonly offered in database management systems. For instance, features such as concurrency control, data security and protection, and, possibly most important, optimized access of data residing in secondary storage, are not part of AI systems. For example, Expert Systems typically load their knowledge base into main storage before the actual ES session begins. This may not have been an important limitation of previous or current Expert Systems; with very few exceptions, their application domains had no need of sophisticated DBMS mechanisms. It is only with the introduction of ESs into the commercial world that their data access requirements have begun to change. These requirements are identified and classified in the next section.

3.0 CLASSIFICATION OF ACCESS REQUIREMENTS

The data access requirements of Expert Systems can be classified along several dimensions. Among the most important are the volume of data needed to perform effectively, the origin of this data, and the timing of the decision as to which subset of the data is required. In this section we discuss these dimensions and illustrate them with examples.

Data Volume. - Historically, the knowledge bases in Expert Systems have been relatively small in size, small enough, in fact, to fit in main storage.

One of the largest knowledge bases for major Expert Systems is that of Internist. It is reported in [POPL83] to contain over 500 disease entities (each requiring several records), and 3,500 manifestations (history items, symptoms, physical signs, and laboratory data). [3] However, most ESs developed to date appear to have very modest data needs; for example, the initial production version of the expert system R1, which suggests a design for a computer system configuration, contained about 750 rules [MCDE81]. Even when new data is created through deductions or generate-and-test methods in Expert Systems, e.g., in [NICO83], and [STEF78], main storage is still sufficient to contain the knowledge base.

Recently though, it has become increasingly apparent that ESs may have to manage very large volumes of data. For instance, in CAD applications of Expert Systems large amounts of data are needed for the support of conclusions by an ES [LAFU83]. Also, for commercial applications of ES technology, very large operational databases will need to be consulted for more accurate ES operation [KUNI82, LAFU83, VASS83, JARK84a]. Of course, data volume is also relative to the size of the computer system and its main storage. In one of the first ESs implemented on a microcomputer, the LSI-11, the knowledge base contains data on scientific disciplines and development goals in Portugal, together with their interactions [PERE82]. The knowledge base in this system consists of a hierarchical set of tables representing correspondences between scientific disciplines and government development goals. Since these tables are quite extensive (roughly 26,500 "facts" are being represented), not all of the knowledge base in this system can reside in main storage. However, the storage management strategies developed in this case are appropriate only to the particular domain and are not readily generalized.

In cases like the above, main storage is insufficient--with virtual memories, you may never run out of space, but, eventually, will certainly run out of time.

Database Origin. - Most Expert Systems developed to date use their own database of facts, custom-made to best suit the application-specific requirements. Practically speaking, however, if ESs are to be applied in the commercial world they will need access to "external" data sources. These "external" data are typically operational databases managed by a DBMS and shared by other applications. Issues like data volatility (frequency of database updates), data currency (how important is an up-to-date representation), and data security and protection influence the decision of whether to access the "external" data through the DBMS, or whether that data can be duplicated, restructured, and permanently stored as part of the ES's own knowledge base.

A representative example is the case of PROBWELL, an ES for the detection of problems in oil wells [OLSO82], which requires data from a large operational database under IMS. Also, in an NYU project on Expert Systems for Business, it was determined that a life-insurance underwriting expert needs data from several external data sources (large customer databases, actuarial tables, etc. [JARK84a]).

It is mostly speculation whether other ESs reported in the literature might have profited from access to data stored in a DBMS. But since the mechanisms for such linkage were not available, this need may have been buried. It seems reasonable to suppose, however, that as ESs find wider commercial applications, we will see more interaction between ES and DBMS.

Determinism in Data Access Requirements. - Let us assume that the the database is large enough that only portions of it can reside in main storage at any one time. The knowledge of what particular information will be relevant to the

----

[3] Roughly, an entity in Internist corresponds to a tuple of a relation in a relational database, and a manifestation corresponds to an attribute.

decision-making process during an ES session is in some cases available in advance, while in other situations it can only be determined during the course of the user/system interaction. If the data requirements can be pre-determined, this directly implies the possibility of making "static" decisions, as to which portion of the database is actually needed by the ES. An example of where "static", pre-determined decisions are not feasible is the life-insurance underwriting expert at NYU. In each ES session, the customer profile as defined by the insurance application is completely different, thus requiring separate actuarial tables and related customer-account records. Furthermore, as each piece of data is examined in light of the evolving customer profile, additional data requirements are dynamically generated. In general, the use of "variables" as parameters in data access is a strong indicator of non-determinism in ESs.

4.0 STRATEGIES FOR DATABASE ACCESS IN EXPERT SYSTEMS

Four strategies for establishing a cooperative communication between the deductive and database access components of an expert system have been identified in [VASS83]. The spectrum of possible enhancements of an expert system with data management facilities is essentially a continuum. Starting from elementary facilities for data retrieval, e.g., a file system, we progress to a generalized DBMS within the expert system, to a 'loose' coupling of the ES with an existing commercial DBMS, and finally to a 'tight' coupling with an external DBMS. The four strategies can be considered to be subcases of two general architectures. The deductive and the database access components of an expert system can either be integrated into one system (the ES), or be independent systems which interact through a communications protocol [VASS84]. This is illustrated in Figure 3.

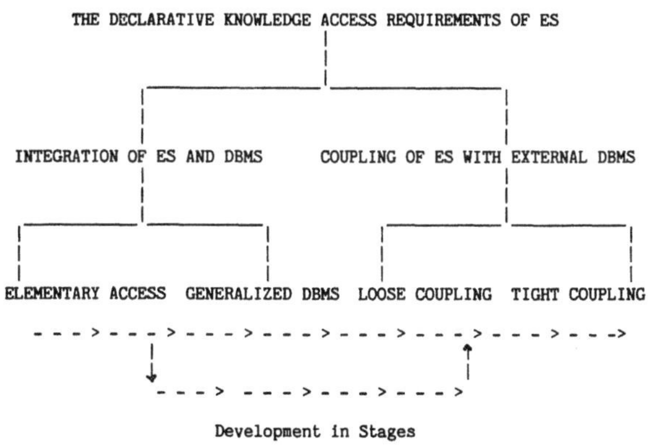

Figure 3: STRATEGIES FOR DATABASE ACCESS BY AN ES

Expert system designers may choose one architecture over another depending on data volume, determinism in data access, and origin of the database, as described above; specific recommendations for the strategy selection problem are given in Section 4.5. These strategies could be developed independently, but in a careful design these successive enhancements would be incremental, allowing for a smooth transition to the next, more sophisticated strategy.

4.1 Elementary Database Access Within An Expert System - Strategy 1

The most commonly employed strategy for data access in ESs is to build an application-specific set of data structures and associated access routines in main memory. Systems like KRL, KLONE, FRL, NETL, and STROBE are used for the representation of the application-domain facts, but also provide data manipulation and simple access mechanisms. Other packages typically used in ESs exist in LISP libraries, e.g., DEFSTRUCT [MOON81], and The Record Package [MASI74]. Frequently, ES designers implement their own application-specific data-handling programs, as in the case of Internist [POPL77]. The direct use of the elementary database features of PROLOG (e.g. the "assert" predicate to add new facts, or the "retract" predicate to delete facts) is also an example of this Elementary Data Access Strategy.

What characterizes all such approaches is the direct manipulation of data objects in main storage. Otherwise, they differ in the degree of generality and data-independence they offer.

4.2 Generalized DBMS Within An Expert System - Strategy 2

In attempting to deal with large data volumes, efforts are underway to implement database management system components for an ES. For example, STROBE is being extended into a DBMS [LAFU83]. Because of its immediate correspondence with relational database concepts, PROLOG has been the favorite language for ES-internal DBMS implementations. For our life-insurance project we have implemented a generalized relational database management system within PROLOG to support a data dictionary with relation schemes, functional dependencies, external file handling, and the query capabilities of a relational algebra or calculus. This type of consolidation of database and programming language systems has also been investigated by [SCHM77]. PROLOG data access extensions to handle external file management are reported in [CHOM83] and [PARS83].

It is worth noting, however, that all these efforts are still early in development, and that they only mention as future plans the extensions of an Expert System to a full-pledged DBMS (i.e. accounting for data sharing, security, protection, etc.). Regardless, extending an ES to provide the facilities of a DBMS is a conceptually elegant approach, which may prove to have practical benefits in the long run.

4.3 Loose Coupling Of The ES With An External DBMS - Strategy 3

Conceptually the simplest solution to the problem of using existing databases managed by an external DBMS is to extract a snapshot of the required data from the DBMS when the ES begins to work on a set of related problems. This portion of the database is stored as the ES's own internal database in combination with any of the two previous access strategies. In current ESs, some form of loose coupling is used with Elementary Data Access mechanisms. Extensive use of this strategy, is limited by the degree of non-determinism in data access requirements, and by the fact that it incurs data-mapping overhead which for a large database can be quite high.

4.4 Tight Coupling Of The ES With An External DBMS - Strategy 4

In this access strategy the ES plays the role of an "intelligent" user of a generalized DBMS that manages a very large database. This is contrasted with loose coupling, where the ES is a one-time, simple user of the DBMS. Utilizing a tight-coupling scenario requires an online communication system between the ES and the DBMS. Queries can be generated and transmitted to the DBMS dynamically, and answers can be received and transformed into the internal knowledge representation. Thus in tight coupling the ES must know when and how to consult the DBMS, and must be able to understand the answers. The consequence of such dynamic use of the communication system is that the external database becomes an "extension" of the ES's knowledge base.

To attain tight coupling, particular care has to be taken to minimize the use of the communication system, and to the data representation and language translation problems. This is the topic of Section 5. To the authors' knowledge, tight coupling to an existing DBMS has not yet been implemented in actual systems, but research efforts are underway [KUNI82, VASS84]. It appears that the impact of logic programming and the commercialization of relational database systems will have a profound effect for tight coupling in future system architectures.

4.5 Recommendations In Choosing An Architecture

The designer of an expert system is faced with many architectural decisions, including how to structure the knowledge base, what form of inference engine is most appropriate, and so forth. We have discussed above the growing trend toward the development of ESs in environments involving very large databases; this introduces another decision for the ES designer, viz. what form of communication path between the ES and the database is appropriate?

Given the three dimensions along which we have analyzed the database access requirements of an ES, and the four strategies for ES-DBMS coupling, it becomes possible to provide some guidance for this decision by examining all of the combinations of system characteristics along these three dimensions, and suggesting appropriate coupling strategies for each. Figure 4 presents these suggestions in the form of a simple decision table. [4] For example, a situation involving very large data volume but no existing database is handled by Rule 3 in the table -- the suggestion for this situation is either to build into the ES generalized DBMS capabilities, or to acquire a DBMS to manage the large data volume, and use a tight-coupling strategy between the two systems. Other possible combinations of characteristics lead to different architectural recommendations.

As anyone who has developed an ES can readily attest, however, there are no really hard and fast rules that apply across the diverse domains to which ES technology has been and will continue to be applied. This table should therefore be viewed as a set of overall recommendations for broad categories of problem domains, rather than as a shortcut for avoiding careful examination of the unique characteristics of the problem at hand. For example, a recent paper [LAFU83] presents some empirical evidence that particular characteristics of the environment (both of the problem space itself and of the available hardware) often override an architectural decision made on purely theoretical grounds.

----

[4] The terminology used is the table is: At the condition part, N, Y denote NO and YES respectively and a dash "-" denotes that the entry could be either. At the action part, an X denotes that this action should be taken. It should be noted that, more than one X's in the same column (rule), imply that there is a choice of actions.

RULES

CONDITIONS	1	2	3	4	5
Is there a very large data volume?	N	N	Y	Y	Y
Is there an existing database?	-	-	N	Y	Y
Are the data access requirements determined during the session?	N	Y	-	N	Y
ACTIONS					
Strategy 1: Elementary Data Access	X	X			
Strategy 2: Extension of ES to Generalized DBMS		X	X		
Strategy 3: Loose Coupling with External DBMS	X			X	
Strategy 4: Tight Coupling with External DBMS			X		X

Figure 4: DECISION TABLE FOR THE DETERMINATION OF AN ES ARCHITECTURE

5.0 OPTIMIZATION REQUIREMENTS

The problem of optimizing database accesses by expert systems does not arise in all of the previously presented architectures. If strategy 1 is selected, the expert system will handle the database of specific facts in the same way as the general rules of the knowledge base. Strategy 2 (a DBMS within the expert system) permits the adaptation of any query processing strategies to the particular needs of the expert systems language. In strategy 3 (loose coupling), the expert system acts like any normal user of a DBMS and can be treated accordingly.

Optimization of the ES-DBMS interactions therefore becomes an issue only when a tight-coupling architecture (strategy 4) is employed. The way an expert system uses its data is typically very different from what a database management system is designed for. On the one hand, an expert system may issue a sequence of closely related calls, for instance, when using recursion in a logic-based representation. On the other hand, an expert system typically considers only one fact at a time whereas a relational DBMS can also work efficiently when confronted with set-oriented queries. Furthermore, this fact-at-a-time access requests will result in a very inefficient use of the communication system, as is demonstrated in [VASS84]. Since tight coupling has rarely been used to date in ES-DBMS, we shall limit the following discussion to a review of some recent work at NYU [VASS83, VASS84, JARK84b] for interfacing a Prolog-based expert system with a relational database system which supports an SQL interface.

During the conversion of Prolog predicates into SQL queries, the above-mentioned problems are solved by use of an intermediate language. This language mediates between Prolog and SQL in the sense that it is a (variable-free) subset of Prolog but - like SQL - gives a set-oriented description of the desired data in terms of stored base relations rather than views (as in the original Prolog version).

The optimization process can thus be divided into three steps [JARK84b]. First, a preprocessing mechanism collects ES requests for data while simulating the ES deduction process [VASS83]. As soon as a database-related request is encountered in the expert system, it stops its reasoning process and gives control to a higher, or meta-language, program, which simulates the continuation of the database-related reasoning to collect similar database requests. In effect, this mechanism delays the submission of individual tuple-oriented queries by converting them into more "optimizable" set-oriented ones, expressed in the intermediate language.

In the second step, the intermediate language expressions are optimized. Two techniques are employed: semantic query simplification, and common subexpression optimization in recursive calls. Query simplification (described in the introductory chapter by Jarke in this book) removes redundant subexpressions from a query, based on idempotency laws in connection with the detection of certain tautologies and contradictions in a query. Semantic query simplification employs integrity constraints such as value bounds for attributes, functional dependencies, and subset dependencies between primary and foreign keys in relations to detect more such simplifications than those visible from the original syntactic form of the query.

To optimize recursive calls, we exploit the case when the answer to each query step submitted to the database constitutes part of the input to subsequent queries. To avoid re-calculations, the result of each step in the recursion is kept as an intermediate result until the entire recursive query has been evaluated. The complete answer -- later used in the further reasoning process after the meta-language processing -- is composed as the union of the results at each intermediate step.

The optimized query is then translated to the DBMS query language and executed by the DBMS. The answer is loaded into the internal expert system database, or -- if that is too small -- into a temporary database relation. Garbage collection may be required to preserve the internal database as a rapidly accessible buffer in the presence of multiple unrelated database calls.

Only after all this has been completed does the meta-level evaluation stop and return control to the object-level of the expert system. The latter can now continue its reasoning with all the relevant data for the current search process provided in the internal database. If a new branch (backtracking from the start of the meta-level evaluation) of reasoning is considered, a new database call may be issued.

It should be noted at this point that this solution is not the only possible approach. Although not in the immediate context of expert systems, various compilation methods have been proposed for so-called deductive databases, i.e., systems in which a special-purpose expert system is superimposed upon a particular database system. Compilation is quite easy in the context of non-recursive reasoning [REIT78, GRAN81] but requires the presence of iteration constructs in the target language otherwise [HENS82]. In [JARK84a], an overview of such approaches is presented in the general context of database-expert systems interaction.

6.0 CONCLUDING REMARKS

The issue of Expert System interaction with Database Management Systems is emerging as an area for research, and one which can provide both practical and theoretical payoffs as the problems become identified and solutions are proposed. It can be expected that both areas will profit from this interaction. Expert systems will become more robust as they provide more of the facilities that are considered standard in commercial DBMSs: centralized storage and control of valuable data, efficient storage and access routines for large volumes of data, the ability to support multiple users, rollback and recovery strategies, and so forth. Database Management Systems will become more intelligent as they adopt more powerful knowledge representation schemes. and by means of the deductive capabilities of Expert Systems, they will provide much more sophisticated querying and decision-making capabilities than mere information management.

We have described a number of different strategies for interfacing these two types of systems, from one extreme of merging the two systems into one, to a dynamically controlled interaction between two independent systems at the other end of the spectrum. Criteria that are relevant to the determination of the appropriate strategy to adopt for a particular problem domain were identified and discussed. The reader should bear in mind that there are very few real systems in operation today that have addressed the problems discussed in this chapter. It is clear that as interactions between knowledge-based systems and database management systems become more widespread, more issues will be identified and additional solutions proposed.

References

(BOBR77) (BOWE72) (BRAC79) (BROD84) (BROW81) (CHOM83) (CLIF83) (DAVI81) (ERMA80) (FAHL79) (FORG80) (GALL78) (GEVA82) (GOLD77) (GRAN81) (HART78) (HAYE83) (HENS82, see HENS84) (HEWI71) (JARK84a) (JARK84b) (KOWA79) (KUNI83, see KUNI82) (LAFU83) (MASI74) (MCDE81) (MINS75) (MOON81) (MYLO84) (NAU82) (NICO83) (OLSO82) (PARS83) (PERE82) (POPL77) (POPL83, see POPL84) (REIT78) (SCHM77) (SMIT83) (TSIC82) (VANM79) (VASS83) (VASS84, see VASS85) (WATE79) (WONG77, see WONG77a)

A Query Language for Statistical Databases

Z. Meral Ozsoyoglu and Gultekin Ozsoyoglu

ABSTRACT

In this chapter we describe a high level, screen-oriented database query language, Summary-Table-by-Example (STBE) for manipulating summary data in statistical databases. STBE uses aggregate functions, relations with set-valued attributes and summary tables to extract and format summary data in tabular form. STBE is similar to Query-by-Example, and is a superset of another language, Aggregates-by-Example (ABE). Summary tables are shown to be information equivalent to a set of relations. This equivalency allows STBE to convert a summary table referenced in a query into a set of relations and to evaluate the query in a uniform manner. The expressive power of STBE is at least that of the relational calculus that allows set-valued attributes and aggregate functions. STBE is compared with ABE and SQL. Access path selection in STBE is discussed briefly.

1. INTRODUCTION

A statistical database system (SDB) is a database system that supports statistical data analysis. Statistical data analysis ranges from simple summary statistics (e.g., SUM, COUNT, MEDIAN, etc.) to advanced statistical techniques such as factor analysis or hypothesis testing. SDBs are used in various application areas such as economy and business, medical research and social sciences.

One of the basic functions of SDBs is to obtain, maintain and manipulate summary data from the raw or other summary data in the database. Tabular representations of summary data, hereafter called <u>summary tables</u>, are widely used in various application areas. Summary tables are maintained (most often manually) for bookkeeping, compared and evaluated perhaps periodically. As such, integrated summary table generation and manipulation features are needed in SDBs. Figure 1 shows an example summary table.

Most of the statistical software packages currently available provide only the capability to create summary tables from a single file. An exception is the Table Producing Language system (TPL) of the U.S. Bureau of Labor Statistics [USLB 80] that has powerful commands to produce summary tables. However, TPL does not manipulate or store summary tables, and is executed as a stand-alone system in batch mode.

Set-valued attributes are very useful in summary tables since information in summary tables is almost always categorized and aggregated over groups of data items. A majority of the commercially available network database systems (e.g., ADABAS [ADAB 80]) allow set-valued fields to be defined and manipulated by users. However, commercially available relational systems permit only simple-(i.e. atomic) valued attributes, for example, INGRES [STON76] and SQL/DS [SQL81]. We propose to extend the relational model with set-valued attributes to provide integrated summary-table manipulation facilities.

Summary tables are obtained by aggregating data in the database using aggregate functions such as SUM, MAX, COUNT, etc. Until recently, aggregate functions have

*This research is supported by the National Science Foundation under grant MCS-8306616.

been incorporated in an ad hoc manner into the query languages of databases. The relational algebra and the relational calculus query languages introduced by Codd [CODD72] do not formally incorporate aggregate functions and set-valued attributes. This is not true of more recent languages [KLUG82a, JACO82, JAES82, OZSO83c, OZSO83a]. Klug [KLUG82a] extends the relational algebra and relational calculus by incorporating aggregate functions, and shows that the extended languages have the same power. Jacobs' [JACO82] database logic allows defining and manipulating relations which may have relations as tuple components. Jaesche and Schek [JAES82] define an extension of relational algebra for non-First Normal Form relations (i.e., a tuple component may be a set or a set of sets, etc.). Ozsoyoglu and Ozsoyoglu [OZSO83c] extend the relational algebra for summary tables by incorporating set-valued attributes and aggregate functions. Ozsoyoglu, Matos, and Ozsoyoglu [OZSO83a] extend the tuple relational calculus with set-valued attributes and aggregate functions, and show that this relational calculus is equivalent in expressive power to the modified relational algebra of [OZSO83c].

Ohio	Ashtabula	Female	63.5
		Male	77.2
	Cuyahoga	Female	81.5
		Male	56.2
	Medina	Female	61.8
		Male	62.4
	Ashtabula		68.9
	Cuyahoga		60.4
	Medina		62.0
Pennsylvania	Allegheny	Female	79.3
		Male	70.2
	Susquehanna	Female	66.0
		Male	70.0
	Allegheny		75.4
	Susquehanna		68.1

Figure 1. An example summary table, AVERAGE-HOUSE-PRICES in thousands of dollars.

In this chapter, we discuss a screen-oriented query language for statistical databases, called Summary-Table-by-Example (STBE). Our investigation of query languages for statistical databases is part of a project for constructing a highly secure and user-friendly statistical database system, called the System-for-Statistical-Databases (SSDB) [OZSO83b]. The SSDB project involves the design of a data model and an architecture of a secure statistical database system as well as a testbed implementation. STBE is designed to be the query language for the SSDB.

STBE is a screen-oriented language and uses the example query concept of Query-by-Example (QBE) [ZLOO77]. The "subquery with parameters" concept of another graphical database language, Aggregates-by-Example (ABE) [KLUG81] is also utilized in STBE. The main difference between ABE and STBE is that ABE does not deal with summary tables or relations having set-valued attributes (see Figure 2), and allows only conjunctive queries. STBE is based on the domain relational calculus version of the extended tuple relational calculus proposed in [OZSO83a], and has a formally defined expressive power.

In Section 2, we modify the relational model with set-valued attributes and the summary table object. Section 3 illustrates STBE queries. In Section 4, we discuss output formatting of summary tables. The expressive power of STBE is discussed in Section 5. Section 6 compares STBE with ABE and SQL [SQL81]. Section 7 discusses access-path selection strategy for STBE queries. Section 8 is the conclusion.

2. SET-VALUED ATTRIBUTES, SUMMARY TABLES AND AGGREGATE FUNCTIONS

A database is a collection of relation instances and summary table instances. A relation instance (or simply, a relation) is a table with each column labeled by a distinct attribute. Each row (tuple) of a relation is unique, i.e., a relation is a set of tuples. A relation scheme of a relation is the set of attributes labeling the columns of that relation. A tuple component in a column labeled by a set-valued attribute is a set of elements, where an element may be an integer, a real number or a string. On the other hand, a tuple component in a column labeled by a simple-valued attribute is an element. Figure 2 shows a relation r with the relation scheme R(A,*B,C) where *B is a set-valued attribute, and A and C are simple-valued attributes.

r

A	*B	C
a1	{b1,b2}	c3
a2	{b1,b3}	c1
a3	{b2}	c2

Figure 2. A relation instance r with a set-valued attribute *B

Informally, a summary-table scheme is a two-dimensional table of cells. The rows and columns of a summary table have some attributes called category attributes. Category attributes in a row (or column) are structured as a forest of trees whose nodes are attributes. In addition to category attributes, a cell also has an attribute, called cell attribute. Example 2.1 illustrates a summary table scheme.

Example 2.1: The scheme for the summary table AVERAGE-HOUSE-PRICES in Figure 1 is given below.

AVERAGE-HOUSE-PRICES			
STATE	COUNTY	SEX	PRICE1
	COUNTY		PRICE2

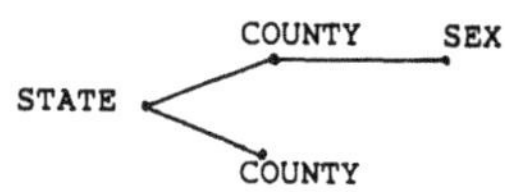

This summary table has two cells with cell attribute names PRICE1 and PRICE2, one tree in the row category attribute forest and no column category attributes (which is represented by an empty box).

In a summary table, attributes which appear in a root-to-leaf path in a row or column category attribute tree are called row category attributes or column category attributes, respectively, of a cell. In example 2.1, STATE, COUNTY and SEX are the row category attributes of the cell PRICE1. Similarly, STATE and COUNTY form the row category attributes of the cell PRICE2.

More formally, a summary-table scheme is a 4-tuple S(Fr,Fc,Ac,M) where Fr and Fc are row and column category attribute forests, Ac is an ordered set of cell attributes, and M is a mapping function. Fr and Fc are ordered forests of ordered trees (Fr or Fc may be empty but not both). A nonempty category attribute forest F is denoted as F=<T1,...,Tk> where each Ti = (Vi,Ei) is an ordered tree whose vertex set is Vi and edge set is Ei. Each cell in S has a pair of ordered sets of attributes as row and column category attributes. The row and column category attributes of a cell appear in a root-to-leaf path of a tree in Fr and Fc, respectively. The function M maps a pair of category attribute sets for a cell into an attribute in Ac, which is the cell attribute of the cell. The function M is one-to-one and onto.

Example 2.2: For the summary table scheme AVERAGE-HOUSE-PRICES in Example 2.1,

Fr = <(V1,E1),(V2,E2)>, V1={STATE,COUNTY,SEX}, V2={STATE,COUNTY}

E1={(STATE,COUNTY), (COUNTY,SEX)} and E2={(STATE,COUNTY)}

Fc = < >

Ac = {PRICE1, PRICE2}

M maps ({STATE,COUNTY,SEX}, { }) to PRICE1, and

({STATE,COUNTY}, { }) to PRICE2.

For notational convenience, we omit the function M and assume that the mapping from pairs of category attribute sets to cell attributes is done as follows. Let leaves in Fr and Fc be numbered from 1 to m and from 1 to n, respectively. (Top leaf of Fr and leftmost leaf of Fc are both numbered 1.) Then category attributes in the path from a root to the i-th leaf in Fr and category attributes in the path from a root to the j-th leaf in Fc map to the (n*(i-1)+j)-th cell attribute in Ac where $1 \le i \le m$, $1 \le j \le n$. Having fixed the mapping function M, we use S(Fr,Fc,Ac) to denote a summary-table scheme.

A category attribute may be set-valued or simple-valued. A cell attribute is a simple-valued attribute. A summary table instance (or simply, a summary table) for S(Fr,Fc,Ac) is a two-dimensional table of cell instances corresponding to cells in S. A cell instance has row and column category attribute values and a cell attribute value. Figure 1 shows an instance of the summary table scheme AVERAGE-HOUSE-PRICES.

An aggregate function takes a group of values (i.e. a simple-valued column of a relation) as input, and produces a single value as output. Notice that there may be duplicate values in the input to an aggregate function.

3. STBE QUERIES

In STBE, the user formulates a query by building an example of a possible answer on the screen. This is achieved by filling in skeletons (i.e. graphical schemes) of empty relations and summary tables in hierarchically arranged windows (i.e., subqueries*). The user constructs an output summary table or output relation skeletons, and "opens" windows. Example elements are used to match and retrieve data in the database, and to bind relations and summary tables in different windows.

Below we illustrate major features of STBE by a number of examples. All examples use a country-wide house-ownership survey database with four relation schemes, where the underlined attributes are keys,

PERSON (pid, pname, income, sex)
HOUSE (hid, owner, *oldowners, price, age, cid)
COUNTY (cid, county, state)
STATE (state, population, acreage)

*The term "subquery" in SQL is used for nested SQL queries.

and one summary-table scheme

SUM-PRICE-82 ((state,county), (*age), (price))

Attributes pid, hid, and cid stand for person-id, house-id and county-id. Attributes county and state form a key for COUNTY relation.

Example 3.1: Produce the summary table of the counts of houses by statename and countyname

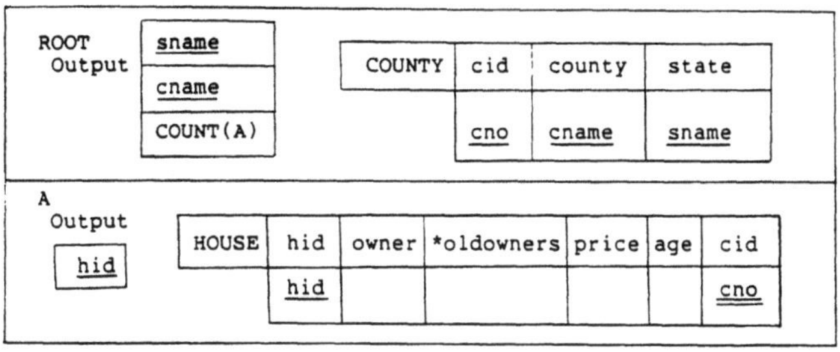

This query has two windows, ROOT and A. (The top window is always named ROOT.) For each window, output specifies the output of that window. Output of all windows except ROOT must be a relation; ROOT output may be a relation or a summary table. Since A is referenced in ROOT (i.e. COUNT(A)), A is an immediate descendant of ROOT. Windows are hierarchically arranged by the immediate descendancy relationship.

Singly-underlined items denote free (i.e., nonfixed) variables; doubly-underlined items denote fixed variables. Assume a free variable x is specified in window A. Then x can not be specified in any other window. Moreover, the fixed variable x can be specified only in windows that are descendants of A. The fixed variable x is said to be bound to the free variable x. The difference between fixed and free variables and their relationships stem from the way they are instantiated (to be discussed below).

Aggregate functions are specified by the name of the function followed by, in parentheses, the name of the relation or the window over which the aggregation is to be done, and the column number (if needed).

Instantiation of variables is by matching and binding. Let x be a free variable in column A of a relation skeleton R. x matches (i.e., it can take the value of) the A-component of any tuple in the current instance of R. Similarly, *x appearing in column *A of R matches *A-component of any tuple in R.

If x appears in column *A of R then x matches any element in *A-component of any tuple in R. Now, consider a fixed variable x appearing in column B of a relation S. If x is bound to a free variable x then x matches B-component of only those tuples t in S where t[B] equals the current value of x. If *x appears in column *B of S and is bound to *x then the matching and binding rules of *x is the same as above. A fixed variable x appearing in column B of S can also be bound to *x. In this case, x matches B-components of those tuples t of S where t[B] is an element of the current value of x. The other cases such as x appearing in *B, or *x bound to x, etc. are not allowed. The matching and binding rules for variables are summarized in Table 1.

A summary table with one cell (i.e., there is at most one row and one column category attribute tree, and each has at most one leaf) can be visualized as a relation whose attributes are the union of row and column category attributes and the cell attribute. Tuples of such a relation (possibly having null components) correspond one-to-one to cell instances of the summary table. Such summary tables are called primitive summary tables in [OZSO83c]. A summary table in general is represented by a collection of primitive summary tables where each cell corresponds to a primitive summary table. Thus a summary table can be visualized as a collection of relations. Consequently, we only need to discuss the instantiation of variables appearing in relation skeletons.

Matching rules for a free variable in a relation or a summary table skeleton:

	simple variable x	set-valued variable *x
simple-valued attribute A	x can take any value in column A of the skeleton	not allowed
set-valued attribute *A	x can take any value which is an element of a set value in column *A of the skeleton	*x can take any value in column *A of the skeleton

Matching and binding rules for fixed variables:
Assume x appears in column A, and x appears in column B.

	x in B	x in *B	*x in B	*x in *B
x in A	x takes the current value of x	not allowed	not allowed	not allowed
*x in *A	x takes any value which is a member of the current value of *x	not allowed	not allowed	*x takes the current value of *x
x in *A	x takes the current value of x	not allowed	not allowed	not allowed

Table 1. Matching and Binding Rules for free and fixed variables

In the above query, the free variables cno, cname and sname match cid, county and state components of a tuple in relation COUNTY. Once cno, cname and sname are instantiated, an output cell with column category attribute values sname and cname is produced by evaluating COUNT(A). This in turn requires the evaluation of subquery A. In A, cno is a fixed variable, and its value is bound to the current value of cno. Thus hid matches to hid-component of any tuple in HOUSE whose cid-component is cno (i.e., the current value of cno). That is, the evaluation of A for the current value of cno produces the set of all hid-components of tuples in HOUSE whose cid-component is cno. Then COUNT is evaluated on the output of A, and this completes the production of one cell instance in the output summary table of ROOT. Note that county and state uniquely determines cid. Hence for each different pair of sname and cname the subquery A is executed once. Thus for each different pair of sname and cname values matching to components of the same tuple in COUNTY, a new cell instance is produced.

A constant matches only itself. A row in a relation skeleton matches when all of its nonempty items (i.e., constants and variables) match a tuple of the corresponding relation instance in the database. Similarly, a cell of a summary table matches when all of its nonempty items for the category attributes and cell attributes match the corresponding summary-table instance in the database. If a component of a row in a relation skeleton, a category-attribute box or a cell-attribute box in a summary-table skeleton is empty, it can match any value in the corresponding position of the relation or summary table in the database.

Information in different skeletons (relation or summary table) of the same window can be related by using the same variable in relevant positions of different skeletons. When a free variable occurs in several skeletons of the same window, all of its occurrences match the same value. Similarly occurrences of the same fixed variable in a window match the same value.

Once all conditions are satisfied, the output of a query is produced. If the output is a relation, a tuple is produced by using current values of free variables, fixed variables, constants, arithmetic expressions and aggregates in the output-relation skeleton. The same process of matching variables, evaluating aggregates and conditions is repeated for other output tuples in an arbitrary order. Query evaluation is complete when no more tuples can be added to the output set. Similarly, if the output is a summary table, a cell is produced from the output summary-table skeleton using current values of free variables, fixed variables, constants, aggregates and arithmetic expressions. The cell is put into an initially empty set S, and the same process is repeated until there are no more cells to be put into S. S contains the information content of the summary table to be produced.

In summary, a window W is evaluated by

(a) matching constants and free variables with the corresponding tuple components of relations or cells of summary tables in the database,
(b) matching and binding fixed variables of W,
(c) evaluating aggregate functions,
(d) satisfying conditions (if any) specified in a box called the <u>condition box</u>, and
(e) retrieving the output items from the database.

<u>Example 3.2</u>: Produce the summary table of house counts by price (in $1,000) and the number of oldowners.

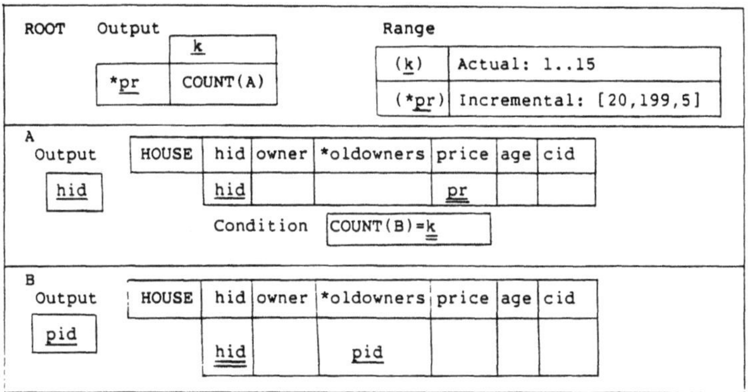

This query illustrates the use of range and condition boxes. A range box has two functions. First, it is used to define a single-column relation over which a set- or simple-valued variable ranges. This feature is useful for defining the domains of category attributes in output summary tables and is not available in QBE or ABE. In this example, *pr is defined as a set-valued free variable ranging over the set values {20,21,22,23,24}, {25,26,27,28,29},...,{195,196,197,198,199}. Also, the range box assigns a range 1,...,15 for k to range over. (This is similar to the user-defined subrange data type of PASCAL programming language.) The second function of the range box is to define the range of variables to be computed relations (which may be the union of two relations, or a relation computed as the output of a subquery). This function of the range box is discussed in Example 3.3.

For a given instantiation of k and *pr in ROOT, A returns the hid values of the houses with a price in the range of *pr and having exactly k oldowners. For an instantiation of hid in A, B returns the pid values of the oldowners of that house. Thus, for each house whose price is in the range of the current value of *pr, B is evaluated in order to find the number of oldowners of that house. If COUNT(B) is the same as the current value of k (i.e., the condition in the condition box is satisfied) then the hid value of that house qualifies to be in the output of A. Note that, during one evaluation of A, for a given value v of *pr in ROOT, pr takes each and every element of v as a value.

In this query, evaluation of ROOT requires evaluation of A, and evaluation of A in turn requires the evaluation of B. Thus the immediate descendancy relationship induces the directed acyclic graph (DAG) structure ROOT-->A-->B. Because of the way in which an STBE query is evaluated, we require the following rule to be enforced:

(R1) Within the directed acyclic graph (DAG) representing the immediate descendancy relationship in an STBE query, if there is more than one directed path from window A to window B then none of the free variables in windows along a path between A and B can appear as fixed variables in window B.

To understand the need for (R1), consider the following DAG of an STBE query.

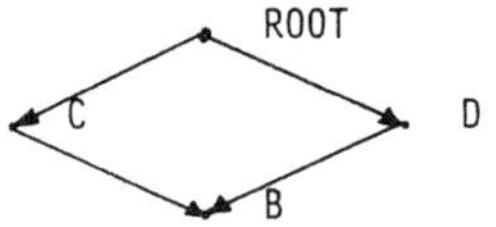

Let x be a free variable in C. Assume x appears as a fixed variable x in B. Then if the evaluation order is ROOT, D and B, the query can not be evaluated since x is undefined during the evaluation of B.

Example 3.3: Produce the summary table of average house prices in thousands of dollars by (statename,countyname) and by (statename,countyname,sex of the owner)

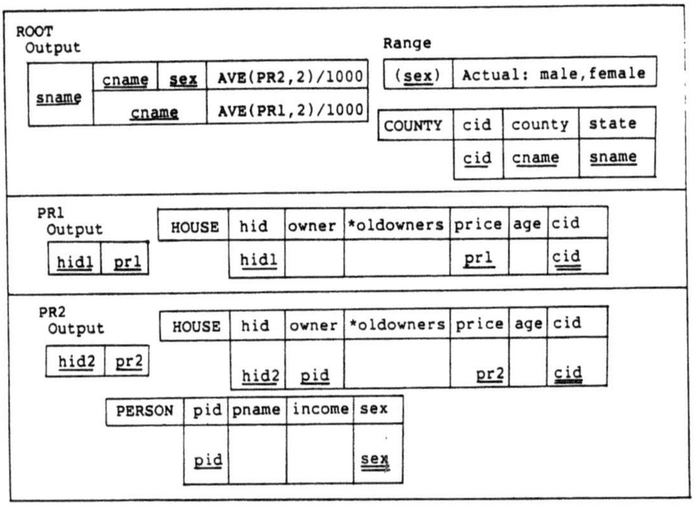

The range box specifies a relation with two tuples (i.e., {(Female), (Male)}) over which sex ranges. AVE(A,2) returns the average of values in the second column of the current output relation for A.

Given instantiations for sname and cname (and thus for cid) from COUNTY, and sex from the range box in ROOT, PR1 returns hid values and prices of houses in that county; and PR2 returns, for that county, hid values and prices of the houses owned by people having sex attribute value equal to the current value of sex.

A possible instance of the output summary table of this query is given in Figure 1.

Example 3.4: For each state s and for each average house price p in a county of s, find the number of counties in s with the average house price p.

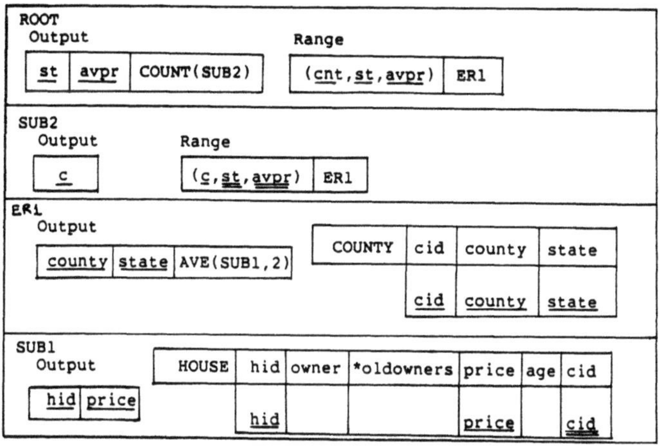

For a given county, SUB1 returns hid values of houses in that county and their prices. ER1 tabulates the average house price for each state and each county in that state. In ROOT, st and avpr are instantiated by matching components of tuples of the relation produced by ER1, as specified in the range box. (ER1 is called an external root query, which will be discussed below.) Subquery SUB2 is referenced in the output of ROOT. Given a pair of values for st and avpr, SUB2 returns the counties in st having avpr as the average house price. Thus, COUNT(SUB2) counts the number of such counties, and is tabulated along with the statename and the average house price.

This query illustrates the use of a range box for specifying computed relations as the range of variables. The second position in a range box contains a union of window names and/or relation names. Any window name in the range box (e.g., window ER1 in the range box of SUB2) is called an external root and forms, together with its descendants, an external root query (ER-query). In this example, the DAG induced by the immediate descendancy relationship, ER1-->SUB1, represents an external root query. Evaluation of an ER-query does not require any information (i.e. fixed variables) from outside the ER-query.

An ER-query satisfies the following conditions:

(a) The output skeleton of an external root is a relation skeleton

(b) An external root does not have any fixed variables

(c) A fixed variable in a subquery of an ER-query can only be bound to a variable in a subquery or external root of that ER-query+

(d) A fixed variable in a subquery outside of an ER-query can not be bound to a variable in that ER-query.

+Matching and binding rules for free and fixed variables in an ER-query are the same as those in Table 1.

Example 3.5: Produce the summary table of the sum of house prices in 1983 by statename and house age groups.

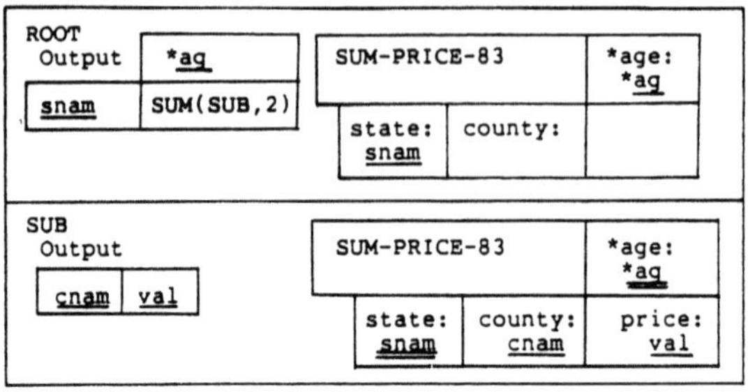

This query illustrates the use of a summary table in the database to obtain another summary table.

4. OUTPUT FORMATTING OF SUMMARY TABLES

We now discuss a way of generating the output summary table. If category attribute A's values are defined by the range box then those values form the instance set of A. Otherwise the instance set of A is the set of values in cells of S appearing as category attribute values for A. For each attribute tree in Fc or Fr, instance trees are generated by

(a) starting from the root v,

(b) replacing v by a set of vertices whose values come from the instance set of the category attribute corresponding to v,

(c) attaching all subtrees of v in the attribute tree to each newly created vertex w that replaced v and

(d) repeating the process recursively by treating each immediate descendant of w as v until no more descendants of w exist.

Instance trees for different attribute trees are sorted in the order of appearance of their corresponding attribute trees in the summary table scheme. Also vertices of category attribute values having the same immediate parent vertex in an instance tree are lexicographically sorted. Roots of instance trees corresponding to the same attribute tree are also lexicographically sorted. (An ordering of category attribute values specified in the range box overrides the sorted order for that category attribute.)

Consider a path P from the root to a leaf in an instance tree T corresponding to an attribute tree in Fr (Fc). The summary table row corresponding to the path P is printed if either all category attributes corresponding to vertices in P are specified in the range box or there exists at least one cell in S whose category attribute values for defining its row (column) are the same as the values of the corresponding vertices in P. All printed cell boxes in the summary table are initialized as blanks first, and then each cell attribute value in S is put into the corresponding cell box by using its category attribute values. Finally, STBE provides dummy labels for category attribute values of summary tables in order to remove potential ambiguity of not being able to distinguish rows or columns.

5. THE EXPRESSIVE POWER OF STBE

Excluding the summary tables, incremental and actual range definitions, and arithmetic expressions in output skeletons, STBE is equivalent in expressive power to an extended version of the relational calculus query language, called the Extended Domain Relational Calculus (EDRC) [OZSO83d]. Relational calculus originally introduced by Codd [CODD72] uses an alpha expression that consists of a target list and a formula. In order to dynamically define ranges for variables, Klug [KLUG82a] extended the relational calculus by replacing the formula by range formula(s) and a qualifier, where a range formula itself is allowed to be a (closed) alpha expression. EDRC extends the relational calculus (as defined by Klug) mainly by

(i) allowing set-valued terms and variables,

(ii) introducing a new range formula to permit variables to range over elements of set-valued tuple components, and

(iii) providing the capability to output tuples with set-valued components.

The correspondence between components of STBE and EDRC are as follows:

(a) the ROOT output skeleton is the target list,

(b) A range formula is either a row in a relation or the union of ER-queries in a row of the range box, and

(c) relation skeletons and the condition box together specify the qualifier.

With the exception of quantification (i.e., existential and universal quantifiers), the correspondence between STBE and EDRC is explicit. For user friendliness, STBE does not have explicit quantifiers. However, by using set-comparison operators, it provides implicit quantification.

In [OZSO83a], the tuple calculus version+ of EDRC is shown to be equivalent to an extended version of relational algebra, called the Extended Relational Algebra (ERA). Various operators of ERA are given in [OZSO83c]. The set of basic operators of ERA include the five basic operators of the relational algebra (union, set difference, cartesian product, selection and projection) extended for set-valued relations, and the operators aggregation-by-template, pack and unpack.

In [CODD72], Codd defines relational completeness of a query language as the capability to formulate queries specified in relational calculus. Extending the relational completeness notion as the capability to formulate queries in EDRC, one can show that STBE is relationally complete. This is accomplished by giving STBE queries that implement each operator of ERA.

5.1 Representation of Summary Tables by Relations

A summary table where each of the row- and column-attribute forests consists of a single chain of attributes (i.e. a tree with one leaf) is called a primitive summary table. In other words, a primitive summary table scheme has exactly one cell. Primitive summary tables are basic building blocks of summary tables since each cell in a summary table scheme corresponds to a primitive summary table. For example, the output summary table in Example 3.3 consists of two primitive summary tables.

A relation, possibly with set-valued attributes, can be used to represent a primitive summary table excluding the order and the type (i.e., row or column) of category attributes. We now give the properties of such a relation in terms of functional dependencies and embedded join dependencies. Let X and Y be disjoint sets of attributes in row- (Fr) and column-attribute forests (Fc), respectively, of a primitive summary table ST with the cell attribute C. Then a relation R with the

+ I.e., variables take on tuples as values (rather than taking on tuple components as values).

attributes X U Y U {C} can be used to represent ST such that each tuple t in R corresponds to a cell occurrence in ST whose row and column category attribute values are tuple components in t[X] and t[Y] respectively, and whose cell attribute value is t[C]. Let R be such a relation representing a primitive summary table ST. Then the functional dependency XY--> C holds+ in R since each cell occurrence in ST is uniquely identified by category attribute values. Moreover, the embedded join dependency *(X,Y) also holds++ in R since there is a cell occurrence in ST for every pair of X,Y values. If R is such a relation representing a primitive summary table ST, we say that R and ST are information equivalent. Similarly given an instance for R(X,Y,C) satisfying XY--> C and *(X,Y) and a scheme for the corresponding primitive summary table ST, an instance for ST can be directly constructed.

The information equivalency of relations with primitive summary tables within an arbitrary summary table permits STBE to process queries involving summary tables in a very simple manner. Whenever a primitive summary table ST within a summary table S is specified in a window of the STBE query then S is retrieved; and the relation scheme R and its instance r information equivalent to ST are constructed on the spot for the evaluation of the query. Similarly for the output summary table ST, first the relations information equivalent to primitive summary tables of ST are obtained and then the ST instance is constructed.

6. COMPARISONS WITH OTHER LANGUAGES

In this section we compare STBE with ABE and SQL. ABE is chosen since the structure of STBE is very similar to ABE. SQL is chosen as a representative of query languages for commercial relational database management systems.

6.1 Aggregation-by-Example (ABE)

ABE is a screen-oriented language similar to QBE [ZLOO77]. The main feature of ABE is to use free variable subqueries to express aggregations instead of grouping operators as in SQL. An ABE query consists of a ROOT query and several subqueries. Each query (subquery or ROOT) has an output relation skeleton, one or more relation skeletons, and an optional condition box. ABE is a proper subset of STBE. The main features of STBE that are not in ABE are (a) set-valued relations, (b) summary tables, (c) range boxes.

For the examples in this section, we modify the country-wide house survey database given in Section 3 so that there are no set-valued relations and summary tables. The example database has four relations where the meanings of the attributes are either self-explanatory or as defined before.

HOUSE (hid, owner, price, age, cid)
COUNTY (cid, sname, cname)
STATE (sname, population, acreage)
PERSON (pid, pname, income)

Example 6.1: For each county find the number of houses with price > \$100K in the county, and print the statename, the countyname and the count.

The corresponding ABE query is:

+Let V and W be subsets of a relation scheme R. The functional dependency V--> W holds in R if for any instance r of R, r has no two tuples which agree on V components, but disagree on one or more W components.

++ Let R1,...,Rk be nonempty subsets of the attributes in R such that R1 U...U Rk=R. A join dependency *(R1,...,Rk) is satisfied by a relation r over R if and only if the natural join of the projections of R onto Ri's equals R. If R1 U...U Rk=V where V ⊆ R, and a join dependency *(R1,...,Rk) is satisfied by the projection of r for R onto V then *(R1,...,Rk) is called an embedded join dependency in r.

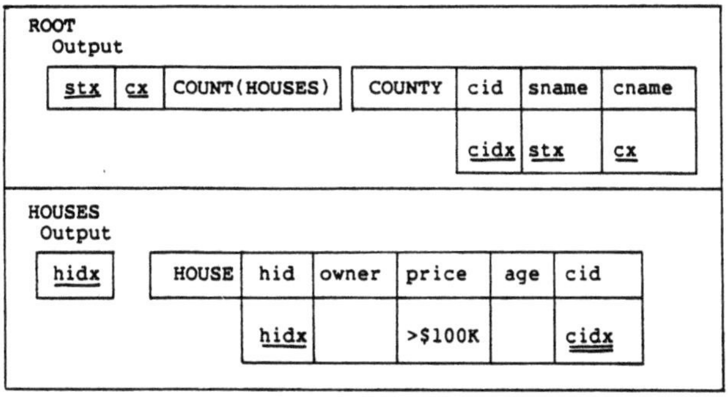

Notice that, if there is no house with price > $100K in a county, the output of the subquery HOUSES for that county will be an empty relation; and in the output of the ROOT, the count for such counties will appear as zero.

The following example illustrates nested aggregations.

<u>Example 6.2</u>: For each state S and for each county C in S, find the number of houses with price > $100K in C; then for each state S, find the average number of such houses over the counties in S. Print names of the states and the corresponding averages.

The corresponding ABE query is:

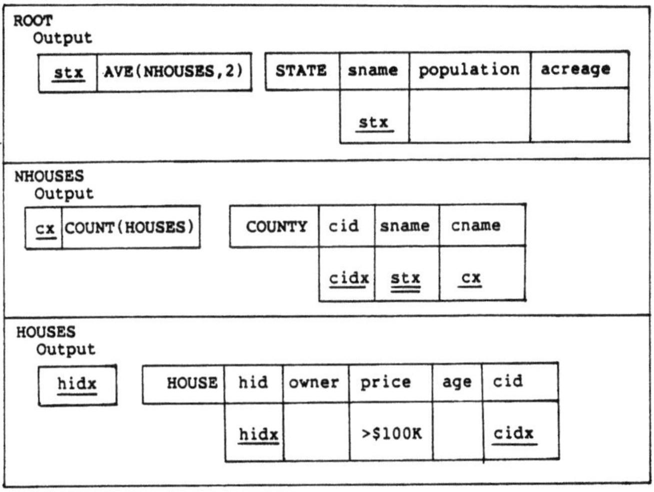

ABE can express conjunctive relational calculus queries and has the capability of expressing aggregations in a natural way. However, ABE can not express a simple union query (e.g. union of two existing relations). STBE expresses such a query using range box.

Other than queries with union, there are some other simple queries which requires the use of range box (see the discussion in Section 3). One of the main uses of the range box in STBE is to range variables on computed relations. For example, consider the following query on the example database above.

"For each county compute the average price of the houses. For each state, compute the number of counties in the state having the same average house price. Print the state name, average house price and the number of such counties."

The STBE version of this query, given in Example 3.4, uses a range box. The use of a range box for this query is necessary for the following reasons. The computation of the number of counties in a state having the same average house price requires a relation containing the average house prices for the counties of a state. In both STBE and ABE, relations having a column which is computed by aggregation can be produced only in the output of a subquery (or ROOT query). The output relations can not be used as relation skeletons, i.e. variables can not range over output relations. However, computing the number of counties with the same average house price, (because of the way STBE and ABE computes aggregations) requires the capability to range variables on the computed relation which is an output of a subquery. This is handled in STBE by using a range box which permits ranging variables over the output of an external root query. Since ABE does not have the range box, such a query can not be expressed in ABE.

6.2. System-R Query Language (SQL):

The general form of a SQL query is

```
SELECT <target list>
FROM <relation list>
[WHERE <boolean condition>]
[GROUP BY <field list>]
[HAVING <boolean condition>]
```

We assume the reader is familiar with the syntax of SQL, and emphasize the differences between SQL and STBE in handling aggregations. In SQL, aggregate expressions of the form "aggregate function (attribute)" may appear in the target list. GROUP-BY clause is used to partition the qualified tuples by the given fields, and the aggregate is applied to each partition. However, empty partitions are automatically eliminated from the output. This limitation of aggregation by partitioning was observed by Klug [KLUG81].

<u>Example 6.3</u>: SQL version of the query in Example 6.1:

```
SELECT  H.cid, C.sname, C.cname, COUNT(*)
FROM  HOUSE H, COUNTY C
WHERE  H.price > 100K
AND  H.cid = C.cid
GROUP BY  (H.cid, C.sname, C.cname)
```

The GROUP BY operator partitions those tuples of the cartesian product of the relations HOUSE and COUNTY which satisfy the conditions in the WHERE clause. Each partition has the tuples with the same cid value. For each partition, a tuple with sname, cname and the number of houses in the county is produced in the output. Naturally, there may be counties in which the price of every house is less than 100K. However, such counties will not appear in the result of this SQL query. Since the query (see Example 6.1) requires for each county the number of houses with price >100K, the result of the SQL query above is only a part of the required answer. There seems to be no natural way to overcome this limitation in a query expressed by partitioning type aggregates.

Another limitation of SQL appears in the computation of nested aggregations as in the query of Example 6.2. This query requires the average by state of the number of houses in counties. In SQL, the GROUP BY operator can not be used to partition the tuples of a computed relation which has a column computed by an aggregate function in conjunction with another GROUP BY operator. Consequently, nested aggregations as described above can not be expressed using a single query in SQL. Note that, in ABE (as well as in STBE) such nested aggregations can be expressed by a single query, since an ABE query can use the output of a subquery which may have aggregated columns for further aggregations.

7. STBE QUERY PROCESSING

An STBE query specifies what is required as an output rather than how it will be constructed. It is the query processor's responsibility to select the appropriate order of operations for the query and to select the access paths that will allow these operations to be carried out efficiently.

In this section, we will briefly discuss the query processing and access-path selection techniques of System R and ABE that can be extended to STBE. Then we will discuss some new techniques for processing STBE queries. A formal treatment of STBE query processing is beyond the scope of this discussion.

Three steps are taken in processing an STBE query. First, the query is parsed and the parse tree is modified through algebraic manipulations to improve the running time of the query. Internal nodes of the parse tree are the extended algebra operators [OZSO83c]. The external nodes may be stored relations, relations with a single column defined in the range box, or relations representing the primitive summary tables of the summary tables referenced in the query. The rules for algebraic manipulations of expressions involving extended algebra operators are given in [OZSO83c]. These transformation rules are similar to those in [ULLM82] for relational algebra operators, except that the properties of aggregate functions are utilized as well as the operators.

The main theme of the algebraic manipulation is to combine the operations that can be performed by a single scan of the relation(s) as well as to reduce sizes of the intermediate results [ULLM82]. There may be different orders of operations implementing the same STBE query which can not be compared without considering the way relations are stored (such as the availability of indexes, the feasibility of sorting or constructing indexes) and different ways of implementing various operators (such as nested loops or sort-merge for joins).

The second step consists of generating the access plans that implement the query by considering the storage structures and different ways of implementing the operators involved. Finally, cost estimates of access plans are determined from the statistics kept in the data dictionary, and the one with the minimum cost is selected.

As in System R [GRIF79] and ABE [KLUG82b], STBE access paths are constructed from a basic set of access procedures and functions. The access procedures in System R (such as, sequential scan and indexed scan of a file, sort, merge scan of two files, etc.) are extended in ABE for aggregate function evaluation. In System R, the join of two relations, R1 and R2, is implemented by one of the two methods, the nested loops and the merge scan.

In ABE, two new procedures (one for nested loops and one for merge scan) are introduced to compute the aggregate functions while computing joins. In System R, the aggregate function is evaluated after the join is computed. Note that, this is one of the reasons why aggregations on empty partitions (such as, the number of houses in counties having no house with price > $100K in Example 6.1) do not appear in the output of a SQL query.

In System R, in computing joins of two relations, either one of the two relations can be the outer relation, which is decided by the cost estimates. However, in ABE and STBE, if a relation R1 in a subquery Q1 is to be joined with a relation R2 in a subquery Q2, where Q2 is a descendant subquery of Q1, then R1 must be the outer relation in computing the join of R1 and R2 for the correct evaluation of the query.

Another important difference between System R and ABE is that in System R access-path selection is done on a query-block basis [KLUG82b]. That is, first the order of evaluating query blocks is decided, and then access paths for each query block are determined separately. The correlation subqueries (i.e. a subquery with a reference to a higher level query block) are always re-evaluated for each candidate tuple in the higher level query block. This is very similar in effect to that of using nested loops as the only access path for joins of relations that are in different query blocks. In ABE, on the other hand, access-path selection is done for the whole query, and the merge scan access path as well as nested loops are possible candidates for joins of relations that are in different subqueries [KLUG82b]. This feature of ABE is also adopted in STBE.

For summary tables and set-valued relations in STBE, new storage structures and access procedures are required. The data dictionary contains schema information for summary tables and set-valued relations as well as for normalized relations. Storage for a summary-table instance consists of different structures for cell instances and category attribute tree instances that are related by the schema of the summary table. A category attribute forest is extended to a tree by a dummy root with a single instance so that a summary table can have at most two category attribute trees; one row, one column. For each such category attribute tree, one super instance is constructed and stored which contains every instance of the tree appearing in that summary table. Due to the root-to-leaf paths that are in the super instance of a category attribute tree but are not in a given instance of the tree, cell instances of the summary are extended by null entries. The cell instances are stored in the form of a compressed file [SHOS82]. Thus, storage is not wasted for null entries while non-null cell entries can be located by straightforward array index manipulations. Such a storage structure is especially useful when the summary table is large and the category attribute tree instances are largely overlapping.

When a summary table is referenced in an STBE query, first the portions of the summary table (in the units of primitive summary tables) that are used by the query are determined. Then relation instances that are information equivalent to these primitive summary tables are constructed. The operators to extract a primitive summary table and to construct the corresponding relation are given in [OZSO83c]. Access procedures for these operators are also included in STBE.

Storage structures for files with records having repeating groups (such as those discussed in [ULLM82]) can be used for storing set-valued relations. The problem arises when the key attribute(s) or the join attribute(s) are set-valued attributes. For efficient access of a set-valued relation through a set-valued attribute, we currently employ two methods. The first is an inverted index. For example, suppose A is a set-valued attribute in a relation R. Let D be the union of the A-components of tuples in the current instance of R. An index on D is constructed and used for attribute A. Given a value for A, the corresponding tuple(s) are located by first retrieving the pointers to tuples for all the elements of A and then forming the intersection of these pointers.

The second method is the use of a bit matrix. This method employs Bloom Filters [SEVE76]. The bit vector in differential files is extended to a two-dimensional bit matrix by using more than one hashing function.

8. CONCLUSION

We have presented a database query language, called Summary-Table-by-Example (STBE), that manipulates summary tables and relations with set-valued attributes. STBE is based on an extended relational calculus language that allows aggregate functions and set-valued relations.

Presently, the display manager and the access path selection routines for STBE are being implemented. We are also investigating ways to incorporate more advanced statistical procedures such as regression into STBE.

References

(ADAB80) (CODD72, see CODD72b) (GRIF79) (JACO82) (JAES82) (KLUG81) (KLUG82a) (KLUG82b) (OZSO83a) (OZSO83b) (OZSO83c) (OZSO83d) (OZSO84a) (SEVE76, see SEVE76b) (SHOS82) (SQL81) (STON76) (ULLM82) (USLB80) (ZLOO77)

Section VI

Techniques for Optimizing the Processing of Multiple Queries

Common Subexpression Isolation in Multiple Query Optimization

Matthias Jarke

Abstract: The simultaneous optimization of multiple queries submitted to a database system may lead to substantial savings over the current approach of optimizing each query separately. Isolating common subexpressions in multiple queries and treating their execution as a sharable resource are important prerequisites. This chapter presents techniques for recognizing, supporting, and exploiting common subexpressions in record-oriented, relational algebra, domain relational calculus, and tuple relational calculus query representations. It also investigates preconditions that transaction management mechanisms must satisfy to make multiple query optimization effective.

1.0 INTRODUCTION

The joint execution of batches of queries and update operations has been a standard technique in the conventional, record-at-a-time file systems of the sixties and early seventies. However, with the introduction of interactive database systems based on direct access to specific subsets of data, the research focus has changed towards optimizing individual, set-oriented data requests. With few exceptions, the art of multiple query processing has not survived the cultural jump from file to database processing. Recently, however, there has been renewed interest in exploiting the potential advantages of resource sharing in query optimization. Two concepts can be distinguished.

Batching. Sharing the cost of operations by jointly executing multiple queries submitted at approximately the same time is viable in a shared database, where a batch of queries can be composed and executed within reasonable response time limits (a few seconds [BARB83]), or in a non-interactive database programming environment. The sharing objective distinguishes batching from simple parallelism of data access, as investigated, e.g., in [CHES83].

Repetitive queries. (Partially) repetitive queries can share common resources even in a one-user environment if these resources (usually called access paths) are kept over an extended period of time. Speaking in business terms, we have an investment problem: the more queries will use a resource, the more initial investment is justified. Support for repetitive queries on a long-term scale, mostly through indexes, has been the focus of much research on the file system level, but less so for high-level queries.

One of the obstacles preventing a more extensive use of these opportunities in database systems has been uncertainty about what constitutes a sharable resource. This chapter assumes (the evaluation of) common subexpressions in queries to be the sharable resource and investigates methods for isolating and exploiting them. A subexpression is a part of a query that defines an intermediate result used during the process of query evaluation. In the relational framework adopted in this paper, subexpressions are defined in relational calculus or as results of relational algebra operations. For the sake of brevity, relational notations as introduced in [JARK84b] will not be repeated here.

In traditional file systems, where records are retrieved one-at-a-time, a query or update is simply defined by a particular key value. Common subexpressions are characterized by the same key value. Section 2 reviews multiple query optimization for such record-oriented systems. Section 3 motivates and defines more general common subexpressions. Sections 4 through 6 present specific methods for common subexpression representation and analysis in three popular query language environments: relational algebra, domain relational calculus (including languages such as QBE and Prolog), and tuple relational calculus (including languages such as SQL and QUEL). For the latter representation, a database programming language construct, called selector, is used to represent subexpressions and access paths supporting their execution.

Finally, section 7 briefly considers a new research problem resulting from multiple query optimization. If the scope of query optimization is extended beyond transaction boundaries, query evaluation strategies may interfere with concurrency control algorithms, leading to an inefficient overall architecture. The need for global transaction optimization integrates the two hitherto separated research areas of query optimization and concurrency control.

2.0 MULTIPLE QUERY OPTIMIZATION IN RECORD-ORIENTED SYSTEMS

In a traditional file system, each query retrieves at most one record, which is described by its file (relation) name and a unique key value. Many such systems are still in use, e.g., in banking applications or reservation systems, in which each user transaction addresses only one data object (e.g., bank account) at a time. One can represent a request for the record of relation 'rel' with the key value 'keyval' in an array-like notation [SCHM83],

rel[keyval].

For example, if social security number is the key for an employee file, a user may ask for 'employee[115-66-3331]'.

In a multiple query environment, information must be provided to determine, to which query the answer should be delivered. A query can be represented by a record

<userid, timestamp, opcode=read, rel[keyval]>.

Consequently, a batch of queries can be stored in a relation, the so-called 'transaction file'. The timestamps become important when the same user submits the same request several times, for example, because of intervening updates. However, we shall ignore this possibility for the moment and will return to it only in section 7.

Under what conditions is batching advantageous? In a paged random access environment, the main profit stems from clustering accesses to the same physical page. Little is gained by batching non-clustered queries which access different pages. (See [SHNE76] for a quantitative analysis of the worst case of random queries to a large file.) Two queries to a relation obviously access the same page if they request the same key value. Therefore, the transaction file should be grouped by relation names and key values; this is typically best achieved by sorting. Sorting has the side benefit of achieving optimal clustering if the database relation to be accessed is sorted by the same criteria (e.g., organized in some indexed sequential fashion).

If, on the other hand, sequential processing is necessary, batching almost always makes sense. As [SHNE76] demonstrate, the expected savings factor of processing a batch of k queries together rather than separately can be approximated by 1-2/(k+1) for large files. For example, a batch of just five queries will already lead to savings of about 66.7%, as compared to evaluating each of them separately: each of the five queries, separately processed, will require scanning about 1/2 of the file (for a total of 5/2 file scans), whereas only 5/6 of the file have to be scanned on the average to retrieve five (randomly selected) elements.

The advantages of batching in average processing time per query generally grow with batch size, in particular with the size of clusters (i.e., the number of accesses to the same page). On the other hand, batch size is limited by the maximum response time acceptable for the first queries submitted to the batch, as well as by storage constraints.

3.0 GENERALIZED COMMON SUBEXPRESSIONS

The key-oriented techniques for multiple query processing do not easily generalize to queries retrieving more than one record. In principle, one can decompose a set-oriented query into many record-oriented ones. For multiple query optimization, however, this approach has major disadvantages:

Unless secondary indexes are available, the set of key values for each query is unknown before accessing the database, and hence the comparison of key values cannot be used to determine sharable accesses. One might argue that unknown key values usually require sequential scans, which should make multiple query optimization even more desirable. However, there is now a 'distribution' problem: it is not known in advance, to which of the queries in a batch a certain record will be relevant. Therefore, sharing is limited to the original scan of base data -- none of the intermediate results required for processing complex queries can be shared. This problem arises even if the key set for each query can be enumerated (e.g., because secondary indexes are available).

The solution adopted in this chapter involves access abstraction mechanisms [SCHM83], which reduce the problem of recognizing common physical access requirements to the simpler task of identifying common logical access paths, i.e., subexpressions. Common <u>sub</u>expressions will be used since one can hardly expect two queries to address exactly the same set of tuples as in the record-oriented case.

A few definitions are needed at this point. We define a <u>query</u> as a relation-valued language expression, that is, the evaluation of a query, q, maps a database state into a relation V(q), the <u>value</u> or result of the query. The <u>readset</u>, S(q), of a query is the set of all data to be accessed during the evaluation of q. Note, that S(q) depends on data structures and query evaluation algorithms, whereas V(q) depends only on the state of the database. Let Q = [q1, ..., qn] be a set of queries. Then, a query, c, with non-empty value is called a <u>common subexpression</u> of Q if S(c) is a subset of the intersection of all the S(qi), i = 1, ..., n.

An <u>access path</u> is the value of a query or of a set of queries; access paths are used to support the evaluation of other queries. For example, a secondary index represents the set of results of those queries that ask for all relation elements with a given value in the indexed attribute; the use of the index provides a fast way to process other queries that contain queries on the indexed attribute as subexpressions. Often, access paths are stored in a specific representation form to avoid redundancy and reduce maintenance problems. However, the special representation is usually invisible to the user who just experiences better performance for certain queries. A language construct for the abstract representation of access paths based on this observation will be introduced in section 6.

An access path defined by a query, ap, is applicable to the evaluation of a subexpression, se, if S(se) is a subset of S(ap), or -- in other words -- if the selection predicate of se implies the selection predicate of ap. In this case, we also say somewhat loosely that ap is applicable to a query containing se.

These definitions are very general. The detection of common subexpressions or of the applicability of access paths may be computationally intractable or even undecidable if arbitrary subexpressions are considered. Of course, in a finite database, one can always detect common subexpressions 'after the fact', i.e., by tracing the query execution. But that does not help in ex-ante query optimization where one would like to analyze the query rather than its value. Most published procedures follow a two-step heuristic: (a) decompose each query into a (partially ordered) set of 'suitable' subexpressions, and (b) identify common subexpressions and applicable access paths. What constitutes a 'suitable' subexpression depends on the query language. The next sections discuss three popular representation forms for relational expressions, i.e., algebra, domain calculus, and tuple calculus.

As a running example, we shall use a simplified version of the infection control database in a hospital. Such databases are used for tracing the flow of infecting organisms in case of epidemics, and for identifying persons under risk of infection. A patient is characterized by the ward he/she is located in, by the day of surgery, by observed symptoms indicating an infection, and by the quantity of pathogenic organisms isolated from certain sites of the human body (e.g., surgical wounds, the blood, or the respiratory tract). Employees are characterized by their status (e.g., doctor, nurse, administration) and assigned ward, as well as by their assignment to operating teams on certain days. The schema consists of seven relations:

```
patient  (pname, ward)
isolated (pname, organism, site, qty)
observed (pname, symptom)
relevant (symptom, site)
employee (ename, status, ward)
surgery  (pname, day)
opteam   (ename, day)
```

4.0 COMMON SUBEXPRESSION ANALYSIS IN RELATIONAL ALGEBRA

In relational algebra notation, a single algebra operation is the natural unit of interest. A more complex subexpression corresponds to a sequence of operations. Since an operation is meaningful only if all of its inputs are known, common subexpression detection is a bottom-up procedure, collapsing common subtrees in the operator tree for the algebra query. This procedure, introduced in [HALL76] for single query optimization, can be extended to multiple query optimization by considering a set of operator trees.

As an example, consider the queries: "which wards are members of the Monday operating team assigned to?", and: "what doctors were on the Monday operating team?" Figure 4-1(a) demonstrates collapsing common subtrees for operator trees corresponding to query formulations which follow the heuristic of moving restrictions as far down as possible [SMIT75]. Only the common restriction of opteam by 'day=monday' can be shared in this case. This shows that an unfortunate sequencing of operations may prevent the detection of larger common subexpressions. In Figure 4-1(b), the restriction on employee in the second query has been moved upward beyond the join, such that the sharable subexpression includes the join operation. It is not easy to find a query standardization that automates such algebra transformations. [HALL76] presents some heuristics. In other cases, collapsing small common subexpressions in the beginning of the procedure may prevent the detection of larger ones later on.

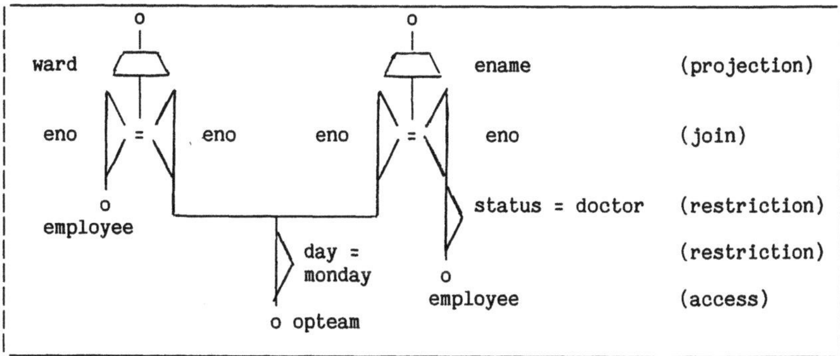

Figure 4-1(a): A simple common algebra subexpression

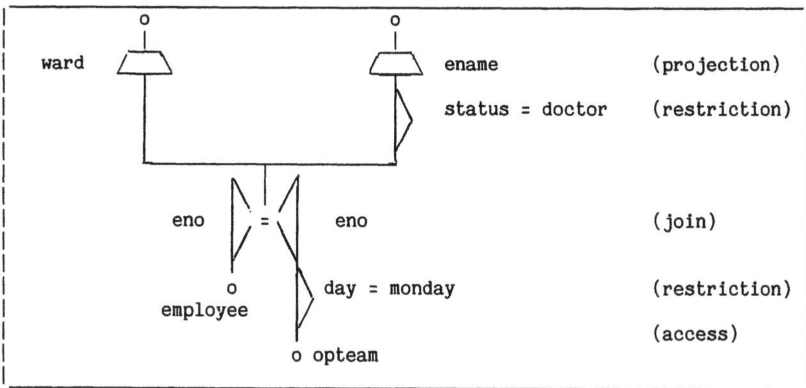

Figure 4-1(b): A better common subexpression

5.0 COMMON SUBEXPRESSION ANALYSIS IN DOMAIN RELATIONAL CALCULUS

Predicate calculus representations offer more control over the level of abstraction, on which common subexpressions can be defined. Domain calculus is used in connection with logic programming, for instance, if Prolog is used as a database language [KOWA81]. In this representation, variables range over attribute domains, and relations are represented as predicates. Relation values are defined as sets of assertions that look like the example schema provided in section 3. An arbitrary hierarchy of parameterized and maybe recursive view definitions can be superimposed on the original database relations through the use of Horn clauses with variables. For example, in the infection database, Prolog definitions of the concepts of an infected patient, and of personnel contact with a patient look as follows:

A patient is said to be infected at a certain body site if pathogenic organisms have been isolated there or relevant symptoms have been observed.

```
infected(Pname, Site) :- isolated(Pname, Organism, Site, Qty).
infected(Pname, Site) :- observed(Pname, Symptom),
                         relevant(Symptom, Site).
```

A employee is said to have been in contact with a patient, if he/she was either on an operating team the same day the patient had an operation, or he/she is a nurse assigned to the patient's ward.

```
contact(Ename, Pname) :- opteam(Ename, Day),
                         surgery(Pname, Day).
contact(Ename, Pname) :- employee(Ename, nurse, Ward),
                         patient(Pname, Ward).
```

In these parameterized view definitions, variable names begin with capital letters and constants begin with lower-case letters. Variables are used to store parts of the relations implicitly, or to represent subsets of stored relations. For example, an assertion

```
relevant(fever, Site).
```

means that fever is a relevant symptom for infections at any site, since the variable 'Site' can assume arbitrary values. A concatenation of predicates by a comma indicates AND-connection; the repetition of a left-hand side predicate indicates that one or the other definition may apply, i.e., OR-connection of the right-hand sides.

A query is an expression consisting of the symbol ':-', followed by AND/OR-connected predicates which refer either to views or directly to base relations. Consider first the case where there are no recursive view definitions applying to the set of queries. Following the two-step heuristic mentioned in section 3, each query is first standardized into disjunctive normal form, i.e., into a set of conjunctive queries to base relations. More than one submitted request will just result in a larger set of conjunctive queries.

To simplify subsequent steps, the query set is then partitioned into components such that the readsets of queries in different components are disjoint. The simplest way to guarantee this is to partition the set of queries by the relations they access [GRAN81]. Within each component, common subexpressions among the queries are identified as follows.

Each query within a component is a conjunction of predicates, where each predicate corresponds to access to one relation. Common subexpressions have to contain at least common predicate (= relation) names. Thus, for each pair of queries, we just have to test if pairs of predicates with common relation names are equivalent. In fact, we can test for containment, rather than for exact equivalence, and use the result of one subexpression as an access path for evaluating the other subexpression [GRAN81]. (Similar methods have also been used to optimize tableaux for non-conjunctive queries [SAGI80].)

To illustrate the above procedure, consider the three view queries:

R1. "what patients with Monday surgery have wound infections?"
```
:- infected(Who, wound), surgery(Who, monday).
```

R2. "what patients had the same organisms isolated as Smith?"
```
:- isolated(smith, Commorg, Site1, Qty1),
   isolated(Pat,   Commorg, Site2, Qty2).
```

R3. "who was in contact with wound-infected patients?"
```
:- infected(Infpat, wound), contact(Pers, Infpat).
```

Using the view definitions given above, the translation of these view queries into queries to the base relations given in section 3 yields the seven conjunctive queries listed below. Q1 and Q2 come from R1, Q3 from R2, and the remaining four queries are derived from R3.

```
Q1. :- isolated(Who, Organism, wound, Qty), surgery(Who, monday).
Q2. :- observed(Who, Symptom), relevant(Symptom, wound),
       surgery(Who, monday).
Q3. :- isolated(smith, Commorg, Site1, Qty1),
       isolated(Pat,   Commorg, Site2, Qty2).
Q4. :- isolated(Infpat, Organism, wound, Qty),
       surgery(Infpat, Day), opteam(Pers, Day).
Q5. :- isolated(Infpat, Organism, wound, Qty),
       patient(Infpat, Ward), employee(Pers, nurse, Ward).
Q6. :- observed(Infpat, Symptom), relevant(Symptom, wound),
       surgery(Infpat, Day), opteam(Pers, Day).
Q7. :- observed(Infpat, Symptom), relevant(Symptom, wound),
       patient(Infpat, Ward), employee(Pers, nurse, Ward).
```

All seven queries form one component and are therefore candidates for simultaneous query optimization. Common subexpressions can be identified by comparing predicates with equal names: (a) The first predicate of Q1 is equivalent to the first predicates of Q4 and Q5, and its value is a subset of the value of the second predicate of Q3; (b) Similarly, the conjunction of the first two predicates of Q2 also appears in Q6 and Q7; (c) the surgery predicates in Q1 and Q2 are identical; (d) the second rows of queries Q4 and Q6, as well as of Q5 and Q7 are sharable.

Could we have detected the common subexpressions more efficiently? Yes; we could have predicted many of the common subexpressions by comparing the original view queries directly. For example, that R1 and R3 have a lot in common is obvious from the common predicate 'infected(X, wound)'. This observation could have reduced the set of queries to be investigated. A more systematic analysis of this view-oriented approach will be presented in section 6.3.

An additional opportunity for multiple query optimization by common subexpression analysis, not found in the other two representations used in this chapter, presents itself in the evaluation of queries that are defined on recursive views. Assume that our infection control database contains a base relation 'met(Gname, Sname)' which describes the fact that an individual named Gname met a potential carrier of pathogenic organisms, named Sname. Note, that the Sname--Gname relationship must be hierarchical (i.e., it may not contain cycles) to be evaluable with the depth-first approach of Prolog. We can now define the risk that organisms have been transmitted from a person another one recursively as

```
risk(Pname, Gname) :- met(Gname, Pname),
                      infected(Pname, Anysite).
risk(Pname, Gname) :- met(Gname, Intermediate),
                      risk(Intermediate, Pname).
```

One can now ask for persons exposed to risk by a particular patient, or for the patients putting a particular person at risk. In both cases, the query evaluation generates a sequence of queries, in which each subsequent query contains the previous one as a subquery. For example, the query,

```
:- risk(smith, Gname),
```

is evaluated by the sequence of non-recursive database queries

```
:- met(Gname, smith), infected(smith, Site).
:- met(Gname, C1),
   met(C1, smith), infected(smith, Site).
:- met(Gname, C1),
   met(C1, C2), met(C2, smith), infected(smith, Site).
etc.
```

Each query appears as the second part of the following one; vice versa, the evaluation of each query can use the result of the previous one [JARK84a]. Additionally, it is possible to rephrase recursive queries in a manner that keeps the size of intermediate results small [MARQ84]. A detailed discussion of these approaches, as well as of a large number of additional problems related to recursive query processing, is beyond the scope of this paper; more material can be found in [MINK83] and [HENS84].

6.0 COMMON SUBEXPRESSION ANALYSIS IN TUPLE CALCULUS

6.1 Nested Expressions And The Selector Language Construct

In the tuple relational calculus representation as used in [JARK84b], an interesting set of subexpressions can be generated using range-nested expressions. Recall that the following transformations can be applied to generate nested expressions where p1 and p2 are predicates [JARK83].

```
[EACH r IN rel: p1 AND p2]     <==> [EACH r IN [EACH r IN rel: p1]: p2]
 SOME r IN rel (p1 AND p2)     <==>  SOME r IN [EACH r IN rel: p1] (p2)
  ALL r IN rel (NOT(p1) OR p2) <==>   ALL r IN [EACH r IN rel: p1] (p2)
```

Here, we shall not deal with universally quantified variables. Therefore, we can assume without loss of generality that all queries are conjunctive. Each of the inner nestings represents a potential common subexpression. For the definition of access paths, there is a need to abstract from specific subexpressions. A language construct called <u>selector</u> [MALL84] serves as an abstract representation of subexpressions and their access paths. Let

```
EACH r IN rel:  p(r, s1, ..., sm, t1, ..., tn)
```

be a relational expression where p is a well-formed formula of the relational calculus in which quantified variables t1, ..., tn appear. The s1, ..., sm are formal parameters representing constants in terms of the selection predicate. A selector sp representing the subexpression can be declared in a function-like fashion [1]:

```
SELECTOR sp(s1, ..., sm) FOR rel;
BEGIN
  EACH r IN rel: p(r, s1, ..., sm, t1, ..., tn)
END;
```

Selectors are used in selected variables that appear in relation-valued expressions, using an array-like notation

```
rel[sp(S1, ..., Sm)],
```

where the Si are actual parameter values. For example, the notation 'rel[keyval]', which was introduced in section 2 for identifying single tuples in relations, uses an implicitly defined key selector,

```
SELECTOR sk(keyval) FOR rel;
BEGIN
 EACH r IN rel: r.key = keyval
END;
```

[1] The actual selector definition originally introduced in [MALL84], [SCHM83] refers to relation types instead of relation variables. In the query optimization context considered in this paper, however, the simpler notation presented here is sufficient.

Selectors have two uses in multiple query optimization: naming common subexpressions and supporting their evaluation. From a language viewpoint, a selector can be regarded as the definition of a (possibly parameterized) view, similar to the ones we saw in the domain calculus examples. However, from a system's viewpoint, a selector can also be perceived as the abstract representation of an access path, that -- if provided with appropriate parameters -- returns a set of relation elements. Following the definitions given in section 3, we say that a selector is applicable to a subquery, if actual parameters S1, ..., Sm can be found, such that the predicate of the subquery implies the selection expression of the selector, with S1, ..., Sm substituted for the formal parameters. Furthermore, we say that a selector is supported if an actual physical access path has been created for all queries represented by the selector definition.

Since testing applicability is undecidable in general first-order predicate calculus, and computationally intractable even in some cases where it is decidable [ROSE80], we shall explore several classes of selectors (and consequently of nested subexpressions), for which efficient tests or good heuristics are known.

Selectors can be classified by the values of m and n in the above definition. First, selectors without parameters (m=0) will be investigated; they correspond to traditional database views. This discussion will be subdivided into the cases of extended range expressions (n=0, section 6.2) and general nested expressions (n>0, section 6.3). Afterwards, selectors with parameters (m>0) will be analyzed (section 6.4). This discussion will be brief since one part of it is covered by the other subsections, another part is covered by the literature on index selection, and the remainder is largely unresearched.

6.2 Common Extended Range Expressions

The early execution of one-variable operations, such as restriction and projection, is a well-known heuristic for query transformation [SMIT75], [WONG76]. In the relational calculus framework, this has been modeled by introducing nested expressions that extend the range definition of variables from simple relation names to relational expressions (i.e., queries) that contain restrictive terms over the base relation [JARK82]. Consider the following three queries and their disjunctive prenex normal form representation in Pascal/R [SCHM80]:

R4. "what analyses yielded more than 1000 organisms/ml?"

```
[EACH i IN isolated: i.qty > 1000]
```

R5. "what patients of which wards had at least 2000 organisms isolated?"

```
[EACH p IN patient: SOME i IN isolated
     (p.pname = i.pname AND i.qty >= 2000)]
```

R6. "list doctors in wards with patients who had fever in connection with the isolation of at least 2000 organisms in wounds."

```
[EACH e IN employees:
 SOME o IN observed SOME p IN patient SOME i IN isolated
  (e.ward = p.ward AND p.pname = o.pname AND i.pname = p.pname
   AND o.symptom = fever AND i.qty >= 2000 AND i.site = wound)]
```

Applying the nesting transformation given in section 6.1 converts the two queries R5 and R6 to:

```
R5'. [EACH p IN patient:
      SOME o IN [EACH i IN isolated: i.qty >= 2000]
          (o.pname = p.pname)]

Q6'. [EACH d IN [EACH e IN employees: e.status = doctor]:
      SOME f IN [EACH o IN observed: o.symptom = fever]
       SOME p IN patient
        SOME w2 IN [EACH i IN isolated:
                         i.qty >= 2000 AND i.site = wound]
       (w2.pname = p.pname AND p.pname = f.pname AND p.ward = e.ward)]
```

Nested expressions are conveniently represented by object graphs [FINK82], [JARK83]. Each inner expression corresponds to a node, and each join term corresponds to an edge. Thus, while R4 is represented by only one node, R5' and R6' are represented by trees with two respectively four nodes (figure 6-1).

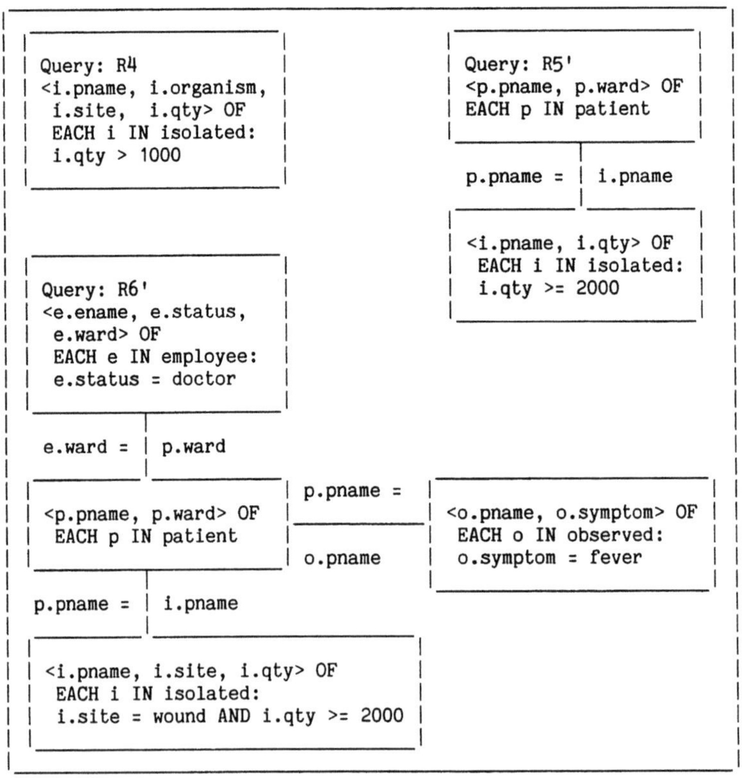

Figure 6-1: Query graphs for extended range expressions

Users often refer to previous queries; for example, the infection control nurse might 'zoom in' on the objects of interest by issuing a sequence of queries R4 to R6. [FINK82] therefore suggests storing object graph representation and query value -- V(q) in the notation of section 3, not s(q)! -- of certain queries in a buffer to be used for evaluating subsequent queries.

Consider first single-node queries such as R4. Such queries are of interest, not only because they occur frequently, but also because most indexes in database systems can be regarded as collections of query results of this type. The stored value of a one-variable query can be used directly as an access path for a new one if two preconditions are satisfied: (a) the selection expression of the new query implies the one of the stored query; (b) the output attributes of the stored query are a superset of the attributes appearing anywhere in the new query. For example, R4 can be used directly for evaluating the second node of R5 since 'i.qty >= 2000' implies 'i.qty > 1000' and both attributes of the relation 'isolated' appearing in R5 also appear in the output of R4.

When condition (b) is violated, using the stored query may still be justified, but a 'backjoin' is required between the stored query result and the base relation to recover missing attribute values. This would happen, for instance, if R4 only requested patient names. The join with a stored relation may be cost-justified if there are fast access paths to perform the backjoin. The backjoin problem may also occur in multi-node queries. The set of patients retrieved in R5' is clearly a superset of the ones retrieved for R6'. However, since the site attribute does not appear in the output of R5', a backjoin of the query value V(R5') with the relation 'isolated' is required.

[FINK82] does not perform general implication tests for multi-node queries (such tests are studied in [MUNZ79] and [ROSE80]) but uses a heuristic, which not necessarily detects all stored query results usable for a given query. In addition, the algorithm also determines eventual backjoins, and compares their costs to the savings expected from using the old query value as an access path. However, [FINK82] does not assume exact foresight of the query optimizer in terms of what future queries to expect.

6.3 Common Nested Expressions

In processing batches of queries, such precise knowledge does exist. Common subexpressions can be supported in a pre-planned fashion by defining appropriate selectors and creating physical access paths supporting them. For example, the batch R4, R5, R6 of the previous subsection could be supported by the selector

```
S1.  SELECTOR org1000 FOR isolated;
     BEGIN
      EACH i IN isolated: i.qty > 1000
     END;
```

This reduces R4 to a single access to an existing query result via the selector

```
     isolated[org1000]
```

and improves the performance of the other queries accordingly. However, it is obvious that the limitation of selector definitions to one-variable expressions does not permit the level of sophistication required for multi-relation queries. This subsection will therefore consider more general selector definitions. For example, with the additional definition of a selector

```
S2.  SELECTOR pat2000 FOR patient;
     BEGIN
      EACH p IN patient: SOME i IN isolated
                          (i.qty >= 2000 AND i.pname = p.pname)
     END;
```

query R6' can be replaced by (notice the backjoin between pi and wi)

```
[EACH doc IN [EACH e IN employees: e.status = doctor]:
 SOME fev IN [EACH o IN observed: o.symptom = fever]
  SOME pi IN patient[org2000]
   SOME wi IN [EACH i IN isolated: i.site = wound]
  (wi.pname = pi.pname AND pi.pname = fev.pname AND pi.ward = doc.ward)]
```

Even this notation is not completely satisfactory since it does not show that one selector can be used to improve the evaluation of another one. We therefore introduce several levels of nesting in selectors.

```
S2'. SELECTOR pat2000 FOR patient : ...;
     BEGIN
      EACH p IN patient: SOME i IN isolated[org1000]
                           (i.qty >= 2000 AND i.pname = p.pname)
     END;
```

Many selectors could be defined for supporting any given query. One can generate these selectors by applying the general range nesting transformations given in section 6.1. In terms of the object graph representation (Figure 6-1), multi-variable selectors can be defined for any subgraph that does not contain the target nodes and is connected to the rest of the query graph by a single edge. For example, in query R6', we could define one selector containing the patient/observed subgraph, one containing the patient/isolated subgraph, or one that contains all three nodes.

All queries in a batch can be described by partially ordered sets of selectors, using a uniform naming scheme for equivalent selectors. The system can then identify common selectors among queries. This looks very similar to the algebra approach of section 4. An important difference is that it is not necessary to trace all possible sequences of operations if other means exist for establishing equivalence among subexpressions.

A similar structure has been proposed as a logical access path schema for database design [ROUS82b]. Roussopoulos introduces an object graph that is the exact complement to an algebra operator graph; that is, the nodes represent the results of algebraic operations and groups of edges the operations themselves. [ROUS82b] presents algorithms similar to [HALL76] but goes further by assigning a weight to each node, based on the frequency of reference to the corresponding selector in a set of queries. The higher the weight, the more profitable is the creation of a special physical access path to support the selector. The latter method is called "view indexing" in [ROUS82a].

6.4 Common Query Structures

The disadvantage of access paths defined through parameter-free selectors as described in the previous two subsections is that they essentially represent only one (sub)query. The usual understanding of indexes is quite different: the exact query is defined by specifying a certain parameter value. For example, most users of the infection control database may be interested only in one type of infecting organism at a time but this type may differ from query to query. Therefore, it pays to define a selector corresponding to a secondary index:

```
SELECTOR the-organism(ORG) FOR isolated;
BEGIN
 EACH i IN isolated: i.organism = ORG
END;
```

A query requesting wards where Klebsiella bacteria were found would then be converted to something like:

```
[<kp.ward> OF EACH kp IN patient:
            SOME k IN isolated[the-organism('klebsiella')]
               (k.pname = kp.pname)]
```

While secondary indexes such as this one are available in most database systems, the selector definition can be more general. For example, if one is always interested in the patients from whom an organism was isolated in certain quantities rather than in the isolation itself, one can define and support a selector, the definition of which spans more than one relation.

```
SELECTOR with-org(ORG, QMIN, QMAX) FOR patient;
BEGIN
 EACH p IN patient: SOME i IN isolated
     (p.pname = i.pname AND i.organism = ORG AND
      i.qty >= QMIN AND i.qty <= QMAX)
END;
```

Obviously, definition and maintenance of such a selector require more sophisticated data structures and algorithms than conventional one-dimensional indexes [NIEV84].

The detection of subexpressions that are supportable by a particular parameterized selector hardly differs from the non-parameterized case; in all places where the formal parameter appears in the selector definition, any domain value may appear in the corresponding position of the query to make the selector applicable.

On the other hand, the problem of choosing a good set of parameterized selectors to be supported by physical access paths is much more difficult than for non-parameterized ones. For single-attribute selectors, and even for general one-variable selectors, the literature on index selection (see [MARC84]) applies. For multiple variable selectors, however, one faces the double problem of choosing a good level of abstraction, and of deciding which query conditions should be parameterized. No solution to this problem is known as of this writing, but several heuristics based on the range nesting procedure of [JARK83] are under study.

7.0 MULTIPLE QUERY OPTIMIZATION AND TRANSACTION MANAGEMENT

When we reviewed batched query processing in record-oriented systems, we excluded update operations from the discussion. In reality, this separation often cannot be accepted; queries and updates may be combined in transactions submitted by the same user or by multiple users. This may lead to problems like inconsistent reads or lost updates which have to be prevented by concurrency control mechanisms [ESWA76].

The only requirement supported by almost all concurrency control methods is serializability, i.e., the outcome of a set of concurrently running transactions has to be equivalent to that of some serial execution of the transactions. Therefore, read and write accesses can follow each other in arbitrary sequence if each transaction concerns only one access to one record. Alternatively, record-oriented file systems often combine batched update with interactive retrieval; the file system is locked completely during the update process. However, certain backout mechanisms for erroneous update transactions have to be provided even in this case [ARDI79].

Once more, consideration of more complex common subexpressions complicates the problem. This section summarizes additional research questions that have to be answered if multiple query optimization is to be integrated into an transaction processing environment that includes interactive update operations.

Consider first a one-user environment (or one in which each user transaction is completely shielded from the others by exclusive locking mechanisms). In such an environment, multiple query optimization is possible only within transactions which consist of more than one query. [HEVN81] studied the influence of general programming language constructs, such as conditional statements and loops, on the composition of query sets to be optimized jointly. As a simple example, consider the following program:

```
IF cond1 THEN Q1; Q2
         ELSIF cond2 THEN Q2; Q3
                     ELSE Q1; Q3
```

Although each query appears twice in the program, any of them will be executed at most once. Creating sophisticated access paths, cost-justified only by multiple usage of any one query, would be a waste of resources.

A second problem in the one-user context is addressed in [KIM81]: the interference of update operations with queries. If the value of a subexpression is changed, the value of queries before and after the update operation will be different. Common subexpressions are defined in [KIM81] on the relation level. As an example, consider a database program that works with queries Qi and altering operations Ai on two relations, R1 and R2:

```
Q1.R1;
A1.R1; A2.R2;
Q2.R1 (Q3.R2);
Q4.R2
```

One can optimize Q3 and Q4 simultaneously but not Q1 and Q2. It is, however, feasible to optimize Q1 and the read part of A1 jointly. Notice that it is quite possible that the actual write set of A1 may be disjoint from the read sets of Q1 and Q2; a detailed analysis of common subexpressions going below the relation level may confirm this.

This argument carries over to the multi-user case. It is well known in concurrency control theory that finer granularity of locks can result in more concurrency [GRAY75], [RIES77]. To identify potential conflicts on a subrelation level, the first requirement is therefore that query optimization and concurrency control mechanisms use the same language, i.e., that predicative concurrency control methods are employed [ESWA76], [REIM83]. Moreover, the focus of multiple query optimization is on sharing rather than just parallelism of data access. Therefore, the introduction of multiple query optimization on a global level creates new problems of integrating query optimization and concurrency control mechanisms.

In the locking approach to concurrency control, shared locks have been proposed to increase concurrency [KEDE83] but sharing is not supported actively. On the other hand, optimistic methods [KUNG81], [REIM83] assume that conflicts are unlikely to occur and validate transactions ex-post; hence, full global query optimization is possible. However, a whole batch of transactions may have to be repeated if one of them cannot be validated.

More flexible scheduling strategies combining locking and optimistic methods are required [BRAE83]. For example, in order to create a safe environment for multiple query optimization, one can schedule read transactions pessimistically (i.e., use locking) while allowing altering transactions to run optimistically.

In addition, we are investigating strategies on the query optimization side that limit the damage done by transaction abortion without sacrificing correctness. Finally, the use of multiversion databases [BERN83] is considered in this context. A radical solution based on multiple versions completely decouples read and write transactions. It allows queries to access only data versions guaranteed to be too old to have been created by any currently active transaction. However, such an extreme solution is hardly acceptable in general.

8.0 SUMMARY AND CONCLUSION

Extending multiple query processing from record handling systems to set-oriented database systems is based on the recognition of and support for common subexpressions in queries. The review of three different language types for relational queries showed that common subexpression analysis is not very hard if only one-relation subexpressions are considered and appropriate tools exist for isolating them. Common multi-relation subexpressions can only be addressed in a heuristic manner. More powerful heuristics, made possible through the introduction of programming language abstractions, allow more than detecting common subexpressions in a purely bottom-up fashion. Where simplistic radical solutions for concurrency control are not acceptable, multiple query optimization requires integrating the hitherto separate areas of query optimization and concurrency control, with the final goal of developing a unified optimization concept for database implementation.

Acknowledgments

The author is grateful to Richard Braegger, Henning Eckhardt, Manuel Reimer, Juergen Koch, and Joachim Schmidt for stimulating discussions, and to the editors for their detailed comments on a previous draft of this paper.

References

(ARDI79) (BARB83) (BERN83) (BRAE83) (CHAK82) (CHES83) (ESWA76)
(FINK82) (GRAN81) (GRAY75) (HALL76) (HENS84) (HEVN81) (JARK82)
(JARK83) (JARK84a, see JARK84b) (JARK84b, see JARK84c) (KEDE83)
(KIM81) (KOWA81) (MALL84) (MARC84) (MARQ84) (MINK83) (MUNZ79)
(NIEV84) (REIM83) (RIES77) (ROSE80) (ROUS82a) (ROUS82b) (SAGI80)
(SCHM80) (SCHM83) (SHNE76) (SMIT75) (WONG76)

Global Optimization of Relational Queries: A First Step

Won Kim

ABSTRACT

Query-processing subsystems in current relational database systems only attempt to minimize the cost of processing single queries. One way to significantly lower the cost of processing a set of queries is to simultaneously process queries which reference the same relation(s). Such a strategy requires global knowledge of the characteristics of the database and the given set of queries. This knowledge makes it possible to determine not only the queries which are amenable to simultaneous processing, but also a near-optimal set of secondary indexes and sorted copies of relations for processing the set of queries.

This chapter first explores opportunities and limitations in exploiting global knowledge. Then it considers a first-cut strategy for global optimization of a set of SQL queries and data manipulation statements. It is expected that the use of such a strategy will result in considerable reduction in the cost of processing a program which contains a fairly large number of 'similar' queries.

1. INTRODUCTION

Query-processing subsystems (optimizers) in current relational database systems attempt to minimize the cost of processing a set of queries sequentially (one query at a time). The cost of sequentially processing a set of n queries is simply the sum of the costs of processing each of the n queries. Processing queries sequentially is usually appropriate for online, interactive uses of a database system. However, this approach may not be suitable for batch processing of queries embedded in conventional high-level, algorithmic programming languages. It may also be inefficient for processing a set of queries which may be explicitly issued as a unit by the user in interactive mode or which may be automatically triggered to check for possible violation of integrity constraints when the user issues a data manipulation statement (update, insert, or delete) [ESWA75, HAMM75, STON75, HAMM78].

One way to significantly lower the cost of processing a set of queries is to simultaneously process queries which reference the same relation(s) when the relation(s) are fetched. Such a strategy requires global knowledge of the characteristics of a given set of queries. Global knowledge of internal database and query characteristics makes it possible to determine a reasonable set of secondary indexes and sorted copies of relations for sequentially processing queries in conventional systems. Further, such knowledge is essential in determining how to group and sequence a given set of queries for simultaneous processing. This chapter examines various issues which arise in developing a global optimization strategy based on simultaneous evaluation of groups of SQL queries [BOYC74, CHAM76].

The symbols used in this chapter are summarized below.

Ri	a relation in the database
Ck	a column of a relation
Qj	a query
Qj.Ri	a query which references Ri
Mj	a data manipulation statement
Mj.Ri	a data manipulation statement on Ri
Pi	size in pages of Ri
Pri	size in pages of the result of a query on Ri
Pxi	size in pages of the portion of Ri which must be retrieved to evaluate a query on Ri

Qri size in pages of the result of Qi
Qxi size in pages of the portion of relations and indexes which must be retrieved to evaluate Qi

The remainder of this chapter is organized as follows. The basic global optimization strategy is outlined in Section 2. Section 3 develops a number of simple rules that guide the strategy. Section 4 describes how these rules are used to derive algorithms for grouping queries for simultaneous processing. Access paths for evaluating groups of queries are considered in Section 5. Section 6 provides a general summary of a global optimization strategy which incorporates the ideas explored in Sections 3, 4 and 5.

2. BASIC STRATEGY

Database application programs in general consist of a sequence of queries and data manipulation statements expressed in high-level, nonprocedural data languages such as SQL [CHAM76] and QUEL [STON76]. Global consideration of a set of queries makes it possible to amortize not only the costs of retrieving relations and indexes, but also the costs of dynamically creating indexes and sorting relations. The following two examples should make this clear.

Example 1. Consider two single-relation queries, Q1 and Q2, which reference relation R1 that occupies P1 data pages. Suppose Q1 requires tuples of R1 whose C1 column values are X, and Q2 requires tuples whose C1 column values are Y. In the absence of an index on the C1 column of R1, conventional systems require 2 * P1 page fetches to process Q1 and Q2. It may be possible, however, to retrieve R1 once and process Q1 and Q2 simultaneously. The cost of processing the two queries is then P1 page fetches.

Example 2. Suppose the tuples of R1 which satisfy Q1 of Example 1 reside on P1/10 data pages and the tuples which satisfy Q2 are also found on P1/10 pages. It takes roughly P1 page fetches to create an index on the C1 column of R1. Of course, it does not make sense for conventional systems to create an index to process a single-relation query. However, once the index is created, it can be repeatedly used to reduce the cost of processing other single-relation queries. The cost of processing the two queries is P1 + 2*P1/10 = 1.2 * P1 page fetches, ignoring the index page fetches.

The above examples suggest a two-stage strategy for optimizing a set of queries and data manipulation statements. This is summarized in Fig. 1. The first stage, the **compile stage**, performs an analysis of query and database characteristics. It consists of two phases. The first phase, phase C-1, determines an optimal set of indexes and sorted copies of relations, while the second phase, phae C-2, derives an optimal grouping of queries and data manipulation statements for simultaneous processing. The compile-time analysis of queries can make use of the access paths determined by the conventional single-query optimizers.

The second stage, the **run stage**, executes the program which contains the set of queries and data manipulation statements. This stage also consists of two phases. During the first phase, phase R-1, each group of queries and data manipulation statements selected for simultaneous processing is executed in the order determined during the compile stage. The results of the preprocessed queries are stored on the disk and the initial program is modified to replace all preprocessed queries by the references to their stored results. During the next phase, phase R-2, the modified program is run in order to process those queries which may have been excluded from processing during phase R-1 and to further process and output the results of the preprocessed queries.

During phase R-1 the main-memory buffer is partitioned into three areas: input buffers, output buffers, and the program area. The input buffers are to hold the data pages that contain tuples of the relation(s) and secondary indexes on the relation(s). The program area is to hold all the procedures required for processing a given set of queries simultaneously. The output buffers are to hold the results of the queries until they are written to the disk.

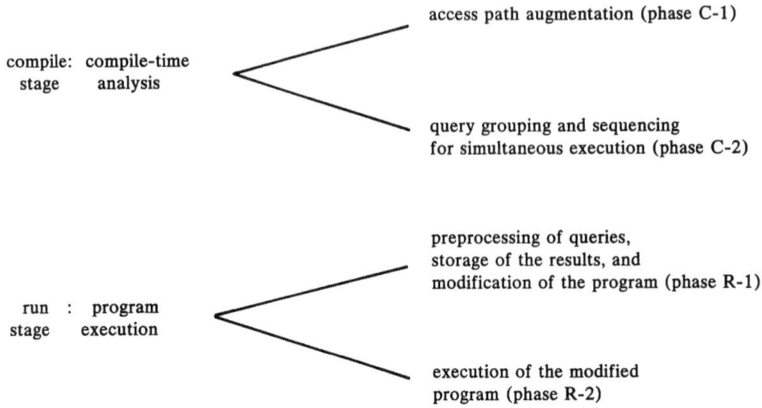

Fig. 1 A strategy for processing a set of queries

3. RULES FOR PREPROCESSING QUERIES

This section explores some fundamental questions that arise in developing a global-optimization strategy based on the simultaneous preprocessing of queries. Consideration of these questions will lead to a number of rules, which in turn will guide the development of the first-order strategy for global optimization of queries in the next sections.

First, consider two single-relation queries Q1 and Q2 which reference relation R1. Suppose the two queries are separated by an insert or a delete statement on R1 as shown below.

Q1.R1
Insert or Delete on R1
Q2.R1

Clearly, Q1 must be processed before the data manipulation statement and Q2 after it.

Suppose Q1 and Q2 are separated by an update statement on the C1 column of R1. If the target list (list of the columns of a relation to be output) and the predicates in Q2 do not reference the C1 column, Q2 may be processed simultaneously with Q1 before the update statement is executed. If the target list and the predicates in Q1 do not reference the C1 column, Q1 can be processed with Q2 after the update statement. An update statement on Ri then does not automatically preclude preceding queries on Ri from being processed simultaneously with those that follow it. However, it is expensive to maintain the target list and the predicates of each query in order to determine whether an update statement affects the result of the query. Therefore, it seems reasonable not to distinguish an update from an insert or a delete. The first rule emerges from this discussion.

Rule 1. Only those queries on Ri that are sandwiched between two data manipulation statements on Ri may be considered for simultaneous processing.

Now consider a set of 3 queries Q1, Q2 and Q3 shown below.

Q1.R1
Q2.R1 (Q4.R2)
Q3.R2

Q2.R1 (Q4.R2) above stands for a nested query of depth 2, defined in [KIM82]. The inner query block, Q4.R2, of some types of nested query must be processed before the outer query block, Q2.R1. Then Q3 and Q4 may be grouped together for simultaneous processing since they reference the same relation, R2. Also Q1 and Q2 may be grouped together. Since Q2 requires the result of processing Q4, it is clear that Q3 and Q4 must be processed before Q1 and Q2. This observation leads to the next rule.

Rule 2. When grouping a set of queries for simultaneous processing, the presence of nested queries gives rise to data dependence which partitions the set of queries and fixes the order in which each subset of the queries may be processed.

Even when it is possible to process n queries simultaneously, it may be counterproductive to do so. The reason is that the result of each query in general has to be written to the disk (during phase R-1) and retrieved for further processing or output (during phase R-2). If the result of a query occupies Pri pages, it costs 2Pri page fetches (and writes) to store and retrieve it.

Rule 3. If it takes Pxi page fetches to retrieve all necessary tuples of a relation referenced by a query and Pxi <= 2Pri, then it may be best to exclude the query from the preprocessing phase and process it during phase R-2.

However, even if Pxi <= 2Pri, it may sometimes be better to process the query during phase R-1. The following set of four queries and one data manipulation statement illustrates the reason.

Q1.R1
M1.R1
Q2.R1
Q3.R1
Q4.R1

It may have been determined by Rule 3 that it is best to postpone the processing of Q1.R1 to phase R-2, but that Q2, Q3 and Q4 may be processed simultaneously during phase R-1. This means that the data manipulation statement M1.R1 must also be executed during phase R-1, before Q2, Q3, and Q4. If Q1.R1 is processed during phase R-2, a snapshot of the version of R1 before M1.R1 is executed must be kept.

Rule 4. If a data manipulation statement on Ri, Mk.Ri, is sandwiched between two sets of queries on Ri, either the set of queries preceding Mk must be processed during phase R-1 or a snapshot of Ri must be taken before Mk is executed (during phase R-1) so that the set of queries may be processed during phase R-2.

How many queries can be grouped together for simultaneous processing? It depends on the size of the main-memory buffer that the designer of a system is willing to allow and the size of the necessary procedures that must be simultaneously main-memory resident, as well as on the nature of the operations to be performed. The following is a discussion of some of the important factors which must be taken into consideration.

If only n single-relation queries which reference the same relation are in the group and the relation is to be sequentially read into the input buffers, only one page may be needed for the input buffers and n pages for the output buffers to buffer the result of each query. The program area may contain a procedure which processes a given set of predicates and isolates an appropriate set of columns for output. It must also contain a procedure which controls the order in which the tuples of the relation fetched into the input buffers are processed against the queries and which directs the partial result of each query to an appropriate output buffer.

What problems arise when two single-relation queries Q1.R1 and Q2.R2 and a 2-relation query Q3.(R1, R2) are to be executed simultaneously? Query Q3 may be processed in two stages: the reduction stage and the join stage. The reduction stage reduces the size of each of the two relations by applying the restriction and projection operations. The join stage then joins the resulting two temporary relations by any of the appropriate methods [BLAS77, SELI79]. It will be assumed through most of this chapter that an n-relation query is processed in two stages. This is a good first-order assumption, since each of the n relations being referenced in the query may be restricted by some simple predicates. Even when no simple predicates restrict a relation, the relation may need to be projected, since the target list of the n-relation query usually includes only a subset of the columns of a relation. Further, if the join stage of an n-relation join is executed during phase R-1, the input buffers must accommodate pages for the n relations and the program area needs to hold a procedure for joining the relations, thereby reducing the main-memory buffer pages that would otherwise be allocated to outputting the results of other queries.

Rule 5. Although it is possible to dynamically determine the number of queries to be simultaneously processed, it is reasonable to determine the number statically and group for simultaneous processing only single-relation queries on the same relation.

Now what if a query appears within a DO-loop or an IF statement? Consider the following situation.

```
IF x THEN DO  Q1.R1  END
     ELSE DO  Q2.R2  END;
```

In general, the value of x can only be determined during phase R-2. However, it is reasonable to try to execute Q1 with other queries which reference R1, and Q2 with other queries which reference R2. The IF statement can then be modified to

```
IF x THEN DO  retrieve Rt1  END
     ELSE DO  retrieve Rt2  END;
```

where Rt1 is the result of processing Q1, and Rt2 the result of processing Q2. If there are other queries which reference R1 or R2 that can be processed simultaneously with Q1 or Q2, the cost of processing Q1 or Q2 may be easily absorbed.

If a query appears within a DO-loop, it is often possible to replace the DO-loop with a set of queries. Consider the following.

```
DO I=1 TO N
QI.R1;
END;
```

The query within the DO-loop can be replaced by the following set of queries.

```
Q1.R1;
Q2.R1;
  ...
QN.R1;
```

However, it is not always possible to replace a DO-loop and preprocess the resulting set of queries during phase R-1. A query within a DO-loop may contain a predicate which can only be defined at run time. Or even the relation which the query references may not be known until run-time [STON76]. This type of query, whether it appears within or outside a DO-loop, must be processed during phase R-2.

4. GROUPING QUERIES

Algorithms for grouping and sequencing queries are outlined in this section. For expository simplicity, it is assumed that no data manipulation statements are present in the application program. The algorithms apply even when the program contains data manipulation statements, as long as no data manipulation statement on Ri logically precedes any query on Ri.

The algorithms will group only single-relation queries, for reasons explored in the previous section. Further, rather than resorting to the rigorous approach developed in [KIM82] for evaluating a general nested query, the algorithm will take the view that a nested query is in essence a multiple-relation query and use the two-stage approach for evaluating an n-relation query. In other words, all relations that appear in the FROM clauses of the query blocks in a nested query will first be reduced by restricting them with simple predicates and projecting them over appropriate columns. All references to the initial relations and their columns in the query blocks will then be replaced by the reduced relations and their columns, and the transformed nested query will be evaluated during phase R-2 by the method of [KIM82]. The merit of this simplistic approach to preprocessing nested queries is that the problem of data dependence caused by nested subqueries is completely circumvented.

As an example, consider the following nested query.

```
SELECT   R1.C1
FROM     R1
WHERE    R1.C2 = V2   AND
         R1.C3 = (SELECT   AVG(R2.C3)
                  FROM     R2)   AND
         R1.C4 IS IN (SELECT   R3.C4
                      FROM     R3
                      WHERE    R3.C5 = R1.C5);
```

The following temporary relations are obtained by restricting and projecting the three relations being referenced in the query blocks.

```
Rt1 (C1, C3, C4, C5) =
     (SELECT   C1, C3, C4, C5
      FROM     R1
      WHERE    C2 = V2) ;

Rt2 = X = (SELECT   AVG(C3)
           FROM     R2) ;

Rt3 (C4, C5) =
     (SELECT   C4, C5
      FROM     R3) ;
```

The initial, nested query is then transformed to reference the reduced, temporary relations, as follows.

```
SELECT   Rt1.C1
FROM     Rt1
WHERE    Rt1.C3 = X   AND
         Rt1.C4 IS IN (SELECT   Rt3.C4
                       FROM     Rt3
                       WHERE    Rt3.C5 = Rt1.C5) ;
```

Algorithm GROUP-1, summarized below, incorporates this simplistic view of nested query processing.

Algorithm GROUP-1

1. Reduce all relations that appear in the FROM clauses of the query blocks in a nested query or nonnested n-relation query by restricting them with simple predicates and projecting them over appropriate columns. Replace all references to the initial relations and their columns in the query blocks with the resulting reduced relations and their columns.
2. Select from the initial set of queries, modified by step 1, only those single-relation queries suitable for simultaneous evaluation during the preprocessing phase. Rules 3 and 4 of the previous section provide criteria for selecting queries for preprocessing.
3. Group the single-relation queries selected on step 2 by the relations they require access to, and compute the sum of the cost of evaluating each group of queries simultaneously during phase R-1. Add to this the cost of sequentially evaluating all other queries in the modifed set of queries during phase R-2.
4. Compute the expected cost of sequentially evaluating the set of queries. Compare this cost to the cost of the preprocessing approach of steps 2 and 3, and select the one with the lower expected cost.

Note that there are a few situations which Algorithm GROUP-1 does adequately deal with. One situation is when a set of queries consists of a number of n-relation queries that can be efficiently merge joined. For example, if a 2-relation query requires the joining of relations R1 and R2 and both relations are already in their join-column order, the reduction stage may be omitted. Algorithm GROUP-1 will postpone the evaluation of the 2-relation query to phase R-2. Clearly, if the given set of queries consists of other queries that can be simultaneously evaluated with the 2-relation query during phase R-1, a reduction in processing time may be achieved.

Another situation is when a given set of queries consists of relatively many nested queries which in turn consist of nested subqueries. The reason why nested subqueries render Algorithm GROUP-1 inefficient is that nested subqueries introduce data dependence between an outer query block and an inner query block, as discussed in [KIM82]. If the relation of the outer query block cannot be significantly reduced in size, Algorithm GROUP-1 will force the evaluation of the outer query block to phase R-2.

The remainder of this section will outline some refinements to Algorithm GROUP-1 by considering the data dependence problem introduced by nested queries. Consider the following set of 5 queries (actually, 3 queries, with one of them being a nested query of depth 3).

Q1.R1
Q2.R1 (Q3.R2 (Q4.R1))
Q5.R2

Information about queries Q1.R1 and Q5.R2 may be symbolically represented as

1.1 and 5.2

respectively. Q2.R1 can be processed only after Q3.R2 has been fully processed, and Q3.R2 after Q4.R1. In other words, there is data dependence between Q4 and Q3 as well as between Q3 and Q2. Q2, Q3 and Q4 are **data dependent** queries. Information about these 3 queries and their relationships are symbolically represented as

->2.1 , ->3.2->(2.1) , and 4.1->(3.2)

respectively. The arrow on the right-hand side of 4.1 indicates that the query in parentheses, 3.2, requires the result of processing 4.1. The arrow on the left-hand side of 2.1 similarly indicates that query 2.1 can be processed only when the result of processing some other query is available. The meaning of the arrows on both sides of 3.2 should be obvious.

It is clear that R1 has to be retrieved at least twice; once for Q4 and later for Q2. That is, queries which reference R1 must be partitioned into two sets, one containing Q4 and the other containing Q2. The set that contains Q4 must be processed first, since the result of processing Q4 is required for processing Q2. Q1 may be put in either set, since it can be processed independently of any other query. Q1 is a **data independent** query. It is also clear that R2 needs to be retrieved only once. Q3 must be processed after Q4 and is a data dependent query. Q5 is a data independent query.

The queries which reference a particular Ri may be data dependent or data independent. Each query block within a nested query is data dependent. A nested query of depth d contains m query blocks which reference Ri, where m <= d. The m query blocks are placed in reverse order into m sets of queries which reference Ri. Each nonnested query on Ri is data independent, and goes into the n-th (n=m+1) set of queries on Ri.

Example 3. The nested query under consideration consists of 2 data dependent queries which reference relation R1: Q2 and Q4. So Q4 is put in the 1st set of data dependent queries on R1, and Q2 in the 2nd set. And Q1 is a data independent query on R1 and goes in the 3rd set. Further, the nested query contains only one query, Q3, which references relation R2. So Q3 goes in the 1st set of queries which reference R2. Q5 is a data independent query and belongs to the 2nd set of queries on R2. The resulting set of groups of queries on R1 is

G1: 4.1->(3.2) | ->2.1 | 1.1

while the set for R2 is

G2: ->3.2->(2.1) | 5.2

Clearly, it is not sufficient to merely generate the set Gi for each of the k relations. What is necessary is an efficient algorithm for deriving a sequence S of groups of queries from the Gi's for simultaneous processing which satisfies the data dependence between queries. Consider the two sets of queries, G1 and G2, obtained in Example 3. Note that | G2(1) | = 1, that is, the 1st set of queries on R2 contains only one query. Moreover, the query, 3.2, has an arrow on its left-hand side, so it cannot be processed until some other query has been processed. Now, G1(1) contains a query, 4.1, which does not have an arrow on its left-hand side. So the first set of queries to be processed simultaneously consists of 4.1 and the data independent query 1.1. This set of two queries becomes S1(1), the first element of an ordered set of query groups, S1. Once query 4.1 has been processed, query 3.2 can be processed. So the left-hand arrow of 3.2 is dropped and queries 4.1 and 1.1 are removed from G1(1) and G1(3). The sets G1 and G2 now look like

G1: ->2.1

G2: 3.2->(2.1) | 5.2

Query 3.2 in G2(1) can now be processed and the set consisting of 3.2 and the data independent query 5.2 becomes S1(2), the second element of S1. Once query 3.2 has been processed, query 2.1 loses its left-hand side arrow, and queries 3.2 and 5.2 are removed from G2(1) and G2(2), respectively. G2 is now empty and G1 looks like

G1: 2.1

Query 2.1 constitutes S1(3), and S1 is the desired sequence of groups of queries.

S1: 1.1 | 3.2 | 2.1
4.1 | 5.2 |

Note that queries within each set, S1(j), can be processed simultaneously. In general, many possible sequences of groups of queries may be derived, and a particular sequence is denoted as Si. The j-th set of queries in Si is denoted as Si(j). S1 for the above set of five queries is a sequence of three groups of queries, two of which reference R1 and one R2. It is computationally difficult to derive all the Si's for a given set of queries. [KIM80] gives a simple heuristic to derive a reasonable sequence of query groups.

In the interest of space, this chapter will not provide a description of general algorithms for grouping queries and deriving a near-optimal sequence of query groups in the presence of data manipulation statements. Interested readers should see [KIM80].

5. ACCESS PATHS

Once queries have been grouped and their order of execution determined, what access paths must be used to process the queries in each of the S(i)'s simultaneously? It is assumed here that the maximum number of single-relation queries to be processed simultaneously has been statically determined to be m.

Suppose n queries are to be processed simultaneously, where n <= m. If any one of the n queries needs to be sequentially retrieved, the remaining n-1 queries can be processed without using indexes. The cost of simultaneously processing queries is the cost of fetching the union of the data pages to which each of the queries requires access plus the sum of the costs of writing out (during phase R-1) and retrieving (during phase R-2) the results of the queries. This cost must be compared with the cost of sequentially processing each of the queries, and the method with the lower expected cost selected.

Example 4. Let m=4 and n=3. Further, let P=100. Suppose Q1 requires sequential retrieval of relation R, but Q2 and Q3 may each be processed via indexes with 40 page fetches. That is, Qx1=100, and Qx2=Qx3=40. Suppose the result of each query is 5 pages, that is, Qri=5, for i=1, 2, and 3. The total cost of sequentially processing the queries is 180 page fetches. The total cost of processing the queries simultaneously and storing the results is 100 + 3 * (2 * 5) = 130 page fetches. The cost reduction amounts to 50 pages.

If n and m are very small and Qri is large compared to Qxi, it may often be more efficient to sequentially process the queries.

Example 5. Suppose the result of each of the queries in Example 4 is 15 pages. The total cost of sequentially processing the queries is still 180 page fetches. But the total cost of processing the queries simultaneously is now 100 + 3 * (2 * 15) = 190 pages.

Now what if n > m (and n is divisible by m)? The next example demonstrates that different orderings of the n queries in general result in different cost savings.

Example 6. Let m=3, n=6, P=100, Qx1 = Qx2 = Qx3 = 100, and Qx4 = Qx5 = Qx6 = 40. Also let Qr1=10, Qr2 = Qr3 = 20, Qr4 = Qr5 = 10, and Qr6 = 15. Suppose the 1st subset of the queries consists of Q1, Q2 and Q3, and the 2nd subset Q4, Q5 and Q6. The cost of processing the 1st subset of queries sequentially is 300 pages and the 2nd subset 120 pages. The cost of processing the 1st subset simultaneously is 100 + 20 + 40 + 40 = 200 pages. The union of data pages retrieved via three indexes for the 2nd subset of the queries is about 80 pages, so the cost of processing the 2nd subset simultaneously is 80 + 20 + 20 + 30 = 150. It is better to process the 2nd subset sequentially. Then the present ordering of queries results in the saving of 100 page fetches.

Suppose now the 1st subset contains Q2, Q4 and Q5, and the 2nd subset Q1, Q3 and Q6. The cost of sequentially processing the 1st subset is 180 pages. The cost of processing it simultaneously is 100 + 40 + 20 + 20 = 180 page fetches. The cost of processing the 2nd subset sequentially is 240 pages. The cost of processing it simultaneously is 100 + 20 + 40 + 30 = 190 page fetches. So the cost reduction achieved by simultaneous processing is 50 pages.

Since the penalty for preprocessing a query Qi is 2Qri, a reasonable way to group n queries of S(j) for simultaneous processing appears to be, as Example 6 demonstrates, to arrange them in descending order of Qxi- 2Qri and compute the cost of processing each of the resulting n/m subsets of queries both simultaneously and sequentially. In fact, an experiment with many examples has indicated that this is an effective strategy.

If n is not divisible by m, the last subset of the queries in S(j) contains r = (n mod m) queries on Ri. It may then be profitable to add m-r of the data independent queries on Ri to the n queries in S(j) and find access paths for the resulting set of n+m-r queries. It may turn out that x of the m-r data independent queries can be more efficiently processed sequentially. Then the x queries are put back into the set of data independent queries on Ri for consideration with the next set of data dependent queries on Ri (before a data manipulation statement on Ri). If the set of data independent queries is nonempty when the last set of data dependent queries on Ri (before a data manipulation statement on Ri) has been reached, all remaining data independent queries on Ri are placed into the last set of data dependent queries on Ri.

Example 7. Suppose there are two sets of queries in S that reference R1, S(1) and S(3). S(1) has two data dependent queries Q1 and Q2, such that Qx1 = Qx2 = 100 and Qr1 = Qr2 = 40. S(2) contains Q3 and Q4, such that Qx3 = Qx4 = 100 and Qr3 = Qr4 = 20. Further, suppose Q5 is a data independent query on R1, and Qx5 = 100 and Qr5 = 20. Assume m = 3.

If Q5 is assigned to S(1), the cost of simultaneously processing Q1, Q2 and Q5 during phase R-1 and the cost of sequentially processing them during phase R-2 are both 300 pages. The cost of simultaneously processing Q3 and Q4 is 180 pages. The total cost of processing S(1) and S(2) is then 480 pages.

Now, if Q5 is assigned to S(2), the cost of sequentially processing S(1) is 200 pages, while the cost of simultaneously processing them is 260 pages. The cost of processing Q3, Q4 and Q5 simultaneously is 220 pages, while their sequential processing costs 300 pages. So the total cost of processing S(1) and S(2) is now 420 pages, 60 pages lower than the other assignment of Q5.

Finally, consider the following sequence of one data manipulation statement and four queries on Ri.

Q1.R1;
Q2.R1;
M1.R1;
Q3.R1;
Q4.R1;

Suppose it has been determined that the set S(1) containing Q1 and Q2 is better to be processed during phase R-2, but the set S(2) of Q3 and Q4 can be more efficiently processed during phase R-1. As has already been pointed out (Rule 4), either S(1) has to be processed during phase R-1 or a snapshot of R1 must be taken before M1 is executed in order to allow S(1) to be sequentially processed during phase R-2. If S(1) is to be processed during phase R-2, the total cost incurred is the sum of the cost of taking the snapshot of R1 and indexes on R1 and the cost of sequentially processing the queries in S(1). The snapshot can be taken when R1 is fetched to execute M1, so it costs P1 + L, where L is the number of pages that hold indexes on R1. This cost must be compared with the cost of processing S(1) during phase R-1and the method with the lower cost selected.

6. CONCLUDING REMARKS

Indexes that can be used to reduce the cost of processing queries sequentially may not be useful when processing the same queries simultaneously. This gives rise to another interesting problem. As suggested in section 2, a strategy for optimizing the performance of many queries can benefit from a compile-time analysis which determines an optimal set of secondary indexes and sorted copies of relations for sequentially processing the queries. Once near-optimal access paths have been determined for a given set of queries and data manipulation statements, algorithms outlined in this chapter can be used to find an optimal sequence of queries for simultaneous processing. Since it is possible that some of the indexes thought to be useful for sequential processing of queries may not be useful for simultaneous processing of the queries, those indexes must be removed from the candidate set of indexes to be dynamically created.

Further, it is possible for the total cost of simultaneously processing groups of queries to be higher than the total cost of processing the initial set of queries and data manipulation statements sequentially. This is because of the need either to take snapshots of relations before they are modified or to process some queries during phase R-1 despite the fact that they would incur lower cost if they were to be sequentially evaluated. Even when no data manipulation statements are in the given set or if the data manipulation statements on Ri do not logically precede queries on Ri, the global optimization technique may still be less efficient than the traditional sequential processing method. Therefore, the total expected cost of processing a given set of queries and data manipulation statements in two stages should in general be compared with the total expected cost of processing it sequentially. A reasonable global strategy for processing a set of queries and data manipulation statements is as follows.

1. Determine a near-optimal set of access paths (indexes, sorted copies of relations) for processing the queries and data manipulation statements sequentially. The problem of selecting an optimal set of secondary indexes on a relation has been rather extensively investigated [HAMM76a, HAMM76b, LUM70, LUM71, SCHK75, STON74, YUE75].
2. Determine S, the near-optimal set of groups of queries and data manipulation statements to be processed simultaneously.
3. Determine the optimal sets of access paths for processing each of the S(i)'s simultaneously.
4. Compare the cost of the preprocessing method with the cost of the sequential processing method. If the preprocessing method is more efficient, remove those indexes that have been determined to be useless (in step 3) from the candidate set of indexes to be created.
5. If the sequential processing method is more efficient, stop. Otherwise, create indexes and sort relations.
6. Process each S(i) using access paths determined in step 3 and store the results of each query. Then modify the initial program by replacing all preprocessed queries by the references to their stored results and, if snapshots of some relations have been taken, modifying some of the queries whose processing has been postponed to phase R-2 to reference the snapshots.
7. Completely process the entire program using the results derived in step 6.

The objective of the global-optimization strategy outlined in this chapter is to take advantage of global knowledge of query and database characteristics and exploit available main-memory buffer space for simultaneous processing of 'similar' queries. It is expected that the use of such a strategy will result in considerable reduction in the cost of processing a program which contains a fairly large number of 'similar' queries, as compared to conventional sequential processing of a set of queries.

References

(BLAS77) (BOYC74) (CHAM76) (CODD70) (ESWA75) (HAMM75) (HAMM76a) (HAMM76b) (HAMM78) (KIM80, see KIM80b) (KIM82) (LUM70) (LUM71) (SCHK75) (SELI79) (STON74) (STON75) (STON76) (YUE75)

Query Processing Using the Consecutive Retrieval Property

Yahiko Kambayashi, Sakti Ghosh

ABSTRACT

In this chapter, we will discuss procedures to handle multiple queries utilizing the consecutive retrieval property. A set of queries is said to have the consecutive retrieval property if the records pertinent to every query in the set are consecutively located in a linear structure file, so that each query can be processed by a single direct access of the file. The consecutive retrieval property can be used to reduce the computation time as well as the storage space. There are many cases when a given query set does not satisfy the property and we need to develop procedures to handle such cases. One approach is to generalize the file structure. Instead of the linear structure various graph structures can be used. Another approach is to permit multiple accesses for queries with low usage frequencies. We give a greedy algorithm to construct a consecutive retrieval file where the preference of queries are given by the frequencies of usage. File organizations with different main memory buffer sizes are also discussed, such as the quasi-consecutive retrieval file organization and the buffer-limited quasi-consecutive retrieval file organization. In these organizations records corresponding to each query are not required to be stored consecutively; instead these records are to be located within the size of the buffer. A multiple query processing method for cost reduction by keeping some records in the buffer is also described.

1. INTRODUCTION

The consecutive retrieval property is a general principle that assures locality of reference. Locality of reference is one of the guiding principles for designing practically useful systems. In computer science, many widely used concepts utilize the locality. In this chapter query processing procedures utilizing the consecutive retrieval property are discussed. The consecutive retrieval (CR) property for organizing files was first introduced by S. P. Ghosh [GHOS72]. If a given set of queries satisfies the CR property, we can organize a file with minimum access time with no redundant storage of records.

In this chapter, we will discuss procedures to handle multiple queries utilizing the CR property. Since redundancy of records causes problems in updating we will discuss file organization with no redundancy.

In Section 2, the basic concepts of the CR property are discussed together with examples. A set of queries is said to have the CR property, if for any query in the set, the pertinent records are consecutively located in a linear structure file and the file organization has no redundancy. The CR property can be used to reduce the retrieval time as well as the storage space.

In Section 3, the CR properties for various kinds of graphs are discussed. Some special cases were handled by [GHOS74] and [LIPS76]. Relations between such general cases and structures of data/files are also presented.

In Section 4, organization of CR files without redundancy are discussed for multiple queries. Basic methods for handling the case when the given query set does not satisfy the CR property are summarized and a procedure to reduce the total number of file accesses without introducing replication of records is discussed. The procedure is "a greedy algorithm" to construct a CR file where the preferences of the queries are determined by the frequencies of their usage.

In Section 5, the CR property for buffered main memory is discussed, which was introduced by Kambayashi [KAMB78] as a generalization of the consecutive retrieval file organization. Since the size of each query is different, we have to prepare a buffer in the main memory which can store the record set corresponding to the query of the maximum size. Thus, a query can be processed by a single access of the file if its pertinent records are contained within the buffer. In this case the consecutiveness is not required. File organization under this model is called the quasi-consecutive retrieval file organization [KAMB78] [TANA79]. On the other hand there may be cases when the size of the buffer is less than the maximum query size. File organization for such cases is called a buffer-limited quasi-consecutive retrieval file organization [KAMB83]. For processing multiple queries, we can reduce the number of direct accesses by keeping some records in the buffer. This method is also discussed in Section 5.

2. BASIC CONCEPTS

Consider a bibliographic information retrieval system where each query is characterized by a Boolean function of keywords. Let R be a set of all records in the system. For simplicity, we will consider the following two keywords: p_1="database" and p_2="computer aided design." Let s_1 and s_2 be the set of records corresponding to the keywords p_1 and p_2, respectively. A query on p_1 and p_2 is expressed by a Boolean function using p_1, p_2 and the Boolean operators ($\vee$(OR),$\wedge$(AND),$^-$(NOT)). The following Boolean functions on p_1 and p_2 are possible.

$$p_1\wedge p_2 \quad \bar{p}_1\wedge p_2 \quad p_1\wedge\bar{p}_2 \quad \bar{p}_1\wedge\bar{p}_2 \quad p_1\vee p_2 \quad p_1\vee\bar{p}_2 \quad \bar{p}_1\vee p_2$$

$$\bar{p}_1\vee\bar{p}_2 \quad p_1p_2\vee\bar{p}_1\bar{p}_2 \quad p_1\bar{p}_2\vee\bar{p}_1p_2$$

The semantics of these queries and the operations to obtain the results are shown next.

$p_1\wedge p_2$: find all records satisfying both keywords, *i.e.,* $s_1\wedge s_2$

$\bar{p}_1\wedge p_2$: find all records with the keyword "computer aided design" but not the keyword "database," *i.e.,* s_2 - s_1

$\bar{p}_1\wedge\bar{p}_2$: find all records not having either of the keywords, *i.e.,* R - s_1 - s_2

Except for the third query, the result is obtained from s_1 and s_2. Boolean functions whose domains are not the whole record set R are called "safe functions" and others are referred to as "unsafe functions." Examples of unsafe functions are as follows

$$\bar{p}_1\vee\bar{p}_2 \quad \bar{p}_1\wedge\bar{p}_2 \quad p_1p_2\vee\bar{p}_1\bar{p}_2\,.$$

In general a Boolean function is said to be safe iff there exists no product term consisting only of negated variables ($\bar{p}_1$, *etc.*) in a sum-of-product form. We usually restrict queries which correspond to safe functions. If only safe functions are considered, we can characterize each query by the set of its properties (keywords in the above example). That is, instead of considering all Boolean expressions we characterize every query by its pertinent record set.

Formal definitions are as follows

$P=\{p_1, p_2, ..., p_n\}$: A set of properties

$Q=\{q_1, q_2, ..., q_m\}$: A set of queries. Each query is expressed by a set of p_i's.

$R=\{r_1, r_2, ..., r_n\}$: r_i is a record containing data items having property p_i.

For simplicity we use p_i instead of r_i.

If all possible queries are considered, m is 2^n-1, which is, in general, very large. We will reduce m by selecting frequently occurring queries.

A set Q of queries is said to have a CR property if there exists a sequence w of p_i's which contain each p_i (*i.e.*, record) at most once, such that for each q_i in Q, there exists a subsequence w_i of w, which contains all records pertinent to q_i.

For example, if $q_1=\{p_1,p_2,p_4\}$, $q_2=\{p_3,p_4\}$, $q_3=\{p_3,p_5\}$, then the query set $Q=\{q_1,q_2,q_3\}$ has the CR property since there exists a sequence $p_1p_2p_4p_3p_5$ which contains the three subsequences $p_1p_2p_4$, p_4p_3 and p_3p_5. If the records are stored in the order

$$p_1\ p_2\ p_4\ p_3\ p_5\ ,$$

then the pertinent record sets corresponding to each query can be retrieved by a single direct access of a subset of the file, since all necessary records for each query are consecutively stored. Since in disks the cost for one seek is much higher than the cost for one search (sequential access), reduction of the number of direct accesses (seeks) is very important for reducing the total access cost. We will use a hypergraph to represent the set of queries, where each vertex corresponds to a property and each hyperedge (which is a set of vertices) corresponds to a query in Q. The hypergraph corresponding to $q_1=\{p_1,p_2,p_4\}$, $q_2=\{p_3,p_4\}$, $q_3=\{p_3,p_5\}$, is shown in Fig. 1, where hyperedges are shown by ellipses.

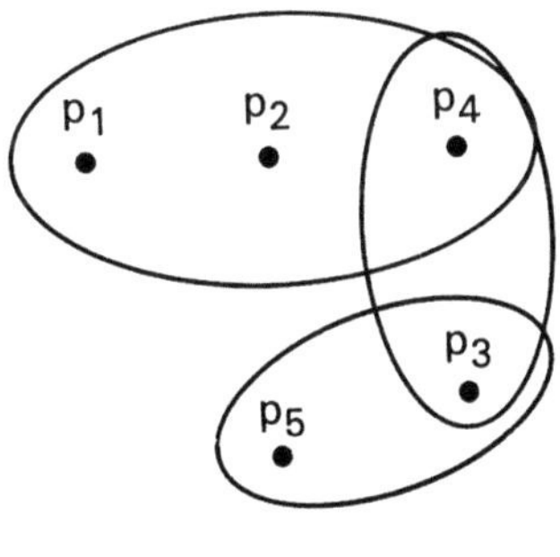

Figure 1. A hypergraph representing a query.

Consider the previous example. When p_1 and p_2 are not consecutively stored in the file, we need two direct accesses to process a query $q=\{p_1,p_2\}$. If they are consecutively located, then p_1 and p_2 can be retrieved by a single direct access. If the system is I/O bound the processing time is mainly determined by the number of direct accesses to the file, the latter case requires only half the processing time as the former. We can further reduce the processing cost of q by combining these two sets s_1 and s_2, where s_i is set of records corresponding to the property p_i. If these records are stored as disjoint subsets shown in Fig. 2(b) instead of storing overlapping subsets as in Fig. 2(a), the following advantages result

(1) The total space required to store s_1 and s_2 is reduced.

(2) Queries like $s_1 \cap s_2$, $s_1 - s_2$, $s_2 - s_1$ can be processed efficiently.

Figure 2(c) shows the case of disjoint partitioning of three consecutive record sets.

In general, the consecutive retrieval file organization has the following advantages

(1) Reduction of the number of direct accesses to the file.

(2) Reduction of the storage space.

There are two methods for storing s_i's in the file, as follows

(a) Store actual records.

(b) Store identification numbers of records.

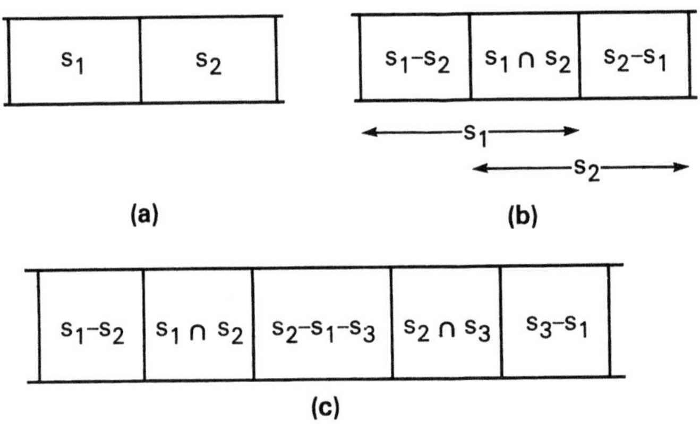

Figure 2. Removal of overlapping subsets.

The first method may have large redundancy because there usually exists many records having more than one property, thus the second method is usually used. In the second method we need a procedure to obtain actual records from a set of identification numbers corresponding to the final result. Although this procedure may require at most one direct access for each identification number, the cost can be further reduced when there are many queries to be processed simultaneously. By combining pertinent identification numbers of the results of these queries, closely located records can be retrieved in a single access. Furthermore, if the number of identification numbers is more than some threshold value, a sequential access of the entire file takes less time than repeated direct accesses [MERR77].

In the second method identification numbers can be stored by the following two schemes

(b-1) Use the integer values corresponding to the identification numbers.

(b-2) Use a bit vector, where the i-th component value (0 or 1) shows nonexistence or existence of the record whose identification number is i.

For example, consider the following queries q_1 and q_2

$q_1=\{p_1, p_2, p_3, p_5, p_7\}$

$q_2=\{p_2, p_4, p_5\}$

Representation by these approaches are as follows

(b-1) {1,2,3,5,7}, {2,4,5}. Here we assume that the identification number of p_i is i.

(b-2) [11101010...], [010110...]. We can reduce the cost by using the run length coding (i consecutive 0's can be expressed by i*0, the tail sequence of 0's can be omitted, *etc.*).

Further reduction may be possible using the CR property. If we change identification numbers so that each set q_i has maximum consecutive numbers, each interval of integers from i to j is represented by i-j. In the above example, if we can change the numbers by 2→4,3→2,4→5,5→3, the two sets become {1,2,3,4,7} and {3,4,5}, which can be expressed by 1-4,7 and 3-5, respectively. This method may also reduce the cost for the bit vector approach, since the result is suitable for the run length coding. This is an example of an application of the CR property to data expression.

3. THE CR PROPERTY FOR GENERAL GRAPHS AND ITS RELATIONSHIP TO THE STRUCTURES OF DATA AND FILES

The CR property of a file is structurally related to such mathematical concepts as consecutive-one property of a 0-1 matrix, connectivity of an interval graph, bipartite graphs, *etc.* Existence of these properties in these mathematical structures correspond to existing of C-R properties of certain file structures. These mathematical structures have been extensively used to identify the existence or nonexistence of CR properties among many file structures [GHOS83a]. They have also enabled mathematical researchers to prove complex CR properties from mathematical theorems and lemmas.

A survey of the relationships between the CR property and interval graphs is given in [LIPS83a]. An interval graph [HAJ057] is defined as a graph each of those vertices corresponds to an interval of real values and there exists an edge between two vertices iff their corresponding intervals overlap.

Booth and Luecker invented an efficient linear-time algorithm for determining whether or not a given set satisfies the CR property [BOOT76]. Complexity of algorithms on related problems have been studied by many researchers and many of these are NP-complete problems [LIPS78] [LIPS83a]. For these problems we need to develop heuristic procedures to get near optimum results in reasonable computation time (see Sections 4 and 5). In this section we will discuss mathematical generalizations of the CR property together with relationships to query processing.

Since the CR property is defined in a chain-type directed graph (see Fig. 3(a)) such that for any set in the given family of sets, there exists a subgraph containing exactly the vertices corresponding to the elements in the set. We can generalize as follows

(1) Handling of ordered sets instead of unordered sets.

(2) Generalization of the graph structure.

If the best order of records in a query (for economical processing) is known, we can use ordered sets instead of unordered sets. A sequence containing all possible sequences of length h consisting of m different records is obtained by a Hamiltonian path of deBruijin graph [VANA51]. The length of such a sequence is m^h+h-1. It has been shown that existence of such Hamiltonian

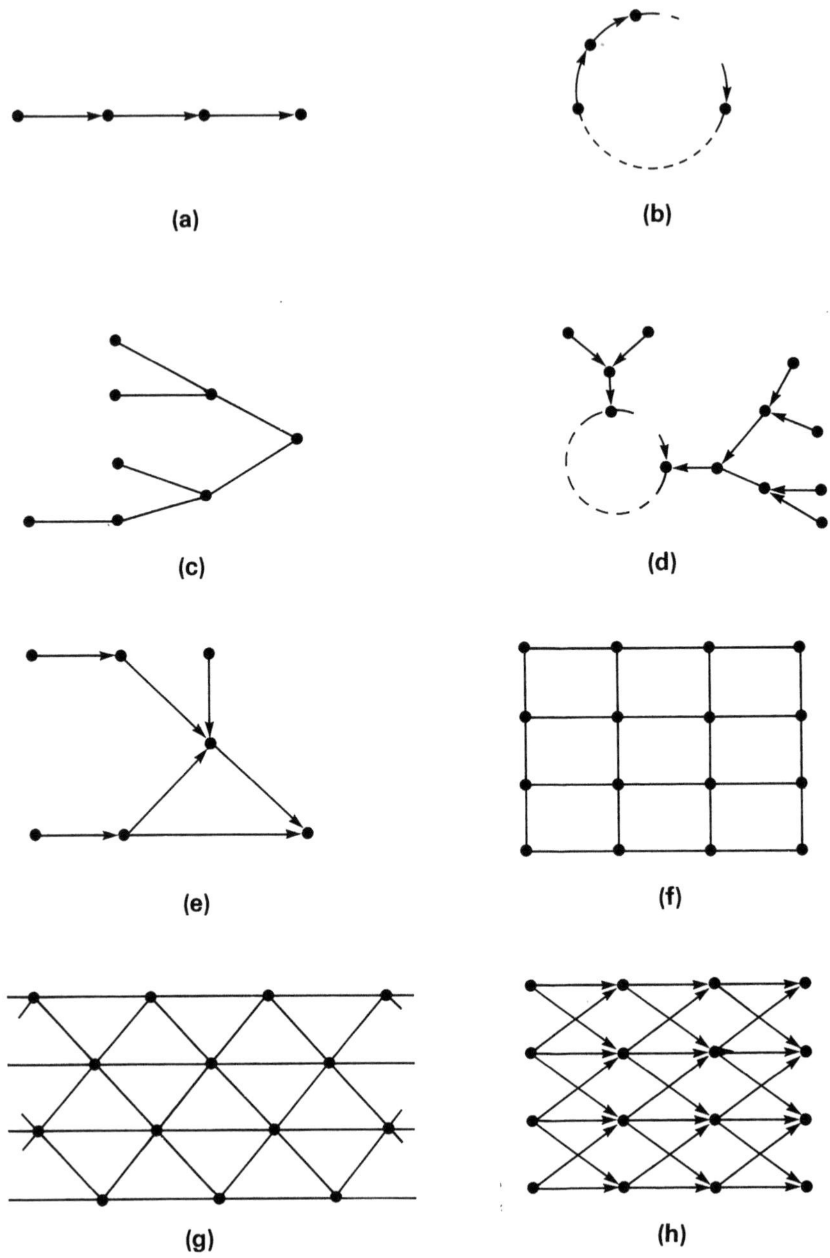

Figure 3. Graphs for the CR property.

paths correspond to existence of CR properties of combinatorial query sets of order h. If we consider ordered sets, the sequence becomes very long in general.

The concept of the CR property is generalized to that of directed graphs where the number of edges going out from each vertex (out-degree of a vertex) is at most one. This type of graph is called f-graphs [LIPS76].. Further generalizations are discussed in this section. In general, combinations of the following cases are possible

(1) Directed graph/undirected graph.

(2) Restrictions on the graph structure. Cycle/Tree/Acyclic.

(3) Restriction on the number of edges connected to each vertex.

The CR property for an arbitrary graph is defined as follows.

For any set in a given family of sets, there exists a path which contains all the vertices corresponding to the set.

Interesting graphs are as follows

(a) Chain graphs: It corresponds to the original CR property (see Fig. 3(a)).

(b) Cycle graphs: A very easy generalization of the CR property is to use a graph consisting of one cycle as shown in Fig. 3(b). In cases (a) and (b), there is no distinction of whether the graph is directed or not. In the case of directed graphs, out-degrees of each vertex is at most one (in case (b), exactly one).

(c) Tree graphs: There are differences between the directed tree problem and the undirected problem. The former is a special case of (e) and the latter is handled by Tanaka [TANA83] (see Fig. 3(c)).

(d) Directed graphs where out-degree of each vertex is at most one (f-graphs): Cases (a), (b) and (c) are special cases of (d). This case is handled by [LIPS76] [TRUS83]. One connected component of such a graph consists of trees (zero, one or more) and at most one cycle as shown in Fig. 3(d). This kind of graphs is known as state diagrams of autonomous sequential machines (precisely speaking, out-degree of each vertex is exactly one and an edge whose starting vertex and terminating vertex are identical is permitted for state diagrams).

(e) Acyclic graphs: A tree is a necessary and sufficient condition for an undirected graph having no cycles. An acyclic directed graph is defined as a directed graph not having cycles (see Fig. 3(e)). The CR property on acyclic graphs where out-degree of any vertex is at most one (acyclic f-graphs) is discussed in [DIET79] and [LONC83].

(f) Degree constraint directed graphs: We can generalize the concept of f-graphs to directed graphs where out-degree of each vertex is at most k for some integer $k(\geq 1)$. We can also give a constraint on in-degrees (the number of edges coming into a vertex).

(g) Two-dimensional regular graphs: Examples of such graphs are shown in Fig. 3(f), (g) and (h).

(h) Degree constrained undirected graphs, planar graphs, *etc.*

(i) Unrestricted graphs.

EXAMPLE 1: The following sets correspond to all paths of length 3 in the graph shown in Fig. 4(a).

1-3-2 1-3-4 1-3-6 2-3-4 2-3-6 3-4-5 3-6-5 4-3-6 4-5-6

If the structure is restricted to a tree, one edge in the cycle is removed. The tree in Fig. 4(b) represents the following sets

1-3-2 1-3-4 1-3-6 2-3-4 2-3-6 3-4-5 4-3-6

The following sets are realized by the directed acyclic graph in Fig. 4(c)

1-3-4 1-3-6 2-3-4 2-3-6 3-4-5 3-6-5

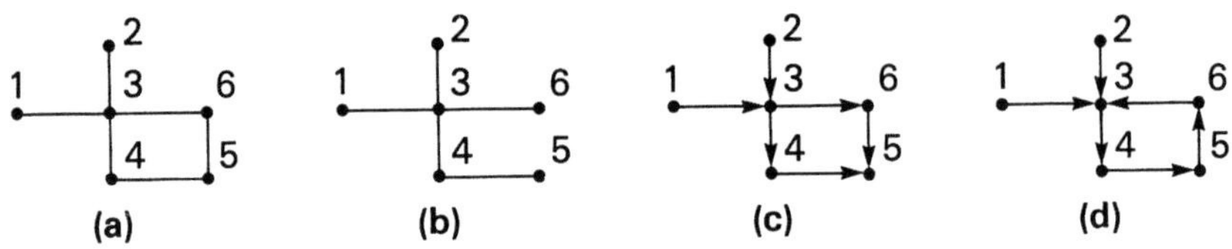

Figure 4. Examples of graphs.

It is not an acyclic f-graph since the out-degree of vertex 3 is two. An example of an acyclic f-graph is shown in Fig. 4(d). The corresponding sets are as follows

1-3-4 2-3-4 3-4-5 4-5-6 5-6-3 6-3-4

Directed graphs correspond to list structures. If the number of pointers is restricted to be one, the structure corresponds to an f-graph. We can, however, permit at most k pointers in each cell for some integer k (case (f) in above). In such a case we need a mechanism to select a proper successor at each cell. The data structure for the graph in Fig. 4(c) is shown in Fig. 5.

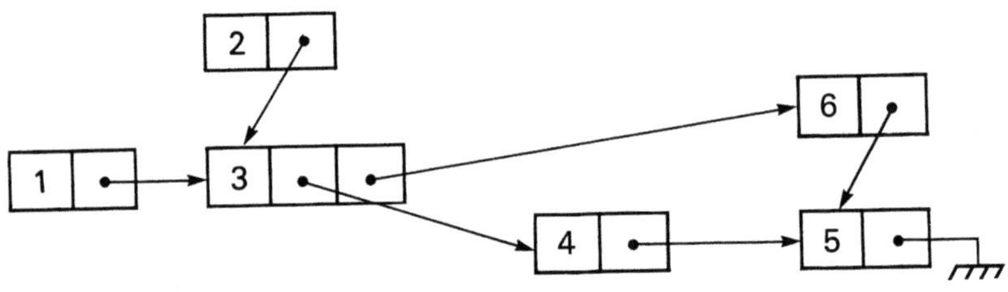

Figure 5. Data structure corresponding to Fig. 4(c).

The model using undirected graphs can be used for the file allocation problem of computer networks. If data required by a query are stored in consecutive sites in a linear order, it can be processed easily (such a query is related to a chain query which is a subclass of tree queries [BERN81]).

Two-dimensional regular graphs correspond to physical organizations of files. The graphs in Fig. 3(f) and (g) correspond to connections realized by LSI circuits. Correspondences between the circuit structures and the connections are shown in Fig. 6(a) and (b), respectively.

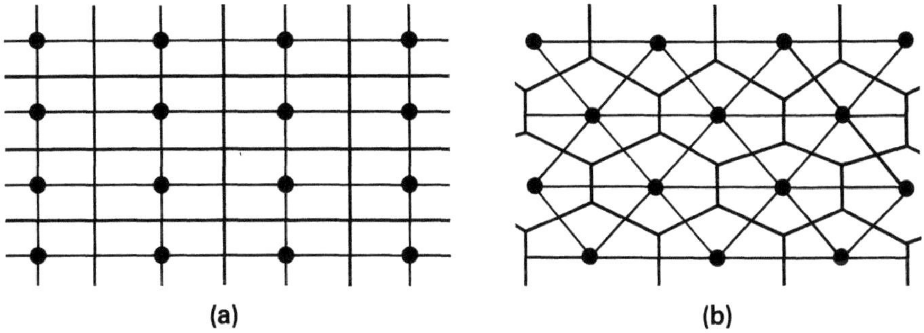

Figure 6. Cell structures for two-dimensional regular graphs.

As typical mass storage systems (tape cartridge type) have the access characteristics of Fig. 6(b), we can use the CR property to minimize the total distance for the movement of the arm for a mass storage system. If the cells storing data required by a query correspond to a path in the graph in Fig. 3(g), the total distance can be minimized.

The graph in Fig. 3(h) is called a two-dimensional CR structure [GHOS74], since it represents the structure of disk devices. Horizontal lines correspond to head movements in identical tracks of a disk and diagonal lines correspond to movements to adjacent tracks. Note that the cost of transition along a horizontal line is smaller than the cost along diagonal lines. This fact will motivate introduction of costs on the edges in the graph. If two-track direct jumps is considered then the cost for such a transition is higher than the cost for moving consecutive tracks. The graph in Fig. 7 represents this situation.

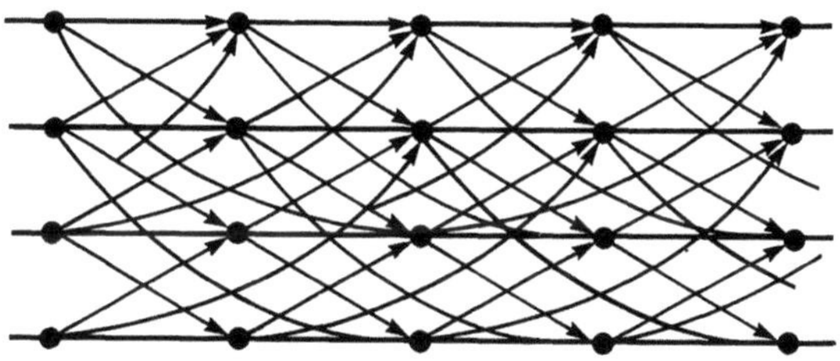

Figure 7. Two-dimensional CR property.

4. ORGANIZATION OF FILES WITH THE CR PROPERTY

In this section we will discuss the organization of CR files which have a linear structure, which corresponds to conventional secondary storage devices. Since the structure is limited, it is usually very difficult to find a CR file representing an arbitrary query set. The following basic methods can be used to solve the problem

(1) Introduction of redundant records [GHOS75]: By duplicating records we can always get a CR file representing a given query set.

(2) Use of multiple accesses [WAKS74]: Instead of introducing redundant records, we can process all queries if the number of direct accesses for some queries is permitted to be more than one.

If all the records pertinent to a query are consecutively located in a file, the query is said to be represented by the file.

EXAMPLE 2: Consider the following set of queries.

$$q_1=\{p_1, p_3, p_4\}$$
$$q_2=\{p_2, p_3, p_5\}$$
$$q_3=\{p_2, p_3, p_8\}$$
$$q_4=\{p_2, p_5, p_7, p_8\}$$
$$q_5=\{p_6, p_7\}$$
$$q_6=\{p_6, p_8\}$$

The hypergraph corresponding to the query set is shown in Fig. 8.

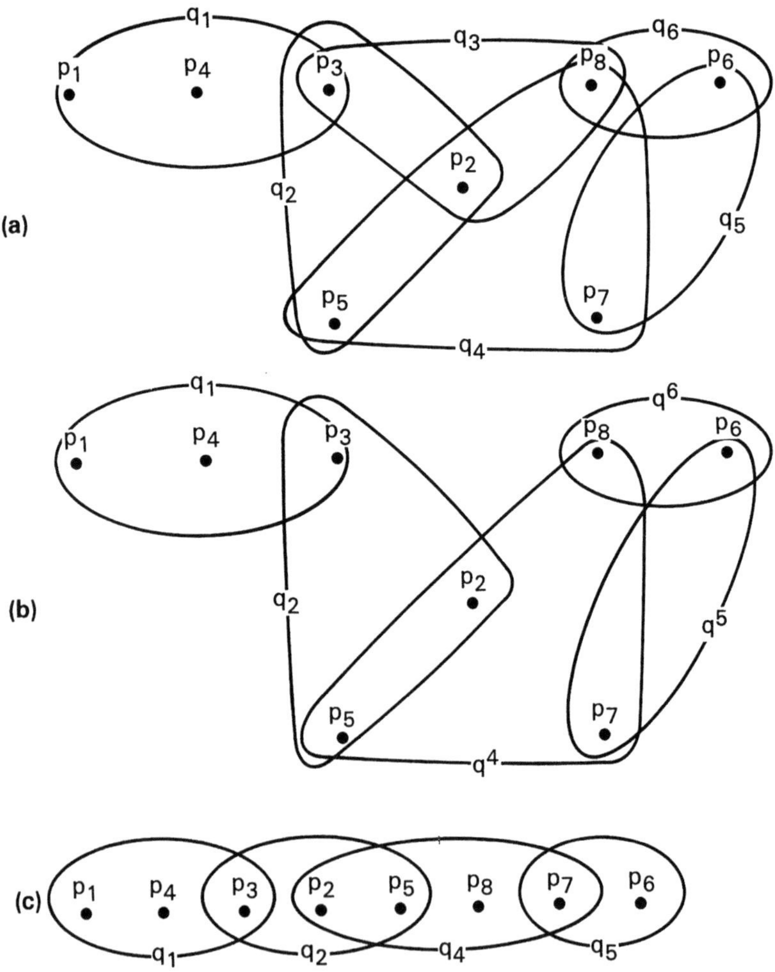

Figure 8. Organization of a CR file.

CR file with repetitions: If we duplicate p_2, p_3 and p_8, the following sequence is obtained

$$p_1\ p_4\ p_3\ p_2\ p_8\ p_6\ p_7\ p_8\ p_2\ p_5\ p_3$$

It corresponds to the following sequence of queries

$$q_1\ q_3\ q_6\ q_5\ q_4\ q_2$$

CR decomposition [YAMA77] [LIPS83b] [SUZU83]: We need not have a single sequence representing all queries. By a mechanism called a CR decomposition we can obtain a set of CR files, each of which does not have duplicated records, and each query is represented by one of the sequences. An example of the CR decomposition is as follows

$$p_1\ p_4\ p_3\ p_2\ p_5\ p_8\ p_7$$

$$p_2\ p_3\ p_8\ p_6\ p_7$$

These sequences correspond to $q_1\ q_2\ q_4$ and $q_3\ q_6\ q_5$, respectively. The CR decomposition is a special case of redundant records in CR files.

Multiple access: The following sequence represents all the queries except q_3 and q_6

$$p_1\ p_4\ p_3\ p_2\ p_5\ p_8\ p_7\ p_6$$

(corresponding to $q_1\ q_2\ q_4\ q_5$)

We need two direct accesses to process q_3 or q_6.

Mixed method: In order to represent all the queries we need three redundant records, but by introducing only one redundant record all the queries except q_3 can be represented

$$p_1\ p_4\ p_3\ p_2\ p_5\ p_8\ p_7\ p_6\ p_8$$

(corresponding to $q_1\ q_2\ q_4\ q_5\ q_6$)

Thus there is a trade-off between the number of redundant records and the number of direct accesses.

If there are frequent updates, introduction of redundant records are not suitable, since all replicated records must be updated. We discuss the second approach in this situation.

For the selection of queries which require multiple accesses, we can use the frequencies of the queries. Let f_i be the frequency of query q_i. We will try to include queries with large f_i's in the file organization in order to reduce the average access count.

If q_i is divided into k_i sequences, the total number of direct accesses for q_i is $k_i f_i$. The following problem is discussed in this section: Obtain a CR file for a given set of queries by finding a sequence such that $\Sigma k_i f_i$ is minimized.

We need a branch-and-bound method to obtain an optimum solution for the problem, which is in general very time consuming. We will give heuristic procedures instead. First some useful properties are shown.

PROCEDURE 1: Simplification of the query set

If there exists queries q_i and q_j such that $q_i \supseteq q_j$ (the records pertinent to q_j are also pertinent to q_i), then we can remove q_j from the query set, since q_j can be processed by retrieving all the records pertinent to q_i. After the removal of q_j, f_i is replaced by f_i+f_j.

After applying Procedure 1, the query set contains only those queries each of which is not contained in another query. That is, every query is maximal. If every query in the given query set is maximal, the set is said to satisfy the maximal query condition.

EXAMPLE 3: If we have the following query in addition to the queries in Example 2,

$$q_7 = \{p_1, p_3\},$$

it can be removed since $q_1 \supseteq q_7$. The frequencies are assumed as follows

$$f_1=50, \quad f_2=200, \quad f_3=40, \quad f_4=100, \quad f_5=150, \quad f_6=50, \quad f_7=40$$

After the removal of q_7, f_1 becomes $f_1+f_7=90$.

The following properties are useful:

(1) If the given query set satisfies the maximal query condition and there exists a record pertinent to more than two queries, only at most two of the queries can be represented by a CR file.

(2) If a subset of queries forms a cycle in the query hypergraph, at least one of the queries in the subset cannot be represented by a CR file.

EXAMPLE 4: Consider the record set of Example 3. The query set satisfies the maximal query property after the removal of q_7 as shown in Example 3. Each of p_2, p_3 and p_8 is contained in three queries

p_2 is contained in $\{q_2, q_3, q_4\}$
p_3 is contained in $\{q_1, q_2, q_3\}$,
p_8 is contained in $\{q_3, q_4, q_6\}$.

By (1) above at most two queries in each set can be represented by a CR file. Since q_3 contains all the records, we will not represent q_3 in a CR file. After removing q_3 the hypergraph in Fig. 8(b) is obtained.

This hypergraph contains a cycle consisting of q_4, q_5 and q_6. By (2) above we have to give up at least one of the three queries. By removing any one of the three queries, a sequence representing the other queries is obtained. Figure 8(c) shows the case when q_6 is removed. We can use frequencies to determine which queries should be removed.

A connected CR file representing more than one query which satisfies the maximal query condition has two external queries. In Fig. 8(c), q_1 and q_5 are external queries. In general a CR file consisting of k separate sequences usually has 2k external queries. Records in external queries not contained in any other queries are called external records. Other records are called internal records. In Fig. 8(c), p_1, p_4 and p_6 are external records. The following properties are obvious

(i) For a CR file, if a query containing one or more internal records is added, the result is not a CR file.

(ii) If a query which contains external records and does not contain any internal records of a CR file is added, the following three cases arises:

(ii-1) If these external records are contained in one external query of the CR file, addition of the query to the CR file results in a new CR file.

(ii-2) If these external records are contained in two external queries in two different sequences of the CR file, a new CR file is generated by adding the query to the CR file.

(ii-3) Otherwise (the query containing two external records in two different external queries of one connected sequence in the CR file is added), a cycle is formed.

(iii) For a CR file if a query which does not contain any record in the CR file is added, the number of separate sequences in the CR file will be increased by one.

We will develop a procedure for constructing a CR file by adding a query one by one using (ii-1), (ii-2) and (iii). Consider the case when there is more than one candidate satisfying (ii-1).

Figure 9(a) shows the case when there are external records p_1, p_2, ..., p_h in one external query of a CR file consisting of more than one query. By (ii-1), any query which contains at least one of the external records and not containing any other records in the CR file is a candidate to be added. After the addition of one query, all the records p_1, p_2, ..., p_h becomes internal records (see Fig. 9(b)). Thus, only one of the candidate queries can be added and all the other queries cannot be added afterwords. We use the frequency to select a query.

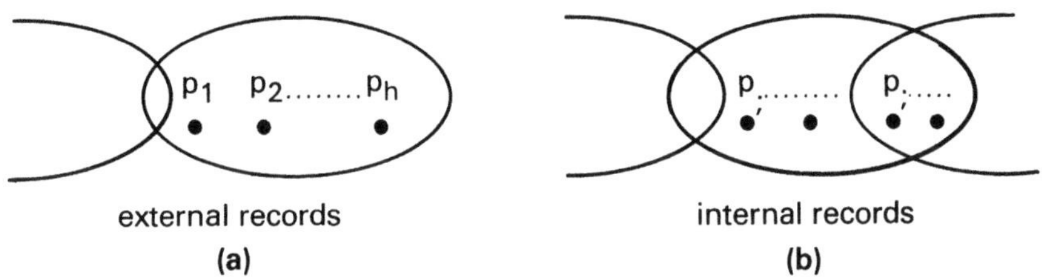

Figure 9. Effect of the addition of one query.

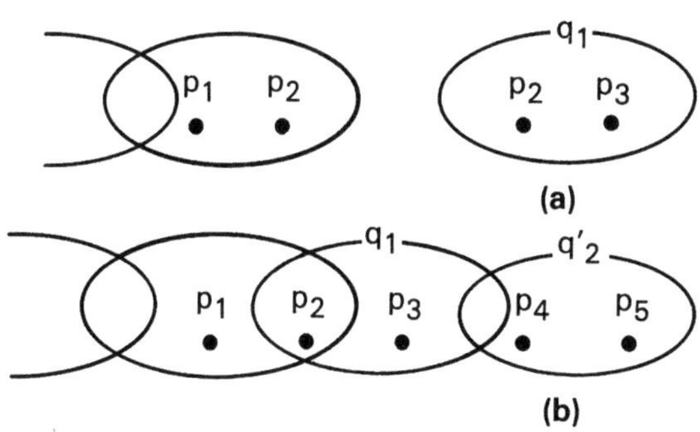

Figure 10. Example 5

EXAMPLE 5: Consider the case shown in Fig. 10(a), where there are external records p_1 and p_2. We assume that there are two candidate queries, $q_1=\{p_2, p_3\}$ and $q_2=\{p_1, p_4, p_5\}$, to be added. If q_1 is selected, q_2 is replaced by $q_2'=\{p_4, p_5\}$ (Fig. 10(b)). If q_2' is represented by the final file, the total cost of processing q_2 is $2f_2$, where f_2 is the frequency of q_2.

As shown in the above example, if a query is not selected it is divided into two subqueries and the cost of processing the query will be increased by the frequency of the query. Thus we select a query with the maximum frequency.

PROCEDURE 2: Organization of a CR file using frequencies of queries

(1) Select a query with the highest frequency and form a CR file containing the query.

(2) Select all the candidate queries satisfying the conditions (ii-1), (ii-2) or (iii) for the current CR file.

(3) Among the candidates select one with the highest frequency and form a new CR file.

(4) Candidates which are known not to be represented by the CR file are replaced as follows. q_i is replaced by q_i-X, where X is the record set contained in the current CR file. Its frequency is unchanged. We can apply Procedure 1 to the resulting set of queries.

(5) Go to (2) and repeat this process until all the records are included in the CR file. Note that a CR file may consist of more than one sequence.

EXAMPLE 6: For the query set in Example 2, suppose that the following frequencies are assigned.

$$f_1=90,\ f_2=200,\ f_3=40,\ f_4=100,\ f_5=150,\ f_6=50$$

q_2 is selected first since f_2 is maximum, and the following file is obtained

$$p_2\ p_3\ p_5$$

q_1, q_3, q_4 are candidates. If q_4 is selected, we have the following file

$$p_3\ p_2\ p_5\ p_7\ p_8$$

We need two accesses of this file for q_3. For external records p_7 and p_8, there are two candidates q_5 and q_6. If q_5 is selected, we have the following file

$$p_3\ p_2\ p_5\ p_8\ p_7\ p_6$$

q_6 needs tow accesses. For another external record p_3, we can add q_1. The CR file obtained is as follows

$$p_1\ p_4\ p_3\ p_2\ p_5\ p_8\ p_7\ p_6$$

EXAMPLE 7: Consider the same set of queries as the previous example with different frequencies

$$f_1=50,\ f_2=100,\ f_3=200,\ f_4=80,\ f_5=50,\ f_6=50$$

q_3 is selected first and the following file is obtained

$$p_2\ p_3\ p_8$$

q_1, q_2, q_4 and q_6 are candidates. If q_2 is selected, the file becomes

$$p_8\ p_2\ p_3\ p_5$$

and q_1 and q_4 are replaced by the new sets

$$q_1=\{p_1, p_4\} \quad q_4=\{p_5, p_7\}$$

q_4 is the candidate for the external record p_5

$$p_8\ p_2\ p_3\ p_5\ p_7$$

Original q_4 can be processed by two accesses. q_6 is a candidate for external record p_8 and q_5 is a candidate for external record p_7, but we cannot add both. If q_5 is selected, the following file is obtained

$$p_8\ p_2\ p_3\ p_5\ p_7\ p_6$$

q_1 forms an isolated sequence

$$p_1\ p_4$$

The above two sequences form the resulting CR file.

5. THE CR PROPERTY FOR BUFFERED MAIN MEMORY AND A SCHEDULE FOR A QUERY SET

In the previous section we showed that a given query set can be simplified by eliminating queries which are contained in other queries. If q_j is eliminated because $q_i \supseteq q_j$, the records pertinent to q_j may not be consecutively located in the file, although the records pertinent to q_i are consecutively located. We can, however, process q_j by retrieving all the records pertinent to q_i. This idea can be extended to queries not contained in other queries.

Assume that a buffer memory can hold w records. A query can be processed by a single direct access if records pertinent to it is contained in a subsequence of length w. These records are not required to be consecutively located. This is the essence of the quasi-consecutive retrieval (QCR) property. The CR file organization discussed so far requires a buffer which can hold all the records pertinent to any query. Thus we can assume that the buffer size is at least the size required by the largest (pertinent records maximum) query.

EXAMPLE 8: In Fig. 8(c) if we assume that the buffer size is 4 then any query can be processed by a single direct access. As a CR file q_3 and q_6 are not represented. q_3 can be processed by retrieving four records $p_3\ p_2\ p_5\ p_8$ and q_6 can be processed by retrieving three records $p_8\ p_7\ p_6$.

For organizing a QCR file we have to address the following problems:

(i) Internal records must be considered to check if they are located within the buffer size.

(ii) By adding a new query to a QCR file, more than one query may be represented by the resulting QCR file.

These cases are shown in Example 9.

To organize a QCR file the following approach is used

(1) Use a procedure to organize a QCR file, which is similar to Procedure 1.

(2) Improve the file by permuting adjacent records.

Instead of giving a procedure for (1) we will show an example. For the second step see [TANA79].

EXAMPLE 9: Consider the following CR file representing q_1 and q_2 ($q_1=\{p_1,p_3,p_4\}$, $q_2=\{p_2,p_3,p_5\}$) and we will select a query to be added to the file. The buffer size is four

$$p_1\ p_4\ p_3\ p_2\ p_5$$

(i) In order to find queries for external records p_2 and p_5, we have to consider the internal record p_3, since the buffer size is four. For example, if there is a query $\{p_3,\ p_6\}$, it can be processed using either of the following files

$$p_1\ p_4\ p_3\ p_2\ p_5\ p_6$$

$$p_6\ p_1\ p_4\ p_3\ p_2\ p_5$$

(ii) For the query set of Example 2, q_3 and q_4 are the candidates. By adding q_4, q_3 is also represented and the QCR organization is:

$$p_1\ p_4\ p_3\ p_2\ p_5\ p_8\ p_7$$

If there exists a query consisting of many records, these records may not be stored in the buffer. The concept of the buffer-limited QCR (BL-QCR) property is introduced to handle such cases [KAMB83].

EXAMPLE 10: If the buffer size is three, we need two direct accesses to process q_4 in Example 2. If q_4 is decomposed into two queries, $q_{41}=\{p_2,p_5\}$ and $q_{42}=\{p_7\ p_8\}$, we have the following file

$$p_1\ p_4\ p_3\ p_2\ p_5\ p_6\ p_7\ p_8$$

Here, q_3 and q_4 require two accesses.

If the buffer size is small, some queries cannot be processed. In the above example, if q_4 is an OR query, $p_2 \vee p_5 \vee p_7 \vee p_8$, we must store all records in $p_2 \vee p_5 \vee p_7 \vee p_8$. We can assume that if the pertinent records of a query require more space than the buffer it will be decomposed. The decomposition, however, may not be done arbitrarily.

The concept of utilizing buffers can also be used in a query processing schedule for a set of queries. So far we have discussed the organization of files considering frequently used queries. When multiple queries are processed simultaneously we can use the following method to reduce the total processing time

(1) A set of queries, whose pertinent records can be held in the buffer, can be processed by a single direct access.

(2) By retaining some records in the buffer the number of direct accesses can be reduced.

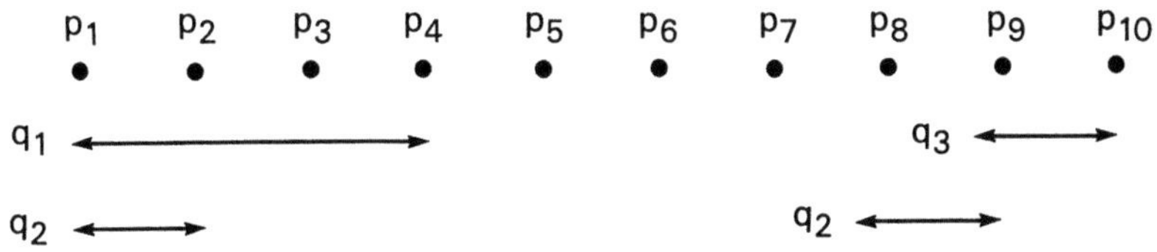

Figure 11. Processing of a set of queries.

EXAMPLE 11: Consider the following query set and the structure of the file is given as Fig. 11

$$q_1=\{p_1, p_2, p_3, p_4\}$$
$$q_2=\{p_1, p_2, p_8, p_9\}$$
$$q_3=\{p_9, p_{10}\}$$

Suppose that the buffer size is five. To process q_1, q_2 and q_3 separately, we need 1, 2, 1 accesses, respectively. We need, however, only two accesses to process all the three queries

(1) Retrieve p_1 p_2 p_3 p_4. q_1 can be processed. Keep p_1 p_2 in the buffer.

(2) Retrieve p_8 p_9 p_{10}. Since the buffer contains p_1 p_2 p_8 p_9 p_{10}, both q_2 and q_3 can be processed.

At the second step we kept some records to reduce the number of direct accesses.

6. REMARKS

Several interesting CR concepts have been discussed in this chapter. In Section 3, organizations of CR files based on various kinds of graphs are discussed. In Sections 4 and 5, organizations of CR and QCR files on linear structured graphs are discussed. Applications of these concepts to various kinds of graphs such as the QCR property on f-graphs, organization of a graph considering multiple accesses, *etc.*, have been introduced for the first time.

It is always challenging to find new application areas of the CR property. In this chapter, data composition (Section 2), data structure design, file allocation, mass storage systems (Section 3) are briefly discussed. Depending of the application area, the CR property or the QCR property is selected. For KWIC index, we use the CR property and the QCR property is not suitable, since titles containing the same keyword should be consecutively arranged [KONI83]. On the other hand for logic circuit layout, the QCR property gives a better result [KAMB83]. Note that some applications like KWIC index and logic circuit layout, reconstructing is not required although it is required by files due to the updating of data.

References

(BERN81, see BERN81a) (BOOT76) (DIET79) (GHOS72) (GHOS73) (GHOS74) (GHOS75) (GHOS77) (GHOS83a) (GHOS83b) (HAJO57) (KAMB78) (KAMB83, see KAMB83b) (KONI83) (LIPS76) (LIPS78) (LIPS83a) (LIPS83b) (LONC83) (MERR77) (MERR83) (SUZU83) (TANA79) (TANA83) (TRUS83) (VANA51) (WAKS74) (YAMA77)

Section VII

Query Processing in Database Machines

The Intelligent Database Machine (IDM)

Michael Ubell

Abstract

This paper presents an overview of the software and hardware architecture of Britton-Lee Corporation's Intelligent Database Machine (the IDM). The IDM was designed to provide quality database performance at a moderate cost. Communication between the host computer and the IDM is discussed, as are the issues involved in dividing the total work load between the host computer and the IDM backend machine. In addition, certain performance characteristics of the IDM are presented.

1. Introduction

The concept of a 'database machine' has been described in many places, including a number of design proposals. With the exception, however, of the ICL CAFS [MITC76] and the Intel iDBP [LOWE82], both shipped only in small quantities, none of these have ever been built and marketed. The Intelligent Database Machine (the IDM) is the first of these special-purpose computers to reach the general marketplace in quantity. The IDM is also the first database machine to be designed with the intent of providing a fast, complete relational database management system at low cost.

The IDM is a backend machine that provides a host-independent facility for managing data; data possibly shared by several heterogeneous host computers. The intelligence required by the host computer to manage normal user communications is provided by the IDM Host Software; software which is resident in the host computer

The architecture of the IDM is based on two main observations. First, there are only a few well-defined tasks which a relational DBMS performs often while processing transactions. These tasks are microcoded in the IDM's specially designed processor, the Database Accelerator. Second, any database management system is more efficient in a dedicated environment. Combining these observations leads to a lower cost solution for high performance database management needs.

This paper first discusses how the IDM is combined with one or more host computers to provide all the functions of a relational database management system (Sections 1,2, and 3). Next an outline of the structure of the IDM data management software is presented (Section 4) followed by a discussion of the advantages of a dedicated environment (Section 5). The paper concludes with a brief description of the IDM hardware (Section 6) and the performance characteristics of the entire system (Section 7).

2. Database Management

Database management systems provide many functions. These include validity checking, protection, query optimization, access path selection, logging, and crash recovery. Database management systems also include different ways for users to interact with the system, including various ways of entering, requesting, and presenting data.

A complete IDM database management system is formed by combining the resources of the special purpose IDM backend hardware, including it disks, and the intelligence of the IDM Host Software resident in the host computer(s). The IDM hardware implements all the facilities of a relational database management system, while the IDM Host Software provides the host with the intelligence to manage user communication, including the implementation of language processors, report generators, and the necessary screen handlers. This division of tasks between the host and the IDM provides for the most efficient use of the IDM backend hardware without restricting the user to a particular language or terminal interface.

As part of the general design strategy the host computer, using the IDM Host Software, makes high level requests of the IDM. For example, the host computer requests the IDM to "run a database operation and return the results".

It would have been possible, of course, to define the IDM/host interface at a much lower level, say the "fetch a record" level of the Research Storage Interface in System-R [BLAS81]. If this were done however, the host would have to access the IDM almost as much as it would have accessed its own disk while doing the work itself. In addition, the implementation of concurrency control would have become more difficult.

Using a "record at a time" interface, concurrency control requires the host to declare how much of a relation (or file) will be accessed or updated so that the backend system can determine whether to lock the whole relation or just lock touched pages. This requires additional accesses of the database and increases the communication overhead. Since the IDM processes higher level commands and does the access path selection, it can determine these needs without directives from the host. In addition the IDM takes into consideration the total current access requirements and promotes locking to a higher level when there are too many page level locks requested on a single relation. This type of interface is only possible with a data model like the relational one, in which commands are given at a very high level.

Language processors, report writers, and screen handlers are the type of tasks which general-purpose computers are designed to handle efficiently and these tasks are left to the host and the IDM Host Software. These tasks can be built in a machine independent manner however, and are therefore portable to many environments. Data management functions, on the other hand, must take advantage of various system resources and are harder to port to multiple machine environments. By moving the data management functions to the IDM backend, these functions can be implemented once, in an optimal environment, with no need for compromises to fit various architectures or operating systems.

A software view of a complete IDM data management system is shown in Figure 1. The top of figure 1 shows the programs which interact with users. All of these programs, in one way or another, translate source language database commands into IDM internal commands. The source language may be a query language or even a forms system. For example, the precompilers translate user written application programs, containing embedded query language commands, into intermediate source code without the embedded commands. The precompiler processes the embedded query language statements and stores them in the IDM in internal IDM form while replacing the query statements with procedure calls which activate these pre-stored commands.

The second level of figure 1 represents the interface routines which handle the functions common to all the programs at the higher level. These functions include parsing one or more source query languages, buffering data to and from the next level, and conversion of data types.

3. Communication

The host communicates with the IDM at two levels. The first level is a driver level which uses an internal protocol to guarantee the reliable transmission of data between the two computers. This level depends on the type of interface used and is implemented by a device driver (or handler) which is usually in the host operating system. In some systems, like IBM's Virtual Machine (VM) operating system, this is done in a service virtual machine so that the database resources may be shared.

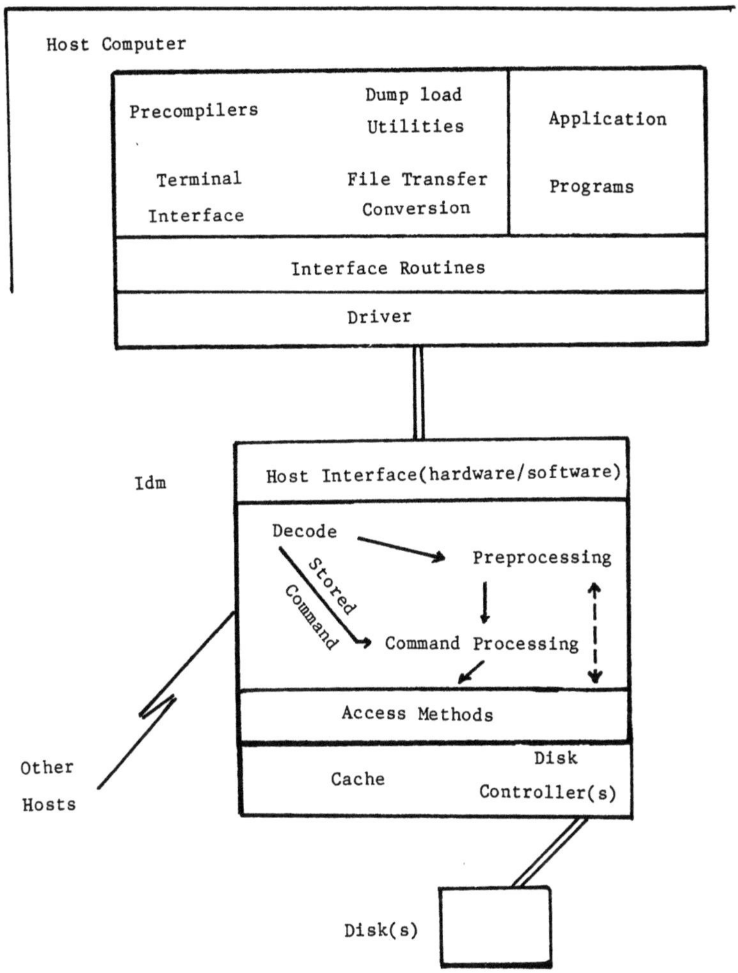

Figure 1: Software view of an IDM data management system.

The second level of communication is an applications level. Using this level a user program sends to the IDM a packet of bytes which is interpreted as a command by the IDM. The IDM returns to the user program any data generated by the command, including error and status messages.

A command packet begins with a command token (RETRIEVE, APPEND, etc.) and any parameters appropriate to the command. The parameters usually include a binary tree which represents the target list (columns affected by the command) and the qualification (records affected by the command). The internal IDM representation is mostly independent of the query language used to express the query and the interface library provides routines that simplify the task of generating command packets and handling returned data.

For example, the following two queries have the same semantics and are handled in a similar fashion. The first query is written in SQL [CHAM76], and the second query is written in IDL [BRIT84] or QUEL [STON76].

```
SELECT name FROM employee
        WHERE dept = 'shoe';

RANGE OF e IS employee
RETRIEVE (e.name)
        WHERE e.dept = "shoe"
```

They can both be expressed by the following IDM command:

```
RETRIEVE
RANGE 0 employee

               ROOT
              /   \
             /     EQ
            /     / \
      RESDOM     /  CHAR shoe
      /    \   VAR 0 dept
    END   VAR 0 name

END_OF_COMMAND
```

The references to the relation "employee" are replaced by the "range variable" 0 which allows multiple references to the same relation in a single command. This also reduces the amount of data that needs to be transmitted to the IDM. Note that the capitalized words are single-byte tokens which can be thought of as "opcodes" for the IDM. Some tokens, like ROOT and RESDOM, are used to maintain the binary structure of the tree, while others, like VAR and CHAR, represent values which are manipulated. When sent to the IDM, the tree is "flattened" by a post-order traversal and constants are preceded by their length, providing a compact, language independent representation of the query. A complete specification of the IDM command language is contained in [BRIT84].

While this representation is best suited for languages like IDL, which do not include nesting, it can also be used to process nested languages such as SQL. This requires the use of the IDM aggregate function facility and some additional processing in the host. In the examples below an SQL query is translated into the equivalent IDL query. In practice, the SQL is translated directly into the IDM internal format.

```
SELECT * FROM a
        WHERE x > ALL (SELECT y FROM b WHERE z = 30);
```

This is equivalent to "x" being larger than the largest value from the inner select. The host must generate the equivalent IDM "tree" for:

```
RETRIEVE (a.all) WHERE a.x > MAX(b.y WHERE b.z = 30)
```

A "less than" comparison is similar. An equals requires that all values of the inner query be the same and is accomplished by counting the unique values:

```
RETRIEVE (a.all) WHERE ANY(a.x BY a.x
                        WHERE a.x = b.y AND b.z = 30) = 1
                   AND COUNT UNIQUE (b.y WHERE b.z = 30) = 1
```

The IDM automatically processes the COUNT first and determines if there is more than one value for "y". An inner select statement must be bound to the outer query with a relational operator and possibly the key words ALL or ANY. If there is no key word then the inner query must return exactly one value or else generate an error. The IDM includes a special aggregate function that traps this condition. Otherwise there is a simple mapping as with the "greater than" operator.

The IDM returns data to the host in block form, rather than one record at a time, while the host interface library contains routines that select the appropriate records, and fields within the records, for host process or display. In order to minimize data transfer overhead, the host specifies to the IDM the size of the data block that it can efficiently handle. The host may also request that the data type and or name of each column be returned in advance of the data which eliminates the need for the host to maintain this information or interrogate the data dictionary.

4. IDM Data Management Software

The high level software in the IDM, for example verification routines, query processing, and sorting, are all built on top of a set of access-method routines which together implement an interface similar to the RSS of system R. This interface is a "fetch a record" level interface and includes commands that open and close relations, search indexes, retrieve the next qualifying record, and append, delete or replace records. These commands reorganize the data pages affected and update indices as necessary.

At the bottom level of these access-method activities are a small set of proprietary routines designed to be executed by a special processor, the Database Accelerator. By isolating the often executed tasks and moving them to specialized hardware great efficiency is achieved. The Database Accelerator is emulated by software routines with a resulting loss in speed in smaller systems.

Upon receiving a command, the IDM verifies the existence requirements and access rights necessary for execution of the command. Data operations are also validated at this time (e.g. the addition of character strings is not allowed).

These functions, typically performed during the parsing phase of a command interpretation, are better performed in the database machine since they require access to the data dictionary. Repetitive parsing and validation only occurs in ad hoc interactive applications. Ordinarily, commands are specified by a user's program, and it is possible to take advantage of the IDM's ability to store preprocessed commands in the database. These commands can then be executed many times by specifying the command names and parameters. This bypasses most parsing and validation activities and increases the efficiency of the system.

Another important IDM facility is the set of routines which handle transactions by recording the updates in a log that is used for recovery and audit tasks. The log is a write ahead log [GRAY78] and the access methods guarantee that the log is written to disk prior to writting any pages which were affected by the updates recorded in the log. The IDM accepts transaction commands (BEGIN TRANSACTION, END TRANSACTION and ABORT TRANSACTION) which can be used to combine multiple commands into a single transaction.

Other higher level routines in the IDM interrogate the data dictionary using the access-method interface to select join strategies and indices to resolve queries. These higher level routines also determine if the access methods should do relation or page level concurrency control.

For each relation an index and search criterion is passed to the access methods which return the qualifying records. The records may need to be processed further and then formatted and returned to the host or used to update the database.

Processing not done by the access methods includes complex qualifications (those including arithmetic operations which cannot be simplified before the access method call) and expression evaluation performed on the returned data.

The IDM implements three access methods.

The first is just a total relation scan. This is done by beginning at the first page of the relation and following the linked list of pages.

A relation may also have one clustered index. A clustered index is a b-tree index in which the data is kept in the bottom level of the tree providing a compact index to the data. This type of index also guarantees that the data is kept sorted on the keys.

A relation may also have up to 200 non-clustered indices. A non-clustered index is a b-tree in which the bottom level consists of the keys and one pointer to each record having that key. Each index may have up to 15 keys.

The IDM uses nested loop substitution and reformatting strategys to process a multi-relation query. Nested loop substitution is a process in which a record from one relation is selected and substituted into the rest of the query. For each relation the IDM will chose an index if one is available. If none is available it may reformat the relation by projecting and restricting it and then building an index on the fields in the remaining query.

5. Dedicated Environment

Operating systems traditionally manage system resources by guessing what an application program is likely to do next. Because DBMS I/O access is very different from most programs [HAWT79], this does not work well for database management systems. The DBMS code, not the operating system, "knows" how to optimally schedule disk accesses or which pages are likely to be re-referenced. The IDM software is designed to take advantage of this knowledge and has all the advantages of a dedicated system environment.

The operating system in the IDM can be best described as an "anarchistic" operating system. The database manager processes cooperate in managing the disk buffer cache, determining which pages should stay in main memory and which should be returned to disk. The operating system will not suspend a process, other than for disk I/O or a concurrency lock, unless the process "volunteers" to be suspended. This feature allows for optimal disk buffering in that a process will never read a page and then not process it before giving up the CPU if it can process it in a "reasonable" amount of time. In other systems a process will be suspended when its quantum is done, possibly requiring it to regain resources when it is able to run again.

The operating kernel schedules the actual I/O and implements a global disk scheduling policy. It is also responsible for allocating memory to processes and maintaining process statistics. The process statistics are used for system tuning and by the data manager processes to determine when it is time to be suspended.

6. IDM Hardware

The hardware of the IDM consists of 6 types of boards communicating on a high-speed bus.

- Host Interface Channels
- Database Processor
- Database Accelerator
- Memory Timing and Control
- Memory Storage
- Disk and Tape Controllers

The exact configuration is site dependent since the number of Controllers and Channels may be varied. Figure 2 is a diagram of one possible hardware organization of the IDM and shows the IDM 500 (in the box) connected to disks, tape and host computers. Commands are passed from the host computers to the Host Interface Channels which buffer messages into the IDM memory. The command is then processed by the Database Processor and the Database Accelerator. Data to resolve the command is either found in memory or read from the disk drives by the Disk Controllers. Tape and the Tape Controller are used by the system for backup and recovery functions.

6.1. Host Interface Channels

One or more hosts communicate with each IDM Channel. The channel implements a communication protocol with the host and buffers data coming into and leaving the IDM. These functions shield the rest of the system from the communication interrupts and allows it to see a uniform command stream. Since it is necessary to have potentially many users from one host making requests to the database machine, the channel must control multiple streams of data to and from the host. This includes keeping track of pending requests, notifying the host of available data, packaging the data into host-specified packet sizes, and error checking and correction. This work could easily use up much of the processing power of the Database Processor if there where no channel to do the work.

Each channel consists of a microprocessor, memory, and the hardware needed to implement a particular type of interface. The channels on the IDM currently support 4 different interfaces.

One type of channel can support 8 serial (rs232c) lines. These can be used to communicate with a host where large amounts of data need not be transferred. A single line can handle about 3 short transactions a second (a short transaction is a simple update or a retrieval which returns about 20 bytes). A serial line can also be used to connect a personal computer to the IDM. Here the speed at which data can be used is typically limited by how fast the person using the computer can read the data.

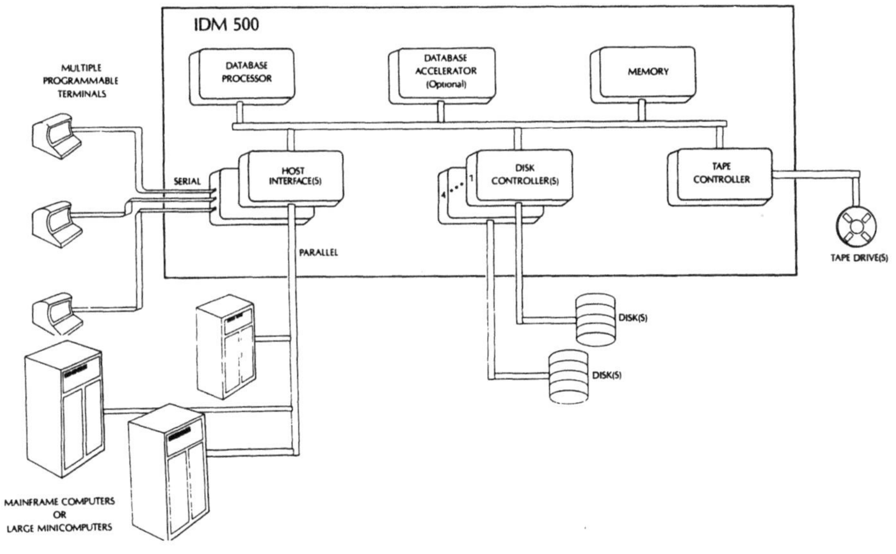

Figure 2. The IDM hardware organization.

A second interface is the parallel (IEEE-488) interface. This interface can handle up to 8 hosts through a shared byte-wide interface. This interface can transfer up to about 100 kilo bytes per second but in most applications a sustained rate of about 30 kilo bytes per second is more typical. This is the interface used to connect mini- and supermini computers to the IDM. It has been shown to sustain at least 25 short transactions per second.

Another interface is the Ethernet channel. This interface allows a large number of hosts to communicate with the IDM. The Ethernet is capable of transferring data at about 1 Megabyte per second. The attainable rate is typically less than this and there is overhead in bytes sent as part of the communication protocol. Ethernet interfaces are available for many different types of computers, from personal computers to mainframes.

The last interface is an interface to the IBM block multiplexer channel. This interface can connect the IDM to IBM and other main-frame computers in the same manner as a disk controller. This interface is capable of about 40 transactions per second and a high data transfer rate.

6.2. Database Processor

Once a command is accumulated in a channel, the channel notifies the Database Processor which transfers it to the main memory for the rest of its processing. The Database Processor is responsible for controlling the other boards in the system and also implements most of the functionality of the system. It uses a standard 16 bit micro-processor chip (Zilog Z8000). It must execute about 55,000 lines of code written in a high level language to implement the relational DBMS. The Database Processor board includes the memory management hardware for the system. This is used to map different areas of the main memory to the address space of the Z8000. Database processes share data and also have a private data area. Most of the shared area consists of the disk and relation descriptor cache. All code is shared among the tasks and is kept resident in memory.

The Database Processor detects the presence of the Database Accelerator at system initialization and overwrites the emulation routines with code that calls the Database Accelerator. The interface to the Accelerator is through memory, with one input register in the Database Accelerator indicating where to find the command. Since the code would otherwise call a subroutine all parameters are placed on the program call stack. The Data Base Processor writes the address of the top of the stack in the input register of the Accelerator. The Accelerator indicates that it is busy in its output register and processes the command. The Database Processor polls for the Accelerator to finish the command. During this time it may run non-user code to schedule disk activity or handle traffic to and from the Channels.

6.3. Database Accelerator

The Database Accelerator is constructed with standard ECL medium scale integrated (MSI) circuits. The most complex components other than memory are the arithmetic logic unit chips. The Accelerator contains 4 Kilo-words of micro-store which is coded to execute database primitives. The routines in the Accelerator are mainly those involved with looking at data within a 2 Kilo-byte page from the database, in other words, the inner loop of most processing activities. It is capable of executing approximately 10 million instructions per second and can run asynchronously with the memory. The Accelerator can request up to 16 bytes from the memory system and then proceed with other non-memory instructions while the data is fetched. Since the Accelerator can execute about 8 instructions while waiting for memory to start transferring it can overlap bookkeeping activities with the memory latency. Bookkeeping includes such functions as determining if it has reached the end of a page, or calculating the length of a field. Once the data starts arriving the Accelerator can process one byte approximately every 100 nanoseconds. The Accelerator also contains 256 words of register memory which is used to cache data from main memory as well as for general programming variables.

The Accelerator does not process interrupts or manage context switching, which are handled by the Data Base Processor. Once given a command the Accelerator runs to completion. Since it can process a page of data in about 1 millisecond and it is not given more than a few pages to process at a time this does not pose a scheduling problem. A general purpose high speed processor would need to be much more complicated, since it would run arbitrary code and would need to be interruptible.

6.4. Memory System

The IDM can hold up to 6 Megabytes of memory. The Memory Timing and Control board handles the timing for the memory and does the error detection and correction. The memory system can correct one-bit errors and detect two-bit errors. This, together with address and data parity on the IDM bus, insures data integrity throughout the system. All correction is done without the intervention of the Database Processor. The memory is used for holding the code executed by the Data Base Processor (about 300 Killobytes), disk and relation caching, buffering of data to and from the communications Channels, and user process data space. The memory system of the IDM provides up to 2 Megabytes for disk caching and additional space for user processes and host I/O buffering.

The memory has two modes of operation; one is byte- and word-oriented for the Data Base Processor and the other, faster, mode is block-oriented for the Accelerator and Disk Controllers which deal in streams of data. In block mode, the memory and the bus can handle the needs of 5 controllers and the Accelerator. The Data Base Processor gets whatever time is left. The streaming nature of the memory system allows the use of standard-speed memory components.

6.5. Controllers

The IDM Disk Controller interfaces to up to four Storage Module Device disk drives. Such drives are currently available in sizes up to about 600 Megabytes. The Disk Controller is responsible for the reliable transfer of data to and form the disk. It implements burst error correction and retry without any intervention from the Database Processor. There can be up to 4 Disk Controllers on the IDM with a total of 16 disks. While this limits the storage capacity to about 9 Gigabytes with current disk technology, the IDM can address up to 32 Gigabytes of disk storage when disk drives become denser. In addition there can be 1 Tape Controller for 1 or 2 tape drives at up to 160 Killobytes per second. The tape drives are used for database backup and loading.

7. Performance Characteristics

This Section presents certain IDM system performance statistics.

On simple retrievals and updates to a relation with a two level b-tree index, processing times between 30 and 60 milliseconds are common. The IDM can process more than 20 of these simple retrieval commands a second when more than one command is active to allow the overlapping of the disk I/O and the processing time. A two level clustered index on the IDM can access over 1.6 million 200 byte records using 2 byte keys.

A retrieval which scans 24000 records, counting those which qualify to 4 restrictions, can run in about 3 seconds when the data is not in memory and runs in about 1 second when the data is in memory. In our particular tests the retrieval found about 1000 qualifying records. The effect of the Database Accelerator in such queries is quite noticeable.

The Accelerator can find the qualifying records on a page in between about 200 and 3000 microseconds, depending on the number of keys and the number of qualifying records. The routines which run in the Database Processor take from between about 1300 and 44000 microseconds to do the same work if there is no Accelerator in the

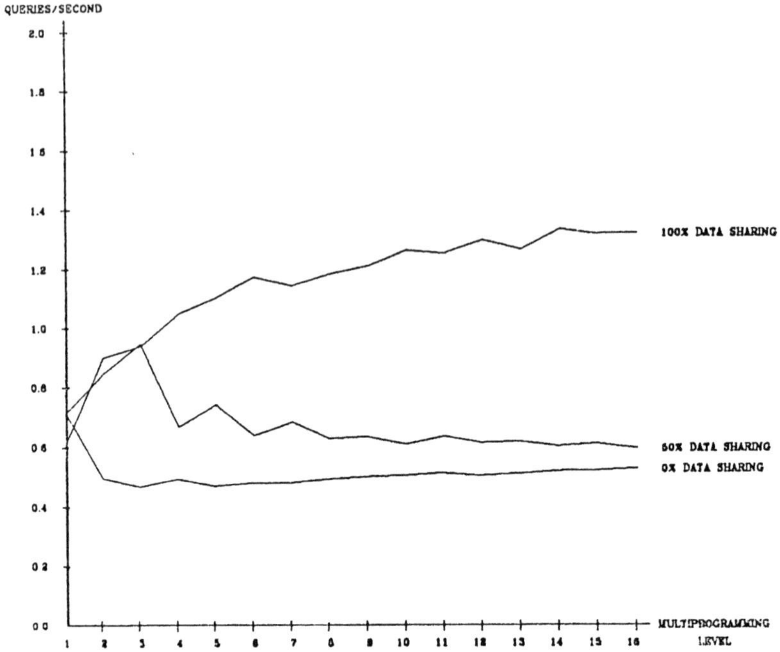

Figure 3. Retrieving 100 records through a non-clustered b-tree index

system. In some cases the Database Accelerator does the work 30 times faster.

The performance of the IDM in a multiuser environment shows no "thrashing" characteristics. When the maximum capacity of the system is reached the throughput declines slowly rather than falling off sharply [BITT83]. This desirable characteristic is due to the disk cache scheduling and the high degree of data sharing among the user processes.

Figures 3 and 4, from [BORA84], shows the throughput of the system in multiuser environments. In these experiments from 1 to 16 processes on a mini-computer submitted similar queries to the IDM retrieving data from 1 to 16 relations each with 10,000 records using random keys. There were 1000 data pages per relation and room for 475 disk cache pages in memory. The degree of sharing was controlled by dividing the process among different relations with the same characteristics. For 100% data sharing every process used the same relation, and for 0% data sharing each process used a different relation.

The first test was retrieving 100 records through a non-clustered index form a 1000 page relation, a task which is I/O bound. A single query of this type takes about 2.4 seconds when there are no pages from the relation in the disk cache. Even with no data sharing the average response time is about 2 seconds indicating that there is still some effective caching. The drop off at the beginning of the curves in Figure 3, where there is less than 100% data sharing, is due to increased contention for the disk cashe.

Figure 4 shows the retrieval of 1 record through a 2 level b-tree index. Note that the throughput increases until the Data Base Processor and Accelerator are saturated and then remains fairly constant.

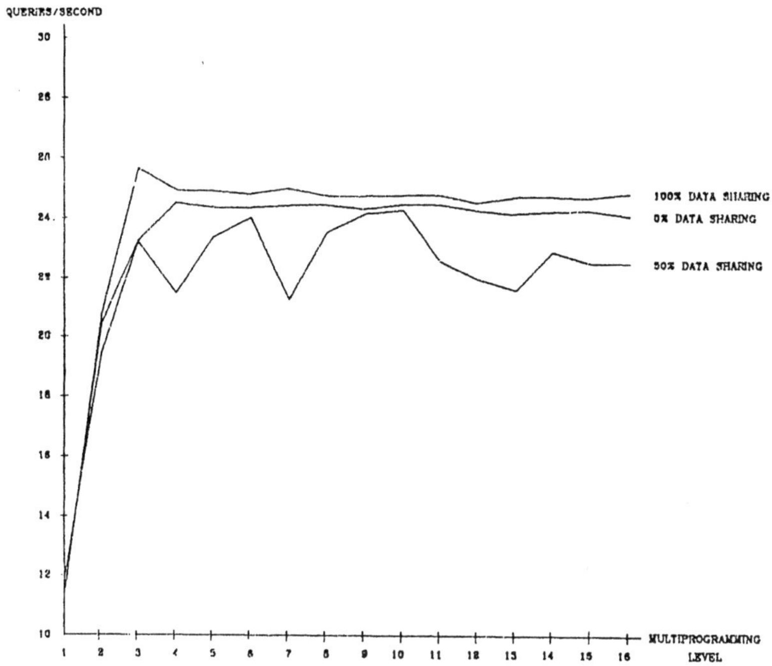

Figure 4. Retrieving 1 record through a clustered b-tree index.

8. Summary

This article has described the architecture and query processing scheme of Britton-Lee Corporation's Intelligent Database Machine. Database machines do not replace general purpose computers but offload specialized database work while adding new functional capacity.

The IDM sells for $35,000 to $100,000, depending on the configuration. Combined with a moderately priced minicomputer, or even a cluster of micro-computers, the IDM provides efficient data management solutions for problems which would be otherwise solvable only at a much greater cost.

When combined with a super-mini or mainframe computer, the IDM can offload the more expensive processor and provide data management services at a lower cost.

References

(ASTR76) (BITT83) (BLAS81, see BLAS79) (BRIT84) (BORA84) (CHAM76)

(GRAY78) (HAWT79) (LOWE82) (MITC76) (STON76)

Relational Query Processing on the Non-Von Supercomputer[1]

David Elliot Shaw

Abstract

The central focus of this chapter is the highly efficient execution of relational database queries using a particular nonstandard machine called NON-VON. NON-VON is a massively parallel, non-von Neumann "supercomputer", portions of which are now being implemented in the Computer Science Department at Columbia University. The machine is intended to support the rapid execution of many large scale data manipulation tasks, including relational database operations and a number of other functions relevant to commercial data processing.

The NON-VON architecture includes a tree-structured primary processing subsystem, which we are implementing using custom nMOS VLSI circuits, along with a secondary processing subsystem based on a bank of intelligent disk drives. A high-bandwidth parallel interface provides for rapid data transfer between the two subsystems. This chapter briefly describes the organization of the NON-VON machine, and considers in somewhat greater detail the manner in which it is used for the high-speed processing of relational database queries.

1 Introduction

Simply stated, the goal of a computer systems engineer is to construct a system that

1. Does what the user wants done.

2. Does it as quickly as possible.

The concurrent realization of these two goals, however, is often impeded by a peculiar sort of "chicken-and-egg" problem. On the one hand, it is difficult to decide which operations should be made highly efficient without identifying those operations which are most frequently executed by a real body of users. Real users, on the other hand, avoid performing operations that require a great deal of time; if these features are essential to the system, they often avoid using

---

[1]This research was supported in part by the Defense Advanced Research Projects Agency under contract N00039-80-G-0132.

the system entirely. The systems engineer is thus left with a distorted view of the intrinsic preferences of his or her users. Moreover, this distortion systematically favors the status quo, since the engineer is unable to identify currently unpopular features that would be used, if only they were more efficiently implemented.

It is our feeling that the present complexion of the market for database management software and hardware may reflect just such a circular distortion of user preferences. In particular, we believe that the many advantages of the relational model of data [CODD71] would by now have led to a nearly uniform adoption of relational database systems in industry were it not for serious problems of efficiency. Conversely, we believe that machines capable of supporting the highly efficient execution of relational database operations might well be commercially available today if a sufficiently large market for such hardware had been identified a decade or so ago.

Within this framework, the efforts of researchers interested in the implementation of database machines [OZKA75, SU75, MCGR76, HSIA77, DEWI78, SHAW79, BABB79, KIM80, SONG81] capable of supporting the relational model of data may be viewed as an "act of faith". Because we believe that relational database systems, and in particular, their most time-consuming operations, would be employed by a great many users if only they could be made much more efficient, we have adopted as one of our central goals the efficient, cost-effective support of the these operations on NON-VON.

In Section 2, we briefly sketch the architecture of the NON-VON machine. Section 3 describes some of the fundamental operations employed in typical NON-VON algorithms, while Section 4 outlines the basis for NON-VON's use as a relational database machine. Section 5 details the manner in which small relations are manipulated; the processing of large relations is described in Section 6. We conclude with a summary of NON-VON's potential utility and a word of caution regarding the formulation of premature conclusions.

2 The NON-VON Architecture

This section outlines the bare essentials of the latest version of the NON-VON family of supercomputers, NON-VON 4. While it is hoped that this description will prove sufficient for an understanding of the algorithms and analysis presented later in the chapter, readers unfamiliar with the NON-VON architecture may wish to review the details of an earlier version of the machine, which have been presented elsewhere [SHAW82].

The top-level organization of the NON-VON machine is illustrated in Figure 1.

NON-VON has two principal components, known as the primary processing subsystem and the secondary processing subsystem. In a typical configuration, the machine would be connected to a host machine, a general purpose computer serving as a front end device for interactions with the user.

The primary processing subsystem is organized as a binary tree consisting of a large number of small processing elements (SPE's). Using a (currently feasible) nMOS process with 2 micron feature size, 16 SPE's can be implemented on a single VLSI chip. Each SPE contains a simple eight-bit ALU, a 64-bit RAM, and communication connections to three neighboring SPE's, which are known as the parent, left child, and right child. In addition, each SPE is capable of communicating, within a single instruction cycle, with two additional SPE's, called the left neighbor and right neighbor. These neighbors are the predecessor

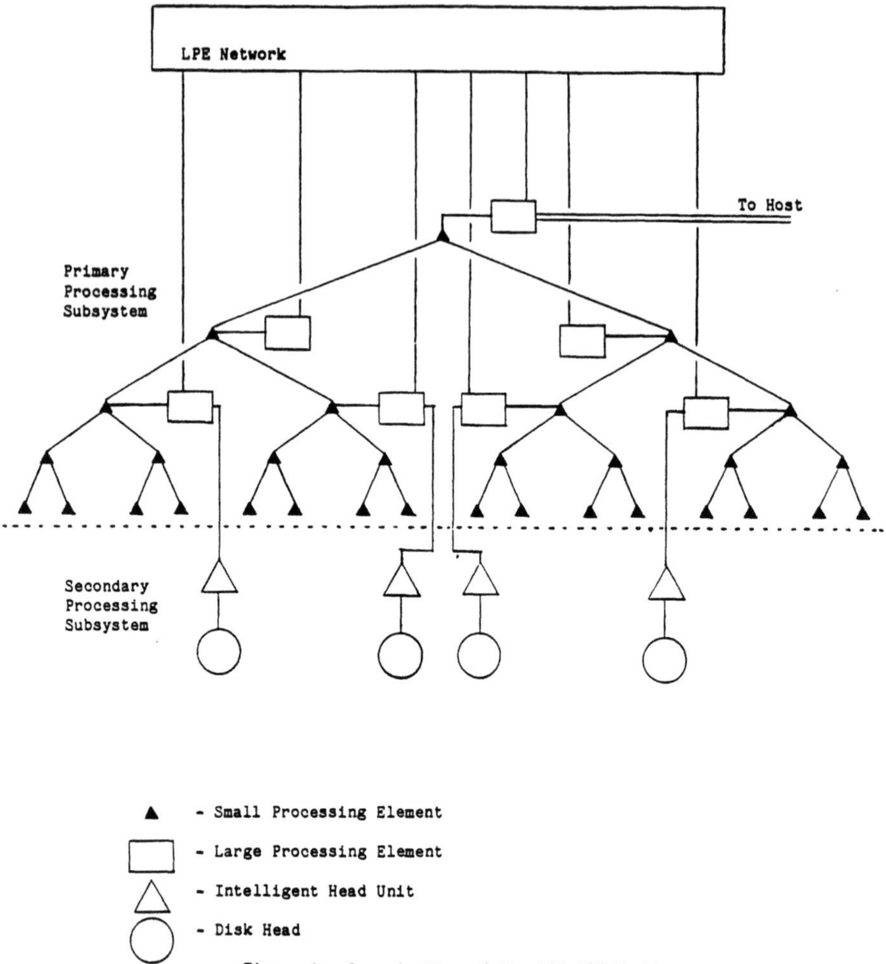

Figure 1: Organization of the NON-VON Machine

and successor in an inorder traversal of the primary processing subsystem tree. Among the uses of NON-VON's physical (tree) and logical (linear) neighbors is the support of tuples whose length exceeds the capacity of a single local RAM.

The SPE's do not store programs locally. Rather, they receive instructions that are broadcast to them from higher up in the primary processing subsystem tree and function in a strictly synchronous manner. Within the top five to ten (depending on the configuration) levels of the primary processing subsystem, each SPE is connected to a _large processing element_ (LPE). Each LPE incorporates a general-purpose microcomputer with a larger RAM, and is thus capable of storing programs locally. The LPE and SPE are designed in such a way that data may be loaded rapidly into the latter from the former.

The LPE's may execute programs independently and asynchronously. In particular, LPE's at the roots of several subtrees of the primary processing subsystem (possibly at different levels) may broadcast separate instruction streams to the SPE's below them, giving NON-VON the capability for what is called _multiple-SIMD_ execution. Each LPE includes a small amount of specialized hardware to perform instruction broadcast and to generate control signals for the SPE's. The LPE from which a given SPE is currently receiving its instructions is referred to as its _control processor_.

The LPE's are connected by a high-bandwidth interconnection network. The precise type of network has not yet been determined; among the candidates are several kinds of logarithmic-stage networks of the butterfly/omega/banyan family and certain configurations based on crossbar switches. While the detailed architecture of the LPE network does not comprise a central part of our research, the use of such a high-bandwidth network is essential to a number of high-performance NON-VON algorithms involving large collections of data, including some reported in this chapter. It should also be noted that, in a typical configuration, the NON-VON machine would be connected to a _host machine_, which would be responsible for such functions as query parsing and optimization and various user interface functions.

The secondary processing subsystem incorporates a substantial number (perhaps between 16 and 256) of disk drives, each of moderate size. Each drive is connected via an _intelligent head unit_ to an LPE in the primary processing subsystem, providing a very high bandwidth interconnection between these two subsystems. In addition to the reading and writing of data to and from disks, intelligent head units perform certain computationally simple operations (hash coding, for example) "on the fly", passing results to the associated LPE's. By way of illustration, a partial match operation (equivalent to the relational algebraic operator _select_) may be executed, passing on to the primary processing subsystem only those tuples that satisfy certain attribute/value criteria.

We are now constructing a prototype primary processing subsystem containing a single LPE and at least 4,096 SPE's. This machine will be connected to a VAX 11/750, which will serve as host. Ultimately, we hope to construct a machine having multiple LPE's and a larger primary processing subsystem.

3 Fundamental Operations

In order to understand the essential operations employed in NON-VON's algorithms for database operations, it would be useful to briefly review certain aspects of the NON-VON SPE and its instruction set. Of central importance is a mechanism that allows an LPE to selectively enable certain of its SPE's. Each SPE contains a one-bit flag called the _enable bit_. When the enable bit is set to 1, the SPE is said to be _enabled_; in this state, it responds to any instruction broadcast by its control processor. When the enable bit is 0, the SPE is _disabled_, and will ignore any such instructions.

The selective enabling of various SPE's is essential to a number of fundamental NON-VON operations. One of these operations involves the parallel comparison of strings stored in a number of SPE's against a string broadcast by their common control processor. All SPE's in which the match fails are disabled, while all matching SPE's remain enabled. Using a single machine language instruction that compares one byte, increments the SPE's memory address register, and disables the SPE in the event of a match failure, NON-VON is able to perform such comparisons at a rate of one byte per instruction cycle (about 400 nanoseconds). This operation is used in all of the relational operations described in the remainder of this chapter.

Another operation used in some of the algorithms described below is the rapid identification of a single SPE from among a set of SPE's in which a given match has succeeded. NON-VON's RESOLVE instruction turns off a particular one-bit flag in all SPE's except the one occuring first in an inorder traversal of the tree. Using this instruction, the members of a set of "marked" SPE's may be sequentially enumerated.

The REPORT instruction causes the contents of a particular register in a single enabled SPE to be transferred to its control processor. This instruction is meaningful only when exactly one SPE in the subtree controlled by a given LPE is enabled. (Note that this condition is always satisfied immediately following the execution of a RESOLVE instruction.) The REPORT and RESOLVE operations are used in several of the database algorithms described below.

4 NON-VON as a Database Machine

The utility of the NON-VON supercomputer in database management applications stems largely from its highly efficient execution of the operators of the _relational algebra_ [CODD71]. Specifically, NON-VON supports highly efficient parallel algorithms for the relational algebraic operators

- Selection
- Projection
- Join
- Union
- Intersection
- Set difference

Update, insertion and deletion operations are also supported in a highly efficient manner. In addition, the machine supports the efficient execution of summation, aggregation, sorting, and various statistical operations, all of which find use in numerous database applications. In this chapter, however, we will restrict our attention to the relational algebraic operators.

In the sections that follow, we will outline the algorithms NON-VON uses to evaluate each of the relational algebraic primitives, both in the case where the arguments can fit entirely within primary storage (the case we call internal evaluation), and where they reside on secondary storage (external evaluation). Space does not permit a detailed explication of the internal evaluation of all of the relational algebraic operators enumerated above, and of the time complexity of each one. Our treatment will thus be abbreviated, and somewhat informal. Readers interested in further details may wish to examine material published elsewhere [SHAW80], [HILL83]. Furthermore, we will not consider the problems of locking and recovery, which are of considerable importance in a realistic multi-user database management system subject to periodic hardware and software failures.

5 Internal Evaluation of the Relational Algebraic Operators

In the discussion that follows, we will assume that each SPE contains a single tuple of an argument relation. In fact, NON-VON supports both packed tuples, several of which are stored in a single SPE, and spanned tuples, which are too large for a single SPE, and must be split among two or more [SHAW82a]. Spanned tuples are supported by splitting a very long tuple into a number of pieces, which are stored within successive (in linear communication order) PE's. Linear communication primitives are employed to pass incomplete matching information between the PE's storing successive pieces of the tuple. Details of the techniques for spanned and packed tuple manipulation are, however, orthogonal to and beyond the scope of the current discussion.

Of the six relational algebraic operators listed above, the simplest to implement on NON-VON is relational selection. To select those tuples of a relation that satisfy some attribute/value criterion, NON-VON simply compares the required values of each attribute simultaneously against the appropriate field in each SPE in the primary processing subsystem, disabling all SPE's that do not match. One instruction cycle is required to match each byte in the specified value string. When performing such an operation, the NON-VON primary processing subsystem functions as a simple content addressable memory. At the end of the select operation, only those tuples that satisfy the given attribute/value specification remain enabled. These tuples may be either enumerated sequentially using the RESOLVE and REPORT instructions or used as the arguments for other relational algebraic operations, depending on the problem at hand. NON-VON also allows selections based on more complex predicates. The retrieval of all employee records satisfying the condition "SALARY + COMMISSION > 30000", for example, would require only a few instructions, independent of the number of employee records.

The execution of projection operations on NON-VON is more interesting. The removal of selected fields from each tuple is straightforward even on a von Neumann machine. The difficult aspect of projection arises from the fact that the deletion of these attribute values may make two previously distinct tuples identical. Since relations are, by definition, sets, all duplicate tuples must be removed from the result relation in a true projection.

The project algorithm begins by issuing a RESOLVE against all tuples in the relation, thus marking an arbitrary tuple as the "current tuple". Using a sequence of REPORTS, the projected values from the current tuple are then sent to the control processor. The projected tuple is included in the result relation. In order to remove any duplicate tuples before they are enumerated, these values are also broadcast to all remaining tuples in the relation, and all matching tuples are marked as "excluded", as is the current tuple itself. These steps are then repeated for all tuples not yet excluded, until all tuples have been excluded.

It should be noted that this algorithm is actually sublinear (under the assumption that all input data is already present in the primary processing subsystem). This follows from the fact that the time required for projection is proportional not to the size of the input relation, but to the size of the result relation, since duplicate tuples are eliminated in parallel before they have a chance to initiate an execution of the program loop.

In practice, the join algorithm is typically the most expensive of the relational algebraic primitives. The NON-VON join algorithm, however, is both efficient and simple, corresponding closely to the "naive" sequential algorithm, but with its inner loop replaced by a single associative operation. The tuples of both relations are initially stored in arbitrary locations within the PPS. (The tuples of a given relation need not be stored together.) The algorithm enumerates each tuple of the first relation in turn using the RESOLVE and REPORT instructions. Only the values of the join attributes of the current tuple are reported to the control processor. These values are then broadcast to all tuples in the second relation. All matching tuples concurrently mark themselves, and are read out in turn and concatenated with the current tuple from the first relation to form a partial result. The process is then repeated for each tuple in the first relation.

Note that the total running time of this algorithm is linear in the size of the smaller argument relation (which may be chosen to be the "first relation") and the result relation. It should be noted, however, that the result relation may, in the worst case, be quadratic in the size of the argument relations; this limits the worst case running time of a join on any machine, whether sequential or parallel, that must enumerate its output sequentially. Fortunately, join operations in most applications of practical interest tend to produce result relations of the same order of magnitude as the argument relations. Providing this constraint is satisfied, the NON-VON join algorithm has time complexity linear in the size of the argument relations.

The NON-VON algorithms for the three set theoretic operations are somewhat simpler. In each case, each tuple from one of the argument relations is broadcast in turn, again using RESOLVE and REPORT instructions, for simultaneous comparison against all the others. The three algorithms differ only in the choice of tuples to be included in the output.

The set union algorithm enumerates the tuples in the first relation and compares each such tuple in parallel against all tuples in the second relation. All matching tuples are simultaneously marked as excluded, thus preventing the appearence of duplicate tuples in the result. After the last tuple in the first relation has been processed, the set of non-excluded tuples from the first and second relations constitutes the result relation. Because union is a commutative operation, the argument relation having a smaller cardinality may be chosen to be the "first", resulting in a running time proportional to the number of tuples in the smaller of the two arguments.

The algorithm for intersection is identical to that for union, except that the result is the set of tuples that match, rather than the set of all tuples that do not match. Once again, the outer loop consists of an iteration over the smaller of the two relations. Running time is thus again proportional to the cardinality of the smaller of the two arguments.

While the set difference operation is not commutative, execution time proportional to the number of tuples in the smaller relation can still be achieved. In the case where the cardinality of the minuend exceeds that of the subtrahend, the outer loop consists of an enumeration of the tuples of the subtrahend, each of which is compared in parallel with all tuples in the minuend; if a match occurs, the matching minuend tuple is marked as excluded. The set of all minuend tuples not excluded by any subtrahend tuple comprises the result. If, on the other hand, there are more subtrahend than minuend tuples, the outer loop effects an enumeration of all tuples of the minuend relation; if a given minuend tuple fails to match against some subtrahend tuple, it is included in the result.

It may prove instructive to compare the aymptotic running times of these NON-VON algorithms with the best known algorithms for a conventional computer system. With the exception of the selection operator, all of these operators are (in the absence of either special constraints or index mechanisms having very high storage and update costs) typically accomplished on a von Neumann machine by first <u>sorting</u> the argument relation(s). In the case of the three set theoretic operators, the entire tuple is used as a key. Projection is accomplished by pre-sorting on the projected attributes, while the join attributes serve as keys for sorting the arguments to the join operator. The sorting process moves identical key values to adjacent locations, where they may be easily processed in linear time. The sorting step itself, which requires O (n log n) time, thus dominates the complexity of each of the sequential algorithms.

On NON-VON, on the other hand, there is no need to pre-sort the relations, and each of the relational algebraic primitives requires only linear time (again with the exception of selection, which is faster). Intuitively, this follows from the fact that NON-VON is able to make equality (and other) comparisons against an arbitrary number of operands in constant time, independent of the size of the argument relations, thus obviating the need to sort.

Selection is a special case. On a von Neumann machine, the naive algorithm for selection requires linear time. Simple hashing can not reduce this time to constant unless 2^k hash tables are constructed and (at great expense) maintained, where k is the number of attributes. More sophisticated techniques have reduced the time required to between O (1) and O (n), depending on the number of specified attribute/value pairs, but at the expense of extra storage and extra processing at the time of tuple insertion. NON-VON, on the other hand, is able to perform general relational selection in constant time, regardless of the number of attribute/value pairs, with no need for either auxilliary data structures or additional insertion time.

6 Internal Insertion, Deletion and Update

NON-VON effects the modification of relations stored internally in an extremely efficient manner. Specifically, the insertion, deletion or update of a single tuple is performed in a constant amount of time, independent of the size of the relation being modified.

To support tuple <u>insertion</u>, we adopt the convention that every PE currently being used to store a tuple (or, in the case of spanned tuples, part of a tuple) is marked by setting a <u>tag bit</u>. To insert a new tuple in the relation, a RESOLVE operation is executed to find an arbitrary free PE (or PE's). The values of each attribute of the new tuple are then broadcast, and are stored in the selected PE, whose tag is then set. Because no indexing is used internally, this operation requires only constant time.

The <u>deletion</u> of tuples is also straightforward on NON-VON. The tuple to be deleted is first identified associatively (in an application-specific manner). The tag bit is then set to 0, causing the tuple to be ignored by all relational operators and freeing the PE's in which it was stored to be used for the storage of other tuples. Again, only constant time is required, independent of the size of the relation from which the tuple is deleted.

The update of a particular tuple in a relation occurs in manner closely related to the algorithms for insertion and deletion. The tuple in question is first identified associatively, and all other tuples are disabled. The new values of all attributes whose values are to be changed are then broadcast in a manner similar to that employed in tuple insertion. As in the previous two operations, only constant time is required for a single update operation, independent of the cardinality of the argument relation.

7 External Evaluation of the Relational Algebraic Operators

In most database applications, the argument relations are too large to fit entirely within the primary processing subsystem. In the case of relational selection, this presents no problem, since, as noted above, the intelligent head units associated with each disk head are themselves capable of performing relational selection dynamically on the tuples passing beneath them. The other relational operators, however, involve "global" comparisons that can not be performed by a single intelligent head unit having little storage and processing capacity. In particular, the disposition of a given tuple may be affected by a tuple in another part of the file, which may well pass under a different intelligent head unit at different point in time.

NON-VON attacks such problems by decomposing the argument relations into a number of partitions, each small enough to be processed within the primary processing subsystem, and constructed in such a way as to guarantee that no reference need be made to some other partition. By way of illustration, let us consider the case of external projection. Here, we wish to partition the (single) argument relation in a way that guarantees that any identical tuples that may be present after projecting out the specified attributes will wind up in the same partition. If this can be guaranteed, it will be possible to transfer each partition into the primary processing system in turn, so that all duplicate tuples in that partition can be detected and eliminated.

This process, which we have termed key-disjoint partitioning [SHAW79] is accomplished by hashing the key (the projected tuple, the compound join attribute, or, in the case of the set theoretic operators, the whole tuple) onto a real number in the range [0, 1]. The interval is divided into a number of partitions somewhat larger than the size of the argument relation(s) divided by the capacity of the primary processing system. All tuples (of both relations, in the case of the binary operators) falling within a given partition are processed simultaneously in the primary processing subsystem.

The manner in which this key-disjoint partitioning is accomplished is as follows. Recall that tuples of the argument relation(s) are distributed among the various disks in the secondary processing subsystem. The relation is scanned by all disk heads in parallel, and the intelligent head units hash the key of each tuple as it passes under the corresponding head. Each tuple is then sent through the LPE network to an LPE determined by the hashed key value, and is transferred from that LPE to the corresponding disk. At the end of this process (which requires time proportional to the size of the relation in bytes divided by the number of disk heads in the secondary processing subsystem), the file has been segmented into key-disjoint partitions, each of which is stored as a temporary relation on some target disk drive.

Because a full-scale NON-VON configuration would incorporate a relatively large number of moderate-sized disk drives, most files would be divided into enough partitions that each one would be small enough to fit entirely within the primary processing subsystem. In this case, each partition would be transferred (serially, in this case, since each partition would reside on a different disk drive) into the primary processing subsystem for internal evaluation.

In the case of extremely large files, however, a single partition might exceed the capacity of the primary processing subsystem. In this case, the partitioning procedure would be applied to each partition, thus dividing the size of each partition again by a factor roughly equal to the number of disk heads. The resulting sub-partitions would then be processed internally in the same manner. In its most general form, the algorithm provides for an arbitrary number of levels of sub-partitioning; in practice, however, the large "fanout" at every stage would make the need for more than two or three levels quite rare. Formally, the algorithm has time complexity O (n log n), assuming the argument relations can truly be of arbitrary size; the constant factors, however, are such that the effect of the (log n) term should in practice be of limited significance.

Consider the case in which the argument relation(s) are no larger than the product of the capacity of the primary processing subsystem and the number of disk drives. The single hash partitioning step contributes little to the complexity of the algorithm. Specifically, this step requires time proportional to the size of the argument relation(s) divided by the number of disk drives (since both hashing and routing through the LPE network occur in parallel over all drives). The remaining steps dominate the running time of the algorithm; they require time proportional to the length of the argument relation(s), since each partition must be read into the primary processing subsystem in turn and subjected to internal evaluation. Since internal evaluation is quite rapid, the total running time of the algorithm should typically be a small constant multiple of the amount of time that would be required simply to read the argument relation(s) from disk in a conventional system.

When the argument relations are very large, it has been noted that the partitions must themselves be divided into sub-partitions. This process is somewhat more expensive than in the case we have just analyzed, since the original data is distributed evenly among the various drives, while the sub-partitioning process operates on data stored on a single drive. The effect of this difference, however, is only to make the running time of the partitioning step comparable to that of the remaining steps. Since no more than two, or for extremely large files, three recursive sub-partitionings are likely to be required in practice, the total running time of these algorithms should in practice be a fairly small multiple of the length of time that would be required to input the arguments.

8 Conclusion

Based on our work to date, we believe that the NON-VON supercomputer could provide significant performance improvements over conventional machines of comparable cost in the execution of the essential operations involved in relational database management. Potential performance improvements appear to be greatest in the case of large and very large databases. Central to NON-VON's predicted performance advantages in such applications is the use of associative processing techniques supported by NON-VON's VLSI-based primary processing subsystem and the utilization of "intelligent disks" to partition the input data using a technique based on hash coding.

It should be emphasized, however, that there has been little investigation to date of a number of functions which would appear to be critical to the practical application of such a machine in a real database management environment. Among these functions are the logging of database transactions for purposes of error recovery, locking procedures to prevent various kinds of database inconsistencies in a multi-user environment, and the provision of a user-friendly environment for the formulation of database queries. In addition, only limited research has been done in area of query optimization for this sort of parallel machine. Further analytical studies, performance evaluations, and experimental development will be necessary before NON-VON's utility in realistic database management applications can be assessed with confidence.

References

(DEWI78) (HILL83) (HSIA77) (KIM80 see KIM84a) (MCGR76) (OZKA75)
(SHAW79) (SHAW80) (SHAW82, see SHAW82b) (SHAW82a) (SONG81) (SU75)

Section VIII

Physical Database Design

Progress Toward Automating The Development of Database System Software*

D. S. Batory

ABSTRACT

Recent advances in physical database modeling suggest that it may be possible to develop significant portions of a DBMS's software, specifically the physical database component, automatically from a small set of specifications. These advances are based on the Unifying Model and the Transformation Model, both of which are reviewed in this paper. The Unifying Model deals with file structures and record linking mechanisms; the Transformation Model deals with conceptual-to-internal mappings. We illustrate their concepts with models of the storage architectures of two very different commercial DBMSs: INGRES and RAPID. We then explain how the Unifying Model/Transformation Model framework can provide a basis for automating the development of physical database software.

1. Introduction

In recent years it is become evident that there are many important database applications that do not conform to the familiar debit-credit scenario of business-oriented transactions. Statistical databases ([IEEE84]), CAD and engineering databases ([IEEE82]), textual databases ([Ston82]), and databases for artificial intelligence ([IEEE83]) are examples. Owing to their unusual requirements, it is not surprising that existing general-purpose DBMSs do not support these applications efficiently; special-purpose database management systems are needed.

Database system software has been customized in two ways: existing systems have been enhanced ([Hask82], [Ston83]) and new DBMSs have been developed ([John83]). In either case, it is well-known that developing special-purpose database software is an exceedingly difficult, costly, and not always successful undertaking. There is a definite need for tools that simplify and aid the development of database software. Presently such tools are lacking.

Within the next ten years, we may witness a revolution in the way database system software is developed. Recent work in physical database modeling points the way to these advances.

Physical database software handles the placement and retrieval of data on secondary storage. The topic of physical databases has traditionally dealt with file structures and record

* This research was supported by the National Science Foundation under Grant MCS-8317353.

linking mechanisms, but more generally it encompasses buffer management, query processing, concurrency control, and recovery algorithms.

Models of physical databases have progressed to the point where they are accurate enough to be used as blueprints for physical database software development. The models to which we refer are the Unifying Model (UM) and the Transformation Model (TM), both of which are reviewed in this paper ([Bato82b], [Bato84b]). It is believed that a technology based on these models can be realized in which the physical database software for a DBMS can be developed automatically from a small set of specifications. The impact of such a technology is potentially significant. Special-purpose DBMSs that are optimized to handle specific classes of applications can be built quickly and inexpensively; modifications to existing DBMSs (constructed using this technology) could be accomplished just as easily. As an added benefit, it would facilitate the development of prototype DBMSs in which new algorithms (e.g., concurrency control, file structure, query processing, buffer optimization) could actually be tested and evaluated, thereby providing a vehicle to help tie physical database theory to practice.

Earlier models of physical databases did not exhibit such possibilities. A progression of increasingly more sophisticated and realistic general-purpose models were proposed prior to 1983 ([Hsia70], [Seve72], [Senk73], [Yao77], [Marc81], [Bato82b]).[1] Unfortunately, none could accurately account for the diversity and variety of structures and algorithms that are present in operational DBMSs in a simple and comprehendible way. Even so, these works were quite important for they laid the foundation for the modeling techniques that we present in this paper.

In the following sections, we will review concepts that are fundamental to physical database modeling. We will show how these concepts have been used to model the physical databases, or *storage architectures,* of two operational DBMSs: INGRES and RAPID. We will then explain how these concepts can underly a technology which may help automate the production of physical database software.

2. The Unifying Model

Since 1970, many studies have contributed to the articulation and understanding of major performance and design issues in files and databases. Such studies have addressed hash-based files ([Seve76a], [Bato82a]), B+ trees ([Naka78], [Bato81]), transposed files ([Hoff76], [Marc83]), batched searching ([Shne76]), performance evolution of files as records are inserted and deleted ([Bato82a], [Heym82]), index selection ([Schk75], [Ande77]), differential files ([Seve76b]), generalized access path structures ([Haer78]), and file reorganization ([Bato82a]), among others. Although many studies seemed quite unrelated, it was shown that all were instances of a single framework, called the Unifying Model (UM) [Bato82b].

The UM had two distinct submodels. One enabled the file structures and physical databases (i.e., networks of interconnected files) that had been investigated in earlier works to be described parametrically. Among the parameters that were used were file structure type (e.g., dynamic hash-based, indexed-sequential, etc.), file size, blocking factors, average length of overflow chains, and file structure height. The other submodel was a set of cost equations which utilized these parameters to predict database performance. These equations were shown to generalize earlier analyses. In this paper, we will concern ourselves only with the descriptive

[1] It is worth noting that at one time DIAM was believed to be sufficiently general and accurate to be used as the basis for DBMS software production ([Senk73]). Since then, it has become evident that DIAM's modeling constructs have two fundamental limitations. First, they are inadequate to represent the conceptual-to-internal mappings of existing DBMS software. Second, they are simply too general to be useful in describing the complexities of DBMSs in a comprehendible way. As a result, few research contributions on physical databases have relied on the DIAM framework.

submodel; its basics and subsequent generalizations are explained below.

Physical databases can be ***decomposed*** into a collection of internal files and internal links. An ***internal file*** is a file of records that are instances of a single ***internal record type***. Records of internal files are actually stored. A relationship between one or more internal files is an ***internal link***. (We draw a distinction here between conceptual files and links, which are defined in database schemas, from internal files and links. We will see later that there is a significant difference between files and links that are conceptual and those that are internal).

The basic structures of a physical database are simple files and linksets. A ***simple file*** is a structure that organizes records of one or more internal files. Classical simple file structures include hash-based, indexed-sequential, B+ trees, dynamic hash-based, and unordered files. A ***linkset*** is a structure that implements one or more internal links. Classical linkset structures include pointer arrays, inverted lists, ring lists, and IMS's hierarchical sequential lists ([Date82]). [2] Catalogs of known simple files and linksets are given in [Bato84b].

Because internal files, internal links, simple files, and linksets are easy to comprehend, the structure of a physical database can be specified by a straightforward procedure. First, the physical database is decomposed into its constituent internal files and internal links. Second, the linkset implementation of each internal link is specified, and third, the simple file implementation of each internal file is specified. Here are two examples.

Consider a file of records of type DATA. A DATA record has n fields $F_1 \cdots F_n$. This file is stored as an inverted file with attributes F_j and F_k indexed. Decomposition of the inverted file reveals three internal files and two links. There is the DATA file and two index files $INDEX_j$ and $INDEX_k$, one for each of the indexed attributes. Each INDEX file is connected to the DATA file by precisely one link. Figure 1.dsd shows these relationships graphically in a ***data structure diagram (dsd)***, where boxes represent files and arrows are links (drawn from the parent file to the child file).

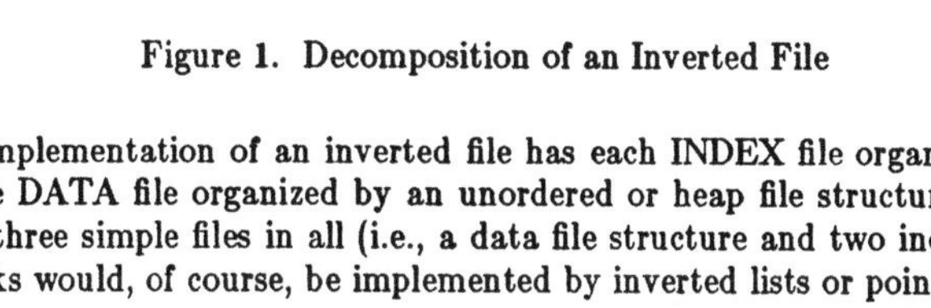

Figure 1. Decomposition of an Inverted File

A typical implementation of an inverted file has each INDEX file organized by a separate B+ tree and the DATA file organized by an unordered or heap file structure. In our example, there would be three simple files in all (i.e., a data file structure and two index file structures). The internal links would, of course, be implemented by inverted lists or pointer arrays.

To describe the implementation in more detail, two additional diagrams are used. One is a ***field definition diagram (fdd)***, which shows the fields of the internal record types. Figure 1.fdd shows the DATA record type to consist of data fields $F_1 \cdots F_n$. It also shows the $INDEX_j$ record type to have two fields: a data field F_j and an inverted list field P_{I_j}. P_{I_j} is called the ***parent field*** of linkset I_j. The $INDEX_k$ type has a similar format to $INDEX_j$.

The other diagram is an ***instance diagram (id)***, which is used to illustrate both the data structure and field definition diagrams. Figure 1.id shows an $INDEX_j$ record with data value v and its inverted list which references all DATA records that have v as its F_j value.

As another example, suppose the DATA records were organized as a multilist file, where again fields F_j and F_k are indexed. Decomposition results in the same data structure diagram as in the inverted file example (Fig. 2.dsd). However, their distinction lies in the link implementations: multilist files use multilist linksets. The distinction can also be seen in the field definition and instance diagrams. Figure 2.fdd shows DATA records to have two additional fields C_{I_j} and C_{I_k}. These fields are respectively the *child fields* of links I_j and I_k. Their purpose is to contain linkset pointers to the next DATA record on a list of DATA records. Figure 2.id shows the same link instance of Figure 1.id, except that a multilist structure connects an $INDEX_j$ record to its DATA records.

As a general rule, the presence and function of parent and child fields in record types that are linked is determined solely by the linkset that materializes the link. In the case of inverted list linksets (Fig. 1), a parent field appears in every parent record. For multilist linksets (Fig. 2), both fields are present. IMS logical parent pointers are linksets that are implemented solely by parent pointers ([Date82]); only child fields are used. Sequential linksets do not require either parent or child fields (i.e., parent and child records are linked by contiguity). Thus, a linkset can introduce parent fields, child fields, both, or neither.

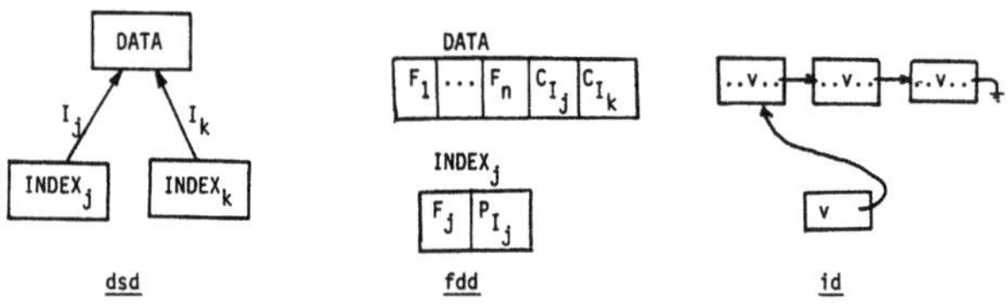

Figure 2. Decomposition of a Multilist File

The decomposition approach to modeling physical databases is intuitive and seemed quite powerful. Virtually all works published prior to the UM used similar, though not as extensive, techniques for modeling database structures. However, common to all models (including the UM) was the assumption that conceptual to internal mappings were simple. That is, given a data structure diagram of the conceptual record types and links, the mapping to the corresponding internal record types and links was obvious. In many commercial and specialized DBMSs, this is definitely not the case. New modeling concepts are required in order to capture the conceptual-to-internal mappings of actual DBMSs. The Transformation Model (TM) was developed in response to this need.

3. The Transformation Model

A primary function of a DBMS is to map conceptual files and operations to their internal counterparts. INGRES [Ston76], for example, maps relations and relational operations onto inverted files. RAPID [Turn79] and SYSTEM R [Date82] also begin with relations, but RAPID maps to transposed files and SYSTEM R maps to inverted files with record clustering.

An intuitive understanding of conceptual-to-internal mappings comes from recognizing that mappings can be modeled as a sequence of database definitions that are progressively more implementation-oriented. The sequence begins with definitions of the conceptual files and their links, and ends with definitions of the internal files and their links. Each intermediate definition contains both conceptual and internal elements, and thus can be identified with a *level of abstraction* that lies *between* the 'pure' conceptual and 'pure' internal levels. It follows that physical databases can be modeled at different levels of abstraction.

What does it mean for a DBMS to have different levels of abstraction? It means that the DBMS's physical database software (the software that accomplishes the conceptual-to-internal mappings) was written (or could have been written) by nesting abstract data types. That is, the outer-most types define the conceptual record types, their links, and operations. These types are defined in terms of 'primitive' abstract data types, and these primitive types in turn are based on even more primitive types, and so on, terminating with abstract data types that define the internal record types, their links, and operations. Thus, levels of abstraction have a practical interpretation. [2]

Recognizing different levels in a DBMS and mapping from one level to an adjacent level turns out to be straightforward. In the DBMSs that the author is aware, only ten different primitive mappings, here called *elementary transformations*, have been utilized. Elementary transformations are used singly or in combination to map records and links from one level of abstraction to the next lower level. In principle, this means that the conceptual-to-internal mappings of a software-based DBMS can be modeled by 1) taking the generic conceptual record types and links that the DBMS supports, and 2) applying a well-defined sequence of elementary transformations to produce the internal record types and links of the DBMS. For example, in the case of RAPID, INGRES, and SYSTEM R, all three begin with the same conceptual record types (i.e., relations), but are distinguished by different sequences of transformations (and hence different sets of internal record types and links). We will briefly describe each of the known elementary transformations later.

The use of elementary transformations to define conceptual-to-internal mappings is the basis of the Transformation Model (TM) [Bato84a-b]. This model is related to the UM in the following way. The UM relies on decomposition to identify the internal files and links of the physical database. Implementations for each internal file and link can then be specified. In contrast, the TM starts with the conceptual files and links that are supported by a DBMS and shows how their underlying internal files and links are derived. Thus, the TM supplants the intuitive process of physical database decomposition with a conceptual-to-internal mapping process that, it is believed, closely models the way DBMS software is written.

Ten elementary transformations were discovered as a natural consequence of modeling the conceptual-to-internal data mappings used in the ADABAS ([Gese76]), CREATABASE ([NDX81]), DMS-1100 ([Sper75]), IDMS ([Cull81]), IMS ([IBM80]), INGRES ([Ston76]), INQUIRE ([Info79]), RAPID ([Turn79]), SPIRES ([Stan73]), SYSTEM 2000 ([Casa81]), and TOTAL DBMSs ([Cinc79]), among others. Each transformation maps an abstract structure (e.g., record type, file, link) to one or more concrete structures. (It is possible for a record type/file to be 'concrete' at one level of abstraction and 'abstract' at a lower level). A brief description of each transformation is given below. More complete descriptions are given in [Bato84b]. Abstract records can be:

- *augmented* by metadata (e.g., delete flag, record type identifier, etc.);
- *encoded* for purposes of compression, encryption, or searching (e.g., SOUNDEX encoding);
- *collected* onto a single link occurrence (similar to the DBTG concept of a singular set);
- *segmented* along field boundaries to produce two or more (sub)records. A link occurrence connects the primary record to all of its secondary records;
- *divided* without respect to field boundaries to produce two or more (sub)records. A link occurrence connects the primary record to all of its secondary records;
- mapped directly to a concrete record by the *null* transformation. Null transformations arise when the application of a sequence of transformations is conditional.

---

[2] Conversely, levels of abstraction also provide new insight into how DBMSs can be implemented using abstract data types. Although this particular topic has been studied before (e.g., [Hamm76], [Rowe79], [Baro81]), the mechanism by which modular design concepts are applied at the internal level is still not well understood. Improvements and clarifications of such mechanisms - based on our notion of levels of abstraction - are presented in [Wise83].

Fields of abstract records can be:

- *extracted.* This produces an index or dictionary for the field's data values. Index or dictionary records each contain a distinct value and are connected via a link to all abstract records that have that value.

Links between abstract record types can be:

- *actualized.* That is, the materialization of an abstract link is expressed in terms of one or more concrete links.

DBMS storage architectures can be

- *layered.* A page at one level of abstraction is mapped to a distinct record at a lower level; the address of the page becomes the primary key of the record. Thus a page fetch is translated to a record retrieval, and a page write is translated to a record update.

Files of abstract records can be:

- *horizontally partitioned* into two or more subfiles.

To illustrate and explain the effects of elementary transformations, we again use data structure, field definition, and instance diagrams. Besides the usual conventions, there are two additions. First, abstract objects (typically record types) are indicated by dashed outlines in data structure diagrams. Figure 3 shows a data structure diagram of an abstract record type W and its materialization as the record types F and G and link L.

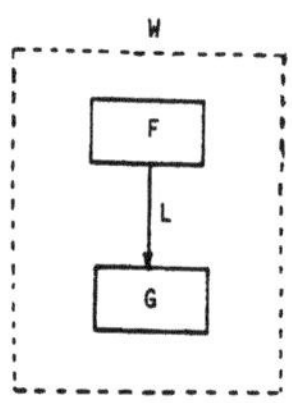

Figure 3. A Materialization of Abstract Record Type W

Second, pointers to abstract records arise naturally. These pointers, however, must ultimately reference internal (concrete) records. To indicate how pointer references are transformed, we rely on the orientation of record types within a dsd. The orientation of F and G in Figure 3, for example, shows that F *dominates* G. This will mean that a pointer to an abstract record of type W will actually reference its corresponding internal (concrete) record of type F. (For almost all transformations, there is a 1:1 correspondence between abstract records and their dominant concrete records; the only known exception, to be considered later, is full transposition). The dominant concept is recursive; that is, if F records are abstract, a pointer to an F record will reference its dominant concrete record, and so on. In this way, pointers to abstract records are mapped to concrete records.

We will illustrate the TM approach in the following sections by presenting models of the storage architectures of two very different relational database systems: INGRES and RAPID. During this exercise, the reader should note the level of detail that is captured using the UM and TM framework. Later we will examine the role this framework can play in the automation of physical database software.

4. Applications

4.1 INGRES

INGRES was among the first major DBMSs that were based on the relational model. It was developed in the mid-1970's at the University of California, Berkeley, and is now marketed by Relational Technology, Inc.

The generic CONCEPTUAL record type supported by INGRES consists of n scalar and elementary fields (see Fig. 4). n is user-definable. Data values and their respective fields have fixed lengths. Relationships between two or more CONCEPTUAL record types are realized by join operations, rather than by physical structures. Thus, the underlying storage structures used by INGRES can be understood by examining how records of a single conceptual type are stored.

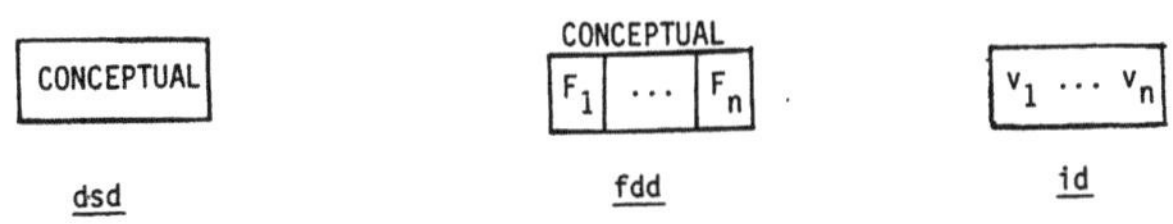

Figure 4. Generic CONCEPTUAL Record Type of INGRES

CONCEPTUAL records are materialized in the following way. INGRES allows elementary and compound fields to be indexed. (A *compound field* is defined in INGRES to be a field that consists of two to six elementary fields). Field F_i is indexed by ***segmenting*** it with duplication from CONCEPTUAL records. (That is, the field to be indexed is 'copied', leaving the CONCEPTUAL record intact). This produces an *ABSTRACT_INDEX$_i$* record type connected to an ABSTRACT_DATA record type by linkset I_i (see Fig. 5). I_i is a singular pointer. (A ***singular pointer*** is a pointer array that contains precisely one pointer. The value of this pointer is called the ***tuple id*** of the CONCEPTUAL or ABSTRACT_DATA record). All fields are indexed in this manner. (The notation ( )... in Figure 5.dsd means that zero or more fields may be indexed).

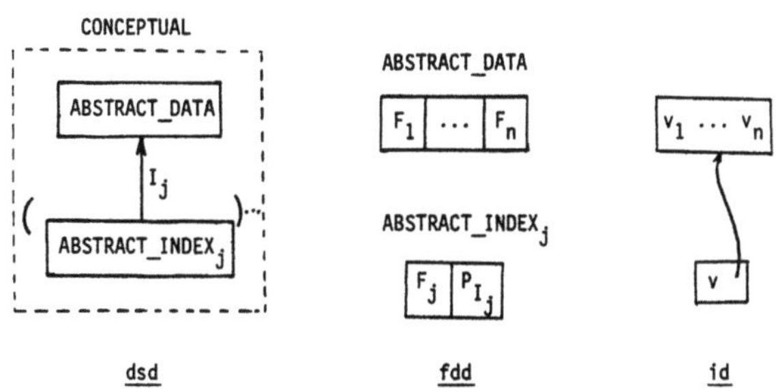

Figure 5. Segmentation of CONCEPTUAL Record Type

INGRES treats ABSTRACT_INDEX files as special normalized relations consisting of a data value field and a pointer field. This treatment actually simplifies the implementation of INGRES, for ABSTRACT_INDEX and ABSTRACT_DATA records are materialized by the same sequence of transformations. To avoid defining this transformation sequence twice, we will define it in terms of a generic record type, ABSTRACT_REC.

Let ABSTRACT_REC consist of m fixed length fields $G_1 \cdots G_m$ (see Fig. 6). ABSTRACT_REC is materialized by ***segmenting*** fields $G_1 \cdots G_m$ from ABSTRACT_REC. The LINE_REC and REC record types connected by link L are produced as a result (see Fig. 7). LINE_REC is fixed-length and contains only the field P_L. REC is identical to its ABSTRACT_REC counterpart. L is a singular pointer with special parent-child clustering properties (to be explained shortly).

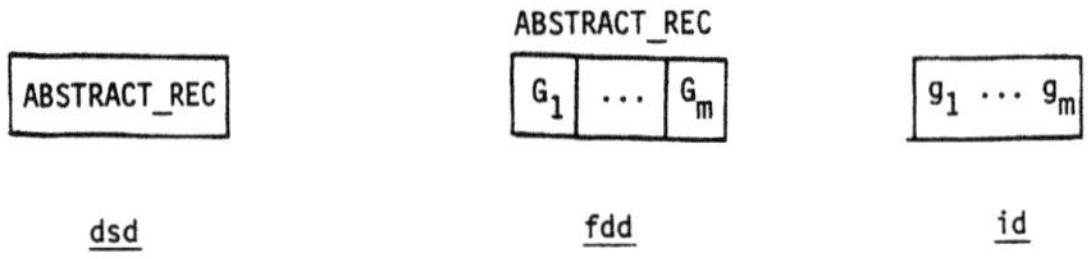

Figure 6. ABSTRACT_REC Type

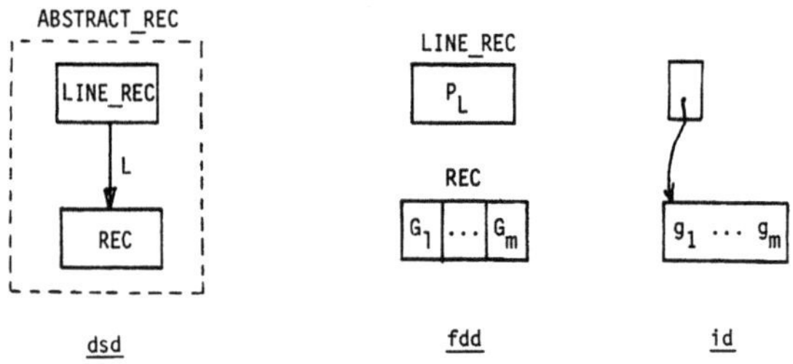

Figure 7. Segmentation of ABSTRACT_REC Type

The database administrator can declare whether or not instances of REC are to be compressed. (INGRES compresses records by eliminating trailing blanks from character fields). If REC is compressed, it is materialized by the ***encoding*** transformation. The COMPRESSED_REC type results. If compression is not requested, REC is materialized by the *null* transformation. The UNCOMPRESSED_REC type results (see Fig. 8).

The above composite sequence of transformations for materializing ABSTRACT_REC will be referred to as the *INGRES transformation*. This transformation is used to materialize both ABSTRACT_INDEX and ABSTRACT_DATA records. The conceptual-to-internal mappings of INGRES are summarized in Figure 9. As a general rule, INDEX records are not compressed.

The simple files that are used to organize the internal records of INGRES can be understood in terms of the INGRES transformation. When an ABSTRACT_REC is materialized, two internal record types result. One is LINE_REC. The other is either COMPRESSED_REC or UNCOMPRESSED_REC. In either case, INGRES *always* stores related records of both types on the same page (see Fig. 10). The storage locations of LINE_REC records are fixed

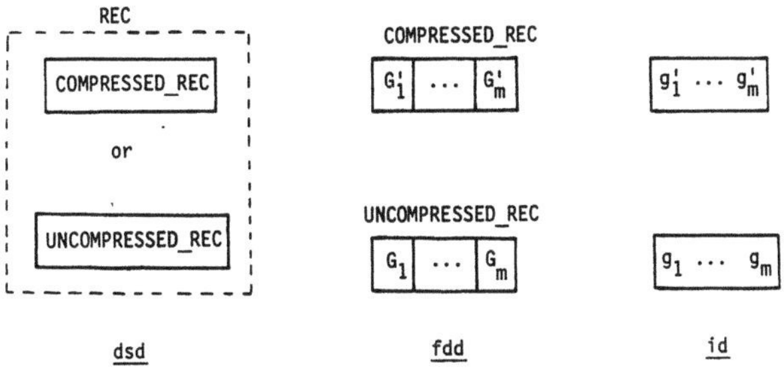

Figure 8. Compression of Null Transformation of REC Type

(but for an exception described below) and do not change with time; the storage location (within a page) of COMPRESSED_REC and UNCOMPRESSED_REC records may change with time. With this notion of parent and child clustering in mind, instances of related record pairs may be organized by an indexed-aggregate, hash-based, or unordered file structure. [3] As a general rule, COMPRESSED_INDEX and UNCOMPRESSED_INDEX records are usually organized by index-aggregate files.

It is worth noting that LINE_REC records maintain the 1:1 correspondence between tuple ids and the storage location of COMPRESSED_REC and UNCOMPRESSED_REC records. This correspondence allows COMPRESSED_REC and UNCOMPRESSED_REC records to be relocated (within the pages in which they are stored) without altering the INDEX records that reference them. (Recall the pointers of INDEX records are tuple ids). Relocations within blocks occur naturally as a consequence of updates, insertions, and deletions. Relocations beyond block boundaries occur when there is no room in a block to accommodate an expanded COMPRESSED_REC record. Such expansions happen when a CONCEPTUAL record is modified. In such cases, the CONCEPTUAL record is assigned a new tuple id. This means that the corresponding COMPRESSED_REC is moved to another block which can accommodate it and its LINE_REC record. Furthermore, all INDEX records that reference the CONCEPTUAL record must be updated to reflect the change in tuple id. This particular design reflects the belief that interblock movements do not occur often.

The storage architecture of INGRES is summarized in Figure 9. Source materials used in the derivation were [Held75], [Ston76], and [Butt83].

---

[3] An *indexed-aggregate* structure is a variation of indexed-sequential structures. When a data record is stored, it is never moved and thus has a fixed storage address. In indexed-sequential files, records are maintained in primary key sequence, and hence are often moved.

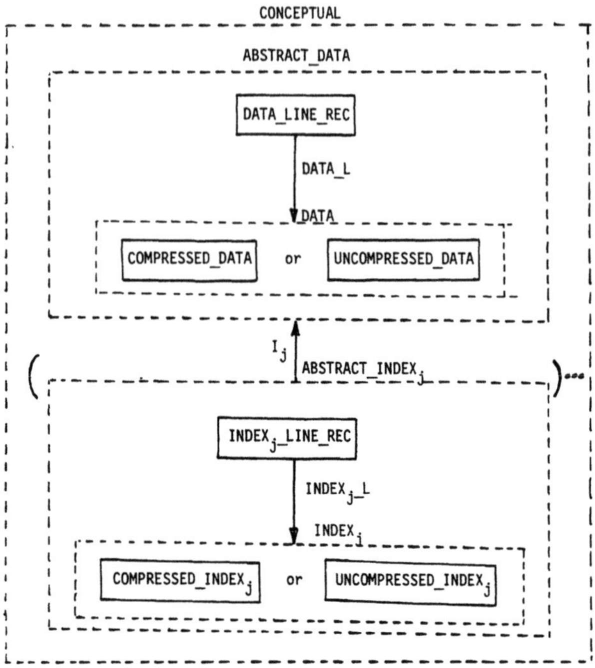

Internal and Aggregate Internal Record Types and Links	Implementation
ABSTRACT_DATA aggregate, $ABSTRACT\_INDEX_j$ aggregate	hash-based, indexed-aggregate, or unordered
I_j, DATA_L, $INDEX_j\_L$	singular pointer

Figure 9. The Storage Architecture of INGRES

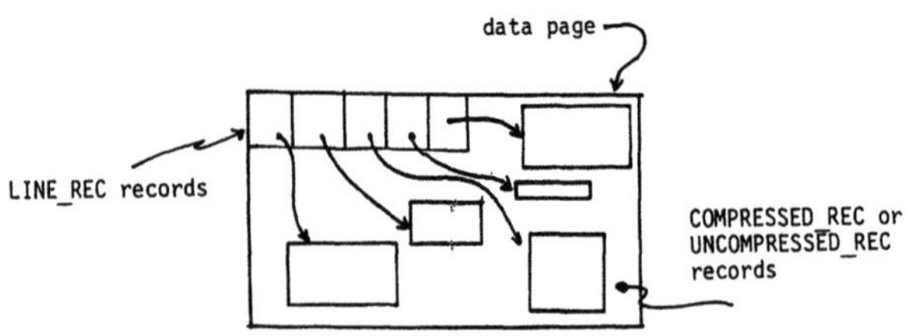

Figure 10. Clustering of LINE_REC, COMPRESSED_REC, and UNCOMPRESSED_REC Record

4.2 RAPID

RAPID was developed by Statistics Canada to support the processing of major surveys and censuses conducted by the Canadian Government. It is among the best known and most sophisticated statistical DBMSs presently in operation.

RAPID has a two-layer architecture. Both layers have well-defined conceptual record types and internal record types. We begin at the higher layer.

RAPID is based on the relational model. Its generic CONCEPTUAL record type is identical to that of INGRES (Fig. 11). CONCEPTUAL records are normally referenced by their contents. However, in RAPID they may also be directly referenced by their *record indexes*, RAPID's name for a tuple identifier.

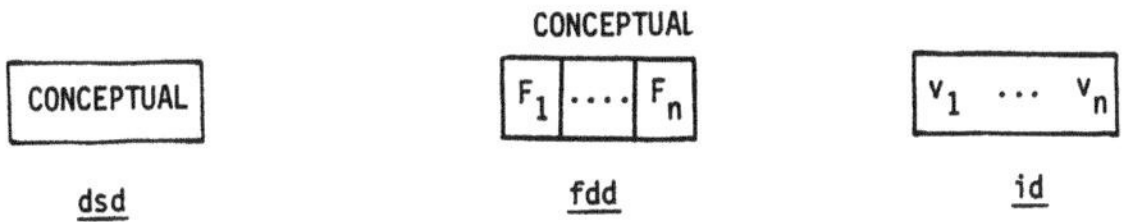

Figure 11. Generic CONCEPTUAL Record Type of RAPID

RAPID allows selected fields of CONCEPTUAL records to be compressed by an index encoding technique ([Alsb75], [Bato83]). When a CONCEPTUAL record type is defined in a RAPID schema, the values of a field's domain can be listed by enumeration. The index position at which a data value is located in the list is its index code. RAPID substitutes fixed-length index codes for data values thereby compressing CONCEPTUAL records.

Index encoding field F_i is modeled by *extracting* F_i from CONCEPTUAL. $DICTIONARY_i$ and IE_CONCEPTUAL (Index-Encoded CONCEPTUAL) record types, connected by link D_i, are formed as a result (see Fig. 12). D_i is an index encoded linkset, a linkset that is implemented solely by parent pointers. (The parent pointers in this case are index codes). All fields are index encoded in this manner. [4] Note that the notation ( )... in Figure 12.dsd means that zero or more fields may be extracted (i.e, index encoded).

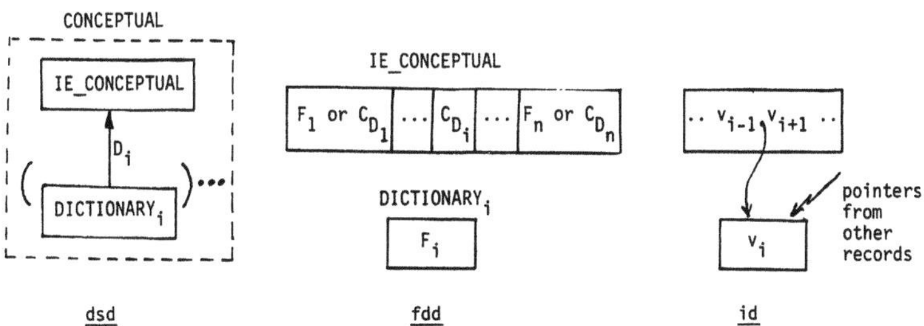

Figure 12. Extraction of CONCEPTUAL Fields

[4] Note that the extraction is performed partially by the database administrator when the domain is enumerated during schema definition. Although some DBMSs, such as CREATABASE ([NDX81]), have internal routines that perform the entire task of index encoding, RAPID's design reflects a typical statistical application need to define the set of data values associated with a given field *prior* to database loading ([McCa82]).

RAPID allows elementary or compound fields to be indexed (see Fig. 13). Field F_k is indexed by ***segmenting*** it with duplication from IE_CONCEPTUAL records. This produces the KEY_COLUMN_k record type which is connected to the ABSTRACT_DATA type by link I_k. I_k is a singular pointer. Other fields are indexed in a similar manner. Note that ABSTRACT_DATA is identical to its IE_CONCEPTUAL counterpart.

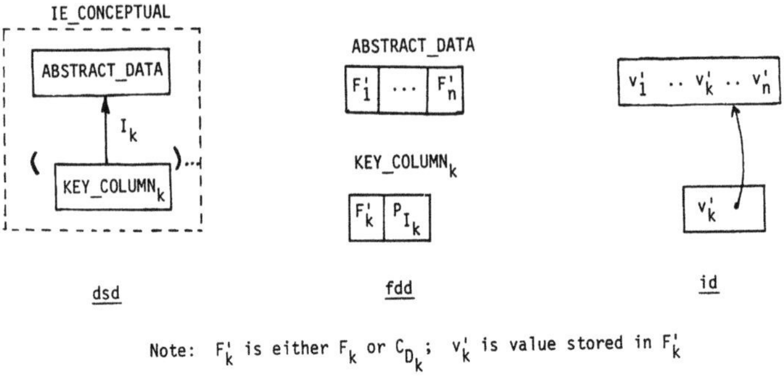

Figure 13. Segmentation of IE_CONCEPTUAL Type

The ABSTRACT_DATA record of Figure 13 is materialized in two steps (see Fig. 14). First, a metadata field containing a delete flag is ***augmented*** to each record. The flag is cleared initially and is set when the record is deleted. Second, each field is ***segmented*** from all other fields. (This is commonly known as ***full transposition***). n+1 record types result; each contains precisely one field. Because all fields are treated identically, the resulting record types are not distinguished as being either 'primary' or 'secondary'. RAPID refers to the record type that contains data field F_i as $COLUMN_i$ and the DELETE_FLAG field as $$$$ROOT.

Link R, which connects the COLUMN and $$$$ROOT record types, is a transposed linkset. A ***transposed linkset*** does not connect related records of different types together by actual pointers. Rather, a connection is implied by the sharing of a common record index. That is, related records share the same relative index position within their respective files. Thus, there is precisely one record instance for each of the $COLUMN_1 \cdots COLUMN_n$ and $$$$ROOT types for

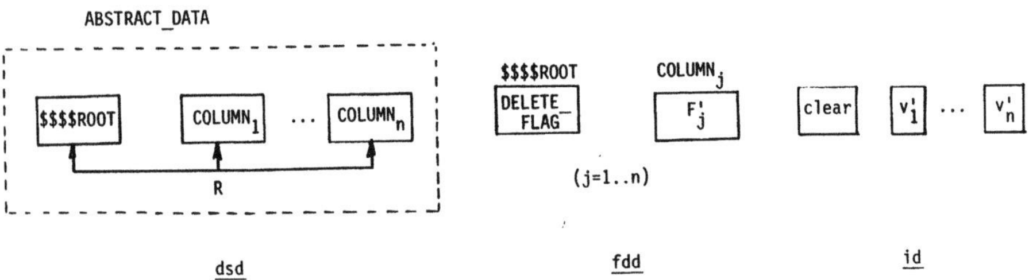

Figure 14. Augmentation and Transposition of ABSTRACT_DATA Type

every ABSTRACT_DATA record. The concatenation of the n+1 records that have record index i reconstructs the ABSTRACT_DATA record (with augmented delete flag) whose record index is i. Owing to this arrangement, a pointer to an ABSTRACT_DATA record may be treated as a pointer to any or all of its $COLUMN_1 \cdots COLUMN_n$ or $$$$ROOT records.

Finally, uncompressed data fields that contain text, such as comments, are now compressed by RAPID. This involves the elimination of trailing blanks. The *TEXT_COLUMN$_j$* records that result from the *encoding* (compression) of *COLUMN$_j$* records are variable in length. *COLUMN$_j$* records whose fields do not contain text are mapped to *NONTEXT_COLUMN$_j$* records by the *null* transform (see Fig. 15).

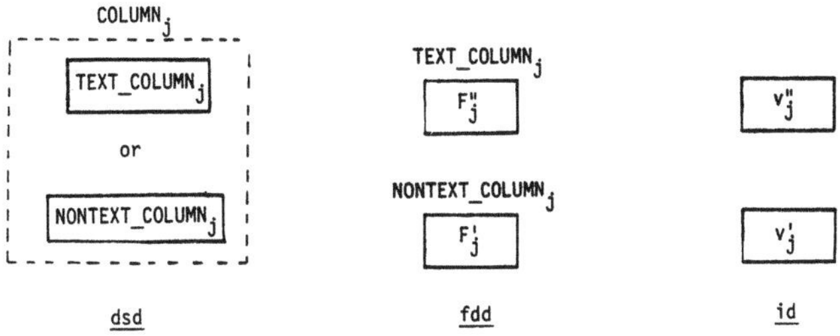

Figure 15. Encoding or Null Transformation of COLUMN Record Types

The internal record types of RAPID at this layer are the KEY_COLUMN, DICTIONARY, TEXT_COLUMN, NONTEXT_COLUMN, and $$$$ROOT. A distinct file structure is used to organized the records of each type. KEY_COLUMN records are organized by B+ trees; DICTIONARY, $$$$ROOT, TEXT_COLUMN, and NONTEXT_COLUMN records are organized by unordered files. [5] Records in an unordered file are addressed by their relative location keys (i.e., their index positions relative to the start of the file). The record index of a CONCEPTUAL record is the relative location key of its corresponding $$$$ROOT record. Similarly, the relative location key of a DICTIONARY record is its index code.

The storage architecture of the upper layer of RAPID is summarized in Figure 16.

The file structures used by RAPID rely on the physical sequentiality of their blocks. This allows the addressing of a record in an unordered file, for example, to be accomplished by a simple indexing operation. Because RAPID files are expected to grow, allocating disk space would not be a difficult problem if there were but one file. However, there are at least n+1 growing files and preserving the sequentiality of their blocks is no longer a simple problem. The designers of RAPID adopted a two-layer architecture as a solution.

The address space of the upper layer was assumed to be virtual and of enormous size. By assigning the starting block addresses of sequentially growing files far enough apart, the interference among the storage requirements for different files could be eliminated. However, virtual secondary storage addresses ultimately have to be mapped to actual addresses. This was accomplished in the following way.

A 1:1 correspondence was defined between blocks on the upper layer and conceptual records of type ABSTRACT_BLOCK on the lower layer. (This is modeled by the *layering* transformation). A ABSTRACT_BLOCK record consists of two fields: BLOCK_ADDRESS and BLOCK_CONTENTS (Fig. 17).

[5] The DICTIONARY, $$$$ROOT, and NONTEXT_COLUMN structures resemble BDAM (1-level unordered) files. TEXT_COLUMN structures resemble RSDS (multilevel unordered) files.

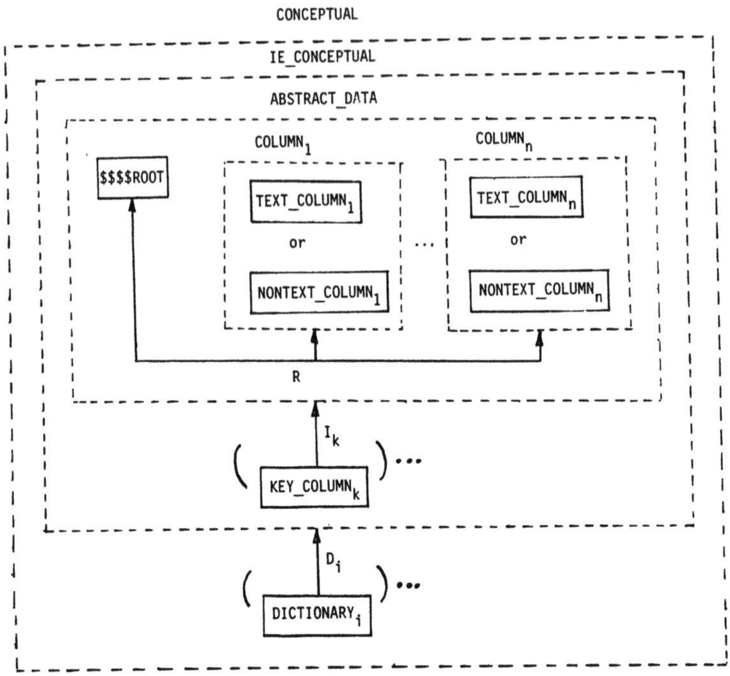

Internal Record Types and Links	Implementation
KEY_COLUMN_k	B+ tree
$\$\$\$\$ROOT, TEXT\_COLUMN_j, NONTEXT\_COLUMN_j, DICTIONARY_i$	unordered
R	transposed linkset
I_k	singular pointer
D_i	relational linkset with parent pointers

Figure 16. Upper Layer Storage Architecture of RAPID

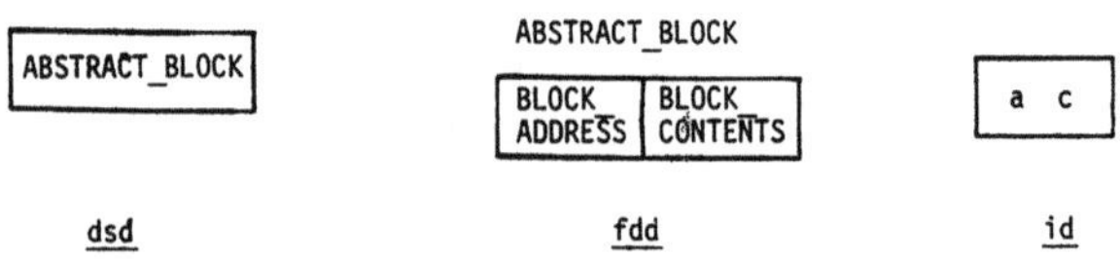

Figure 17. Lower Layer Generic Record Type

ABSTRACT_BLOCK is materialized by segmenting BLOCK_ADDRESS from BLOCK_CONTENTS (see Fig. 18). This produces the internal record types ADDRESS and BLOCK, which are connected by link AB. AB is a singular pointer.

ADDRESS records are organized by a B+ tree and BLOCK records are organized by an unordered file. Figure 18 summarizes the lower layer architecture of RAPID.

Source materials used in the derivation were [Turn79], [Stat81], and [Hamm82].

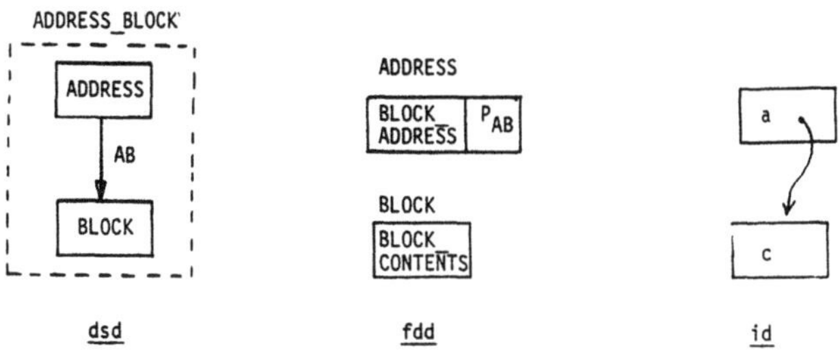

Figure 18. Lower Layer Storage Architecture of RAPID

4.3 Comments

The models of INGRES and RAPID are typical of those of other commercial DBMSs; storage architectures are described by sequences of elementary transformations. It is natural to ask how such sequences are generated, and what, if any, is the justification for using a given sequence. Clearly such questions are significant for they raise a fundamental point about what storage architectures are better than others. No answer can yet be given. The state of the research at this moment is to examine as many storage architectures as possible. Once a sufficient knowledge base has been collected, it is hoped that the underlying methodology for generating and justifying transformation sequences will become evident.

5. Data Operations, Locking, Query Processing, and DBMS Compilers

Elementary transformations, abstract data types, and automated software development are closely related. The idea of abstract data types is to encapsulate a record type definition and operations on the type with their mappings to lower level types and operations. We have explained elementary transformations as rules for mapping abstract structures to concrete structures. Alternatively, each transformation could have been explained in terms of mapping abstract operations (e.g., retrieval, updates, locks, etc.) to their concrete counterparts. It therefore seems possible that the data and operation mappings associated with each elementary transformation could be encapsulated as an abstract data type. It follows that the software which implements the storage architectures of commercial DBMSs may be described as a composition of abstract data types. It is believed that this connection between elementary transformations and abstract data types will lead to an automated development of internal DBMS software.

With this in mind, the models of the previous section can be used as blueprints for writing 'INGRES' and 'RAPID' software. In the process of writing such software, one will end up defining:

1) how conceptual operations on data are mapped to their internal counterparts,

2) how conceptual record and conceptual file locks are mapped to their internal counterparts, and

3) how query processing is accomplished.

At first glance, it is not clear how any of these processes can be automated or introduced into our modeling framework. However there is a way, and we will consider each of the above points in turn.

Consider the division transformation and its rule for mapping data. This transformation takes an abstract record and divides it into one or more segments. One segment is the primary segment; the remaining are secondary segments. The primary segment is connected to its secondary segments by a link occurrence. Figure 19 shows the data mapping induced by the division transformation on record type REC. In Figure 19.id, the link is implemented by a list linkset, and the example REC record was divided into three segments; one primary and two secondary.

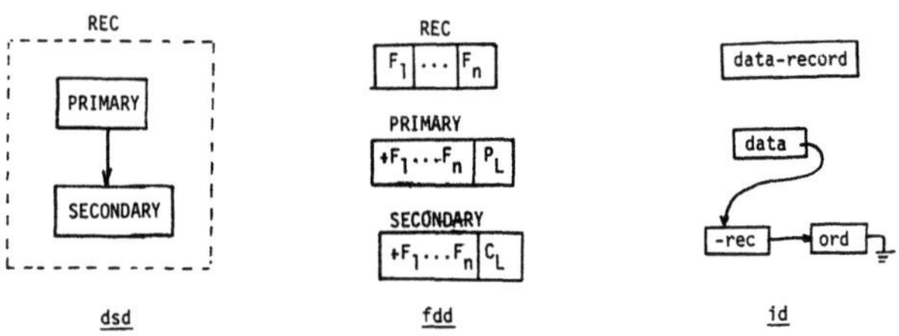

Figure 19. The Division Transformation

Consider the 'Access REC at rec-addr' operation which retrieves the record (of type REC) that is identified with the physical address rec-addr. At the level where REC is a concrete record type, this operation is a primitive. At a lower level (Fig. 19), the operation becomes:

1) Access PRIMARY at rec-addr;
2) Follow the link L occurrence to retrieve all related SECONDARY records;
3) Remove the parent and child fields of linkset L from the PRIMARY and SECONDARY records. Concatenate the records and return the result.

As this example shows, supplying a rule that defines how an abstract operation (Access REC) is mapped to a sequence of one or more concrete operations (e.g., Access PRIMARY) is fairly straightforward. It is often the case that several different rules can be supplied for each transformation. For example, in each of the following works [Kenn73], [Hoff76], [Niam78], [Bato79], a different algorithm for searching transposed files was presented. Each of these algorithms could be expressed as an operation mapping rule for the full transposition version of the segmentation transformation. The same holds for other elementary transformations.

In order for such rules to be valid at all levels of abstraction, the set of operations on abstract records (structures) must be identical to the set on concrete records (structures).

To see how this is possible, recall the basic ideas of the Unifying Model. At any level of abstraction, one is dealing with a physical database whose internal record types and links can be modeled by a data structure diagram. Just as physical databases can be decomposed into their constituent internal record types and links, so too can operations on physical databases be decomposed into a sequence of basic operations on internal record types and links. The total number of basic operations is quite small. Basic operations on record types include record retrieval, modification, insertion, access (as defined above), and deletion. Basic operations on links include the retrieval of the child records of a given parent, the retrieval of the parent record(s) of a given child record, and record linking and unlinking. With the aid of supplementary operations (e.g., record concatenation), level-independent transformation rules for mapping operations can be specified. The first phase of this research has already been completed

([Wise83]).

Now consider the 'Lock REC at rec-addr using lock-type' operation which locks the record (of type REC) that is identified with the physical address rec-addr. The locking mode is lock-type (e.g., exclusive or shared). Again, at the level where REC is concrete, this operation is a primitive. At a lower level (Fig. 19), the operation becomes:

Lock PRIMARY at rec-addr using lock-type.

There is no need to lock the corresponding SECONDARY records since the only way such records can be accessed is through their PRIMARY record. Rules for other transformations can be defined in a corresponding way.

Not all locks originate at the conceptual level. Locks on index records, for example, are not requested by DBMS users (since index records are invisible at the conceptual level). Instead, they are set by internal level routines. DBMSs also use special locks, called *cursor* or *currency* locks, which are imposed on records when a internal routine is examining a record as a candidate for retrieval ([Cull81], [Gray78]). (Retrievals often require a DBMS to examine many more records than are actually returned). A cursor lock is converted to a shared or exclusive lock if the record is returned to the user; otherwise it is released once the cursor (currency) is changed. Research is presently underway to define protocols for internal locking mechanisms and general rules for mapping locks according to elementary transformations.

How will such research differ or contribute to existing results? Many locking protocols have already been advanced in the literature. Some protocols are suitable only for restricted data structure diagrams, such as trees ([Silb80]); others are not restricted, such as two-phase locking ([Eswa76]). In our framework, these protocols are seen as concurrency control mechanisms that apply at the conceptual level. Protocols for lock mapping rules apply at levels below the conceptual. In this way, research on lock transformations should complement existing research.

How will research on query processing fit into the framework? The Unifying Model starts with the assumption that operations (e.g., retrievals, joins, etc.) on physical databases can be expressed as sequences of basic operations on internal record types and links. How these operations are sequenced in order to traverse multiple record types and links is often decided by a query optimizer which has knowledge of conceptual records and available links and indices. (The optimizer also relies on cost modules which predict the costs of traversing these links and accessing indices and 'conceptual' files. Such predictions *are* based on knowledge of the 'pure' internal level). Therefore, many query processing and query optimization algorithms work at a level of abstraction which lies immediately below the 'pure' conceptual level, but usually much above the 'pure' internal level. Further research on this topic is necessary.

It is evident that many difficult problems must be solved before physical database software development can be automated. But it should also be evident that software automation is possible. It is envisioned that a compiler of DBMSs would accept as input the transformation sequence that defines the conceptual-to-internal mappings of the target DBMS. Descriptive specifications about the transformations, such as limits on record lengths, compression algorithms to use, and internal record type and link implementations, would also be input. The output of the compiler would be the physical database component of the target DBMS, i.e., the software that stores, retrieves, etc. conceptual files and links according to the specified storage architecture. The generated software could include concurrency control and recovery mechanisms.

The compiler would rely on an extensive library of software modules. These modules would contain the code of different transformation rules, algorithms for different data compression techniques, support for each simple file and linkset structure (e.g., there would be module for index-sequential files, B+ trees, pointer arrays, etc.), a general recovery manager (using shadow paging or logging), different lock managers (based on different protocols), and different query processors (for different processing strategies), etc. The compiler would use its input to select among the available modules and synthesize special software (based on the transformation sequence) to integrate them. If a special module is needed (e.g., support code for a special-purpose file structure), it would have to be added to the library before it could be used in DBMS development.

6. Conclusions

An advance in physical database modeling has been the recognition that conceptual-to-internal mappings can be explained as a sequence of primitive mappings called elementary transformations. This has enabled the storage architectures (i.e., physical databases) of many different operational database management systems to be modeled in a uniform, simple, and comprehendible way. Prior to the introduction of elementary transformations, it was difficult - and in many cases impossible - to account for the complexity of the storage architectures of commercial systems.

We have reviewed two models of physical databases in this paper: the Unifying Model (UM) and the Transformation Model (TM). The UM defines and characterizes file structures and record linking mechanisms; the TM explains conceptual-to-internal mappings. Taken together, they were used to describe the storage architectures of two commercial DBMSs: INGRES and RAPID.

It is believed that models of storage architectures are now accurate enough to be used as blueprints for DBMS (physical database) software development. In this paper we have indicated how this may be done. However, many problems still remain to be solved. Further advances in query processing, physical database modeling, and concurrency control are needed before this goal is satisfactorily attained.

References

(ALSB75) (ANDE77) (BARO81) (BATO79) (BATO81) (BATO82a) (BATO82b)
(BATO83) (BATO84a) (BATO84b) (BUTT83) (CASA81) (CINC79) (CULL81)
(DATE82) (ESWA76) (GESE76) (GRAY78) (HAER78) (HAMM76, see HAMM76c)
(HAMM82) (HASK82) (HELD75, see HELD75b) (HEYM82) (HOFF76) (HSIA70)
(IBM80) (IEEE82) (IEEE83) (IEEE84) (INFO79) (JOHN83) (KENN73) (MARC81)
(MARC83) (MCCA82) (NIAM78) (NAKA78) (NDX81) (ROWE79) (SCHK75) (SENK73)
(SEVE72) (SEVE76a) (SEVE76b) (SILB80) (SHNE76) (SPER75) (STAN73)
(STAT81) (STON76) (STON82, see STON82b) (STON83) (TSIC77, see TSIC77b)
(TURN79) (WISE83) (YAO77, see YAO77a)

Physical Database Design: Techniques for Improved Database Performance

Salvatore T. March and John V. Carlis

ABSTRACT

In recent years, the information processing requirements of business organizations have expanded tremendously. With this expansion, the design of databases to efficiently manage this information has become critical. This paper addresses two areas of physical database design: record structuring (the grouping of data items into records that are physically stored and accessed together) and access path design (the design of algorithms and system structures used to determine the physical location of records and to support content dependent retrieval). The performance of a database system is largely dependent on the design choices made in these two areas. Techniques to support a database designer in making these choices are discussed.

1. INTRODUCTION

Databases exist to meet the information and processing requirements of some community of users. To be effective, a database must not only contain the right information, but it must also provide timely and efficient access to that information [Edel81]. Modern databases are typically large and service user communities with widely divergent information and processing needs.

Database design is commonly viewed at two levels: logical and physical [Nava78]. While the dividing line between logical and physical design is not precise [Lum79], the distinction may be thought of in terms of WHAT versus HOW. Logical database design addresses the WHAT of the database: what is the data content, what are the retrieval and update activities, what are the response time requirements. Physical database design addresses the HOW of the database: how is the data physically organized in secondary memory, how is it accessed, how is it maintained.

This paper addresses techniques for physical database design given a logical database design. The criterion for selecting among alternative database designs is the minimization of total system operating cost. This is typically approximated by the sum of storage, retrieval, and update costs. The data storage cost for a physical database is estimated by multiplying the size of the database by the storage cost per character for the media on which the data is maintained. Retrieval and update costs depend on the retrieval and update activities of the user community as well as the physical database design.

Physical database design is difficult. A myriad of physical design alternatives can support a given logical database. The performance of a particular physical design depends on many factors, such as the database management system (DBMS) software, the retrieval and update patterns of the user community, and the operating costs and accessing characteristics of the computer system. Typically the accessing characteristics of different users are in conflict. Data organizations that are efficient for one user may be inefficient for others. Tradeoffs must be evaluated and a compromise design selected which most efficiently meets all information requirements. Despite much work in the area, physical database design is still an art that relies heavily on human intuition and experience. Consequently, its practice is becoming more difficult as the applications that databases must support become more sophisticated.

Physical database design may be viewed as two interrelated tasks [Wied83, Marc83a]:

(1) record structuring and
(2) access path design.

The record structures of a database define the grouping of data items into records that are physically stored and accessed. The access paths of a database determine how those records are physically organized in secondary memory and they define retrieval criteria that are efficiently supported. Both tasks are discussed in the following sections.

2. LOGICAL AND PHYSICAL DATABASE CONCEPTS

At the logical level a database contains and provides controlled access to descriptions of instances of entities as required by its community of users. An entity is a category or grouping of things [Chen76, Kent78]; entity instances are members of that category. The description of an entity instance is a set of values for selected characteristics or descriptors of the entity instance. Two types of descriptors are distinguished: (1) attribute descriptors (or attributes), which are single valued characteristics of a single entity, and (2) relationship descriptors, which characterize an association between the entity described and some other (describing) entity. A relationship between two entities has two relationship descriptors, one for each direction of the relationship. The degree of a relationship descriptor is the (average) number of instances of the describing entity that exist for each instance of the described entity.

Each entity has some (subset of) data items(s) termed the identifier schema, whose value(s) is(are) used to identify unique entity instances. Each entity also has a cardinality or number of instances. Each attribute descriptor has an (encoded) length. Relationship descriptors may be thought of as "logical connectors" from one entity to another. How they are represented in the database is a physical design decision.

Figure 1 shows a graphical representation of a logical database containing four entities, DEPARTMENT, EMPLOYEE, PROJECT and ASSIGNMENT. The entity PROJECT has three attribute descriptors, proj-no, proj-budget and proj-due-date. It also has two relationship descriptors, MANAGER-OF-PROJECT (associating each project with the EMPLOYEE who manages the PROJECT) and ASSIGNMENT-OF-PROJECT (associating ASSIGNMENTs to PROJECTs). The degree of MANAGER-OF-PROJECT is one; the degree of ASSIGNMENT-OF-PROJECT is M (indicated by "chicken feet" on the ASSIGNMENT side of the relationship). Proj-no is the identifier schema for PROJECT (denoted by the dot on the proj-no arc). Entity cardinality and attribute length are not shown in the figure.

The logical retrieval and update activities of a user community are defined in terms of the logical data content. A retrieval is described by selection (of entity instances), projection (of descriptors pertaining to those instances) and sorting (descriptors used to order the output) criteria, and by a frequency of execution. An update activity is described by selection (of entity instances) and projection (descriptors to be updated for those instances) criteria, and again, by frequency of execution. Insertions and deletions project all descriptors for the selected entities. Retrieval and update activities may be quite complex and involve multiple entities (e.g., joins in a relational algebra).

At the physical level, data items (or fields) corresponding to logical level descriptors are grouped to define database records (or records). Records may be quite complex, containing repeating groups, termed aggregations, of data items describing one or more entities. Conversely, records may contain data items

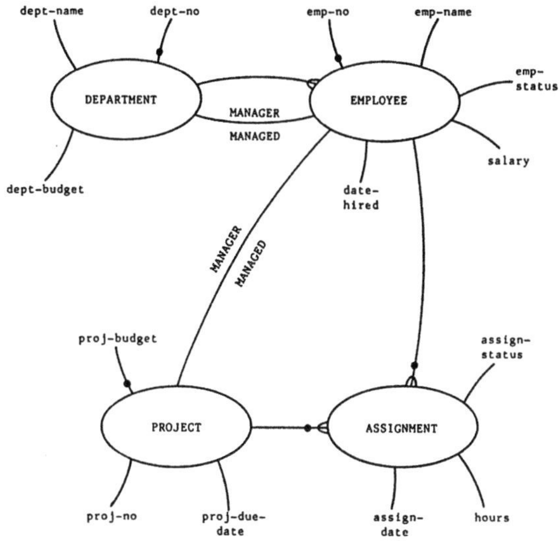

FIGURE 1. AN EXAMPLE LOGICAL DATABASE

corresponding to only a subset of an entity's descriptors. These are termed record segments and are connected either explicitly by pointers or implicitly by physical positioning. Hence a record may describe all or a part of one or more entities.

Many different physical record structures can support the same logical database. To assure that the physical database accurately reflects the entire logical database, each attribute descriptor must have a corresponding data item in some record. Relationship descriptors, on the other hand, may or may not have corresponding data items. Relationship descriptors with corresponding data items are linksets [Bato82] connecting the records describing the appropriate entities. Relationship descriptors may also be represented implicitly by physical proximity, i.e., an aggregation. Finally, since each relationship has two descriptors, no information is lost if only one of them is phyically represented in the database - the other can be derived.

A record instance contains a part of the description of one or more entity instances at the logical level (i.e., strings of bits that represent the values of the appropriate descriptors). A set of record instances for a particular record is called a file. Similarly, a set of all segment instances for a particular record segment is termed a subfile. Files and subfiles reside permanently in secondary memory in groups called datasets; that is, a dataset is a physical allocation of secondary memory in which some number of files and subfiles are maintained.

One of literally millions of record structures that represent the logical database of Figure 1 is shown in Figure 2. The entity EMPLOYEE is represented in two record segments (denoted RS1 and RS2 in Figure 2). These two segments are connected by a symbolic pointer (the identifier item emp-no is contained in both). RS1 also represents part of the entity ASSIGNMENT. The relationship descriptor ASSIGNMENT-OF-EMPLOYEE is implicitly represented by the placement of ASSIGNMENT

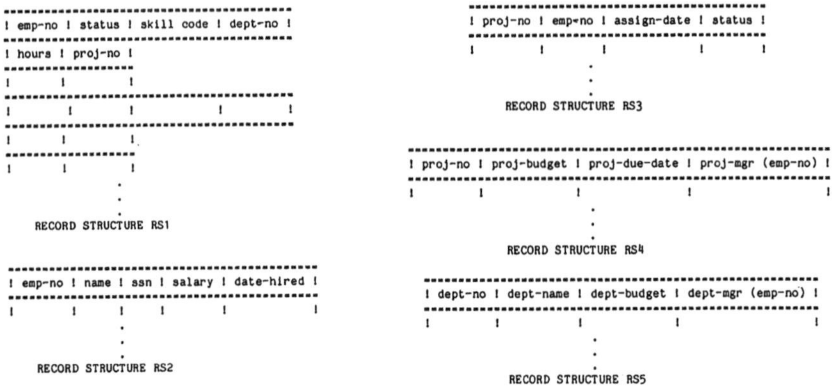

FIGURE 2. A POSSIBLE SET OF RECORD STRUCTURES FOR THE EXAMPLE LOGICAL DATABASE

data. The relationship descriptor DEPARTMENT-OF-EMPLOYEE is represented by a symbolic pointer (dept-no) in RS1. EMPLOYEE-OF-DEPARTMENT is not explicitly represented.

The aggregation (hierarchic arrangement) of ASSIGNMENT data with EMPLOYEE data is an efficient physical arrangement for database activities directed through EMPLOYEE to ASSIGNMENT. Since EMPLOYEEs and their ASSIGNMENTs are physically clustered, this information can be retrieved in the minimum time. If EMPLOYEEs and their ASSIGNMENTs were stored in different files and ASSIGNMENTs were not clustered by EMPLOYEE-OF-ASSIGNMENT, then each ASSIGNMENT for an EMPLOYEE could require a secondary memory access, thus substantially increasing the retrieval time.

The aggregation RS1 does not contain all of the EMPLOYEE data or all of the ASSIGNMENT data - both EMPLOYEE and ASSIGNMENT are segmented. For activities that require EMPLOYEE and ASSIGNMENT data, the retrieval costs depend on the projection criteria of the activity. If only data in RS1 is required, then the retrieval cost is reduced over the aggregation of all EMPLOYEE and ASSIGNMENT data since the subfiles of aggregated segments are smaller than the aggregated files would be. If the data items required by an activity are distributed over multiple segments, then evaluating the cost is more complex. If subfiles are independent and may be processed "in parallel," then cost may still be reduced. However, this is not common in practice; usually access to multiple subfiles proceeds serially and thus at greater cost than access to a single subfile.

While record segmentation may significantly reduce retrieval costs, it can also increase database maintenance costs. In particular, inserting or deleting an instance of a record typically requires access to each of the record's segments. The more segments a record has, the more expensive insertions and deletions become.

The logical retrieval and update activities must be supported by <u>access paths</u> at the physical level. Access paths determine how records are physically organized in secondary memory and they define retrieval criteria that are efficiently supported. A dataset with its associated access paths is termed a <u>file organization</u>. A <u>physical database</u> is a set of interconnected file organizations.

Each access path of a file organization is defined by a record selection criterion which it efficiently supports. A record selection criterion consists of a set of data items, termed the key data items or the database key of the access path, and possibly a set of values for each key data item. Each file organization of a database has exactly one primary access path which dictates the physical positioning of records in secondary memory and some number of secondary or auxiliary access paths, that are used to retrieve subsets of records (segments) which have been stored via the primary access path.

Three types of primary access paths are differentiated: hashed, sequential and indexed sequential [Mart77]. A hashed access path uses an algorithm to transform its database key into the secondary memory location where the record should be stored. A sequential access path provides access only to the next record physically stored in the dataset. An indexed sequential access path (e.g., ISAM or VSAM [IBM74]) logically maintains an ordered sequential file based on its database key and maintains a hierarchic block index to support rapid access to individual records by key value.

Retrievals requiring individual records are most efficiently satisfied by a hashed primary access path. In practice, a hashing algorithm only supports one database key, and hence one selection criterion. If different individual record retrievals have different selection criteria then one may be selected as the key of the primary access path, others must be supported by secondary access paths.

Retrievals requiring a large proportion of the data records are most efficiently met by sequential access paths which retrieve the entire file. In order to eliminate sorting costs, each retrieval would prefer to have the sequential access path ordered by its ordering criterion. Clearly, only one ordering is possible for the sequential access path.

Finally, retrievals which require a small subset of the data records are most efficiently met by an indexed sequential access path. In this way, records are clustered according to the key of the access path and direct access is supplied to clusters by the index. Again, each retrieval would prefer to have its selection criterion define the key of the primary access path.

Since a file organization can only have one primary access path (i.e., a record can only be physically stored in one location), secondary access paths support retrieval activities that are not efficiently supported by the primary access path. Secondary access paths are grouped into two categories: list (or chained) and inverted [Seve77]. A list connects a subset of data records by maintaining a pointer in each data record which is used to locate "the next" record in the list. Membership in a list is determined by the list key; all records with a given (set of) value(s) for a (set of) data item(s) are members. A multilist is a set of mutually exclusive lists each having a different (set of) value(s) for the same key data item(s). Lists and multilists have list headers which denote the (data item, value) pair for the list (or for each list in a multilist) and a pointer to the first record in the list. If there are a large number of lists in a multilist, the list header may be a separate file with its own primary access path (hashing, sequential or indexed sequential).

An inverted access path similarly connects a subset of data records. Rather than maintaining a pointer in each data record, however, the pointers are maintained as a separate file (which has a primary access path). An inverted list is analogous to a list and an inverted file is analogous to a multilist.

If the key for a secondary access path is an identifier, then there is only one record in each subset and the access path is commonly called a full index. The full index has a primary access path, typically hashing or indexed sequential. The terms hashing via a full index and hierarchic full index are used, respectively, for these types of access paths. As a final step, the values of the key data item(s) may be implicitly maintained by position in an inverted file; the resulting structure is commonly termed a scatter table or trie [Come79]. Hashing is typically used as the primary access path for a scatter table. The term hashing via a scatter table is used for this type of access path.

The result of processing multiple inverted access paths prior to data record retrieval is called a virtual access path. This type of processing is extremely important in a class of database management systems called "inverted file" DBMSs [Hoff80]. In such systems the number of records which must be accessed to satisfy a user retrieval request can be reduced, and hence the cost of satisfying that request reduced, by intersecting existing inverted access paths. Consider, for example, a retrieval request that selects records based on two data items, say EMPLOYEE Status and Skill Code. Suppose that 40 percent of the records satisfy the Employee Status criterion and 20 percent satisfy the Skill Code criterion. If an inverted access path with Employee Status as its key was used to satisfy this request, then 40 percent of the records would be accessed; if an inverted access path based upon Skill Code was maintained then only 20 percent of the records would be accessed. If, however, inverted access paths were maintained for both Employee Status and Skill Code, then then these access paths could be intersected and, assuming that values of these data items are independent, only 8 percent of the records would be accessed. This reduction in required records could significantly reduce the cost of satisfying this request. Inverted access paths are preferred over list access paths for the above reasons and because they can be dynamically created and deleted without altering any data records.

Secondary access paths can reduce data retreival time (and hence cost) when the proportion of records required is "small". Otherwise, if the proportion of required records is "large", simply scanning all records may be more efficient [Seve77]. The problem is to determine "how big is small?". This value is a function of dataset, storage device, and computer environment characteristics as well as detailed database design decisions.

The dominant secondary storage device is the moving head disk. Access time on a disk has three components: seek time (to move the head to the proper cylinder), rotational delay or latency time (waiting for the data to move under the appropriate read/write head), and data transfer time (to move data across a channel). The unit of transfer is a block, typically containing several data records. These components of access and the fact that blocks contain multiple records makes the calculation of "how big is small" complicated. In a computer environment where there is no contention for the disk, scanning all records can be done with a minimum amount of disk arm movement and virtually no rotational delay. If there is contention for the disk, then each block accessed could require an average arm movement and an average rotational delay. Secondary access paths, on the other hand, almost always require arm movement and rotational delay for each block accessed.

Consider the disk, dataset, and design decisions shown in Figure 3. What is the dividing line between "large" and "small"? This question is significant for physical database design since the choice of access paths depends on the answer. Figure 4 shows the answer. Assuming no contention and unsegmented records, the dividing line is approximately 2.1 percent. That is, if a retrieval request requires more than 21,000 records, then scanning the million records is as efficient as using a secondary access path. If there is contention for the disk, then the dividing line goes up by a factor of four. If records are segmented, then these proportions are reduced for retrievals requiring only one segment. The amount of the reduction depends on the segment length.

To summarize, just these factors make physical database design difficult:

DISK PARAMETERS

Characters per track	13030 characters
Tracks per cylinder	20
Data transfer rate	1 M chars/sec
Rotation time	24 milliseconds
Average rotational delay	12 milliseconds
Minimal arm access time	10 milliseconds
Average arm access time	25 milliseconds

Dataset Parameters

Number of records	1 million
Record size	500 characters

Implementation Parameters
(Detailed Design Decisions)

Records per block	12
Blocksize	6000 characters
Blocks per track	2
Blocks for the dataset	83,334
Cylinders for the dataset	2,084

FIGURE 3. DISK, DATASET, AND IMPLEMENTATION PARAMETERS

1. there are millions of different possible record structures to choose from for a given logical database,
2. records can be physically organized in secondary memory according to only one database key,
3. access path, segmentation, and maintenance choices are interdependent,
4. the times for random and sequential disk accesses can vary by an order of magnitude, and
5. the unit of disk access is a block, not a record

3. REPRESENTING PHYSICAL DESIGNS IN COMMERCIAL DATABASE MANAGEMENT SYSTEMS

Commercially available database management systems (DBMSs) are differentiated by their underlying data models. The three most common data models are: hierarchic, network (CODASYL) and relational [Date82]. Each type of DBMS requires both record structuring and access path design.

Record structures are termed hierarchic segments in IMS, record types with owner member sets in CODASYL DBMSs and relations in Relational DBMSs. Record structuring may be viewed as the aggregating and segmenting of logically defined data, within the context of a database management system. IMS [McGee77] supports aggregation by permitting multiple hierarchic segments to be stored in the same dataset (termed "dataset group"in IMS). In this case, children segments are physically stored immediately following their parent segments. CODASYL DMBSs [CODA78] support aggregation by allowing repeating groups in the definition of a record type and by permitting the storage of a MEMBER record type in the same dataset (termed "area" in CODASYL) as its OWNER, i.e., "NEAR OWNER". In CODASYL, a SET defines a relationship by connecting OWNER and MEMBER record types (e.g., if EMPLOYEE and ASSIGNMENT are record types, then ASSIGNMENT-OF-EMPLOYEE could be implemented as a SET with EMPLOYEE as the OWNER and ASSIGNMENT as the MEMBER). Storing a MEMBER record type "NEAR OWNER" directs the DBMS to place all MEMBER records physically near (presumably on the same block as) their respective OWNER records and indicates that access to the MEMBER records occurs primarily from the OWNER record via the SET relationship. Most relational DBMSs do not support

Disk Environment	Sequential Scan Time (dataset)	Random Retrieval Time (per record)	Dividing Line Between "large" and "small"
no contention	17.5 min.	49 millisec	2.1%
high contention	68 min.	49 millisec	8.3%

FIGURE 4. THE DIVIDING LINE BETWEEN "LARGE" AND "SMALL"

aggregation per se (i.e., "normalizing" relations requires, among other things, the removal of repeating groups [Date82]); however, substantial efficiencies can be achieved through the use of aggregation. In System R [Cham81], aggregation can be approximated by initially loading several tables into the same dataset (termed "segment" in System R) in hierarchic order and supplying "tentative record identifiers" during INSERT operations to maintain the physical clustering. Several relational DBMSs (e.g., RIM [RIM83]) allow arrays within a relation thus supporting a single level of aggregation.

All three types of DBMSs support record segmentation. In IMS, segmentation is accomplished simply by removing data items from one segment to form new segments, which become that segment's children. Similarly, in a CODASYL DBMS, segmentation is accomplished by removing data items from one record type to form new record types and defining SETs with these new record types as MEMBERS and OWNED BY the original record type. The new (MEMBER) record types are stored VIA SET to maintain the connection but not NEAR OWNER for efficient processing of the OWNER. In addition, a proposed CODASYL physical level specification [CODA78] suggests that record segmentation be supported at the physical level by allowing the definition of multiple record segments, termed <u>storage records</u>, for a single record type. In a relational DBMS, record segmentation is accomplished by breaking up a "base relation" [Date82] into multiple relations, each of which contains the identifier (key) of the original; these then become "base relations".

Given a set of record structures which define a set of interrelated file organizations, the access paths of each file organization must be designed. Commercial DBMSs restrict the types of primary and secondary access paths supported. IMS, for example, supports sequential, indexed sequential (ISAM and VSAM [IBM74]) and hashing as primary access paths and hierarchic full indexes as secondary access paths [Date82]. CODASYL Network DBMSs [CODA78] typically support sequential and hashed (CALC) as primary access paths (at least one CODASYL based system, DMS 1100 [SPER81] also supports indexed sequential as a primary access path). Secondary access paths are created by defining an OWNER record type that only contains pointers to the MEMBER record type to be accessed. This OWNER record type may be sequential (full index scan) or CALC (hashed full index). System R stores records directly in chronological sequence. Again, record clustering may be maintained by supplying tentative TIDs during insert operations. System R also supports hierarchic full indexes as secondary access paths.

4. TECHNIQUES FOR SUPPORTING DATABASE DESIGN DECISIONS

A database designer may understandably be overwhelmed by the many and varied design decisions which must be made; inappropriate database designs often result [Mart77]. This section briefly describes techniques which support physical database design. Techniques for record structuring are presented first, followed by techniques for access path design. Finally, an approach to solving the combined record structuring and access path selection problem is discussed.

4.1 Record Structuring

Record structuring is accomplished by aggregating and segmenting logically defined data within the context of a database management system. March [Marc83a] surveys techniques for solving this database design subproblem. These are briefly described below.

4.1.1 Aggregation

Aggregation is a type of record structuring that physically arranges groups of data items that have been defined by some data model. This section discusses a technique termed hierarchic aggregation. As its name implies, hierarchic aggregation assumes that the logical data structure is expressed in the hierarchic data model. Thus the set of aggregations from which a record structure is selected is restricted to "child" segments being aggregated iteratively into "parent" segments. Such an approach is also possible for the network and relational data models; however, its efficiency is highly dependent on the single parent restriction of the hierarchic model, and this restriction does not apply to the network or relational models.

Schkolnick [Schk77] developed hierarchic aggregation for use in designing IMS databases. The scope of the problem addressed by Schkolnick is restricted to hierarchic organizations of data stored without redundancy in a paged secondary memory environment, and sequentially processed via hierarchic scans. A hierarchic organization of data is simply one which can be represented by a tree structure. The basic element considered is termed a segment. Each segment is described by length (the number of characters required to store the segment) and type (an identifier for the items stored within the segment). Segments are organized into trees by means of a type tree. A type tree is an (m + 1)-tuple T = (S, T_1, T_2, ...,T_m), where S is the root segment of the type tree, T_1, T_2,...T_m are children type trees of S, and m is termed the root fanout of T; if m = 0, then T is called a root tree. The number of instances of a type tree T_j associated with a root segment S, is denoted Z_j and is called the Z-fanout of segment j.

Figure 5 shows a graphical representation of a hierarchy formed from the logical database of Figure 1. To create a hierarchy from a logical database, some relationship representations must be prespecified. Representing DEPARTMENT-OF-MANAGER and PROJECT-OF-ASSIGNMENT by symbolic pointers yields the hierarchy of Figure 5. Many other hierarchies can be created for this logical database, however, to apply the Schkolnick procedure, one hierarchy must be selected.

The hierarchy shown in Figure 5 can be represented by the type tree T = (DEPARTMENT, T_1), where T_1 = (EMPLOYEE, T_2, T_3). T_2 = (ASSIGNMENT) and T_3 = (PROJECT) are root trees. Given such a type tree, a physical storage scheme must be devised which efficiently supports the activity upon that structure. Two storage schemes are immediately obvious. First, one may use the hierarchic preorder [Knut73] to linearize the structure and then simply store segments sequentially, according to that ordering, in a single file organization. Alternatively, one may store each segment in a separate file organization. The first structure has advantages for the retrieval of all information for a particular instance of the main type tree (e.g., all information describing a single department), while the second has advantages for the retrieval of all instances of a single segment tree (e.g., assignment information for all employees).

Schkolnick developed sets of equations to evaluate the cost of retrieval activities based on transitions from one segment to another in retrieval activities (e.g., a retrieval requiring assignment information for an employee requires a transition from the employee segment to the assignment segment).

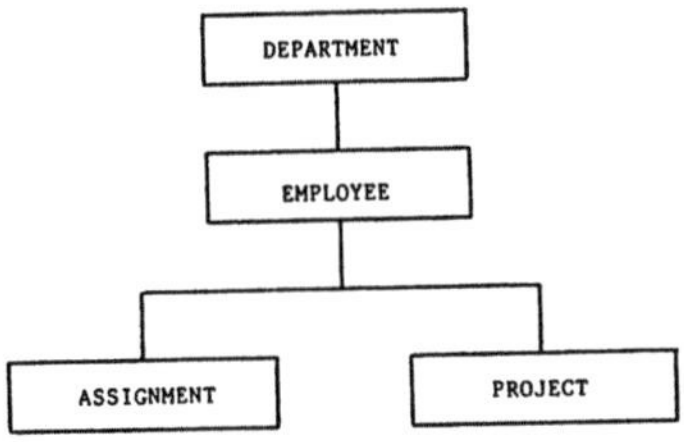

FIGURE 5. A HIERARCHY FORMED FROM THE LOGICAL DATABASE OF FIGURE 1

Specifically he developed cost equations for: parent-child transition, twin transition, and child-parent transition (hierarchic uncle). He characterized the activities on the hierarchy by the number of each type of transition for each segment in the tree. He then developed a branch and bound procedure to efficiently search the space of all possible aggregations. He concludes that the procedure produces record structures which are at least as efficient as those produced by experienced database designers - in some cases they are much more efficient.

This approach was developed only for the restricted case of the hierarchic data model; however, it is also applicable to other data models. Teorey and Fry [Teor82] suggest a two-step approach to aggregating network structures which was later extended by Chiang and Teorey [Chia82]. In the first step, the network structure is broken down into a set of overlapping hierarchies and the Schkolnick algorithm directly applied to each hierarchy. Forming a set of hierarchies from a network structure is relatively straightforward: when a record type is a MEMBER of only one SET, then the OWNER and MEMBER record types are already hierarchically related and no further work need be done; however, when a record type is a MEMBER of more than one SET, then a distinct hierarchy must be formed for each OWNER record type, with the MEMBER record type appearing as a child. Since a record type may appear in more than one hierarchy, it may also appear in more than one aggregation. Assuming that data are stored nonredundantly, then record types appearing in more than one aggregation conflict with the method of implementation. Such conflicts are resolved in the second step of the procedure by simply evaluating all possible combinations of conflicting aggregations. A similar procedure is applicable to any logical database. To insure optimality, the Schkolnick algorithm would have to be applied to all possible hierarchies. The difficulty lies in the number of possible hierarchies that could be created for a given logical database.

4.1.2 Record Segmentation

The aggregation approach discussed above assumes that logical entities will not be decomposed. It is possible that database performance may be improved by <u>segmenting</u> these logical structures.

The record segmentation problem is to determine an assignment of data items to segments (recall that each segment defines a subfile) that will optimize performance for all users of the database. The problem may be formally stated as

$$\min_{A \varepsilon R} \sum_{u_r \varepsilon U} v_r \sum_{s \varepsilon A} X_{rs} RC(r,s) + \sum_{s \varepsilon A} SC(s),$$

where R is the set of all possible segmentations (i.e., assignments of data items to segments), A is one particular segmentation, s is a segment of the segmentation A, v_r is the frequency of retrieval request u_r, and X_{rs} is a boolean variable defined as follows:

$$X_{rs} = \begin{cases} 1, & \text{if segment s is required by user request } u_r; \\ 0, & \text{otherwise} \end{cases}$$

RC(r,s) is the cost of retrieval for the subfile defined by segment s for the retrieval request u_r and SC(s) is the cost of storage for segment s, including overhead space required for its access paths (if any).

Three major techniques have been suggested for the determination of efficient record segmentations: clustering, iterative grouping refinement, and bicriterion programming. Each technique varies in the assumptions it makes about access paths and the secondary memory environment it considers. These variations yield significantly different problem formulations. Each, however, is restricted to a single flat file representation, and none permit the replication of data.

Mathematically, clustering is simply the grouping together of things which are in some sense similar. The general idea behind clustering in record segmentation is to organize the data items physically so that those data items that are often required together are stored in the same segment; in a processing sense, such data items are "similar". Conversely, data items that are not often required together are stored in different segments; they are "dissimilar". In this way user retrieval requirements can be met with a minimal amount of extraneous data being transferred between main and secondary memory. Unfortunately, user retrieval requirements are typically diverse, and a method of evaluating tradeoffs among user requirements must be determined.

Hoffer and Severance [Hoff75a,Hoff75b] developed a heuristic procedure for the record segmentation problem that uses a mathematical clustering algorithm and a branch-and-bound optimization algorithm. Their procedure is restricted to sequential access paths but includes a detailed costing model of secondary memory (in a moving-head disk environment). The solution to this problem is an assignment of data items to segments such that the sum of retrieval, storage, and maintenance costs is minimized.

Their approach first establishes a measure of similarity between each pair of data items. This measure reflects the performance benefits of storing those data items in a common segment. It then forms initial segments by using a mathematical clustering algorithm [McCo72] to group data items with high similarity measures. Finally, a branch-and-bound algorithm selects an efficient merging of these initial segments to define a record segmentation.

Hammer and Niamir [Hamm79] developed an heuristic procedure for the record segmentation problem which iteratively forms and refines record segments based on a stepwise minimization ("hill climbing") approach. Their procedure considers the number of page accesses for multiple record segments that have been stored nonredundantly. Access may be either sequential or random via any combination of predefined secondary indexes (i.e., direct access paths), each of which is associated with exactly one data item. In order to evaluate random retrieval, they define the selectivity S_i of a data item as the expected proportion of records that contains a given value for S_i. The selectivity of a data item is estimated by the inverse of the number of distinct values the data item may assume. If an index exists for a data item, then the selectivity of the index is equal to the selectivity of the data item.

The performance of a segmentation is evaluated by the number of pages that must be accessed in order to satisfy all user requests. Several expressions exist to estimate the number of pages that must be accessed to satisfy a retrieval request [Yao77]. An exact expression is given by:

$$\frac{N}{b}\left(1 - \frac{C_s^{N-b}}{C_s^N}\right)$$

where C_j^k is the number of combinations of k objects taken j at a time, N is the number of records in the file organization, b is the blocking factor (i.e., segments per page) for the subfile, and s is the number of segments required from the subfile.

The record structuring proceeds as follows. An initial segmentation is formed, with each data item stored in a separate segment. This is termed the trivial segmentation. The procedure iteratively defines new segments by selecting the pair of existing segments that, when combined, yields greatest performance improvement. When no pairwise combination of existing segments yields improved performance, all single data item variations of the current segmentation are evaluated. A single data item variation moves one data item from its current segment to another segment. If any variation is found that improves the performance, then the procedure is repeated, using that variation as the initial segmentation; otherwise, the procedure terminates. While it is possible for the procedure to cycle a large number of times, experimental evidence suggests that for reasonable design problems it is not expected to cycle more than once before terminating with an efficient, if not optimal, record structuring.

Eisner and Severance [Eisn76] proposed a mathematical programming approach to the record segmentation problem, which was extended by March and Severance [Marc77,Marc78]. This approach views record segmentation as a constrained optimization problem in which the objective is to minimize the sum of retrieval and storage costs.

Based on a behavioral model of database usage that predicts subsets of "high"-use and "low"-use data items, the procedure is restricted to considering at most two segments: "primary" and "secondary." Data items with high usefulness, relative to their storage and transfer costs, are isolated and stored in a primary segment; the remaining data items are stored in a secondary segment. All activity must first access the primary subfile, and may access the secondary subfile (at additional cost) only if the request cannot be satisfied by the primary subfile. The possibility of retrieving data items by accessing only the secondary subfile is not considered.

Eisner and Severance [Eisn76] analyze this design problem by assuming that activity to the primary subfile is either all random (with both subfiles unblocked) or all sequential (with a blocked primary subfile and an unblocked secondary subfile). In addition, they assume that pointers stored in the primary segments link the corresponding secondary segments. They formulate the program as a bicriterion mathematical program and develop a parametric solution procedure based on a network flow model.

Consider a database with N records and assume that primary and secondary subfiles are both unblocked. Let a_1 be the cost of a single access to the primary subfile, t_1 be the unit cost of data transfer from the primary subfile, and s_1 be the unit cost of primary subfile storage over the time interval T. Similarly define a_1, t_2, and s_2 for the secondary subfile. Given a specific segmentation A and assuming that the primary and secondary subfiles are both sequentially processed, then

$$\begin{aligned} Cost_A = N((a_1 + t_1W_A)V \\ + (a_2 + t_2\overline{W}_A)\overline{V}_A \\ + s_1W_A + s_2\overline{W}_A) \end{aligned}$$

where W_A is the length of the primary segment, $\overline{W}_A$ is the length of the secondary segment, V is the total retrieval frequency and $\overline{V}_A$ is the retrieval frequency for the secondary subfile.

Defining R to be the set of all possible record segmentations, the design problem becomes:

$$\min_{A \varepsilon R} N((a_1 + t_1W_A)V + (a_2 + t_2\overline{W}_A)\overline{V}_A + s_1W_A + s_2\overline{W}_A).$$

This expression can be reduced to one in W_A and $\overline{V}_A$ to yield

$$\min_{A \varepsilon R} K3 - K4(K1 - W_A)(K2 - \overline{V}_A),$$

where

$$K1 = W + a_2/t_2,$$
$$K2 = (t_1V + s_1 - s_2)/t_2,$$
$$K3 = N(a_1V + s_2 + t_2K1K2),$$
$$K4 = Nt_2.$$

For reasonable values of a_i, t_i, and s_i, K1, K2, K3, and K4 are nonnegative constants and the objective function is minimized by that segementation which solves:

$$\max_{A \varepsilon R}(K1 - W_A)(K2 - \overline{V}_A).$$

This expression is termed a <u>bicriterion mathematical program</u> because its objective function is the product of two expressions (i.e., $(K1 - W_A)$ and $(K2 - \overline{V}_A)$).

Geoffrion [Geof67] has shown that if $K1 \geq W_A \geq 0$, $K2 \geq \overline{V}_A \geq 0$ and R is a continuous convex set, then a solution A* with a maximum value for the objective:

$$\max_{A \varepsilon R} c(K1 - W_A) + (1 - c)(K2 - \overline{V}_A)$$

all $c \varepsilon [0,1]$ also solves the above bicriterion program.

By using standard network theory, Eisner and Severance developed a procedure that produces a family of "parametric" solutions for the parameter c. On the basis of conditions established by Eisner and Severance [Eisn76] the procedure terminates either with a parametric solution, which is known to be optimal, or with the best parametric solution and a lower bound on the optimal solution. If the best parametric solution is not "sufficiently close" to the lower bound, a branch-and-bound procedure is used to find the optimal solution.

March and Severance [Marc77] extended this work in the area of blocked sequential retrieval. They generalized the analysis to a situation in which primary and secondary subfiles are arbitrarily blocked, subject to the constraint of a limited buffer area; they then presented an algorithm that determines an optimal combination of record segmentation and block size, given a fixed main memory buffer allocation.

4.2 Access Path Design

The problem of access path selection has been addressed by many authors. Cardenas [Card75,Card77], Hulten and Soderlund [Hult77], and Anderson and Berra [Ande77] all address the problem of secondary index selection by providing models with which to evaluate the costs of alternative choices of key data items to be indexed. They do not provide algorithms which optimally or nearly optimally select which data items to index nor do they evaluate alternative types of access paths.

Gerritsen [Gerr75] and Gambino and Gerritsen [Gamb77] provide an evaluator for alternative access paths; however, it is restricted to CODASYL based [CODA78] database management systems (DBMSs). Hoffer [Hoff80] characterizes the process of key selection for inverted file DBMSs, but like others provides no support for selecting among the numerous alternatives.

Duhne and Severance [Duhn78] proposed a branch-and-bound approach to this problem which was utilized by March and Severance in a computer aided file organization design system [Marc78]. The class of access paths considered, however, is limited; individual record retrieval is not supported and inverted files and multilist structures are not considered. In addition, the algorithm is lengthy and complex.

As an example of access path selection techniques, the procedure developed by March [Marc83b] is briefly discussed. The procedure has three major components. First, a set of "potentially useful" access paths is automatically generated based on the set of selection data items required by each retrieval and on a set of file generation constraints imposed by the designer. Multiple types of both primary (sequential, ISAM, hashed) and secondary (inverted files, inverted lists, lists, multilists, hashing via scatter tables, and hashed and hierarchic full indexes) access paths are generated as required. Next, a file organization costing model is used to evaluate the fixed cost of storage and maintenence and the variable cost of retrieval for each access path generated. Finally, these evaluations are used in a mathematical program which selects a set of access paths that minimizes total operating cost.

The access path selection problem is formulated using the network representation illustrated in Figure 6. AP is the set of potentially useful access paths to be considered and EX is the set of user retrieval requests or extracts to be supported. Access paths and extracts are each represented by nodes in the network. In Figure 6 there are 8 access paths and 4 extracts. Access paths and extracts are connected via a set, G of generated access paths. A generated access path is either a real or a virtual access path. The concept is used in the costing model to represent the cost of record retrieval required to satisfy an extract. Each generated access path, g, is connected to a set of access paths $APG(g) \subset AP$, each of which must be implemented in order to use that generated access path. In Figure 6 there are 11 generated access paths. Generated access paths 1 through 8 require one access path each (access paths 1 through 8 respectively); they are real access paths. Generated access paths 9 and 11 require two access paths each and generated access path 10 requires three access paths; they are virtual access paths. Virtual access paths are used to model the processing of multiple inverted access paths to satisfy a single extract. Each extract, ex, is connected to a set of generated access paths, $GEX(ex) \subset G$, any of which can be used to satisfy the extract. In Figure 6, extract 3 can be satisfied by generated access paths 6, 8, or 10. If it is satisfied by generated access path 10, then access paths 6, 7, and 8 must be implemented (presumably they are inverted access paths which are processed together).

Associated with each access path, $ap \epsilon AP$, is a cost AC_{ap} required to store and maintain that access path for one period. Associated with each (generated access

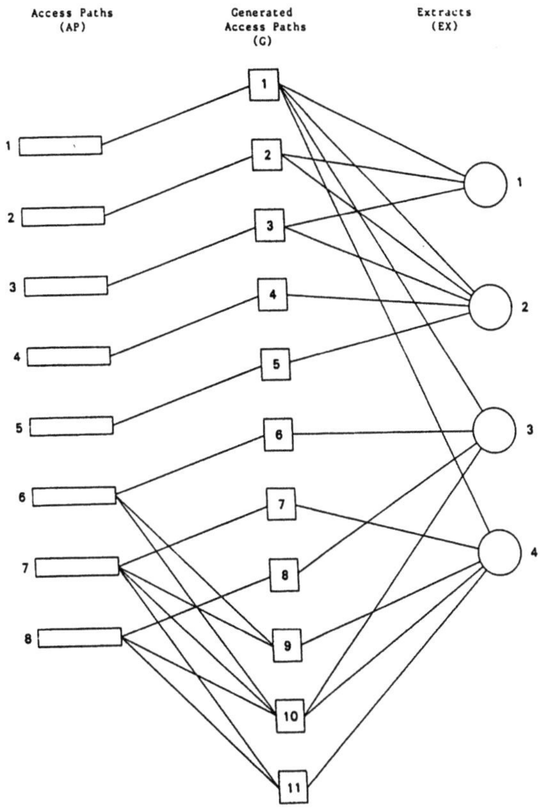

FIGURE 6. A NETWORK REPRESENTATION OF THE ACCESS PATH SELECTION PROBLEM

path, extract) pair, (g,ex)(exεEX, gεGEX(ex)), is cost, $GC_{g,ex}$, incurred when extract ex is retrieved via generated access path g; both record retrieval and extract sorting costs are included. The problem of access path selection is to assign each extract to a generated access path so that the sum of fixed and variable cost is minimized.

Equations for calculating the fixed and variable costs for various types of access paths were briefly discussed earlier and have been presented in detail elsewhere (see, e.g., [Hoff75b,Ande77,Marc78]). Given such costs, the task of access path selection may be formulated as a constrained, integer, linear program [Marc83b]. The objective may be stated as:

$$\text{Min} \sum_{ap \in AP} AC_{ap} X_{ap} + \sum_{ex \in EX} \sum_{g \in GEX(ex)} GC_{g,ex} Y_{g,ex}$$

where $$X_{ap} = \begin{cases} 1 & \text{if access path ap is implemented} \\ 0 & \text{otherwise;} \end{cases}$$

and

$$Y_{g,ex} = \begin{cases} 1 & \text{if extract ex is obtained via generated file g,} \\ 0 & \text{otherwise} \end{cases}$$

Two sets of constraints are also required. First, each extract must be retrieved from some generated access path, that is, one member of each set GEX(ex) must have a value of 1. Given that all $Y_{g,ex}$ are binary, these constraints may be stated

$$\sum_{g \in GEX(ex)} Y_{g,ex} = 1 \text{ for all } ex \in EX.$$

Second, all access paths required by a generated access path from which any extract is retrieved must be implemented; that is, if g is used for any extract then all members of the set APF(g) must have a value of 1. Again, given that all X_{ap} are binary, and that the $Y_{g,ex}$ variables are 1 if and only if g is used for ex, these constraints must be stated:

$$X_{ap} \geq Y_{g,ex} \quad \begin{array}{l} \text{for all } ex \in EX \\ \text{and } g \in GEX(ex) \\ ap \in APG(g). \end{array}$$

A file organization must have one primary access path which accounts for the cost of data record storage and maintenance. To assure the inclusion of a primary access path, the set of extracts is augmented by an extract which may be retrieved from any primary access path, but NOT from any secondary access path. Its frequency of execution is zero times per month; hence it does not impact the total cost.

This integer program does not explicitly limit the number of primary access paths to one. An additional constraint could, of course, enforce this requirement. We do not include such a constraint because the selection of more than one primary access path indicates that data duplication is cost justified and should be considered. That is, each primary access path includes the cost of data record storage and maintenance. If more than one is selected then the retrieval cost reduction exceeds the storage and maintenance cost increase associated with the data duplication. Hence the designer should consider multiple duplicate file organizations. If this is not acceptable, then the designer may simply eliminate one of the selected primary access paths and resolve the integer program.

This integer program may be solved by evaluating all possible combinations of access paths and selecting that combination with minimal cost. Unfortunately there are 2NA possible combinations of access paths, where NA is the number of access paths under consideration. While not all of these combinations will be feasible (i.e., meet all user information requirements) this approach is clearly inadequate for reasonably sized problems.

As an alternative approach, the program can be relaxed by removing the integer constraints; it can then be solved using classical linear programming techniques (see, e.g., [Baza77]). If the solution is integer, then the solution to the relaxed problem also solves the integer program. Otherwise, the solution to the relaxed problem provides a lower bound on the optimal solution. An upper bound may be obtained by simply rounding up all non-zero X_{ap} variables, then assigning each extract to the least cost generated file available, and finally eliminating any access paths which are not used.

If the upper and lower bounds are "sufficiently close" then use the current solution (the objective in database design is to select an "efficient" not necessarily optimal solution); otherwise apply a branch and bound procedure which alternately forces access paths into and out of the solution (by adding constraints of the form $X_{ap} = 1$ and $X_{ap} = 0$ respectively) and again solves the relaxed problem. If at any branch, the solution to the relaxed problem is either integer or not "significantly" less than a known upper bound then that branch may be pruned.

Theoretically the procedure discussed above may become rather time consuming due to the potential for branch and bound. However, in a series of 40 experiments using the procedure (discussed in [Marc83b]) the linear program produced an optimal solution 24 times. In the remaining 16 experiments the maximum difference between the lower bound obtained from the linear program and upper bound obtained by the rounding heuristic described above was less than 1 percent. While this does not guarantee that branch and bound will never be required, it does suggest that this approach is of practical significance for real world design problems.

4.3. The Combined Record Structuring and Access Path Selection Problem

As discussed above, record structuring and access path selection are interrelated problems. Record structuring techniques assume a given set of access paths; the cost evaluations associated with access path selection techniques depend on the record (segment) lengths.

An approach to the combined problem has been presented by March and Severance [Marc78] as part of a more global file organization design procedure. They first heuristically generate a set of access paths and use the Eisner-Severance procedure to determine an optimal record segmentation for the assumed set of access paths. Using that segmentation; an efficient set of access paths is selected using a branch and bound procedure developed by Duhne [Duhn78]. Using this set of access paths, the record segmentation algorithm is applied again. If the segmentation has not changed, then the procedure stops, otherwise, if the segmentation has changed, the access path selection algorithm is repeated with the new segmentation.

Theoretically this procedure could cycle many times and never converge. March and Severance limit the number of cycles to a maximum of 2 and select the record segmentation and set of access paths which minimize cost. The procedure is heuristic and cannot guarantee optimality; however, the physical design selected in a series of experiments have been intuitively reasonable and considerably more efficient than the simplistic designs to which they were compared (see [Marc78]).

Carlis and March [Carl83b] took a similar approach to this problem; however, the branch and bound algorithm was replaced by the linear programming approach discussed above. In addition, they suggest a heuristic procedure to generate potentially useful record aggregations prior to applying the segmentation and access path selection techniques.

5. SUMMARY AND DIRECTIONS FOR FURTHER RESEARCH

This paper has discussed techniques for physical database design. Specifically the subproblems of record structuring and access path selection were addressed. Techniques for record structuring include hierarchic aggregation, which seeks to group logically defined records and three segmentation techniques (clustering iterative grouping - refinement and bicriterion programming), which seek to partition logically defined records. Techniques for access path selection include evaluation procedures and optimization procedures utilizing branch and bound and linear programming. Finally, an approach to the combined record structuring-access path selection problem was presented.

We believe that the integration of record structuring with the selection of data access paths is a major area for future research. What is needed is a comprehensive model that will include both aggregation and segmentation and explicitly incorporate the effects of alternative data access paths. Such a model would serve as the basis for a more integrated approach to database design optimization than has previously been possible.

A second area for future research is integrating the database design and the software design activities. The activities on the physical database depend in part on the procedures used to access data. Alternate implementations for various queries could significantly impact the selection of record structures and access paths. This type of analysis is the subject of query optimization; however such techniques have not as yet been applied to the database design problem.

A third area for research is that of determining the effects of update operations. The costs associated with doing update operations are significantly different from those of retrieval operations and therefore affect the selection of record structures and access paths in different ways. In addition, alternative record structures and access paths vary greatly in their requirements for backup and recovery procedures. A record structure that isolates all data items that are subject to update may reduce backup and recovery costs; however, it may increase retrieval costs.

Finally, in any database serving a diversified user community, the question of data security must also be considered. Although in certain cases segmented record structures may be more expensive to implement, for security reasons it may be desirable to isolate sensitive data items in a high-security segment, perhaps stored on a separate disk device and requiring specific access authority. Similarily, some efficient access paths may not be implemented due to data security considerations.

References

(ANDE77) (BATO82, see BATO82b) (BAZA77) (CARD75) (CARD77) (CARL83a) (CARL83b) (CHAM81) (CHEN76) (CHIA82) (CODA78) (COME79) (DATE82) (DUHN78) (EDEL81) (EISN76) (GAMB77) (GEOF67) (GERR75) (HAMM79) (HOFF75a) (HOFF75b) (HOFF80) (HULT77) (IBM74) (KENT78) (KNUT73) (LUM79) (MARC77) (MARC78) (MARC83a, see MARC83) (MARC83b) (MART77) (MCCO72) (MCGE77) (NAVA78) (RIM83) (SCHK77) (SCHK79) (SEVE77) (SPER81) (TEOR82) (WIED77, see WIED83) (YAO77, see YAO77a)

The Property of Separability And Its Application to Physical Database Design

Kyu-Young Whang, Gio Wiederhold, and Daniel Sagalowicz

Abstract A theoretical approach to the optimal physical design of a large multifile database is presented. The approach is based on the concept that, given a set of access structures and transaction processing methods that satisfy a certain property called *separability*, the problem of optimally assigning access structures to the whole database can be reduced to the collective subproblems of optimizing individual (smaller) objects in the database independently of one another. The formal concept is introduced, and applications to both relational and network model database systems are discussed. The approach presented significantly reduces the complexity of the design problem which has the potential of being combinatorially explosive.

1. Introduction

The problem of physical database design addresses designing the underlying storage structures that support logical databases. Since a good physical design of the database has a vital influence on the database performance, the physical design problem has long been a subject of intense research and interest. The research in this area has been performed in several directions–such as file modeling and selection [SENK69, CARD75, HSIA70, SEVE75, YAO77, BATO82], access structure selection [TEOR78, HONE71, GERR77, GAMB77, MITO75, DE78], and index selection [LUM71, KING74, STON74, COME78, SCHK75, HAMM76].

Among these issues, we concentrate on the access structure selection problem in this chapter. A major premise in this problem is the existence of a database management system (DBMS) that provides various features to be utilized in physical database design. Thus, we are not concerned with designing these features themselves; it is assumed that they have already been implemented according to the specific technique employed by the DBMS which is being considered.

We now formally define two terms First, we define *access structures* as the features that a particular DBMS provides for the physical database design. For instance, access structures can be indexes, hashed organizations, clustering of the records, etc. Second, we define the term *access configuration* of a logical object–such as a relation in a relational database, a record type in a network model database, or an entire database–to mean the aggregate of access structures specified to support that logical object. Thus, the access configuration is an abstraction of the physical database.

A typical approach to access structure selection is to design a cost evaluator that produces the total cost of processing transactions† acting upon a specific access configuration. Using this cost evaluator, an optimal access configuration can be found by exhaustively searching through all possible access configurations–by designer's intuition or by trial-and-error. Teorey and Oberlander [TEOR78] presented a database design evaluator as a design aid to Honeywell's IDS [HONE71]. Gerritsen and Gambino [GERR77, GAMB77] developed a database design support system based on the DBTG model [CODA71]. Other papers on the design support system for network model databases appeared in [MITO75, DE78].

A common problem in most past research is that an optimal solution can be found only by exhaustively searching through all possible access configurations. The number of possible access configurations, however, can be prohibitively large even for a small database. Example 1 illustrates this point.

Example 1: In this example we consider a very simplified design process of a small database based on an exhaustive-search algorithm. We assume that the only access structure available is the clustering property. A column of a relation is said to have the *clustering property*, if records of the relation is stored according to the order of the column values. Although the clustering property can be assigned to a combination of columns, in this example we assume for simplicity that it is assigned only to a single column.

---

† Here the term *transaction* is used as a generic term for both queries and update activities against the database.

Using this access structure, for a given set of transactions as input information, we want to find an optimal access configuration for the database consisting of relations R_1 and R_2 each of which has only two attributes. We have nine possible access configurations as in Figure 1, in which dashed lines show the position of the clustering column.

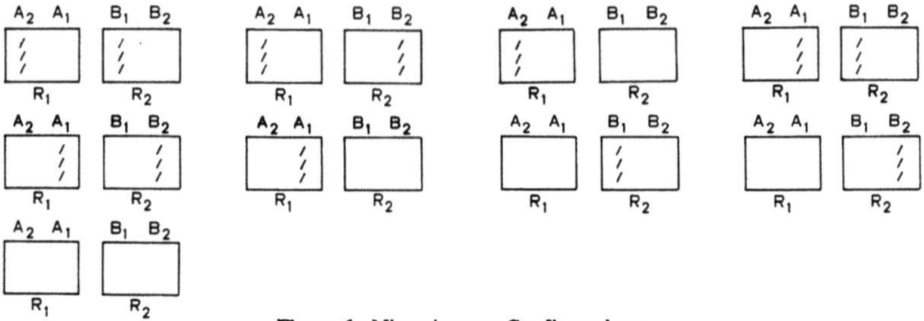

Figure 1: Nine Access Configurations.

The optimal access configuration can be found as follows:

1. For each of the nine configurations do
   a. find the best processing methods for each query
   b. obtain the total processing cost
2. Select the configuration that yields the minimum processing cost

In this simple design example, we have only nine possible access configurations ($(d + 1)^2$) when d is the number of attributes in a relation); but, the number of access configuration is explosive if we have more relations, more attributes in a relation, and various access structures such as the clustering property, indexes, links, etc. For instance, if we have five relations having five attributes each, with indexes and the clustering property as available access structures, the number of possible access configurations becomes

$$(6\times6\times6\times6\times6)\times(2^5\times2^5\times2^5\times2^5\times2^5) = 2.6\times10^{11}$$

($(d + 1)^r\times(2^d)^r$ where r is the number of relations)). □

In an effort to accomplish automatic design of physical database without an exhaustive search, Schkolnick and Tiberio [SCHK79] developed an algorithm based on partial exhaustive search. A certain number of intermediate solutions that are the best at any design stage are saved, and an exhaustive search is performed starting from those intermediate solutions to a predefined depth in the search tree. The same number of best solutions in the results are saved and the procedure is repeated. Although this algorithm improves the time complexity over the exhaustive-search approach, it still has the potential of being excessively time-consuming when a very large database is designed. As pointed out in [GERR77], a relevant partitioning of the entire design is necessary to make the optimal design of the physical databases a practical matter.

In this chapter we shall develop a methodology for the physical design of multifile databases applicable to many situations with reasonable efficiency and accuracy. In particular, we discuss the issues involved in designing the access configuration of a physical database to minimize the total processing cost of transactions. In calculating the processing cost we only consider the number of I/O accesses; the cost due to the CPU time is not included. Our approach is somewhat formal and mathematical, deliberately avoiding excessive reliance on heuristics. Our purpose is to render the whole design phase manageable and to facilitate understanding of the underlying mechanisms.

We proceed by first developing a design theory called *separability* that enables us to partition the design problem into disjoint subproblems. We then discuss application of the theory to two major types of database systems: relational and network model database systems. Specifically, we show that important subsets of features provided by both types of database systems satisfy the conditions for separability. Thus, if features are restricted to these subsets, the optimal design of access configurations of multifile databases can be reduced to the collective optimal designs of smaller objects. In principle, these smaller objects, which we call *logical objects*, can be any subsets of the database scheme being designed. In practice, however, the most convenient partition would be the set of individual relations for relational systems and record types for network model database systems.

In Section 2 we develop the skeleton of the theory of separability and prove the separability theorem. We then investigate, in Section 3, how the theory can be applied to relational database systems. Application of the theory to network model database systems is presented in Section 4. An interesting application of the theory to a relational database system appears in [BONF83].

2. Theory of Separability

In this section we present the theorem of separability. The theorem states that, given a set of access structures and transaction processing methods that satisfy certain conditions, the problem of optimally designing the access configuration of the entire database can be reduced to the subproblem of optimizing individual logical objects in the database independently of one another. Before introducing the theorem we need the following definitions.

Definition 1: The procedure of designing the optimal access configuration of a database is *separable* if it can be decomposed into the tasks of designing the optimal configurations of individual logical objects independently of one another. □

Definition 2: A *partial-operation* cost of a transaction is the part of the transaction processing cost that represents the accessing of only one logical object, as well as of the auxiliary access structures defined for it. □

Definition 3: A *partial operation* is a conceptual division of the transaction whose processing cost is a partial-operation cost. □

Theorem 1: (Separability) The procedure of designing the optimal access configuration of a database is *separable* if the following conditions are satisfied:

Condition 1: The partial-operation cost of a transaction for a logical object is independent of the access configuration specified and the partial operations used for the other logical objects.

Condition 2: A partial operation for a logical object can be chosen regardless of the access configuration specified and the partial operations used for the other logical objects.

Condition 3: Access structures for a logical object can be chosen independently of access configurations of the other logical objects.

Proof: Condition 2 states that, in selecting a partial operation of a transaction for a logical object, we are not constrained by the access configurations of and the partial operations used for the other logical objects. Similarly, Condition 3 says that we are not constrained by the access structures chosen for the other logical objects in selecting an access structure for a logical object. Furthermore, since the partial-operation cost of a particular logical object is not affected by the access configurations of and the partial operations used for the other logical objects, neither the specific access structures assigned to the other logical objects nor the partial operations used for them can affect the design decisions for this logical object. □

Many database management systems satisfy Condition 3 in the sense that they do not put restrictions in assigning the access structures to a different logical object because of access structures of other logical objects. Therefore, from now on, we exclude Condition 3 from our consideration.

Condition 1 is easy to check if we have specific cost formulas; but is somewhat difficult otherwise. In the latter case, we have the following sufficient conditions which are easier to check.

Sufficient conditions for Condition 1: Each item below is independent of the access configurations specified for and the partial operation used for the other logical objects.

1.A. Cardinality of the set of records accessed in the partial operation

1.B. The order of accessing these records

1.C. Relative placement of these records in the storage medium

Conditions 1.A, 1.B, and 1.C together form a sufficient condition for Condition 1 of Theorem 1 since the partial-operation cost can be determined from them. These conditions are not necessary ones because, although unlikely, partial-operation costs could be the same even though some of the conditions are not satisfied.

3. Separability in Relational Database Systems

In this section† we investigate how the theory introduced in Section 2 can be applied to relational database systems. In particular, we shall prove that a set of practically important join methods satisfies the conditions for separability. The implication is that, if the available join methods are restricted to this set, the optimal design of the access configuration of a multifile database can be reduced to the collective optimal designs of individual relations.

3.1 Approaches and Assumptions

We assume that the DBMS we consider provides indexes and the clustering property of a single relation as access structures. Clustering of two or more relations, as in many hierarchical organizations, is not considered. For simplicity, we consider only the indexes and the clustering property defined for single columns. Multicolumn indexes and clustering property can be incorporated by defining virtual columns and treating them as separate columns that have certain dependencies in the physical database design process [WHAN83a].

The database is assumed to reside on disk-like devices. Physical storage space for the database is divided into fixed-size blocks [WIED83]. The block is not only the unit of disk allocation, but is also the unit of transfer between main memory and disk. We assume that a block contains tuples of only one relation. Furthermore, we assume that the blocks containing tuples of a relation, which comprise a file, can be accessed serially. However, the blocks do not have to be contiguous on the disk. For simplicity, we assume that a relation is mapped into a single file. Accordingly, from now on, we shall use the terms *file* and *relation* interchangeably; nor shall we make distinction between an attribute and a column or between a tuple and a record.

We shall develop a simple cost model of the storage structure in Section 3.3, and use various cost formulas based on this model for case studies. We assume that no block access will be incurred if the next tuple (or index entry) to be accessed resides in the same block as that of the current tuple (or index entry); otherwise, a new block access is necessary. We also assume that all TID (tuple identifier) manipulations can be performed in main memory without any need for I/O accesses.

Relations can have various relationships depending on the characteristics of the domains of the attributes that are related. For example, if we relate a key attribute (or a set of attributes) in relation R_1 and a nonkey attribute (or a set of attributes) in relation R_2, then R_1 and R_2 have a one-to-many relationship with respect to these attributes. In this chapter, we consider only one-to-many (including one-to-one) relationships between relations, since we believe that many-to-many relationships between relations are less important for optimization. Let us note however that a many-to-many relationship among entity sets is extremely important in representing the semantics of the data [WIED79], but is different from a many-to-many relationship between relations. A many-to-many relationship among entity sets at the conceptual level is often structured with an additional intermediate relation (called an association in [WIED79]) representing the many-to-many relationship. In this case, however, the relationships between relations still will be either one-to-many or many-to-one. In contrast, a many-to-many relationship between relations may be relatively trivial. It is shown in [WHAN83] that, for a relation scheme R any of whose relation instance is a join of two relation instances whose relation schemes have a many-to-many relationship with respect to a set of attributes A, a multivalued dependency (MVD) [ULLM82] holds. We assume that the only predicate that relates these two relations is the one for join based on A. Intuitively, if an MVD $A \twoheadrightarrow B$ (accordingly $A \twoheadrightarrow A \cup B$ and $A \twoheadrightarrow R-B$)) holds for relation scheme R, where A and B are sets of attributes in R, then in a specific relation instance r of R, given a specific value of A, the values of R−B are completely replicated for every distinct value of AUB. Because of this replication, sets of attributes AUB and R−B tend not to have a meaningful relationship, and thus it does not make much sense to have both sets of attributes together in a single relation (say, in the result of a query involving a join).

† A preliminary version of this section appeared in [WHAN84a].

Finally, we consider only one-variable and two-variable queries and update transactions. Consideration of transactions of more than two variables needs a more complex treatment. In principle, however, a heuristic approach can be employed to decompose those transactions into sequences of two-variable transactions [WHAN83a].

3.2 Transaction Evaluation

3.2.1 Queries

The class of queries we consider is shown in Figure 2. This query class includes two relations, R_1 and R_2 , and equijoin based on the attributes A and B, and restriction predicates P_1 and P_2.

```
SELECT <list of attributes>
FROM   R1, R2
WHERE  R1.A = R2.B AND
       P1          AND
       P2
```

Figure 2: General Class of Queries Considered.

Query evaluation algorithms, especially for two-variable queries, have been studied in [BLAS76] and [YAO79]. The most important parts of query processing algorithms in relational databases are those for processing joins. Restrictions and projections can be processed with joins in an integrated manner. Therefore, from now on, we call query processing algorithms in relational databases simply join algorithms. Before discussing the various join methods, let us define some terminology. Given a query, an index is called a *join index* if it is defined for the join column of a relation. Likewise, an index is called a *restriction index* if it is defined for a restriction column. We use the term *subtuple* for a tuple that has been projected over some columns. The restriction predicate in a query for each relation is decomposed into the form $Q_1 \wedge Q_2$, where Q_1 is a predicate that can be processed using indexes, while Q_2 is one that cannot. Q_2 must be resolved by accessing individual records. We shall call Q_1 the *index-processible predicate* and Q_2 the *residual predicate.*

Some algorithms for processing joins that are of practical importance are summarized below (see also [BLAS76] and [SELI79]):

- *Join Index Method:* This method presupposes the existence of join indexes. For each relation, the TIDs of tuples that satisty the *index-processible predicates* are obtained by manipulating the TIDs from each index involved; the resultant TIDs are stored in temporary relations R_1 and R_2. TID pairs with the same join column values are found by scanning the join column indexes in the order of join column values. As they are found, each TID pair (TID_1,TID_2) is checked to determine whether TID_1 is present in R_1' and TID_2 in R_2'. If they are, the corresponding tuple in one relation, say R_1, is retrieved. When this tuple satisfies the *residual predicate* for R_1, the corresponding tuple in R_2 is retrieved and the residual predicate for R_2 is checked. If qualified, the tuples are concatenated and a subtuple is constructed for output.

- *Sort-Merge Method:* The relations R_1 and R_2 are scanned–either by using restriction indexes, if there is an index-processible predicate in the query, or by scanning the relation directly–and temporary relations T_1 and T_2 are created. Restrictions, partial projections, and the initial step of sorting are performed while the relations are being initially scanned and stored in T_1 and T_2. T_1 and T_2 are sorted by the join column values. The resulting relations are scanned in parallel and the join is completed by merging matching tuples.

- *Combination of the Join Index Method and the Sort-Merge Method:* One relation, say R_1, is sorted as in the sort-merge method and stored in T_1. Relation R_2 is processed as in the join index method, storing the TIDs of the tuples that satisfy the index-processible predicates in R_2'. T_1 and the join column index of R_2 are scanned in the order of join column values. As matching join column values are found, each TID from the join index of R_2 is checked against R_2'. If it is in R_2', the corresponding tuple in R_2 is retrieved and the residual predicate for R_2 is checked. If qualified, the tuples are concatenated and the subtuple is constructed.

- *Inner/Outer-Loop Join Method:* In the two join methods described above, the join is performed by scanning relations in the order of the join column values. In the inner/outer-loop join, one of the relations, say R_1, is scanned without regard to order, either by using restriction indexes or by scanning the relation directly, and, for each tuple of R_1 that satisfies predicate P_1, the tuples of relation R_2 that satisfy predicate P_2 and the join predicate are retrieved and concatenated with the tuple of R_1. The subtuples desired are then projected.

Let us note that, in the combination of the join index method and the sort-merge method, the operation performed on either relation is identical to that performed on one relation in the join index method or in the sort-merge method. We call the operations performed on each relation *join index method (partial)* or *sort-merge method (partial)*, respectively; whenever no confusion arises, we call these operations simply *join index method* or *sort-merge method.* According to the definitions, the join index method actually consists of two join index methods (partial) and, the sort-merge method similarly consists of two sort-merge methods (partial).

3.2.2 Update transactions

We assume that the updates are performed only on individual relations, although the qualification part (WHERE clause) may involve more than one relation. Thus, updates are not performed on the join of two or more relations. (If they are, an ambiguity arises as to which relations to update [KELL81].) The class of update transactions we consider is shown in Figure 3.

UPDATE R_1
SET $R_1.C$ = <new value>
FROM R_1, R_2
WHERE $R_1.A = R_2.B$ AND
P_1 AND
P_2

Figure 3: General Class of Update Transactions Considered.

The meaning of this class of transactions is as follows. Tuples in relation R_2 are restricted by restriction predicate P_2. Let us call the set of resulting tuples T_2. Then, the value for column C of each tuple in R_1 is changed to <new value> if the tuple satisfies the restriction predicate P_1 and has a matching tuple in T_2 that satisfies the join predicate. In a more familiar syntax [CHAM76], the class of update transactions can be represented as in Figure 4. The equivalence of the two representations has been shown for queries in [KIM82].

UPDATE R_1
SET $R_1.C$ = <new value>
WHERE P_1 AND
$R_1.A$ IN
(SELECT $R_2.B$
FROM R_2
WHERE P_2)

Figure 4: An Equivalent Form of the General Class of Update Transactions.

Deletion transactions are specified in an analogous way. It is assumed that insertion transactions refer only to single relations. From now on, unless any confusion arises, we shall refer to update, deletion or insertion transactions simply as update transactions.

The update transaction in Figure 3 can be processed just like queries except that an update operation is performed instead of concatenating and projecting out the subtuples after relevant tuples are identified. In particular, all the join methods described in Section 3.2.1 can be used for update transactions as well. But, there are two constraints: 1) The sort-merge method cannot be used for the relation to be updated since it is meaningless to create a temporary sorted file for that relation. 2) When the inner/outer-loop join method is used, the direction of the join must be from the relation to be updated (R_1) to the other relation (R_2) because, if the direction were reversed, the same tuple might be updated more than once. Let us note that, although two-relation update transactions are not joins, the join predicates can be processed using the join methods defined for processing joins.

3.3 Cost Model of the Storage Structure

To calculate the cost of evaluating a query, we need a proper model of the underlying storage structure and its corresponding cost formula. Although the theory does not depend on the specifics of cost models, it is helpful to have a simple cost model for illustrative purposes.

We assume that a B^+tree index [BAYE72] can be defined for a column or for a set of columns of a relation. The leaf-level of the index consists of (key and TID) pairs for every tuple in that relation. The leaf-level blocks are chained according to the order of indexed column values, so that the index can be scanned without traversing the index tree. Entries having the same key value are ordered by TID.

An index is called a *clustering index* if the relation on which this index is defined is physically clustered according to the index column values. With a clustering index, we assume that no block is fetched more than once when tuples with consecutive values of the indexed column are retrieved. Except for this ordering property, no other difference in the structure is assumed between a clustering and a nonclustering index. The clustering property can greatly reduce the access cost, especially when a join column has a clustering index. Unfortunately, only one column of a relation can have the clustering property, since clustering requires a specific order of records in the physical file. One of the objectives of designing optimal physical databases is to determine which column will be assigned the clustering property.

The access cost will be measured in terms of the number of I/O accesses. The following notation will be used throughout this chapter:

R	:A relation.
Other(R)	:The relation to be joined with R.
C	:A column.
n_R	:Number of tuples in relation R (cardinality).
p_R	:Blocking factor of relation R.
L_C	:Blocking factor of the index for column C.
F_C	:Selectivity of column C or its index.
cc	:Subscript for the clustering column.
m_R	:Number of blocks in relation R, which is equal to n_R/p_R.
im_C	:Number of blocks that the index for column C occupies.
t	:A transaction.
$H_{t,R}$	:Projection factor of transaction t on relation R.

By using the simplified model above, the cost of various operations can be obtained as follows:

- Relation Scan Cost: Cost for serially accessing all the blocks containing the tuples of a relation:

  $$RS(R) = n_R/p_R = m_R$$

- Index Scan Cost: Cost for serially accessing the leaf-level blocks of an entire index:

  $$IS(I,R) = \lceil n_R/L_C \rceil$$

- Index Access Cost: Cost for one access of the index tree from the root:

  $$IA(I,R) = \lceil \log_{L_C} n_R \rceil + (\lceil F_C \times n_R/L_C \rceil - 1)$$

  Here the first term estimates the cost of traversing the index tree from the root to a leaf node; the second the cost of scanning the remaining leaf nodes that contain the index entries having the key value.

- Sorting Cost: Cost for sorting a relation, or a part thereof, according to the values of the columns of interest:

  $$SORT(NB) = 2 \times \lceil NB \rceil + 2 \times \lceil NB \rceil \times \lceil \log_z \lceil NB \rceil \rceil$$

  Here we assume that a z-way sort-merge is used for the external sort [KNUT73]. NB is the number of blocks in the temporary relation containing the subtuples to be sorted after restriction and projection have been resolved. It will be noted that SORT(NB) does not include the initial scanning time to bring in the original relation, while it does not include the time to scan the temporary relation for the actual join after sorting (see [BLA76]).

3.4 Design Theory

In this section we investigate the property of separability for relational database systems. In particular, we shall prove that the set of join methods consisting of the join index method, the sort-merge method, and the combination of the two satisfies the conditions for separability under certain constraints. We illustrates the concepts through a series of examples and by case analysis, using the cost model developed in Section 3.3. Observations resulting from this procedure are formalized and proved in Section 3.4.3.

Our approach to physical database design is based on the premise that at execution time the query processor will choose the best processing method for a given query. We call this processor an *optimizer*. Since the behavior of the optimizer at execution time critically affects the physical database design, we investigate .this issue and discuss how it is related to the design.

We define the influence of the restriction on one relation to the number of tuples to be retrieved from the other relation the *coupling effect*. Starting with a case in which coupling effects between relations are excluded, we then proceed to those cases in which they are included.

3.4.1 Cases without coupling effects

Example 2: Figure 5 describes two relations R_1 and R_2 with their access configurations. Dashed lines (/) represent clustering indexes, dotted lines (:) nonclustering indexes. Columns without either type of line have no indexes. We would like to find the best method of evaluation–which the optimizer would choose at query-processing time, for the following query:

SELECT A_1, A_2, B_2
FROM R_1, R_2
WHERE $R_1.A_2$ = 'a_2' AND
$R_2.B_2$ = 'b_2' AND
$R_1.A_1 = R_2.B_1$

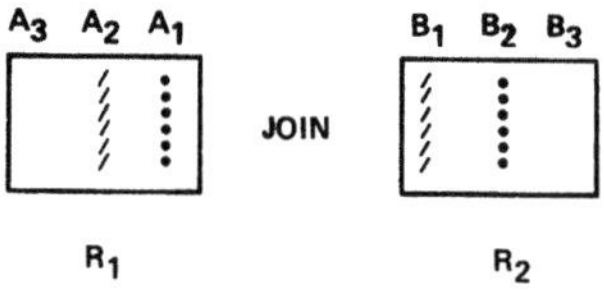

Figure 5: Relations R_1 and R_2.

For this example only, it is assumed that all tuples in each relation participate in the join.

Given the above access configuration, the optimizer could try all possible combinations of the join methods, evaluate the cost of each, and then select the one that costs the least. We have the following combinations:

	R_1	R_2
1.	Join index method (partial)	Join index method (partial)
2.	Sort-merge method (partial)	Sort-merge method (partial)
3.	Join index method (partial)	Sort-merge method (partial)
4.	Sort-merge method (partial)	Join index method (partial)

Using the cost model developed in Section 3.3, the following formulas give the cost (number of block accesses) for each of the four cases above. In each formula the first and the second bracketed expressions represent the cost of accessing relations R_1, and R_2 respectively. Bracketed expressions in the formulas are given arbitrary values for illustrative purposes. Those expressions whose form is identical are given the same value.

$$\text{Cost} = [IA(I_{A2},R_1) + IS(I_{A1},R_1) + F_{A2} \times n_{R1}] + \qquad :100 + \qquad (1)$$

$$[IA(I_{B2},R_2) + IS(I_{B1},R_2) + b(m_{R2},p_{R2},F_{B2} \times n_{R2})] \qquad :20$$

$$\text{Cost} = [IA(I_{A2},R_1) + F_{A2} \times m_{R1} + SORT(F_{A2} \times H_{R1} \times m_{R1})] + \qquad :60 + \qquad (2)$$

$$[IA(I_{B2},R_2) + b(m_{R2},p_{R2},F_{B2} \times n_{R2}) + SORT(F_{B2} \times H_{R2} \times m_{R2})] \qquad :50$$

$$\text{Cost} = [IA(I_{A2},R_1) + IS(I_{A1},R_1) + F_{A2} \times n_{R1}] + \qquad :100 + \qquad (3)$$

$$[IA(I_{B2},R_2) + b(m_{R2},p_{R2},F_{B2} \times n_{R2}) + SORT(F_{B2} \times H_{R2} \times m_{R2})] \qquad :50$$

$$\text{Cost} = [IA(I_{A2},R_1) + F_{A2} \times m_{R1} + SORT(F_{A2} \times H_{R1} \times m_{R1})] + \qquad :60 + \qquad (4)$$

$$[IA(I_{B2},R_2) + IS(I_{B1},R_2) + b(m_{R2},p_{R2},F_{B2} \times n_{R2})] \qquad :20$$

Here b(m,p,k) is a function that computes the number of block accesses, where k is the number of tuples to be retrieved in TID order. An exact form of this function and various approximation formulas are summarized in [WHAN83b]. The function is approximately linear in k when k<<n, and approaches m as k becomes large. A familiar approximation suggested by Cardenas [CARD75] is $b(m,p,k) = m[1-(1-1/m)^k]$. F_{A2} and F_{B2} are the selectivities of the columns $R_1.A_2$ and $R_2.B_2$, respectively. In Equation (1), $F_{A2} \times n_{R1}$ and $b(m_{R2},p_{R2},F_{B2} \times n_{R2})$ represent the numbers of blocks accessed that contain data tuples of relations R_1 and R_2, respectively. Since retrieving tuples by scanning a nonclustering join index will access the tuples randomly, the same block will be accessed repeatedly if it contains more than one tuple. Therefore, one block access is needed to retrieve each tuple. Hence we get $F_{A2} \times n_{R1}$ for the number of data blocks fetched from relation R_1. On the other hand, for relation R_2, the join index is clustering and thus the tuples will be retrieved in TID order. Therefore, even though a block contains more than one tuple, each block will be fetched only once. We thus get $b(m_{R2},p_{R2},F_{B2} \times n_{R2})$ for the number of data blocks fetched from R_2, where $F_{B2} \times n_{R2}$ is the number of tuples selected by the restriction.

In Equation (2), $F_{A2} \times m_{R1}$ and $b(m_{R2},p_{R2},F_{B2} \times n_{R2})$ represent the numbers of blocks accessed during the initial scan of the relation prior to sorting. Since the restriction index is clustering in relation R_1, the initial scan through this restriction index will access $F_{A2} \times m_{R1}$ blocks. In relation R_2, a nonclustering restriction index is used to access the relation initially. This restriction results in random distribution of TIDs of the qualified tuples over the blocks. Since these tuples are then accessed in TID order, the access cost is $b(m_{R2},p_{R2},F_{B2} \times n_{R2})$.

The factor H_{R2} used in Equation (3) represents the projection effect upon relation R_2. Since the projection selects only part of the attributes from the relations, the tuple is usually smaller after projection. The cost of writing the final result is not included since it is the same regardless of the join method used.

With the specific values of the access cost given, Equation (4) gives the minimum access cost. We note that the access costs for each relation do not depend on any parameter of any other relation, and that each part of the cost of Equation (4) becomes the local minimum. That is, the first part of the cost incurred by accessing relation R_1 is the minimum of the costs of the join methods used for R_1, while the second part is the minimum of those for R_2. This implies that the optimizer can determine the optimal join method on one relation without regard to any properties of other relations. □

The foregoing observation is extremely important because, if we can determine the optimal join method for one relation without regard to other relations, we can also determine the optimal access configuration for the relation without regard to other relations, using the following procedure:

1. Consider each possible access configuration for a relation in turn.
2. Find the best join method of each transaction given the particular access configuration.
3. Calculate the total cost for processing all transactions, using their expected frequencies of occurrence.
4. Repeat this procedure for all other possible access configurations, finally selecting the one that yields the minimal total cost.

The result of this will be to reduce designing an optimal access configuration of a database to that of single relations. Therefore, local optimal solutions for individual relations constitute an optimal solution for the entire database.

In Example 2 we considered only the cases without coupling effects. It will be shown in the following discussion that the problem is similarly reduced even when coupling effects are present. Before further discussion, we need the following definition and example.

Definition 4: The *join selectivity* J(R,JP) of a relation R with respect to a join path JP is the ratio of the number of distinct join column values of the tuples participating in the unconditional join to the total number of the distinct join column values of R. A *join path* is a set (R_1, R_1.A, R_2, R_2.B), where R_1 and R_2 are relations participating in the join and R_1.A and R_2.B are the join columns of R_1 and R_2, respectively. An *unconditional join* is a join in which restrictions on either relation are not considered. □

Definition 5: A *connection* is a join path predefined in the schema [WIED79]. □

3.4.2 Cases with coupling effects

Let us analyze the four cases shown in Example 2–using the same query, join methods, and access configuration defined as in Figure 5, but now with coupling effects. In fact, we shall consider coupling effects throughout our subsequent discussions. We shall also assume that R_1 and R_2 have a 1-to-N relationship (1 for R_1 and N for R_2).

Case 1: The join index method is applied to both relations R_1 and R_2. With coupling effect, the join will be performed as follows: If a tuple of relation R_1 does not satisfy the restriction predicate for R_1, the corresponding tuples of R_2 that have the same join column values are not retrieved. Hence, we have the coupling effect from R_1 to R_2. If there are only index-processible predicates in the query, the situation is symmetric–in the sense that, for the tuples in relation R_2 that do not satisfy the restriction predicate for R_2, the corresponding tuples of R_1 are not retrieved either. We have this symmetry because we can resolve all index-processible predicates by using TIDs only, without any need to access the tuples.

Since both $R_1.A_2$ and $R_2.B_2$ have indexes, the restriction predicates in the WHERE clause are index-processible. Therefore, the cost of evaluating this query, including the coupling effect, will be as follows:

$$\text{Cost} = [IA(I_{A2},R_1) + IS(I_{A1},R_1) + \{<J_1 \times b(1/F_{B1},F_{B1} \times n_{R2},F_{B2} \times n_{R2})/(1/F_{B1})> \times F_{A2} \times n_{R1}\}] \quad (5)$$

$$+ [IA(I_{B2},R_2) + IS(I_{B1},R_2) + b(m_{R2},p_{R2},\{<J_2 \times F_{A2}> \times F_{B2} \times n_{R2}\})]$$

Here J_1 and J_2 represent the join selectivity of relations R_1 and R_2, respectively, for the join path considered. Expressions in braces represent the numbers of tuples accessed in relations R_1 and R_2, respectively. In the first part of the formula, the expression in braces represents the number of blocks accessed in relation R_1. This follows the argument of Example 2.

F_{B1} is the selectivity of column $R_2.B_1$ and $1/F_{B1}$ represents the number of groups of tuples that have the same join column values in relation R_2– which is essentially the same as the number of distinct join column values.

The expression $b(1/F_{B1},F_{B1} \times n_{R2},F_{B2} \times n_{R2})$ represents the number of groups selected by restriction F_{B2}. Although the b function estimates the number of block accesses in which a certain number of tuples are randomly selected, the same function is used for estimating the number of logical groups selected–if the latter are assumed to be of uniform size. Note that the clustering or nonclustering of tuples in a group is irrelevant. $F_{B1} \times n_{R2}$, the number of tuples in one logical group, plays a role similar to that of the blocking factor.

The expression $b(1/F_{B1},F_{B1} \times n_{R2},F_{B2} \times n_{R2})/(1/F_{B1})$ represents the ratio of the number of groups selected by restriction F_{B2} to the total number of groups in relation R_2. Since every tuple participating in the unconditional join in R_1 has a unique join column value and, therefore, exactly one corresponding group in R_2 ,this ratio correctly represents a special restriction upon R_1 caused by the coupling effect originating in R_2.

In the second part of the cost formula, we simply use F_{A2} to represent the coupling effect directed from R_1 to R_2. Since in R_1 every tuple has a unique join column value, if a tuple is selected according to the restriction, the corresponding group in R_2 that has the same join column value (if it exists) will be selected on the basis of this special restriction resulting from the coupling effect. Hence, F_{A2} represents the ratio of the number of groups selected as a consequence of the coupling effect to the total number of groups in R_2 participating in the unconditional join. That ratio, in turn, has the same value as the ratio of tuples, selected according to the coupling effect, to the total number of tuples participating in the unconditional join in R_2. □

The coupling effect is formally defined as follows:

Definition 6: The *coupling effect* from relation R_1 to relation R_2, with respect to a transaction, is the ratio of the number of distinct join column values of the records of R_1, selected according to the restriction predicate for R_1, to the total number of distinct join column values in R_1. □

If we assume that the join column values are randomly selected, the coupling effect from R_1 to R_2 is the same as the ratio of the number of distinct join column values of R_2 selected by the effect of the restriction predicate for R_1 to the number of distinct join column values in R_2 participating in the unconditional join.

Definition 7: A *coupling factor* Cf_{12} from relation R_1 to relation R_2, with respect to a transaction, is the ratio of the number of distinct join column values of R_2, selected by both the coupling effect from R_1 and the join selectivity of R_2, to the total number of distinct join column values in R_2. □

According to Definition 7, a coupling factor can be obtained by multiplying the coupling effect from R_1 to R_2 by the join selectivity of R_2. Intuitively, the coupling factor represents the influence of restriction predicates for a relation on the tuples selected from the other relation through join. This factor contains all the consequences of the interactions of relations in the join, since it includes both coupling and join filtering effects. Let us note that, although the coupling factor can be obtained in any case, it does not always contribute to the reduction of the tuples to be retrieved. We will see an example of this in Case 2 below (Equation (6)). A coupling factor is said to be *effective* if the coupling effect actually contributes to the reduction of the tuples to be retrieved. In Case 1, the expressions in angle brackets (Equation (5)) represent the coupling factors from R_2 to R_1 and from R_1 to R_2, respectively. Hence,

$$Cf_{12} = J_2 \times F_{A2},$$

$$Cf_{21} = J_1 \times b(1/F_{B1}, F_{B1} \times n_{R2}, F_{B2} \times n_{R2})/(1/F_{B1}).$$

One important observation here is that the coupling factors do not depend on the specific access structures present in either relation, nor on the specific join method selected, but rather (and solely) depend on the restriction and data characteristics. Such characteristics include the side the relation is on in the 1-to-N relationship, the average number of tuples in one group, and the join selectivity–which will be known before we start the design phase.

Now let us investigate the remaining cases in which coupling effects between relations are present.

Case 2: The sort-merge join method is applied to both relations, in the same situation as in Figure 5. The cost formula is then as follows:

$$\text{Cost} = [IA(I_{A2},R_1) + F_{A2} \times m_{R1} + SORT(F_{A2} \times H_{R1} \times m_{R1})] \qquad (6)$$

$$+ [IA(I_{B2},R_2) + b(m_{R2},p_{R2},F_{B2} \times n_{R2}) + SORT(F_{B2} \times H_{R2} \times m_{R2})]$$

It will be noted that the coupling factors do not appear in the cost formula. This is because, when the sort-merge join method is used, an initial scan and the sort are performed before the join is resolved; indexes are not used any more while the join is being actually resolved, since relation scan is done upon the sorted temporary relations. The coupling effect can arise only when the join is being actually resolved and only when the join index is used. Thus, the coupling factor is not effective in this case.

Case 3: The sort-merge join method is used for R_1, the join index method for R_2. The join will be performed as described in Section 3.2, under the heading "Combination of the Join Index Method and the Sort-Merge Method." Note that the coupling factor is effective from R_1 to R_2, but not from R_2 to R_1. Thus, we obtain the following cost formula:

$$\text{Cost} = [IA(I_{A2},R_1) + F_{A2} \times m_{R1} + Sort(F_{A2} \times H_{R1} \times m_{R1})]$$

$$+ [IA(I_{B2},R_2) + IS(I_{B1},R_2) + b(m_{R2},p_{R2},Cf_{12} \times F_{B2} \times n_{R2})]$$

Case 4: The join index method is used on R_1, the sort-merge method on R_2. We obtain the following cost formula:

$$\text{Cost} = [IA(I_{A2},R_1) + IS(I_{A1},R_1) + Cf_{21} \times F_{A2} \times n_{R1}]$$

$$+ [IA(I_{B2},R_2) + b(m_{R2},p_{R2},F_{B2} \times n_{R2}) + SORT(F_{B2} \times H_{R2} \times m_{R2})]$$

In all the case analyses we note that the access cost for each relation is independent of any parameters of the other relation. Thus, when the optimizer chooses the least costly join method, it can compare the costs for only one relation at a time.

3.4.3 Formalization

So far, we have discussed the property of separability for relational systems through a series of examples and case analyses. The concepts involved are now formalized. To begin with, we rephrase the definitions and the theorem presented in Section 2 to make them suitable for relational systems.

Definition 8: The procedure of designing the optimal access configuration of a database is *separable* if it can be decomposed into the tasks of designing the optimal configurations of individual relations independently of one another. □

Definition 9: A *partial-join cost* is that part of the join cost that represents the accessing of only one relation, as well as the auxiliary structures defined for that relation. □

Definition 10: A *partial-join algorithm* is a conceptual division of the algorithm of a join method whose processing cost is a partial-join cost. □

Theorem 2: The procedure of designing the optimal access configuration of a database is *separable* if the following conditions are satisfied:

1. A partial-join cost for relation R can be determined regardless of the partial-join algorithm used and the access configuration defined for Other(R).
2. A partial-join algorithm can be chosen for R regardless of the partial-join algorithm used and the access configuration defined for Other(R). □

Additionally, we need the following definitions:

Definition 11: The *partial coupling effect* from relation R_1 to relation R_2, with respect to a transaction, is the ratio of the number of distinct join column values of the tuples of R_1, selected according to the index-processible predicate for R_1, to the total number of distinct join column values in R_1.□

Definition 12: A *partial coupling factor* PCf_{12} from relation R_1 to relation R_2 with respect to a transaction is the ratio of the number of distinct join column values of R_2, selected by both the parital coupling effect from R_1 and the join selectivity of R_2, to the total number of distinct join column values in R_2.□

Definition 13: The *restricted set* of relation R with respect to a transaction is the set of tuples of R selected according to the restriction predicate for R. □

Definition 14: The *partially restricted set* of relation R with respect to a transaction is the set of tuples of R selected according to the index-processible predicate for R. □

Definition 15: The *coupled set* of relation R_1 with respect to a transaction is the set of tuples in R_1 selected according to the coupling factor from R_2.□

Definition 16: The *partially coupled set* of relation R_1 with respect to a transaction is the set of tuples of R_1 selected according to the partial coupling factor from R_2.□

Definition 17: The *result set* of relation R with respect to a transaction is the intersection of the restricted set and the coupled set. Thus, the tuples in the result set satisfy all the predicates in a transaction. □

Definitions 13 through 17 partition a relation into various subsets according to the predicates they satisfy. The definitions and Theorem 2 above lead to the following theorem, which shows the separability of a relational system.

Theorem 3: The set of join methods consisting of the join index method, the sort-merge method, and the combination method satisfies the conditions for separability under the constraint that, whenever the join index method is used for both relations, at least one relation must have indexes for all restriction columns.

Proof: In the set of join methods considered, there are two partial-join algorithms: the join index method (partial) and the sort-merge method (partial). Since these two can be arbitrarily combined to form a join method, Condition 2 for separability is satisfied. For Condition 1 of separability we prove that each of the three sufficient conditions is satisfied as follows:

Condition 1.a: We prove that the first condition is satisfied by showing that the following statements are true:

1. If the sort-merge method is used, the set of records in R retrieved is the restricted/partially restricted set.

2. If the join index method is used, the set of records in R retrieved is the intersection of restricted/partially restricted set and the coupled set.

Then, we know the set of records of R accessed is independent of the access structures of and the join methods used for Other(R) because the restricted/partially restricted set can be completely determined by local parameters of relation R, and the coupled set can be determined by the coupling effect and the join filtering effect which are independent of the access structures of Other(R) and the partial-join algorithms used for Other(R).

Now, let us examine each of the two statements. First, when the sort-merge method is used, it follows directly from the definition of this join method that the partially restricted set will be accessed if there are residual predicates; the restricted set will be accessed otherwise. Second, when the join index method is used, the optimizer will access the indexes of the relation (say R) having indexes for all restriction columns first. Since all the predicates for R are resolved by using indexes, the coupling factor is effective in Other(R). The records of Other(R) will subsequently be accessed and all the predicates for Other(R) are resolved before accessing records of R. Thus, the coupling factor is also effective in R. Since full–not partial–coupling factors are effective in both relations, the records to be accessed are in the coupled set. These records of R are also in the restricted/partially restricted set because the index-processible predicate is resolved by using indexes before data records are accessed.

Let us note that, if the optimizer accesses the indexes of Other(R) first, then only partial coupling factor is effective in R. But, because this will always cost more than the previous method, the optimizer will always choose the previous one.

Condition 1.b: The order of accessing those records is always the join column order regardless of the access structures and partial-join algorithms used.

Condition 1.c: Since we assumed that a block contains records of only one relation, records of a relation cannot interfere with the placement of records of other relations. □

3.4.4 Separability in cases arbitrary indexes are missing

The set of join methods in Theorem 3 does not have the separability property if, for any transaction, some restriction indexes are missing in both relations. Example 3 further illustrates this point.

Example 3: Let us assume that the join index method is used for both R_1 and R_2, in the same situation as in Figure 5, but that restriction indexes for both R_1 and R_2 are missing. In this situation, since there are no restriction indexes, there is no way of resolving the restriction predicates without accessing the tuples. Therefore, if we access relation R_1 first, the access cost would be

$$\mathrm{Cost1} = [\mathrm{IS}(I_{A1},R_1) + \mathrm{PCf}_{21} \times n_{R1}] + [\mathrm{IS}(I_{B1},R_2) + b(m_{R2},p_{R2},\mathrm{Cf}_{12} \times n_{R2})]$$

On the other hand, if we access relation R_2 first, the access cost would be

$$\mathrm{Cost2} = [\mathrm{IS}(I_{A1},R_1) + \mathrm{Cf}_{21} \times n_{R1}] + [\mathrm{IS}(I_{B1},R_2) + b(m_{R2},p_{R2},\mathrm{PCf}_{12} \times n_{R2})]$$

Here, $PCf_{21} = J_1$ and $PCf_{12} = J_2$ since there are no restriction indexes in both R_1 and R_2. In general, if some restriction indexes are missing in both relations, the coupling factor is effective in one relation while the partial coupling factor is effective in the other relation. The choice depends on which relation is to be accessed first. The optimizer will choose the cheaper one at run time based on the access configurations of both relations. Since this choice depends on the access configurations of both relations, the design is not separable. □

What is implied in the optimal design of the physical database is that those indexes that do not compensate for their maintenance and access costs should not be included in the result. Since Theorem 3 requires the existence of all the restriction indexes in at least one relation for each two-variable transaction, we can inevitably expect that, for some transactions, this constraint is not met during the decision process. In this situation calculation of the cost is no longer separable. Nevertheless, the calculative error caused by the assumption of separability should not be significant because the restriction indexes for both relations that have been dropped must be relatively insignificant–otherwise, the indexes would not have been dropped.

3.4.5 Update cost

We assumed in Section 3.2.2 that updates are performed only on individual relations, although the qualification part (WHERE clause) may involve more than one relation. Suppose that the qualification part–which can be treated as a query–is separated. Then, the remaining part–update operation–depends only on the local parameters of the relation to be updated and on the coupling factor because update operation should only occur after all the predicates are resolved. When processing the qualification part, there are some restrictions as explained in Section 3.2.2. The restriction, however, is independent of the access structures or partial-join algorithms of other relations. Thus, separability can also be applied to the update transactions as well.

3.4.6 Nonseparable join methods

Nonseparable join methods are those not included in the separable set. For instance, the inner/outer-loop join method is a nonseparable join method. The reasons are as follows. First, a partial inner/outer-loop join method cannot be combined with other partial joins. Second, the cost of inner/outer-loop join method depends on the direction of the join. At run time, however, the optimizer chooses the direction of join according to the access structures of both relations to be joined. Thus, the partial-join cost of the inner/outer-loop join depends on the access structures of both relations, violating the condition for separability.

4. Separability in Network Model Database Systems

We discuss, in this section† an application of the theory of separability to network model database systems. In particular, we introduce a cost model originally developed by Gerritsen [GERR77] and prove that the procedure of designing optimal physical databases is separable under this cost model. This model is based on the system specification given in the DBTG proposal [CODA71].

4.1 Access Structures of Network Model Databases

We consider three classes of access structures provided by network model database systems. The first class includes access structures that determine the placement strategy (location mode in DBTG terminology) for storing records of each record type. Three access structures belong to this class:

1. Placement by a CALC key
2. Placement by CLUSTERING VIA SET
3. Placement by CLUSTERING VIA SET NEAR OWNER

These three access structures determine the position of the records to be stored; thus, more than one cannot be specified together. The implementation of the CALC key typically employs the hashing technique to calculate the address of a record. If a record of type R is the member type of a SET S, the placement

† A preliminary version of this section appears in [WHAN84b].

strategy for R can be CLUSTERED VIA SET S. This implies that the records of R in a SET occurrence are stored close to one another. If NEAR OWNER option is specified, the records in a SET occurrence are stored close to their owner record.

The second class includes various SET implementations listed below:

1. Link with next pointer
2. Link with next pointer and prior pointer
3. Link with next pointer, prior pointer, and owner pointer
4. Link with next pointer and owner pointer
5. Pointer array

SET implementations differ according to their use of pointers. A SET that is implemented by a link has the next pointer by default. The prior pointer can be added to form a doubly linked list. The owner pointer makes it easy to retrieve the owner record once one of its member records is identified. A SET can also be implemented by an array of pointers, which is functionally equivalent to the next pointer and the prior pointer combined.

The last class of access structures is the singular SET that connects all the records in a record type. The singular SET enables a scan through all the records in a record type.

4.2 Assumptions

We summarize major assumptions that will be used throughout Section 4. We assume that records of all types are stored in one area, and that they are randomly scattered. It is assumed that the clustering of records of the member type of a SET affects the relative distances between records of that type, but does not affect the distances between records of other types. To make this assumption valid, we exclude the option of clustering member records near their owner record.

Next, we assume that the CALC records are randomly distributed, and that the average number of block accesses required to access one record by CALC key is the same for any record type and for any key, depending only on the overall load factor of the area.

Finally, we ignore any disparity in the size of records of the owner type of a SET that results from various SET implementations, so that a SET implementation affects only the size of member records (because of the space needed for additional pointers).

4.3 Design Theory

In this section we develop a design theory based on the concept of separability. Sepcifically, we reintroduce the definition and the theorem presented in Section 2 by rephrasing them to a form suitable for network model database systems; develop the cost model; and show that the cost model satisfies the conditions for separability. Lastly, update costs are discussed briefly.

4.3.1 Theorem of separability

For network model databases, Definitions 1 to 3 and Theorem 1 can be rephrased by simply replacing the *logical object* by *record type.*

We have two special considerations in applying the theorem to the network model databases. First, we consider various SET implementations to be the access structures that belong to their member record type. Accordingly, the access cost of owner records, when they are accessed through the SET, will be included in the partial-operation cost for the member record type as will be shown in Equation (11). Second, as mentioned in Section 4.2, the placement strategy CLUSTERED VIA SET NEAR OWNER will be excluded because a condition for separability is not satisfied as explained in Situation 1 below. This access structure can be incorporated in the design algorithm by a heuristic method.

Situation 1: Figure 6 describes four record types, R_0, R_1, R_2, and R_3. Set types S_1, S_2, and S_3 are defined among them. If the placement of R_2 records is declared as CLUSTERED VIA SET S_2 NEAR OWNER, then R_2 records will be clustered around R_1 records. Similarly, if the placement of R_3 records is declared as CLUSTERED VIA SET S_3 NEAR OWNER, then R_3 records will be clustered around R_1 records. Let us assume that the placement strategy of R_1 records is CLUSTERED VIA SET S_1. Then, the accessing of the member records (R_1 records) of an occurrence of SET S_1 will be different, depending on whether R_2 or R_3 is clustered via its SET (S_2 or S_3) near the owner R_1, since the intervening records will affect the distances between R_1 records. Thus, the partial-operation cost for R_1 is dependent on the access configurations of R_2 or R_3, which violates the conditions for separability. □

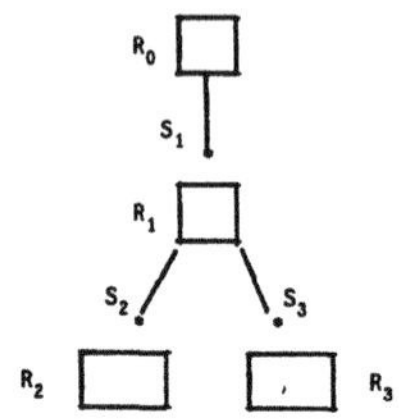

Figure 6: Record Types R_0, R_1, R_2, R_3 with SET Types S_1, S_2, and S_3.

4.3.2 Usage specification

The problem of designing an optimal physical database for network model database systems is difficult because of data dependencies in many of these systems. As an example, let us assume that a singular set is defined in the conceptual schema and programs use it explicitly. Then, the singular set cannot be eliminated without changing all the programs that use it. Similarly, once a CALC key is defined in the schema and used by programs, it cannot be redefined without jeopardizing those programs. Moreover, if a CALC key is used in the usage specification, it in effect forces the presence of the CALC key, thereby rendering the whole physical database design meaningless.

One possible approach to averting these problems would be to employ a high-level usage specification that does not explicitly designate the access structures to be exploited. We would then have to have a hypothetical optimizer to translate the transaction in this form into an optimal sequence of operations using available access structures. In principle, the design can be accomplished as follows:

1. Enumerate all possible access configurations of the physical database.
2. Evaluate the minimum possible processing cost for each configuration using the hypothetical optimizer.
3. Find the access configuration that yields the minimum cost.

If we intially design the optimal physical database structure based on a high-level usage specification, the application programs will be adapted towards the true optimum. A good initial design is particularly important when a full data independence is not provided by the system.

We choose here a the usage specification scheme that is similar to the approach used in [GERR77]. The usage information has two components: frequency of entering the database and the *access path tree*–a high-level description of the transaction.

The usage information for the database entry, $f_{ENT}(T,R)$ is the frequency of entry to record type R in processing transaction T. Associated with f_{ENT} is PRED representing the predicate, which is in the conjunctive normal form, to be applied to record type R. A *simple predicate* is an equality predicate on one data item, such as DATAITEM=DATAVALUE. A *candidate key* is defined as the list of all data items, each of which appears in a conjunct of PRED that is a simple predicate. Only candidate keys are considered as potential CALC keys.

An access path tree represents the record types, connected by access paths, as well as the order of visiting them. Its derivation is consistent with the conceptual schema and is organized in such a way that the preorder traversal matches the order of visiting the nodes. Figure 7 shows an example of such a tree. The nodes marked R_1, R_2, etc. represent the record types. Access paths S_1, S_2, etc. correspond to the SET types. Associated with each record type R are its cardinality, n_R, and a predicate, $PRED_R$, that will be applied to its records. The point of entering the database is marked with DBENTER. In the access path tree we denote the SET type to which the subtree rooted on node R_i (or R) is attached as S_i (or set(R)). The symbol '*' represents the member record type of a SET type.

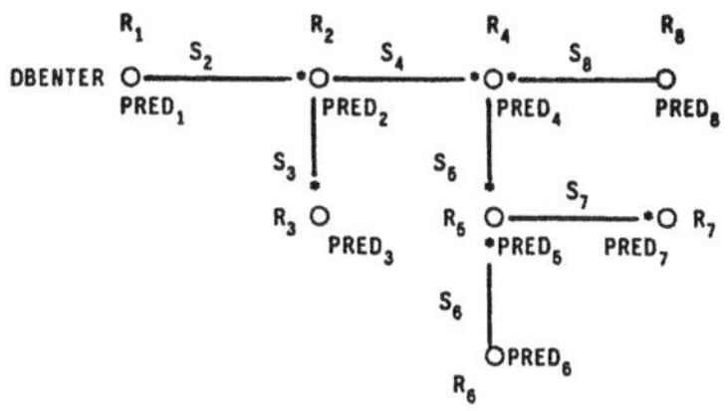

Figure 7: An Access Path Tree.

To proceed we need the following definition and notation.

Definition 19: The *linkage factor* $J_{R,S}$ of a record type R with respect to a SET type S is the ratio of the number of records of type R that are linked in any occurrence of S to the total number of records of type R. (This is similar in concept to the join selectivity in relational systems described in Section 3.) □

n_R	: Number of records of record type R.
$g_{R,S}$	: Number of records of type R in a SET occurrence of SET type S (grouping factor).
owner(R,S)	: The owner record type of SET type S whose member record type is R.
SEL(PRED,R)	: Selectivity of predicate PRED when applied to the records of type R.

4.3.3 Usage transformation

4.3.3.1 Transformation functions

The access path tree together with the frequency of the database entry completely specifies the usage specification. The access path tree, however, is not in a suitable form for cost calculations; it has to be transformed to derive the frequency of traversals of occurrences of each SET type in the tree. Two functions are defined for this purpose:

- $F_{OM}(T,R,S)$ is the frequency of traversal of occurrences of SET type S, in processing transaction T, from the owner to the member (record type R).

- $F_{MO}(T,R,S)$ is the frequency of traversal of occurrences of SET type S, in processing transaction T, from the member (record type R) to the owner.

These functions are further illustrated in Figure 8. Notice that both functions are defined as properties of the member record type (R_2).

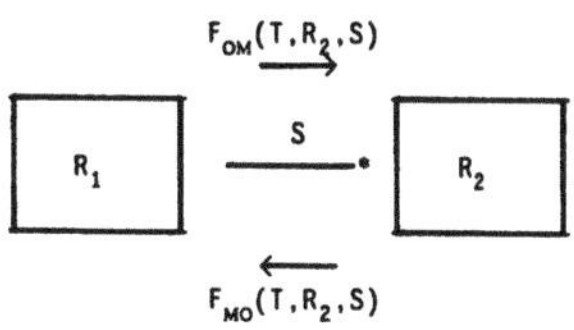

Figure 8: Transformation Functions for SET occurrence Traversal.

To achieve usage transformation we use the concept of *active records* of a SET type in the access path tree. The set of active records of a SET type corresponds to the result of processing the transaction not including the subtree connected by the SET Accordingly, the number of active records determines the frequency of traversals of the SET occurrences to the next record type in the preorder traversal. Thus, the frequency of traversals of the SET occurrences are derived as follows:

$$F_{OM}(T,R,S) = f_{ENT}(T,R_{DB-ENTER}) \times ACTIVE(set(owner(R,S))) \quad (7)$$

$$F_{MO}(T,R,S) = f_{ENT}(T,R_{DB-ENTER}) \times ACTIVE(set(R)) \quad (8)$$

where ACTIVE(S) represents the number of active records of SET type S and $R_{DBENTER}$ is the root of the access path tree.

4.3.3.2 Number of active records

We now proceed to develop an algorithm to obtain the number of active records. We begin with a simple case and extend it to a more complex case. First, we assume that the access path tree is a linear list without any branch; then the number of active records of SET type S_{n+1} can be obtained as follows:

$$\text{ACTIVE}(S_{n+1}) = \text{ACTIVE}(S_n) \times J_{R_{n-1},S_n} \times g_{R_n,S_n} \times \text{SEL}(\text{PRED}_n)$$

$$\text{ACTIVE}(S_2) = n_1 \times \text{SEL}(\text{PRED}_1)$$

Example 4 further illustrates this case.

Example 4:

Consider an access path tree in Figure 9.

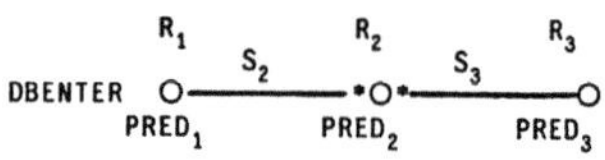

Figure 9: A Simple Access Path Tree without Any Branch.

Associated with the tree are the following data.

$n_1 = 50$	$g_{R1,S2} = 1$	$J_{R1,S2} = 1$	$\text{SEL}(\text{PRED}_1) = 0.1$
$n_2 = 200$	$g_{R2,S2} = 4$	$J_{R2,S2} = 1$	$\text{SEL}(\text{PRED}_2) = 0.5$
$n_3 = 40$	$g_{R2,S3} = 10$	$J_{R2,S3} = 1$	$\text{SEL}(\text{PRED}_3) = 0.5$
	$g_{R3,S3} = 1$	$J_{R3,S3} = 0.5$	

Then, the number of active records for S_2 and S_3 are

$$\text{ACTIVE}(S_2) = 50 \times 0.1 = 5$$

$$\text{ACTIVE}(S_3) = 5 \times 1 \times 4 \times 0.5 = 10. \quad \square$$

To extend the method of obtaining the number of active records to a more general access path tree, we define a procedure LABEL that traverses the tree in preorder, calculate the number of active records, and record the number in the global array of variables ACTIVE[S]. To set up the initial conditions we create a hypothetical record type R_0 and SET type S_1 such that TACTIVE$[R_0] = 1$, $J_{R_0,S_1} = 1$, $J_{R_1,S_1} = 1$, $g_{R_0,S_1} = 1$, $g_{R_1,S_1} = n_1$. Equivalently, record type R_0 has one record that is linked to all the records of R_1 via SET type S_1.

```
procedure LABEL(R, R-PREV)
    begin
    TACTIVE[R] = TACTIVE[R-PREV] x SEL(PRED_R) x g_R,S(R) x J_R-PREV,S(R)
    for every branch B_i
        begin
        ACTIVE[set(Root(B_i))] = TACTIVE[R]
        LABEL(Root(B_i,R))
        TACTIVE[R] = TACTIVE[Root(B_i)]
        end
    end
```

Here, function Root returns the root node of branch B_i. A call to LABEL(R_1,R_0) calculates the number of active records and sets the global variables ACTIVE[S] for all SET types. Here, two arrays of global variables, ACTIVE and TACTIVE, are used. TACTIVE[R] represents the number of active records when the tree traversal has been completed up to record type R; but it changes every time the traversal of a branch of record type R is completed. ACTIVE[S] keeps the value of TACTIVE[R] just before SET type S leading to a branch of R is traversed. The parameter R-PREV represents the record type connected to R via

SET set(R). Let us note that R-PREV is not the record type last visited.

4.3.4 Formulation of partial-operation costs

To formulate the partial-operation cost we define the following notation.

Elementary-Operation Costs

C_{ENT} (R,CALC-key)	The cost of entering the database. Records of type R are accessed by using the CALC-key.
C_{ENT} (R,singular-set)	The cost of entering the database. Records of type R are accessed by using the singular-set.
C_{ENT} (R,area-scan)	The cost of entering the database. Records of type R are accessed by using an area scan.
C_{OM}(R,S)	The cost of traversing one SET occurrence of type S from the owner record to its member records (of type R). The cost of accessing the owner record is excluded since the owner record must have been accessed through other access structures that belong to the owner record type.
C_{MO}(R,S)	The cost of accessing member records and the owner record when traversing one SET occurrence of type S from a member record (of type R) to its owner. The starting member record is assumed to have been accessed already.

Partial-Operation Cost

Given an access configuration of the physical database, the partial-operation cost of transaction T for record type R will be

$$POC(T,R) = Cost_{DB-ENTER}(T,R) + Cost_{SET-TRAVERSE}(T,R), \tag{9}$$

where

$$Cost_{DB-ENTER}(T,R) = f_{ENT}(T,R) \times \min \{C_{ENT}(R,CALC\text{-}key)^{\dagger}, C_{ENT}(R,singular\text{-}set)^{\dagger}, C_{ENT}(R,area\text{-}scan)\}, \tag{10}$$

and

$$Cost_{SET-TRAVERSE}(T,R) = \sum_{S\in\{SET\ types\ whose\ member\ is\ R\}} \{F_{OM}(T,R,S) \times C_{OM}(R,S) + F_{MO}(T,R,S) \times C_{MO}(R,S)\} \tag{11}$$

Entries in Equation (10) marked with the symbol † are considered only when the corresponding access structures (singular set or CALC-key) are available in the given access configuration.

4.3.5 Cost model

The cost model developed by Gerritsen [GERR77] is introduced. Based on a system [GERR76] similar to the one described in the DBTG proposal [CODA71], it is presented here in a slightly modified form, incorporating the assumptions in Section 4.2. The following notation will be used in the cost model:

$x_{R,S}$	1 if the placement strategy of record type R is CLUSTERED VIA SET S, and 0 otherwise.
Z_R	Size in bytes of a record of type R.
B	Size in bytes of a block.
LF	Load factor of the area in which the database is stored. Here it is assumed to be constant throughout the design procedure.
$g_{R,S}$	Number of records of type R (which is the member) in a SET occurrence of type S.
Q_S	1 if SET type S has the owner pointer, and 0 otherwise.
n_R	Number of records of type R (cardinality).
P	Number of blocks in the area.
f	An overflow function indicating the average number of block accesses, in excess of 1, required to retrieve a record by a CALC key.

We define MAC(R,S) (Member-Accessing Cost) as the expected cost of completing the physical accesses required to visit all the members (of type R) of an occurrence of SET type S. Then we have

$$MAC(R,S) = x_{R,S} \times \lceil (Z_R \times g_{R,S})/(B \times (1-0.5LF)) \rceil + (1-x_{R,S}) \times g_{R,S}.$$

The first term calculates the average number of blocks touched when the placement strategy for record type R is CLUSTERED VIA SET S. The factor 0.5 in the denominator is for adjusting the load factor. This factor is obtained based on the assumption that the load factor is 0 when the first SET occurrence is loaded, whereas it is LF when the last SET occurrence is loaded. The second term represents the cost when the placement strategy of the record type R is not CLUSTERED VIA SET S, in which case the records in a SET occurrence are accessed randomly.

Using MAC(R,S), we can obtain the elementary-operation costs as follows:

$$C_{ENT}(R,\text{Calc-key}) = 1 + f(LF) \quad (12)$$

$$C_{ENT}(R,\text{singular-set}) = n_R \quad (13)$$

$$C_{OM}(R,S) = MAC(R,S) \quad (14)$$

$$C_{MO}(R,S) = (1-Q_S) \times 0.5 \times MAC(R,S) + 1 \quad (15)$$

In Equation (15) it was assumed that accessing the owner record causes one block access for each traversal of a SET occurrence. If there is no owner pointer, on the average, half of the member records will be accessed to reach the owner; thus, $0.5 \times MAC(R,S)$ must be added.

4.3.6 Separability for the cost model

To verify that the design of the physical database for our model is indeed separable, we have to show that the partial-operation cost POC(T,R) for record type R is independent of the access structures chosen for the other record types. For this purpose, we shall consider each individual component of the partial-operation cost. First, as shown in Equations (7) and (8), the usage-transformation functions are independent of access structures. They depend solely on the characteristics of the data such as the number of records in a record type, linkage factors, grouping factors, or the selectivity of a predicate for a record type, etc.

Elementary-operation costs for a record type, say R, are not affected by the access structures of record types other than R as we see in Equations (12), (13), (14), and (15). C_{ENT} (R,CALC-key) and C_{ENT} (R,singular-set) are not dependent on the access structures at all. C_{OM}(R,S) differs according to whether R is stored CLUSTERED VIA SET S or not. Placement by CLUSTERED VIA SET S, however, is the access structure of R itself which is the member record type. C_{MO}(R,S) is dependent on the existence of the owner pointer. But, both C_{OM}(R,S) and C_{MO}(R,S) are not affected by the access structures of record types other than R.

Since all the components of the partial-processing cost for record type R are independent of access structures of other record types, so is the partial-processing cost; thus, Condition 1 for separability is satisfied.

Condition 2 in Theorem &networktheorem is satisfied since we are not restricted at all, in our choice of elementary operations (for database entry or SET traversing) for a record type, by choices made for other record types. (In relational systems, however, this condition may be a significant restriction, especially in the selection of partial-join algorithms.)

4.3.7 Update cost

Although a detailed usage specification for update transactions will not be developed here, the following points are worth noting.

An update operation can be viewed as a series of operations that locate the record to be updated as well as those that are accessed on the way of locating it. Thus, usage specifications similar to the ones used in previous sections can be employed for the updates.

As mentioned previously, we included the cost of accessing the owner record through a SET in the partial-operation cost of member record type. By the same token, the cost of updating the pointers (used for a specific SET implementation) of the records of the owner record type of a SET must be included in the partial-operation cost of the member record type. This is because the cost is a function of the specific SET implementation, and the SET implementation is regarded as an access structure of the member record type.

It is not difficult to conclude that, if we separate the costs into partial-operation costs for each record type as defined in Section 4.3, update costs for a record type other than that of SET pointers will not be affected by the access configurations for the other record types.

5. Summary

We introduced the theory of separability as a formal method of partitioning in physical database design. This partitioning has a profound effect on reducing the complexity of physical database design even for a moderate-size database schema. For instance, in Example 1, if the partitioning is applied, the total number of access configurations would be only $5\times(6\times2^5) = 960$, which is 3.7×10^9 times of an improvement over an exhaustive search.

In Section 3, we discussed application of the theory to relational database systems. In particular, we showed that the set of join methods consisting of the join index method, the sort-merge method, and the combination method has the property of separability. The implication is that, if the database system supports only this set of join methods, the physical database can be designed relation by relation independently of one another. Extensions to nonseparable joins such as the inner/outer-loop join methods can be achieved by means of heuristic methods. Interested readers are referred to [WHAN83a] for more details.

In Section 4, we discussed application of the theory of separability to network model databases. We introduced a cost model based on the DBTG proposal [CODA71] and showed that an important set of access structures satisfies the conditions for separability. Thus, if only those access structures are considered, the physical database can be designed record type by record type independently of one another. For this purpose, we introduced a usage specification scheme that is suitable for describing the network model database environment was introduced. The access path tree represents a high-level description of the transaction processing and, together with the frequency of database entry, provides the usage information. This usage information is subsequently transformed to derive the frequencies of traversals of SET occurrences. Problems on applying the theory of separability to a more general network model database system not constrained by this specific cost model are discussed in [WHAN82].

References

(BATO82, see BATO82b) (BAYE72) (BONF83) (CARD75) (CHAM76) (CODA71)
(COME78) (DE78) (GAMB77) (GERR76) (GERR77) (HAMM76, see HAMM76a)
(HONE71) (HSIA70) (KELL81) (KIM82) (KING74) (KNUT73) (LUM71) (MITO75)
(SCHK79, see SCHK79a) (SCHK79, see SCHK79b) (SELI79) (SENK69)
(SEVE75) (STON74) (TEOR78) (WHAN82) (WHAN83a) (WHAN83b) (WHAN84a)
(WHAN84b) (WIED79) (WIED83) (YAO77, see YAO77a) (YAO79)

References

[ADAB80]
ADABAS Reference Manual, Software AG of North America, Reston, VA, 1980
[ADIB77]
Adiba ME, Chupin JC, Demolombe R, Bihan JL, Gardarin G, "Issues in distributed database management systems: a technical overview", *Proc. 3rd VLDB Conference,* Tokyo, 1977, 89-110
[ADIB80a]
Adiba ME, Lindsay BG, "Database snapshots", *Proc. 6th VLDB Conference,* Montreal, October 1980, 86–91. Also available as IBM Research Report FJ2772
[ADIB80b]
Adiba ME, Andrade JM, Fernandez F, Toan NG, "An overview of the Polyphem distributed database management system", *Proc. IFIP Congress 1980,* Tokyo/Melbourne, 1980
[AHO79]
Aho AV, Sagiv Y, Ullmann JD, "Efficient optimization of a class of relational expressions", *ACM Transactions on Database Systems,* 4,4, December 1979, 435–454
[ALSB75]
Alsberg PA, "Space and time savings through large database compression and dynamic restructuring", *Proc. IEEE,* 63,8, August 1975, 1114–1122
[ANDE77]
Anderson HD, Berra BP, "Minimum cost selection of secondary indexes for formatted files", *ACM Transactions on Database Systems,* 2,1, March 1977, 68–70
[APER83]
Apers PMG, Hevner AR, Yao SB, "Optimization algorithms for distributed queries", *IEEE Transactions on Software Engineering,* SE-9,1, January 1983, 57–68
[ARDI79]
Arditi J, "An optimized backout mechanism for sequential updates", *Proc. 5th VLDB Conference,* Rio de Janeiro, 1979, 147–154
[ARMS80]
Armstrong WW, Delobel C, "Decompositions and functional dependencies in relations", *ACM Transactions on Database Systems,* 5,4, December 1980, 404–430
[ASTR76]
Astrahan MM et al, "System R: A relational approach to database management", *ACM Transactions on Database Systems,* 1,2, June 1976, 97–137
[ASTR80]
Astrahan MM, Kim W, Schkolnick M, "Evaluation of the System R access path selection mechanism", *Proc. IFIP Congress 1980*, North-Holland Publishing. 1980. Also available as IBM Research Laboratory RJ2797, San Jose, Calif
[BANC81]
Bancilhon F, Spiratos N, "Update semantics of relational views", *ACM Transactions on Database Systems,* 6,4, December 1981, 557–575

[BARB83]
Barber RE, Lucas HC, "System response time, operator productivity, and job satisfaction", *Communications of the ACM,* 26,11, November 1983, 972–986
[BARO81]
Baroody AJ, DeWitt DJ, "An object-oriented approach to database system implementation", *ACM Transactions on Database Systems,* 6,4, December 1981, 509–539
[BATO79]
Batory DS, "On searching transposed files", *ACM Transactions on Database Systems,* 4,4, December 1979, 531–544
[BATO81]
Batory, "B + trees and indexed sequential files: a performance comparison", *ACM SIGMOD,* 1981, 30–39
[BATO82a]
Batory DS, "Optimal file designs and reorganization points", *ACM Transactions on Database Systems,* 7,1, March 1982, 60–81
[BATO82b]
Batory DS, Gotlieb CC, "A unifying model of physical databases", *ACM Transactions on Database Systems*, 6,4, December 1982, 509–539
[BATO83]
Batory DS, "Index encoding: a compression technique for large statistical databases", *Proc. Workshop on Statistical Database Management*, 1983, 306–314
[BATO84a]
Batory DS, "Conceptual-to-internal mappings in commercial database systems". *Proc. ACM PODS, Conference,* 1984, 70–78
[BATO84b]
Batory DS ,9 "Modeling the physical structures of commercial database systems" to appear in *ACM Transactions on Database Systems*, also TR-83-21, Department of Computer Sciences, University of Texas at Austin, 1983
[BAYE72]
Bayer R, McCreight E, "Organization and maintenance of large ordered indices", *Acta Informatica,* 1, 1972
[BAZA77]
Bazaraa S, Jarvis JJ, *Linear Programming and Network Flows*, John Wiley and Sons, New York, 1977
[BEER81]
Beeri C, Fagin R, Maier D, Mendelzon A, Ullman J, Yannakakis M, "Properties of acyclic database schemes", *Proc. of 13th ACM Symposium on Theory of Computing*, 1981, 355–362
[BERN79]
Bernstein PA, Goodman N, "Full reducers for relational queries using multi-attribute semi-joins", Center for Research in Computing Technology, Harvard University, 1979
[BERN79a]
Bernstein PA, Goodman N, "Inequlity semi-joins", *Computer Corp. of America,* CCA-79-28
[BERN81a]
Bernstein PA, Chiu DM, "Using semi-joins to solve relational queries", *Journal of the ACM,* 28,1, January 1981, 25–40
[BERN81b]
Bernstein PA, Goodman N, "Power of natural semi-joins", *SIAM Journal of Computing,* 10,4, November 1981, 751–771
[BERN81c]
Bernstein PA, Goodman N, "The power of inequality semi-joins", *Information Systems,* 6, 1981, 255–265

[BERN81d]
Bernstein PA, Goodman N, Wong E, Reeve CL, Rothnie JB, "Query processing in a system for distributed databases (SDD-1)", *ACM Transactions on Database Systems* 6,4, December 1981, 602-625

[BERN83]
Bernstein PA, Goodman N, "Multiversion concurrency control – theory and algorithms", *ACM Transactions on Database Systems,* 8,4, December 1983, 465–483

[BERT83a]
Bertino E, Haas LM, Lindsay BG, "View management in distributed data base systems", *IBM Research Report RJ3851*, April 1983. Also available as an extended abstract in *Proc. 9th VLDB Conference,* Florence, Italy, 1983

[BERT83b]
Bertino E, Meghini C, Pelagatti G, Thanos C, "The update problem in the distributed database system HERMES/1", *Proc. 2nd International Conference on Databases,* SM Deen and P Hammersley (Eds), Cambridge, England, 1983

[BITT83]
Bitton D, Martinez R, Turbyfill C, Wiley R, "An experiment in benchmarking database systems", *Proceedings of Fall DECUS Conference,* Las Vegas, Nevada, September 1983

[BLAC82]
Black PA, Luk WS, "A new heuristic for generating semi-join programs for distributed query processing", *IEEE COMPSAC*, 1982, 581–588

[BLAS77]
Blasgen MW, Eswaren KP, "Storage and access in relational data bases", *IBM Systems Journal,* 16,4, 1977. Also available as, "On the evaluation of queries in a relational data base system", *IBM Research Laboratory RJ1745,* San Jose, Calif, April 1976

[BLAS79]
Blasgen MW, et al. "System R: an architectural update". *IBM Research Report RJ2581,* IBM Research Laboratory, San Jose, 1979

[BLAS81]
Blasgen MW, Astrahan MM, Chamberlin DD, Gray JN, King WF, Lindsay BG, Lorie RA, Mehl JW, Price TG, Putzolu GR, Schkolnick M, Selinger PG, Slutzs DR, Strong HR, Traiger IL, Wade BW, Yost RA, "System R: An architectural overview", *IBM Systems Journal,* 20, 1, 1981, 41–62

[BOBR77]
Bobrow DG, Winograd T, "An overview of KRL, a knowledge representation language", *Cognitive Science*, 1,1, 1977, 84–123

[BONF83]
Bonfatt F, Maio D, Tiberio P, "A separability-based method for secondary index selection in physical database design", *Methodology and Tools for Data Base Design,* Ceri S (ed), Chapter 6, North-Holland, 1983

[BOOT76]
Booth KS, Leuker GS, "Testing for the consecutive ones property, interval graphs, and planarity using PO-tree algorithms", *JCSS* 13, 1976, 335–379

[BORA84]
Boral H, DeWitt D, "A database system performance evaluation methodology", *University of Wisconsin Computer Science Technical Report,* Madison, Wisconsin, January 1984

[BOWE82]
Bowen KA, Kowalski RA, "Amalgamating language and metalanguage in logic programming", *Logic Programming,* Clark K, Tarnlund SA (eds), Academic Press, 1982

[BOYC74]
Boyce RF, Chamberlin DD, "SEQUEL: a structured English query language", *Proc. ACM SIGMOD Workshop on Data Description, Access and Control,* May 1974, 249–264

[BRAC79]
Brachman R, "On the epistemological status of semantic networks", *Associative Networks: Representation and Use of Knowledge by Computer,* Findler NV (ed), Academic Press, 1979, 3–50

[BRAE83]
Braegger RP, Reimer M, "Predicative scheduling: integration of locking and optimistic methods", *Bericht 53,* ETH Zuerich, 1983
[BRIT84]
Britton-Lee Inc., *IDM Software Reference Manual Version 1.6,* Los Gatos, California, 1984
[BROD81]
Brodie M, Zilles SN (eds), "Proc. of the workshop on data abstraction, databases and conceptual modelling, *ACM SIGMOD Record* 11,2, February 1981
[BROD82]
Brodie M, Schmidt JW (eds), "Final report of the ANSI/X3/SPARC DBS-SG relational database task group", *ACM SIGMOD Record* 12,4, July 1982
[BROD84]
Brodie M, Mylopoulos J, Schmidt JW (eds), *On Conceptual Modelling: Perspectives from Artificial Intelligence, Databases, and Programming Languages,* Springer-Verlag New York Berlin Heidelberg Tokyo, 1984
[BROW81]
Brown J, Burton R, de Kleer J, "Pedagogical natural language and knowledge engineering techniques in SOPHIE I, II, and III", *Intelligent Tutoring Systems,* Sleeman et al (eds), Academic Press, 1981
[BUTT83]
Butterworth P, *Relational Technology,* Technical Discussion Inc., 1983
[CARD75]
Cardenas AF, "Analysis and performance of inverted data base structures", *Communications of the ACM, 18,5,* May 1975, 253–263
[CARD77]
Cardenas AF, Sagamang JP, "Doubly-chained tree data base organization – analysis and design strategies", *The Computer Journal*, 20,1, 1977
[CARL79]
Carlson CR, Arora AK, "The updatability of relational views based on functional dependencies", *Proc. IEEE COMPSAC,* 1979, 415–420
[CARL83a]
Carlis JV, March ST, Dickson GW. "Physical database design: a DSS approach", *Information and Management,* 6, 1983, 211–224
[CARL83b]
Carlis JV, March ST, "A computer aided physical database design methodology". *Computer Performance*, December 1983
[CASA81]
Casas-Raposo I, "Analytic modelling of database systems: the design of a System 2000 performance predictor", *M. Sc. Thesis,* Department of Computer Science, University of Toronto, 1981
[CASA83]
Casanova MA, Castilho JMV, Furtado AI, "Properties of conceptual and external schemas", *Formal Description of Programming Concepts II,* Bjorner D (ed), North Holland, 1983, 409–430
[CELL80]
Cellary W, Meyer D, "A multi-query approach to distributed processing in a relational distributed data base management system", *Distributed Data Bases: Proc. International Symposium on Distributed Data Bases,* Delobel C, Litwin W (eds), North Holland Publishing Co., March 1980
[CERI82]
Ceri S, Pelagatti G, "Allocation of operations in distributed databases", *IEEE Transactions on Computers,* C-31, January 1982, 119–128
[CHAK82]
Chakravarthy US, Minker J, "Processing multiple queries in database systems". *IEEE Database Engineering*, 5,3, September 1982, 38–43

[CHAM76]
Chamberlin DD et al, "SEQUEL2: A unified approach to data definition, manipulation, and control", *IBM J. Res. and Devel.,* 20,6, November 1976, 560–575
[CHAM81]
Chamberlin DD, Astrahan MM, Blasgan MW, Gray JN, King WF, Lindsay BG, Lorie RA, Mehl JW, Price TG, Putzolu GR, Schkolnick M, Selinger PG, Slutz DR, Strong HR, Traiger IL, Wade BW, Yost RA, "A history and evaluation of System R", *Communications of the ACM,* 24,10, October 1981, 632–646. Also available as IBM Research Laboratory RJ2843, San Jose, Calif., 1981
[CHAM81a]
Chamberlin DD, Astrahan MM, King WF, Lorie RA, Mehl, JW, Price TG, Schkolnick M, Griffiths Selinger P, Slutz DR, Wade BW, Yost RA, "Support for repetitive transactions and ad hoc queries in System R", *ACM Transactions on Database Systems,* 6,1, March 1981. Also available as *IBM Research Laboratory RJ2551,* San Jose, Calif
[CHAN77a]
Chandra AK, Merlin PM, "Optimal implementation of conjunctive queries in relational databases", *Proc. 9th ACM Symposium on Theory of Computation*, Boulder, Co., 1977, 77–90.
[CHAN77b]
Chandy KM, "Models of distributed systems", *Proc. 3rd VLDB Conference,* Tokyo, 1977, 105–120
[CHAN82a]
Chandra AK, Harel P, "Structure and complexity of relational queries", *Journal of Computing System Sciences*, 25, 1982, 99–128
[CHAN82b]
Chang JM, "A heuristic approach to distributed query processing", *Proc. 8th VLDB Conference,* Mexico City, September 1982, 54–61
[CHAN83a]
Chan A, Dayal U, Fox SA, Goodman N, Ries D, Skeen D, "Overview of an Ada-compatible distributed database manager (DDM)", *Proc. ACM SIGMOD Conference,* June 1983, 228–237
[CHAN83b]
Chan MHC, McDonell KJ, "An algorithm for translating updates on relational user views", (submitted for publication), 1983
[CHEN76]
Chen PP, "The entity-relationship model: toward a unified view of data", *ACM TODS,* 1,1, March 1976, 9–36
[CHES83]
Chesnais A, Gelenbe E, Mitrani I, "On the modelling of parallel access to shared data", *Communications of the ACM* 26,3, 1983, 196–202
[CHEU81]
Cheung TY, "Two methods of resolution for general equi-join queries in distributed relational databases", *Tech. Report,* University of Ottawa, Department of Computer Science, 1981
[CHEU82]
Cheung TY, "A method for equi-join queries in distributed relational databases", *IEEE Transactions on Computers,* C-31, August 1982, 746–751.
[CHIA82]
Chiang WP, Teorey TJ, "A method for database record clustering", *Proc. 1982 Conference on Information Systems,* Ann Arbor, MI, December 1982, 57–73
[CHIU80a]
Chiu DM, Ho YC, "A methodology for interpreting tree queries into optimal semi-join expressions", *Proc. ACM SIGMOD, Intl. Conf. on Management of Data,* Santa Monica, 1980, 169–178
[CHIU80b]
Chiu, DM, "Optimal query interpretation for distributed databases, *Ph. D.* Dissertation, Division of Applied Sciences, Harvard University, 1980

[CHIU81]
Chiu DM, Bernstein PA, Ho YC, "Optimizing chain queries in a distributed database system", *TR-01-81,* Harvard University, 1981
[CHOM83]
Chomicki J, "A database support system for PROLOG", *Proceedings of Logic Programming Workshop 83,* Portugal, 1983
[CHRI81]
Christodoulakis S, "Estimating selectivities in data bases", *Ph. D. Dissertation*, University of Toronto, 1981
[CHRI83]
Christodoulakis S, "Estimating block transfer and join sizes", *Proc. ACM SIGMOD Conference,* San Jose, 1983, 40–54
[CHU82]
Chu WW, Hurley P, "Optimal query processing for distributed database systems", *IEEE Transactions on Computers,* C-31, September 1982, 835–850
[CICS]
IBM Corporation, *CICS/VS General Information Manual,* IBM Form No. GC33-0066
[CINC79]
Cincom System, Inc., *TOTAL PDP-11 Programmer's Reference Manual,* Cincinnati, Ohio, 1979
[CLEM78]
Clemons EK, "An external schema facility to support data base updates", *Databases: Improving Usability and Responsiveness,* Academic Press, 1978, 371–398
[CLIF83]
Clifford J, Jarke M, Vassiliou Y, "A short introduction to expert systems", *IEEE Database Engineering*, 6,4, December 1983
[CODA71]
CODASYL, *Data Base Task Group Report,* ACM, New York, 1971
[CODA78]
CODASYL, "Data description language", *Journal of Development,* Hull, Quebec, Secretariat of Canadian Government EDP Standards Committee, 1978
[CODD70]
Codd EF, "A relational model for large shared data banks", *Comm ACM,* 13,6, June 1970, 377–387
[CODD72a]
Codd EF. "Further normalization of the database relational model", *Database Systems,* Prentice Hall, Englewood Cliffs, NJ, 1972, 33–64
[CODD72b]
Codd EF, "Relational completeness of database sublanguages", *Database Systems,* Prentice Hall, 1972, 67-101
[CODD79]
Codd EF, "Extending the database relational model to capture more meaning", *ACM Transactions on Database Systems,* 4,4, December 1979, 397–434
[COME78]
Comer D, "The difficulty of optimum index selection", *ACM Transactions on Database Systems,* 3,4, December 1978, 440–445
[COME79]
Comer D, "Heuristics for trie index minimization", *ACM Transactions on Database Systems,* 4,3, September 1979, 383–395
[CONN79]
Connelly D, "A single-tuple relational interface for CODASYL databases", *Research Report 79–80,* Sperry Research Center, Sudbury, MA, 1979
[COSM83]
Cosmadakis S, Papadimitriou CH, "Updates of relational views", *Proc. 3rd ACM SIGMOD-SIGACT Symp. on Principles of Database Systems,* Atlanta, 1983, 317–331.

[CULL81]
Cullinet Database Systems, Inc., *IDMS Database Design and Definition Guide,* Westwood, MA, 1981

[DANI82a]
Daniels D, "Query compilation in a distributed database system", *IBM Research Laboratory RJ3423,* San Jose, Calif., 1982

[DANI82b]
Daniels D, Selinger PG, Haas LM, Lindsay BG, Mohan C, Walker A, Wilms P, "An introduction to distributed query compilation in R*", *Proc. 2nd International Conference on Distributed Databases,* Berlin, September 1982. Also available as IBM Research Laboratory RJ3497, San Jose, Calif.

[DATE82]
Date CJ, *An Introduction to Database Systems,* Third Edition, Addison-Wesley Publishing Company, Reading, MA, 1982

[DAVI81]
Davis R, "Expert Systems: Where are we? and Where do we Go from Here?", Massachusetts Institute of Technology, AI MEMO no. 665, 1982

[DAYA78]
Dayal U, Bernstein PA, "On the updatability of relational views", *Proc. 4th VLDB Conference,* Berlin, West Germany, 1978, 368–378

[DAYA81]
Dayal U, Goodman N, Landers TA, Olson K, Smith JM, Yedwab L, "Local query optimization in MULTIBASE – a system for heterogeneous distributed databases", *Technical Report, CCA-81-11,* Computer Corporation of America, Cambridge, MA, 1981

[DAYA82a]
Dayal U, Landers TA, Yedwab L, "Global query optimization in MULTIBASE: a system for heterogeneous distributed databases", *Technical Report CCA-82-05,* Computer Corporation of America, Cambridge, MA, 1982

[DAYA82b]
Dayal U, Goodman N, "Query optimization for CODASYL database systems", *Proc. ACM SIGMOD Conference,* Orlando, June 1982, 138–150

[DAYA82c]
Dayal U, Hwang HY, "View definition and generalization for database integration in MULTIBASE: a system for heterogeneous distributed databases", *Proc. 6th Berkeley Workshop on Distributed Database Management and Computer Networks,* February 1982, 203–238. (A revised version appeared in *IEEE Transactions on Software Engineering*, SE-10,6, November 1984, 628-644)

[DAYA82d]
Dayal U, Goodman N, Katz RH, "An extended relational algebra with control over duplicate elimination", *Proc. ACM PODS Conference,* 1982, 117–123.

[DAYA82e]
Dayal U, Bernstein PA, "On the correct translation of update operations on relational views", *ACM Transactions on Database Systems, 8,3,* September 1982, 381–416

[DAYA83a]
Dayal U, "Processing queries over generalization hierarchies in a multidatabase system", *Proc. VLDB Conference,* 1983, 342–353.

[DAYA83b]
Dayal U, "Processing queries with quantifiers: a horticultural approach", *Proc. ACM PODS Conference,* 1983, 125–136

[DAYA85]
Dayal U, "Query processing in a multidatabase system", this volume,

[DE78]
De P et al, "Towards an optimal design of a network database from relation descriptions", *Operations Research, 26,5,* September-October 1978, 805–823

[DEWI78]
DeWitt DJ, "Direct – a multiprocessor organization for supporting relational database management systems", *Proc. 5th Annual Symposium on Computer Architecture*, 1978
[DEWI79]
DeWitt DJ, "Query execution in DIRECT", *Proc. ACM SIGMOD Conference, Boston,* 1979, 13–22
[DIET79]
Dietz P, Furst M, Hopcroft J, "A linear time algorithm for the generalized consecutive retrieval property", *Report TR79-386,* Dept. Computer Science, Cornell University, July 1979
[DUHN78]
Duhne RA, Severance DG, "Selection of an efficient combination of data files for a multiuser database", *Proc. 1978 National Computer Conference,* 47, AFIPS Press, Montvale, NJ, 1978, 843–847
[EDEL81]
Edelman F, "The management of information resources – a challenge for American business", *MIS Quarterly,* 5,1, 17–28
[EGGE80]
Eggers S, Shoshani A, "Efficient access of compressed data", *Proc. 6th VLDB Conference,* Montreal, 1980, 205–211
[EISN76]
Eisner MJ, Severance DG, "Mathematical techniques for efficient record segmentation in large shared databases", *Journal of the ACM,* 23,4, October 1976, 619–635
[EPST78]
Epstein R; Stonebraker M, Wong E, "Distributed query processing in a relational data base system",*Proc. ACM SIGMOD Conference,* Austin, TX, May 1978, 169–180
[EPST80]
Epstein R, Stonebraker M, "Analysis of distributed data base processing strategies", *Proc. 6th VLDB Conference, Montreal,* 1980, 92–101
[ERMA80]
Erman LD et al, "The Hearsay-II speech-understanding system: integrating knowledge to resolve uncertainty", *Computing Surveys,* 12,2, June 1980, 213–253
[ESSL82]
Esslemont P, Gray PMD, "The performance of a relational interface to a CODASYL database", unnumbered *Research Report,* Dept. of Computer Science, University of Aberdeen, Scotland, UK, 1982
[ESWA75]
Eswaran KP, Chamberlin DD, "Functional specification of a subsystem for data base integrity", *Proc. VLDB Conference,* 1975, 48–68.
[ESWA76]
Eswaran KP, Gray JN, Lorie RA, Traiger IL, "The notions of consistency and predicate locks in a database system", *Communications of the ACM,* 19,11, 1976, 624–633
[FAGI83]
Fagin R, "Acyclic database schemes (of various degrees): a painless introduction", *IBM Research Report,* RJ3800, February 1983
[FAHL79]
Fahlman SE, *NETL: A System for Representing and Using Real-World Knowledge,* MIT Press, Cambridge, MA, 1979
[FINK82]
Finkelstein S, "Common expression analysis in database applications", *Proc. ACM-SIGMOD Conference,* Orlando, 1982, 235–345
[FORG80]
Forgy CL, *The OPS5 User's Manual,* Tech. Report, Carnegie-Mellon University, 1980

[FURT77]
Furtado AL, Kerschberg L, "An algebra of quotient relations", *Proc. ACM SIGMOD Conference,* Toronto, 1977, 1–8.
[FURT79]
Furtado AL, Sevcik KC, Santos CS, "Permitting updates through views of data bases", *Information Systems, 4,* 1979, 269–283.
[GALL78]
Gallaire H, Minker J, *Logic and Databases,* Plenum, 1978
[GAMB77]
Gambino TJ, Gerritsen R, "A database design decision support system", *Proc. 3rd VLDB Conference,* Tokyo, 1977, 534–544
[GARD82]
Gardarin G, Valduriez P, "Join and semi-join algorithms for a multiprocessor database machine", *Rapports Techniques* 11, INRIA, Le Chesnay, France, April 1982
[GARE79]
Garey MR, Johnson DS, *Computers and Intractability: A Guide to the Theory of NP-Completeness,* Freeman WH and Company, 1979
[GAVI82]
Gavish B, Segev A, "Query optimization in distributed computer systems", Akoka J (ed), *Management of Distributed Data Processing,* North-Holland, 1982, 233–252
[GELE82]
Gelenbe E, Gardy D, "The size of projections of relations satisfying a functional dependency", *Proc. 8th VLDB Conference,* Mexico City, 1982, 325–333
[GEOF67]
Geoffrion AM, "Solving bi-criterion mathematical programs", *Operations Research,* 15,1, January 1967, 39–54
[GERR75]
Gerritsen R, "A preliminary system for the design of DTGB data structures", *Communications of the ACM,* 18,10, October 1975, 551–557
[GERR76]
Gerritsen R et al, "WAND user's guide", *Decision Sciences Working Paper 76-01-03*, Wharton School, University of Pennsylvania, 1976
[GERR77]
Gerritsen R et al, "Cost effective database design: an integrated model, *Decision Sciences Working Paper 77-12-03,* Wharton School, University of Pennsylvania, 1977
[GESE76]
Gesellschaft für Mathematik und Datenverarbeitung, *ADABAS: Database Systems Investigation Report,* 2,1, Institut für Informationssysteme, Bonn, West Germany, 1976
[GEVA82]
Gevarter WB, "An overview of expert systems", *National Bureau of Standards Report, NBSIR 82-2505, 1982*
[GHOS72]
Ghosh SP, "File organization: the consecutive retrieval property", *Communications of the ACM* 15, 1972, 802–808
[GHOS73]
Ghosh SP, "On the theory of consecutive storage of relevant records", *Information Sciences,* 6, 1973, 1–9.
[GHOS74]
Ghosh SP, "File organization: consecutive storage of relevant records on drum-type storage", *Information and Control,* 25, 1974, 145–165
[GHOS75]
Ghosh SP, "Consecutive storage of relevant records with redundancy", *Communications of the ACM,* 18, 1975, 464–471.

[GHOS77]
Ghosh SP, *Data Base Organization for Data Management,* Academic Press, New York, 1977
[GHOS83a]
Ghosh SP, Kambayashi Y, Lipski Jr. W (Eds), *Data Base File Organization, Theory and Applications of the Consecutive Retrieval Property,* Academic Press, New York, 1983
[GHOS83b]
Ghosh SP, "Future of the consecutive retrieval property", in [GHOS83a]
[GOLD77]
Goldstein I, Papert S, "Artificial intelligence, language and the study of knowledge", *Artificial Intelligence,* 1,1, 1977, 84–123
[GOLD84]
Goldhirsh D, Yedwab L, "Processing read-only queries over views with generalization", *Proc. VLDB,* 1984
[GOOD79]
Goodman N, Bernstein PA, Wong E, Reeve CL, Rothnie JB, "Query processing in a system for distributed databases", CCA Technical Report, Computer Corporation of America, 1979
[GOOD82a]
Goodman N, Shmueli O, "The tree property is fundamental for query processing", (Extended Abstract), *Proc. 1st ACM SIGACT-SIGMOD Symposium on Principles of Database Systems,* March 1982, 40–48
[GOOD82b]
Goodman N, Shmueli O, "Transforming cyclic schemas into trees", *ACM SIGACT Symposium on Principles of Database Systems,* March 1982, 49–54
[GOOD82c]
Goodman N, Shmueli O, "Tree queries: a simple class of relational queries", *ACM Transactions on Database Systems,* 7,4, December 1982, 653–677
[GOUD81]
Gouda MG, Dayal UD, "Optimal semijoin schedules for query processing in local distributed database systems", *Proc. ACM SIGMOD Conference,* Ann Arbor, 1981, 164–175
[GRAH79]
Graham MH, "On the universal relation", *Technical Report,* Univ. of Toronto, 1979
[GRAN81]
Grant J, Minker J, "Optimization in deductive and conventional relational database systems", Gallaire H, Minker J, Nicholas JM (eds), *Advances in Database Theory,* Plenum, New York, 1981, 195–234
[GRAY75]
Gray JN, Lorie RA, Putzolu GR, "Granularity of locks in a shared database", *Proc. 1st VLDB Conference,* Framingham, MA, 1975, 428–451
[GRAY78]
Gray JN, *Notes on Database Operating Systems, Report RJ2188,* IBM San Jose, 1978
[GRAY79]
Gray PMD, Bell R, "Use of simulators to help the inexpert in automatic program generation", *Proc. EURO-IFIP79,* North Holland, 1979
[GRAY81]
Gray J, "The transaction concept: virtues and limitations", *Proc. 7th VLDB Conference,* Cannes, 1981, 144–154
[GRIF79]
Griffiths-Selinger P, et al, "Access path selection in a relational data base management system", IBM Research Laboratory, San Jose, California, 1979
[HAER78]
Haerder T, "Implementing a generalized access path structure for a relational database system", *ACM Transactions on Database Systems,* 3,3, 1978, 285–298

[HAJO57]
Hajos G, "Über eine Art von Graphen". *Internationale Mathematische Nachrichten*, 11, 65, 1957
[HALL76]
Hall PAV, "Optimization of a single relational expression in a relational database", *IBM Journal of Research and Development*, 20, 1976, 244–257
[HAMM75]
Hammer M, McLeod D, "Semantic integrity of a relational data base system", *Proc. 1st. VLDB Conference*, September 1975
[HAMM76a]
Hammer M, Chan A, "Index selection in a self-adaptive data base management system", *Proc. SIGMOD Int. Conf. on Management of Data (ACM)*, 1976
[HAMM76b]
Hammer M, Chan A, "Acquisition and utilization of access patterns in relational data base implementation", *Pattern Recognition and Artificial Intelligence*, Chen C (ed), Academic Press, 1976
[HAMM76c]
Hammer M, "Data abstractions for databases", *Proc. Conf. Data: Abstraction, Definition, and Structure*, SIGPLAN Notices 11, 1976, 58–59
[HAMM78]
Hammer M, Sarin SK, "Efficient monitoring of database assertions", *Proc. ACM SIGMOD Conference*, Austin, 1978, 159–168
[HAMM79]
Hammer M, Niamir B, "A heuristic approach to attribute partitioning", *Proc. ACM SIGMOD International Conference on Management of Data*, Boston, MA, 1979, 93–100
[HAMM80]
Hammer M, Zdonik S, "Knowledge-based query processing", *Proc. 6th VLDB Conference*, Montreal, 1980, 137–147
[HAMM82]
Hammond R, technical discussion, (Statistics Canada), 1982
[HART78]
Hart PE, Duda RO, Einaudi MT, "A computer-based consultation system for mineral exploration", *Technical Report*, SRI International, Menlo Park, Calif. 1978
[HASK82]
Haskin RL, Lorie RA, "On extending the functions of a relational database system", *Proc. ACM-SIGMOD International Conference on Management of Data*, Orlando, 1982, 207–212
[HAWT79]
Hawthorn PB, "Evaluation and enhancement of the performance of relational database management systems", *Ph. D. Dissertation*, University of California, Berkeley, 1979
[HAYE83]
Hayes-Roth F, Waterman DA, Lenat DB, *Building Expert Systems*, Addison Wesley, 1983
[HAYN81]
Haynie MN, "The relational/network hybrid data model for design automation databases", *Proc. 18th Design Automation Conference (IEEE)*, 1981, 646–652
[HELD75a]
Held GD, Stonebraker MR, Wong E, "INGRES: A relational database system", *Proc. AFIPS NCC*, 1975, 409–416
[HELD75b]
Held G, Stonebraker M, "Storage structures and access methods in the relational database managment system INGRES", *Proc. ACM Pacific*, 1975, 26–33
[HENS84]
Henschen L, Naqvi S, "On compiling queries in recursive first-order databases", *Journal of the ACM 31*, 1984, 47–85.

[HEVN79]
Hevner AR, Yao SB, "Query processing in distributed database systems", *IEEE Transactions on Software Engineering,* SE-5,3, May 1979, 177–187
[HEVN80]
Hevner AR, "The optimization of query processing on distributed database systems", *Ph. D. Dissertation,* Department of Computer Science, Purdue University, Lafayette, Indiana, 1980
[HEVN81]
Hevner AR, Yao SB, "Transaction optimization on a distributed database system", *Technical Report HR-81-259,* Honeywell Corporate Computer Science Center, Bloomington, MN, 1981
[HEWI71]
Hewitt C, "PLANNER: A language for proving theorems in robots", *Proc. IJCAI-71,* London, England, 1971
[HEYM82]
Heyman DP, "Mathematical models of database degradation", *ACM Transactions Database Systems,* 7,4, December 1982, 615–631
[HILL83]
Hillyer BK, Shaw DE, Nigam A, "NON-VON's performance on certain database benchmarks", *Technical Report,* Columbia University, Computer Science Department, 1983
[HOFF75a]
Hoffer JA, Severance DG, "The use of cluster analysis in physical data base design", *Proc. 1st VLDB Conference,* Framingham, MA, September 1975, 69–86
[HOFF75b]
Hoffer JA, "A clustering approach to the generation of sub-files for the design of a computer data base", *Ph. D. Dissertation,* Department of Operations Research, Cornell University, January 1975, 276 pages
[HOFF76]
Hoffer JA, "An integer programming formulation of computer database design problems", *Information Sciences,* 11, 1976, 29–48
[HOFF80]
Hoffer J, "Database design practices for inverted files", *Information and Management,* 3, 1980, 149–161
[HONE71]
Honeywell Information Systems Inc., *Integrated Data Store,* 1971
[HSIA70]
Hsiao D, Harary F, "A formal system for information retrieval from files", *Comm. ACM,* 13,2, February 1970, 67–73. Also see *Comm. ACM,* 13,4, April 1970, 266
[HSIA77]
Hsiao DK, Kannan K, Kerr DS, "Structure memory designs for a database computer", *Proc. ACM Annual Conference,* 1977
[HULT77]
Hulten C, Soderlung L, "A simulation model for performance analysis of large shared data bases", *Proc. 3rd VLDB Conference*, New York, 1977
[HWAN81]
Hwang H, Dayal U, "Using the entity-relationship model for implementing multi-model database systems", *Proc. Second Entity-Relationship Conference,* Washington, D.C., October 1981
[HWAN82]
Hwang HY, "Database integration and query optimization in multi-database systems", *Ph. D. Dissertation,* Dept. of Computer Sciences, The University of Texas at Austin, Austin, TX., 1982
[HWAN84]
Hwang HY, Dayal U, "Using semi-outerjoins to process queries in a multidatabase system", *Proc. ACM PODS Conference,* 1984
[IBM]
IBM Pub., *SQL/Data System Application Programming,* SH 24-5018

[IBM74]
IBM Corporation, "Introduction to direct access storage devices and organization methods", *Student Text, No. GC20-1649-8,* IBM Corporation, White Plains, NY, 1974
[IBM80]
IBM, *IMS/VS Version 1: General Information Manual,* 1980
[IEEE82]
IEEE, *Database Engineering,* Katz R, (ed), June 1982
[IEEE83]
IEEE, *Database Engineering,* Kim W, (ed), December 1983
[IEEE84]
IEEE, *Database Engineering,* Batory D, (ed), March 1984
[INFO79]
Infodata Systems Inc., *INQUIRE Basic Training Course,* Pittsford, NY, 1979
[JACO82]
Jacobs BE, "On database logic", *Journal of the ACM,* 29,2, 1982
[JAES82]
Jaeschke G, Scheck HJ, "Remarks on the algebra of nonfirst normal form relations", *Proc. ACM PODS Conference,* 1982
[JARK82]
Jarke M, Schmidt JW, "Query processing strategies in the PASCAL/R relational database management system", *Proc. ACM SIGMOD Conference,* Orlando, 1982, 256–264
[JARK83]
Jarke M, Koch J, "Range nesting: a fast method to evaluate quantified queries", *Proc. ACM SIGMOD Conference,* San Jose, 1983, 196–206
[JARK84a]
Jarke M, Vassiliou Y, "Coupling expert systems with database management systems", Reitman W (ed), *Artificial Intelligence Applications for Business,* Ablex, Norwood, NJ, 1984, 65–85
[JARK84b]
Jarke M, Clifford J, Vassiliou Y, "An optimizing PROLOG front-end to a relational query system", *Proc. ACM SIGMOD Conference,* Boston, 1984
[JARK84c]
Jarke M, Koch J, Schmidt JW, "Introduction to query processing", this volume.
[JARK84d]
Jarke M, "Common subexpression isolation in multiple query optimization", this volume
[JOHN83]
Johnston HR, Schweitzer JE, Warkentine ER, "A DBMS facility for handling structured engineering entities", *Proc. Database Week: Engineering Design Applications Conference,* San Jose 1983, 3–12
[KAMB78]
Kambayashi Y, Hara H, Yajima S, "Systematic organization of quasi-consecutive retrieval files", *Proc. Language and Automata Symp.*, February 1978
[KAMB82a]
Kambayashi Y, "Theory of relational database", *Japan Annual Reviews in Electronics, Computers & Telecommunications, Computer Science & Technologies,* OHMSHA/North Holland, March 1982, 206–226
[KAMB82b]
Kambayashi Y, Yoshikawa M, Yajima S, "Query processing for distributed databases using generalized semi-joins", *Proc. ACM SIGMOD International Conference on Management of Data,* June 1982, 151–160
[KAMB83a]
Kambayashi Y, Yoshikawa M, "Query processing utilizing dependencies and horizontal decomposition", *Proc. ACM SIGMOD Conference,* San Jose, May 1983, 55–57

[KAMB83b]
Kambayashi Y, "The buffer-limited quasi-consecutive retrieval file organization and its application to logic circuit layout", in [GHOS83a], 1983, 165–178
[KAMB84]
Kambayashi Y, "Processing cyclic queries", this volume
[KATZ81a]
Katz R, "Software architecture for heterogeneous database management, *Proc. COMPSAC,* IEEE, 1981, 33–42
[KATZ81b]
Katz R, Goodman N, "View processing in MULTIBASE – a heterogeneous database system", *Entity-Relationship Approach to Information Modelling and Analysis,* Chen PP (ed.), ER Institute, Saugus, CA, 1981
[KATZ82]
Katz R, "A database approach for managing VLSI design data", *Proc. 19th Design Automation Conference (IEEE),* June 1982, 274–282
[KATZ82a]
Katz R, Wong E , "Decompiling CODASYL DML into relational queries", *ACM Transactions on Database Systems,* 7,1, March 1982, 1–23
[KEDE83]
Kedem ZM, Silberschatz A, "Locking protocols: from exclusive to shared locks, *Journal of the ACM*, 30, 4, 1983, 787–804
[KELL81]
Keller AM, "Updates to relational databases through views involving joins", *IBM Research Report RJ3282,* IBM, San Jose, Calif. October 1981
[KENN73]
Kennedy SR, "The use of access frequencies in database organizations, *Ph. Dissertation,* Cornell University, Ithaca, NY, 1973
[KENT78]
Kent W, *Data and Reality,* Amsterdam, North-Holland Publishing Company, 1978
[KERS80]
Kerschberg L, Ting PD, Yao SB, *Optimal Distributed Query Processing,* Bell Laboratories, Holmdel, NJ, 1980
[KERS82]
Kerschberg L, Ting PD, Yao SB, "Query optimization in star computer networks", *ACM Transactions on Database Systems,* 7,4, December 1982, 678–711
[KIM80a]
Kim W, "A new way to compute the product and join of relations", *Proc. ACM SIGMOD Conference,* Santa Monica, 1980, 179–187.
[KIM84a]
Kim W, Gajski D, Kuck DJ, "A parallel pipelined relational query processor", *ACM Transactions on Database Systems,* 9,2, June 1984, 214–242
[KIM80b]
Kim W, "Query optimization for relational database systems", *Ph. D. Dissertation,* Dept. of Computer Science, University of Illinois, 1980
[KIM81]
Kim W, "Query optimization for relational database systems", *IBM Technical Report RJ3081,* San Jose, 1981
[KIM82]
Kim W, "On optimizing an SQL-like nested query", *ACM Transactions on Database Systems,* 7,3 September 1982, 443–469. Also available as *IBM Research Laboratory RJ3063,* San Jose, California
[KIM84b]
Kim W, "Global optimization of relational queries: a first step", this volume

[KING74]
King WF, "On the selection of indices for a file", *IBM Research Report RJ1341,* IBM, San Jose, California, 1974
[KING81]
King JJ, QUIST: "A system for semantic query optimization in relational data bases", *Proc. 7th VLDB Conference,* Cannes, 1981, 510–516
[KLUG81]
Klug A, "ABE – A query language for constructing aggregates-by-example", *Proc. 1st LBL SDB Workshop,* 1981
[KLUG82a]
Klug A, "Equivalence of relational algebra and relational calculus query languages having aggregate functions", *Journal of the ACM,* 29, 1982, 699–717
[KLUG82b]
Klug A, "Access paths in the ABE statistical query facility", *Proc. ACM SIGMOD Conference,* Orlando, 1982, 161–173
[KNUT73]
Knuth DE, *The Art of Computer Programming, Volume 3, Searching and Sorting,* Addison Wesley, Reading, MA, 1973
[KONI83]
Konish O, Kambayashi Y, "Improvement of the KWIC index utilizing the consecutive retrieval property", in [GHOS83a], 1983, 289–299
[KOOI82]
Kooi R, Frankforth, D., "Query optimization in INGRES", [REIN82b], 1982
[KOWA79]
Kowalski RA, *Logic for Problem Solving,* North-Holland, New York, 1979
[KOWA81]
Kowalski R, *Logic as a Database Language,* Imperial College, London, 1981
[KUNI82]
Kunifuji S, Yokota H, "Prolog and relational databases for Fifth Generation Computer Systems", *Proc. Workshop on Logical Bases for Data Bases,* Toulouse, December 1982
[LAFU83]
Lafue GME, "Basic decisions about linking an expert system with a DBMS: a case study", *IEEE Database Engineering Bulletin,* 6,4, December 1983
[LAME84]
Lamersdorf W, "Recursive data models for non-conventional database applications", *Proc. IEEE COMPDEC Conference,* Los Angeles, 1984
[LAND82]
Landers TA, Rosenberg RL, "An overview of MULTIBASE", *Distributed Databases,* Schneider HJ (ed), North Holland, 1982, 153–184
[LANG78]
Langdon JJ, "A note on associative processors for data management", *ACM Transactions on Database Systems 3,* 1982, 148–158.
[LIND79]
Lindsay BG, Selinger PG, Galtieri C, Gray JN, Lorie RA, Price TG, Putzolu F, Traiger IL, Wade BW, "Notes on distributed databases", *Distributed Data Bases,* Draffan IW, Poole F (eds), Cambridge University Press, 1980, 223–247. Also available as *IBM Research Report RJ2571,* July 1979
[LIND81]
Lindsay BG, "Object naming and catalog management for a distributed database manager", *Proc. 2nd International Conference on Distributed Computing Systems,* Paris, France, April 1981. Also available as *IBM Research Laboratory RJ2914,* San Jose, California, April 1984

[LIND83]
Lindsay BG, Haas LM, Mohan C, Wilms PF, Yost RA, "Computation and communication in R*: a distributed database manager", *Proc. 9th ACM Symposium on Principles of Operating Systems,* Bretton Woods, October 1983. Also in *ACM Transactions on Computer Systems* 2,1 (Feb. 1984), 24–38, and available as *IBM Research Report RJ3740*

[LIPS76]
Lipski, Jr W, "Information storage and retrieval – mathematical foundation II (combinatorial problems), *Theoretical Computer Science,* 3, 1976, 183–212

[LIPS78]
Lipski, Jr W, "Generalization of the consecutive ones property and related NP-complete problems", *Rept. ACT 9,* Coordinate Sci. Lab., University of Illinois, September 1978

[LIPS83a]
Lipski Jr W, "The consecutive retrieval property, interval graphs and related topics – a survey", in [GHOS83a], 1983

[LIPS83b]
Lipski Jr W, "A note on decomposing a query set into subsets having the consecutive retrieval property", in [GHOS83a], 1983

[LOHM84]
Lohmann GM, Daniels D, Haas LM, Kistler R, Selinger PG, "Optimization of nested queries in a distributed relational database", *IBM Research Laboratory RJ4260, San Jose, California*

[LONC83]
Lonc Z, Traczyk T, Truszczynski M, "Optimum f-graphs for the family of all k-subsets of an n-set", in [GHOS83a]

[LORI83]
Lorie R, Plouffe W, "Complex objects and their use in design transactions", *Proc. Annual Meeting – Database Week: Engineering Design Applications (IEEE),* May 1983, 115–221

[LORI84]
Lorie R, Kim W, McNabb D, Plouffe W, Meier A, "Supporting complex objects in a relational system for engineering databases", this volume

[LOWE82]
Lowenthal E, "Database systems for local nets", *DATAMATION,* August 1982

[LUK80]
Luk WS, Luk L, "Optimal query processing strategies in a distributed database system," Department of Computer Science, Simon Fraser University, Burneby B.C., Canada, 1980

[LUK81]
Luk WS, Black PA, "On cost estimation in processing a query in a distributed database system", *IEEE COMPSAC,* 1981

[LUK83]
Luk WS, Luk L, "Optimizing semi-join programs for distributed query processing", *Proc. 2nd International Conference on Databases,* Deen SM, Hammersley P (Eds), Cambridge, England, September 1983

[LUM70]
Lum VY, "Multiattribute retrieval with combined indices", *Comm ACM,* 13,11, November 1970

[LUM71]
Lum VY, Ling H, "An optimization problem of the selection of secondary keys", *ACM Natational Conference,* 1971, 349–356

[LUM79]
Lum VY et al., *1978 New Orleans Database Design Workshop. IBM Technical Report Number RJ2554,* IBM, San Jose, 1979

[MAIE83]
Maier D, *The Theory of Relational Databases,* Computer Science Press, 1983

[MALL84]
Mall M, Reimer M, Schmidt JW, "Data selection, sharing and access control in a relational scenario", in [BROD84]
[MANO82]
Manola F, Pirotte A, "CQLF", *Proc. ACM SIGMOD Conference,* Orlando, 1982, 94–103
[MANO83]
Manola F, Pirotte A, "An approach to multi-model database systems", Deen SM, Hammersley P (eds), *ICOD-2: Proc. 2nd International Conference on Databases,* Wiley Heyden, 1983
[MARC77]
March ST, Severance DG, „The determination of efficient record segmentations and blocking factors for shared data files", *ACM Transaction on Database Systems,* 2,3, September 1977, 279–296
[MARC78]
March ST, Severance DG, "A mathematical modeling approach to the automatic selection of database designs", *Proc. ACM SIGMOD International Conference on Management of Data,* Austin, Texas, May 31 - June 2, 1978, 112–126
[MARC81]
March ST, Severance DG, Wilens M, "Frame memory: a storage architecture to support rapid design and implementation of efficient databases", *ACM Transactions on Database Systems,* 6,3, September 1981, 441–463
[MARC83]
March ST, "Techniques for structuring database records", *Computing Surveys,* 15,1, March 1983, 45–79.
[MARC83a]
see [MARC83]
[MARC83b]
March ST, "A mathematical programming approach to the selection of access paths for large multiuser databases", *Decision Sciences,* December 1983
[MARC84]
March ST, "Physical database design: techniques for improved database performance", this volume
[MARQ84]
Marque-Pucheu G, Martin-Gallausiaux J, Jomier G, "Interfacing Prolog and relational data base management systems", Gardarin G, Gelenbe E (Eds), *New Applications of Data Bases,* Academic Press, 1984
[MART77]
Martin J, *Principles of Data-Base Management,* Prentice Hall Inc., Englewood Cliffs, NJ, 1977
[MARY80]
Maryanski FJ, "Backend database systems", *ACM Computing Surveys 12,* 1980, 3–26.
[MASI74]
Masinter LM, in *INTERLISP Reference Manual,* 1974
[MCCA82]
McCarthy JL, "Metadata management for large statistical databases", *Proc 8th VLDB Conference,* Mexico City, 1982, 234–243
[MCCO72]
McCormick WT Jr, Schweitzer PJ, White TW, "Problem decomposition and data reorganization by a clustering technique", *Operations Research,* 20,5, September 1972, 933–1009
[MCDE81]
McDermott J, "R1's formative years", *AI Magazine,* 2,2, 1981
[MCGE77]
McGee WC, "The information management system, ICM/VS, Part II: data base facilities", *IBM System Journal,* 16,2, 1977, 96–122
[MCGR76]
McGregor DR, Thomson RG, Dawson WN, "High performance for database systems", *Systems for Large Databases,* North-Holland, Amsterdam, 1976

[MEIE83]
Meier A, Lorie R, "Implicit hierarchical joins for complex objects", *IBM Research Report RJ3775,* San Jose, February 1983
[MERR77]
Merret TH, "Database cost analysis: a top down approach", *ACM SIGMOD,* Toronto, 1977, 135–143
[MERR83]
Merrett TH, Kambayashi Y, "Join scheduling in a paging environment using the consecutive property" in [GHOS83a]
[MINK78]
Minker J, "Search strategy and selection function for an inferential relational system", *ACM Transactions on Database Systems,* 3, 1978, 1–31
[MINK83]
Minker J, Nicolas JM, "On recursive axioms in deductive databases", *Information Systems*, 8, 1983, 1–13
[MINS75]
Minsky M, "A framework for representing knowledge", *The Psychology of Computer Vision,* Winston PH (ed), McGraw-Hill, New York, 1975, 211–277
[MITC76]
Mitchell RW, "Content addressable file store", *Proc. Online Database Technology Conference,* April 1976
[MITO75]
Mitoma MF, Irani KB, "Automatic data base schema design and optimization", *Proc. 1st. VLDB Conference,* Framingham, MA., September 1975
[MOHA83]
Mohan C, Lindsay BG, "Efficient commit protocols for the tree of processes model of distributed transactions", *Proc. 2nd ACM SIGACT-SIGOPS Symposium on Principles of Distributed Computing,* Montreal, Canada, August 1983. Also available as IBM Research Report RJ3881.
[MOON81]
Moon D, Weinreb D, in *LISP Machine Manual*, 1981
[MOTR81]
Motro A, Buneman P, "Constructing superviews", *Proc. ACM SIGMOD Conference,* Ann Arbor, 1981, 56–64
[MUNZ79]
Munz R, Schneider HJ, Steyer F, "Application of sub-predicate tests in database systems", *Proc. 5th VLDB Conference,* Rio de Janeiro, 1979, 426–435.
[MUTH83]
Muthuswamy B, Kerschberg L, "Distributed query optimization using detailed database statistics", unpublished manuscript, University of South Carolina, May 1983
[MYLO84]
Mylopoulos J, "An overview of knowledge representation", *On Conceptual Modelling,* Brodie ML, Mylopoulos J, Schmidt JW, (Eds), Springer-Verlag, 1984, 3–18.
[NAKA78]
Nakamura T, Mizoguchi T, "An analysis of storage utilization factor in block split data structuring scheme", *Proc. 4th VLDB Conference,* Berlin, 1978, 489–495
[NAU82]
Nau DS, "Expert Computer Systems", *Computer,* February 1982, 63–85
[NAVA78]
Navathe S, Schkolnick, "View representation in logical database design", *Proc. SIGMOD Conference,* Austin, Texas, 1978, 114–156
[NDX81]
NDX Retrieval Systems, Inc., *CREATABASE Performance Manual,* Houston Texas, 1981

[NG82]
Ng P, "Distributed compilation and recompilation of database queries", *IBM Research Report RJ3375,* January 1982

[NGUY80]
Nguyen GT, "Decentralized dynamic query decomposition for distributed database systems", *Proc. ACM Pacific 80: Distributed Processing – New Directions for a New Decade,* San Francisco, November 1980

[NIAM78]
Niamir B, "Attribute partitioning in a self-adaptive relational database system", *Report MIT/LCS/TR-192,* Laboratory for Computer Science, M.I.T., 1978

[NICO83]
Nicolas JM, Yazdanian K, "An outline of BDGEN: a deductive DBMS", Mason RE (ed), *Information Processing 83*, North Holland, Amsterdam, 1983, 711–717

[NIEV84]
Nievergelt J, Hinterberger H, Sevcik KC, "The grid file: an adaptable, symmetric multi-key file structure", *ACM Transactions on Database Systems*, 9,1, March 1984, 38–71

[OBER82]
Obermarck R, "Distributed deadlock detection algorithm", *ACM Transactions on Database Systems,* 7,2, June 1982

[OLSO82]
Olson JP, Ellis SP, "PROBWELL – An expert advisor for determining problems with producing wells", *IBM Scientific/Engineering Conference,* Poughkeepsie, New York, November 1982

[ONUE83]
Onuegbe E, Rahimi S, Hevner AR, "Local query translation and optimization in a distributed system", *Proceedings NCC,* July 1983, 229–239

[OTT82]
Ott N, Horlaender K, "Removing redundant joins in queries involving views", *IBM Heidelberg Scientific Center Technical Report TR-82.03.003,* 1982

[OZKA75]
Ozkarahan EA, Schuster SA, Smith KC, "RAP: An associative processor for database management", *Proc. National Computer Conference, 44,* AFIPS Press, 1975

[OZKA82]
Ozkarahan EA, "Database machines/computer-based distributed databases", *Proc. 2nd International Symposium on Distributed Databases,* Berlin 1982, 61–80

[OZSO80]
Ozsoyoglu M, Yu CT, "On identifying a class of database queries that can be processed efficiently", *Proc. IEEE COMPSAC Conference,* October 1980, 453–461

[OZSO83a]
Ozsoyoglu G, Matos V, Ozsoyoglu ZM, "Extending relational algebra and relational calculus for set-valued atributes and aggregate functions", *Technical Report, CES 83–14,* CWRU, 1983

[OZSO83b]
Ozsoyoglu G, Ozsoyoglu ZM, "Features of SSDB", *Proc. 2nd LBL SDB Workshop,* 1983

[OZSO83c]
Ozsoyoglu, ZM, Ozsoyoglu G, "An extension of relational algebra for summary tables", *Proc. Second LBL SDB Workshop*, 1983

[OZSO83d]
Ozsoyoglu, ZM, Ozsoyoglu G, "An extension of relational algebra", *Technical Report CES 83-03,* CWRU, 1983

[OZSO84a]
Ozsoyoglu ZM, Ozsoyoglu G, "STBE – A database query language for manipulating summary data", *Proc. IEEE COMPDEC Conference,* April 1984

[OZSO84b]
Ozsoyoglu M, Ozsoyoglu G,"A query language for statistical databases", this volume

[PALE72]
Palermo FP, "A data base search problem", *Proceedings 4th Computer and Information Science Symposium,* Miami Beach, 1972, 67–101
[PARS83]
Parsaye K, "Logic programming and relational databases", *IEEE Database Engineering Bulletin,* 6,4, December 1983
[PERE82]
Pereira LM, Porto A. " A Prolog implementation of a large system on a small machine". Departmento de Informatica, Universidada Nova de Lisboa
[POPL77]
Pople H, "The formation of composite hypotheses in diagnostic problem solving: an exercise in synthetic reasoning", *Proc. IJCAI-77,* 1977, 1020–1037
[POPL84]
Pople H, "Knowledge based expert systems: the buy or build decision", *Artifical Intelligence Applications for Business,* Reitman W (ed), Ablex, January 1984
[REIM83]
Reimer M, "Solving the phantom problem by predicative optimistic concurrency control", *Proc. 9th VLDB Conference,* Florence, 1983, 81–88.
[REIN82a]
Reiner DS, Rosenthal A, "Strategy spaces and abstract target machines for query optimization", *Database Engineering,* 5,3, September 1982, 56–60
[REIN82b]
Reiner DS, (ed.), *IEEE Database Engineering,* Special issue on Query Processing, September 1982
[REIN84]
Reiner DS, Rosenthal A, "Querying relational views of networks", this volume
[REIT78]
Reiter R, "Deductive question-answering on relational data bases", *Logic and Databases,* Gallaire H, Minker J, (eds), Plenum New York, 1978, 149–178
[RICH81]
Richard P, "Evaluation of the size of a query expressed in relational algebra", *Proc. ACM SIGMOD Conference,* Ann Arbor, 1981, 155–163
[RIES77]
Ries DR, Stonebraker M, "Effects of locking granularity in a database management system", *ACM Transations on Database Systems,* 2,3, 1977, 233–246
[RIES82]
Ries D, Chan A, Dayal U, Fox SA, Lin WTK, Yedwab L, "Decompilation, and optimization for ADAPLEX: a procedural database language", *Technical Report CCA-82-04,* Computer Corporation of America, 1982
[RIM83]
RIM User's Guide Version 6.0, Boeing Computer Services, Co., 70101-03-017, 1983, 90
[ROSE80]
Rosenkrantz DJ, Hunt MB, "Processing conjunctive predicates and queries", *Proc. 6th VLDB Conference,* Montreal, 1980, 64–74
[ROSE82a]
Rosenthal A, Reiner D, "An architecture for query optimization", *ACM SIGMOD Conference,* Orlando, 1982, 246–255
[ROSE82b]
Rosenthal A, Reiner D, "Querying relational views of networks", *IEEE-COMPSAC Conference.* 1982, 571–580
[ROSE84]
Rosenthal, A, Reiner D, "Extending the algebraic framework of query processing to handle outerjoins", *Proc. 10th VLDB Conference,* Singapore, 1984

[ROTH77a]
Rothnie JB, Goodman N, "A survey of research and development in distributed database management", *Proc. 3rd VLDB Conference*, Tokyo, 1977, 48–62.
[ROTH77b]
Rothnie JB, Goodman N, "An overview of the preliminary design of SDD-1: a system for distributed databases", *Berkeley Workshop on Distributed Data Management and Computer Networks,* Berkeley, 1977
[ROTH80]
Rothnie PA, Bernstein PA, Fox S, Goodman N, Hammer M, Landers T, Reeve C, Shipman DW, Wong E, "Introduction to a system for distributed databases (SDD-1)", *ACM Trans on Database Systems,* 5,1, March 1980, 1–17
[ROUS82a]
Roussopoulos N, "View indexing in relational databases", *ACM Transactions on Database Systems,* 7, 1982, 258–290
[ROUS82b]
Roussopoulos N, "The logical access path schema of a database", *IEEE Transactions on Software Engineering SE-8*, 6, 1982, 563–573
[ROWE79]
Rowe L, Schoens KA, "Data abstractions, views and updates in RIGEL", Proc. *ACM SIGMOD International Conference on Management of Data,* Boston, MA., May 1979, 71–81
[SACC82]
Sacco GM, Schkolnick M, "A mechanism for managing the buffer pool in a relational database system using the hot set model", *Proc. 8th VLDB Conference,* Mexico City, 1982, 257–262
[SAGI80]
Sagiv Y, Yannakakis M, "Equivalences among relational expressions with the union and difference operators", *Journal of the ACM,* 27,4, 1980, 633–655
[SAGI81a]
Sagiv Y, Delobel C, Parker DS Jr, Fagin R, "An equivalence between relational database dependencies and a fragment of propositional logic", *JACM,* 28,3, July 1981, 435–453
[SAGI81b]
Sagiv Y, *Optimization of Queries in Relational Databases,* UMI Research Press, Ann Arbor, 1981
[SANT81]
Santos CS, Maibaum TS, Furtado AL, "Conceptual modelling of data base operations", *International Journal of Computer and Information Sciences,* 10,5, 1981, 299–314
[SCHE82]
Scheck HJ, Pistor P, "Data structures for an integrated data base management and information retrieval system", *Proc. 8th VLDB Conference,* Mexico City, 1982
[SCHK75]
Schkolnik M, "The optimal selection of secondary indices for files", *Information Systems,* 1, 1975, 141–146
[SCHK77]
Schkolnick M, "A clustering algorithm for hierarchical structures", *ACM Transactions on Database Systems,* 2,1, March 1977, 27–44
[SCHK79]
Schkolnick M, Yao SB, "Physical database design", *1978 New Orleans Data Base Design Research Report,* IBM Research Report RF2554 (33154), July 1979
[SCHK79a]
Schkolnick M, Tiberio P, "Considerations in developing a design tool for a relational DBMS", *Proc. International Comp. Soft. & Appl. Conference,* Chicago, IEEE, November 1979, 228–235
[SCHK79b]
Schkolnick M, "The optimal selection of secondary indices for files", *Information Systems,* 1, March 1975, 141–146

[SCHM77]
Schmidt JW, "Some high level language constructs for data of type relation", *ACM Transactions on Database Systems,* 2,3, September 1977, 247–261
[SCHM80]
Schmidt JW, Mall M, "Pascal/R Report", *Report 66,* Fachbereich Informatik, University of Hamburg, 1980
[SCHM83]
Schmidt, JW, Mall M, "Abstraction mechanisms for database programming," *Proc. ACM SIGPLAN Symposium on Programming Languages in Software Systems, SIGPLAN Notices,* 18,6, San Francisco, 1983
[SELI79]
Selinger PG, Astrahan MM, Chamberlin DD, Lorie RA, Price TG, "Access path selection in a relational database management system", *Proc. ACM-SIGMOD Conference,* Boston, May 1979. Also available as *IBM Research Laboratory RJ2429,* San Jose, California
[SELI80]
Selinger PG, Adiba M, "Access path selection in distributed database management systems", *Proc. International Conference on Data Bases,* Deen and Hammersly (eds), University of Aberdeen, July 1980, 204–215. Also available as *IBM Research Laboratory RJ2883,* San Jose, California
[SENK69]
Senko ME et al, *File Design Handbook,* IBM San Jose Research Laboratory
[SENK73]
Senko ME, Altman EB, Astrahan MM, Feder PL, "Data structures and accessing in database systems", *IBM Syst. Journal, 12,1, 1973, 30–93*
[SEVC78]
Sevcik KC, Furtado AL, "Complete and compatible sets of update operators", *Proc. International Conference on Management of Data (ICMOD),* Milan, Italy, June 1978, 247–260
[SEVE72]
Severance DG, "Some generalized modeling structures for use in design of file organizations", *Ph. D. Dissertation,* University of Michigan, 1972
[SEVE75]
Severance DG, "A parametric model of alternative file structures", *Information Systems,* 1, 2, 1975, 51–55
[SEVE76a]
Severance DG, Duhne R, "A practitioner's guide to addressing algorithms", *Comm ACM,* 19,6, June 1976, 314–326
[SEVE76b]
Severance DG, Lohman GM, "Differential files: their application to the maintenance of large databases", *ACM Transactions on Database Systems,* 1,3, September 1976, 256–267
[SEVE77]
Severance DG, Carlis JV, "A practical guide to the selection of record access paths", *ACM Computing Surveys,* 9,4, December 1977, 259–272
[SHAW79]
Shaw, DE, "A hierarchical associative architecture for the parallel evaluation of relational algebraic database primitives", *Stanford Computer Science Department Report STAN-CS-79-778,* October 1979
[SHAW80]
Shaw, DE, "Knowledge-based retrieval on a relational database machine", *Ph. D. Dissertation,* Department of Computer Science, Stanford University, 1980
[SHAW82a]
Shaw, DE, Hillyer BK, "Allocation and manipulation of records in the NON-VON Supercomputer", *Technical Report,* Columbia University, Computer Science Department, 1982

[SHAW82b]
Shaw DE, "The NON-VON Supercomputer", *Technical Report,* Columbia Computer Science Department, August 1982
[SHIP81]
Shipman DW, "The functional data model and the data language DAPLEX", *ACM Transactions on Database Systems,* 6,1, March 1981, 140–173
[SHNE76]
Shneiderman B, Goodman V, "Batched searching of sequential and tree structured files", *ACM Transactions on Database Systems,* 1,3, September, 268–275
[SHOS82]
Shoshani A, "Statistical database: characteristics, problems and some solutions", *Proc. 8th VLDB Conference,* Mexico City, 1982, 208–222
[SILB80]
Silberschatz A, Kedem Z, "Consistency in hierarchical database systems", *Journal of the ACM,* 27,1, 1980, 72–80
[SMIT75]
Smith JM, Chang PYT, "Optimizing the performance of a relational algebra database interface", *Communications of the ACM,* 18,10, October 1975, 568–579
[SMIT77]
Smith JM, Smith DCP, "Data base abstractions: aggregation and generalization", *ACM Transactions on Database Systems,* 2,2, June 1977, 105–133
[SMIT81]
Smith JM, Bernstein PA, Dayal U, Goodman N, Landers TA, Lin KWT, Wong E, "MULTIBASE – integrating heterogeneous distributed database systems", *Proc. AFIPS National Computer Conference,* 5, 1981, 487–499
[SMIT83]
Smith RG, "STROBE: support for structured object knowledge representation", *Proc. IJCAI-83,* Karlsruhe, W. Germany, 1983
[SONG81]
Song SW, "On a high-performance VLSI solution to database problems", *Ph. D. Dissertation,* Department of Computer Science, Carnegie-Mellon University, August 1981
[SPER75]
Sperry Rand Corporation, *DMS 1100 Schema Definition: Data Administrator Reference,* 1975
[SPER81]
SPERRY UNIVAC, *Data Management System DMS 1100 Data Administrator Reference,* Sperry Corporation, UP-7907, 1981
[SQL81]
SQL/Data System, *Concepts and Facilities,* Pub. No. GH24-5013, IBM, White Plains, NY, 1981
[STAN73]
Stanford University, *Design of SPIRES: Vol I and II,* Center for Information Processing, Stanford University, 1973
[STAT81]
Statistics Canada, *RAPID Internals Manual,* Ottawa, Ontario, 1981
[STON74]
Stonebraker, M, "The choice of partial inversions and combined indices", *International Journal of Computer Information Sciences,* 3,2, 1974, 167–188
[STON75]
Stonebraker M, "Implementation of integrity constraints and views by query modification", *Proc. ACM SIGMOD Conference,* San Jose, California, 1975, 65–77
[STON76]
Stonebraker M, Wong E, Kreps P, Held G, "The design and implementation of INGRES", *ACM Transactions on Database Systems,* 1,3, September 1976, 189–222

[STON77]
Stonebraker M, "A distributed database version of INGRES", *Proc. Berkeley Workshop,* May 1977
[STON80]
Stonebraker M, "Retrospection on a data base system", *ACM Transactions on Database Systems,* 6,3, September 1980
[STON82a]
Stonebraker M, Woodfill J, Ranstrom J, Murphy M, Kalash J, Carey M, Arnold K, "Performance analysis of distributed data base systems", *Database Engineering, 5,4, IEEE Computer Society, December 1982, 58–65*
[STON82b]
Stonebraker M et al, "Document processing in a relational database system", *Report UCB/ERL M82/32,* Electronics Research Laboratory, University of California, Berkeley, 1983
[STON83]
Stonebraker M, Rubenstein B, Guttman A, "Application of abstract data types and abstract indices to CAD databases", *Report UCB/ERL M83/3,* Electronics Research Laboratory, University of California, Berkeley, 1983
[SU75]
Su S, Lipovski G, "CASSM: a cellular system for very large databases", *Proc. 1st VLDB Conference,* 1975
[SU79]
Su S, "Cellular logic devices: concepts and applications", *IEEE Computer 12,* 1979, 11–25
[SUZU83]
Suzuki S, Imai H, "On optimum partition of a query set into subsets having the consecutive retrieval property", in [GHOS83a]
[TANA78]
Tanaka K, Le Viet C, Kamabyashi Y, Yajima S, "A file organization suitable for relational database operations", *Lecture Notes in Computer Science 75,* Springer-Verlag, August 1978, 193–227
[TANA79]
Tanaka K, Kambayashi Y, Yajima S, "Organization of quasi-consecutive retrieval files", *Information Systems,* 4, 1979, 23–33
[TANA83]
Tanaka K, "Tree-structured data organization with consecutive retrieval property", in [GHOS83a]
[TEOR78]
Teorey TJ, Oberlander LB, "Network database evaluation using analytical modelling", *Proc. National Computer Conference, 47,* AFIPS, Anaheim, California, 1978
[TEOR82]
Teorey TJ, Fry JP, *Design of Database Structures,* Prentice Hall Inc., Englewood Cliffs, N.J., 1982
[TRUS83]
Truszczynski M, "On admissible families of sets", in [GHOS83a.]
[TSIC77a]
Tsichritzis D, Klug AC, "ANSI/SPARC DBMS Framework", *Report of the Study Group on Data Base Management Systems,* AFIPS Press, Arlington, VA, 1977
[TSIC77b]
Tsichritzis D, Lochovsky F, *Data Base Management Systems,* Academic Press, New York, 1977
[TSIC82]
Tsichritzis D, Lochovsky F, *Data Models,* Prentice Hall, Inc., Engelwood Cliffs, NJ, 1982
[TUCH83]
Tuchermann L, Furtado AL, Casanova MA, "A pragmatic approach to structured database design", *Proc 9th VLDB Conference,* Florence, October 1983, 219–231.
[TURN79]
Turner MJ, Hammond R, Cotton P, "A DBMS for large statistical databases", *Proc VLDB Conference,* 1979, 319–327.

[ULLM82]
Ullman JD, *Principles of Database Systems, Second Ed.*, Computer Science Press, 1982.
[USLB80]
Bureau of Labor Statistics, *Table Producing Language System Version 5,* Washington D.C., July 1980
[VALD84]
Valduriez P, Gardarin G, "Join and semi-join algorithms for a multiprocessor database machine", *ACM Transactions on Database Systems,* 9, 1984, 133–161
[VANA51]
van Aardenne-Ehrenfest T, de Bruijn NG, "Circuits and trees in oriented graphs", *Simon Stevin*, 28, 1951, 203–217
[VANM79]
van Melle W, "A domain-independent production rule system for consultation programs", *Proc. 6th International Joint Conference Artificial Intelligence*, 1979
[VASS80]
Vassiliou Y, Lochovsky F, "DBMS transaction translation", *Proc. COMPSAC IEEE,* 1980, 89–96
[VASS83]
Vassiliou Y, Clifford J, Jarke M, "How does an expert system get its data?", *Proc. 9th VLDB Conference*, Florence, October 1983, 70–72
[VASS85]
Vassiliou Y, Clifford J, Jarke M, "Database access requirements of knowledge-based systems", this volume
[VSAM]
IBM Corporation, *Virtual Sequential Access Method,* IBM Form No. GC26–3838.
[WAKS74]
Waksman A, Green MW, "On the consecutive retrieval property in file organization", *IEEE Transactions on Computers, C–27,* 1974, 173–174
[WARR81]
Warren DHD, "Efficient processing of interactive relational data base queries expressed in logic", *Proc. 7th VLDB Conference,* Cannes, 1981, 171–283
[WATE79]
Waterman D, Hayes-Roth F, (eds), *Pattern Directed Inference Systems,* Academic Press, 1979
[WHAN81]
Whang KY, Widerhold G, Sagalowicz D, "Separability – an approach to physical database design", *Proc. VLDB Conference*, 1981, 320–332
[WHAN82]
Whang K, Wiederhold G, Sagalowicz D, " Physical design of network model databases using the property of separability", *Proc. 8th VLDB Conference,* Mexico City, 1982, 98–107
[WHAN83a]
Whang K,"A physical database design methodology using the property of separability". *Ph. D. Dissertation,* Stanford University, Stanford CA, Rep. STAN-CS-83-968, 1983
[WHAN83b]
Whang K, Wiederhold G, Sagalowicz D, "Estimating block accesses in database organizations – a closed noniterative formula", *Commun. ACM,* 26,11, 1983, 940–944
[WHAN84a]
Whang K, Wiederhold G, Saglowicz D, "Separability - an approach to physical database design", *IEEE Transactions on Computers,* C-33,3, 1984
[WHAN84b]
Whang K, "The property of separability in physical design of network model databases," *Information Systems,* 9,4
[WIED79]
Wiederhold G, El-Masri R, "The structural model for database design", *Proc. International Conference on Entity Relationship Approach,* Los Angeles, Calif., 1979, 247–267

[WIED83]
Wiederhold G, *Database Design,* McGraw-Hill Book Company, New York, Second Edition, 1983

[WILL81]
Williams R, et al, "R*: an overview of the architecture", *IBM Research Report RJ3325,* San Jose, California, 1981

[WILL82]
Williams R, Daniels D, Haas L, Lapis G, Lindsay B, Ng P, Obermark R, Selinger P, Walker A, Wilms P, Yost R, "R*: An overview of the architecture", *Proc. International Conference on Databases: Improving Database Usability and Responsiveness,* Jerusalem, Scheuermann P, (ed), Academic Press, New York, 1982, 1–27. Also available as IBM Research Laboratory RJ3325, San Jose, California

[WILM81]
Wilms PF, Lindsay BG, "A database authorization mechanism supporting individual and group authorization", *Distributed Data Sharing Systems,* van de Riet and Litwin (eds), North Holland, May 1981, Also availabe as *IBM Research Report RJ3137*

[WILM83]
Wilms PF, Lindsay BG, Selinger PG, "'I wish I were over there': distributed execution protocols for data definition in R*, *Proc. ACM-SIGMOD,* San Jose, California, May 1983, 238–244. Also available as *IBM Research Laboratory, RJ3892, San Jose, California*

[WISE83]
Wise T, "A technique to model and design physical database structures", *M. Sc. Thesis,* Department of Computer and Information Sciences, University of Florida, 1983

[WONG76]
Wong E, Youssefi K, "Decomposition – a strategy for query processing", *ACM Transactions on Database Systems,* 1, 3, September 1976, 223–241

[WONG77a]
Wong HK, Mylopoulos J, "Two views on data semantics: data models in artificial intelligence and database management", *INFOR,F 15,3* 1976

[WONG77b]
Wong E, "Retrieving dispersed data from SDD-1: a system for distributed databases", *Berkeley Workshop on Distributed Data Management and Computer Networks,* Berkeley, 1977

[WONG81]
Wong E, "Dynamic rematerialization: processing distributed queries using redundant data", *Berkeley Workshop on Distributed Data Management and Computer Networks,* Berkeley, 1981. *Also in IEEE TOSE, May 1983*

[WONG83]
Wong E, Katz R, "Distributing a database for parallelism", *Proc. ACM SIGMOND,* 1983, 23–29

[YAMA77]
Yamamoto S, Usio K, Ikeda H, Tamari F, Hamada N, "Partition of a query set into minimal number of subsets having consecutive retrieval property", *J. Stat. Plann Inference,* 1, 1977, 41–51

[YAO77a]
YAO SB, "An attribute-based model for database access cost analysis", *ACM Transactions on Database Systems,* 2,1, March 1977, 45–67

[YAO77b]
Yao SB, "Approximating block access in database organizations", *Communications ACM,* 20, April 1977, 260–261

[YAO79]
Yao SB, "Optimization of query evaluation algorithms", *ACM Trans Database Systems,* 4,2, June 1979, 133–155

[YOUS79]
Youssefi K, Wong E , "Query processing in a relational database management system", *Proceedings 5th VLDB Conference,* Rio de Janeiro, 1979, 409–417

[YU79a]
Yu CT, Lam K, Ozsoyoglu M, "Distributed query optimization for tree queries", Dept. of Information Engineering, University of Illinois at Chicago Circle, October 1979
[YU79b]
Yu CT, Ozsoyoglu MZ, "An algorithm for tree-query membership of a distributed query", *IEEE COMPSAC,* Chicago, November 1979, 306–312
[YU82a]
Yu CT, Lam K, Chang CC, Chang SK, "Promising approach to distributed query processing", *Berkeley Workshop on Distributed Data Management and Computer Networks,* Berkeley, 1982, 363–390
[YU82b]
Yu CT, Chang CC, Chang YC, "Two surprising results in processing simple queries in distributed databases", *IEEE COMPSAC,* November 1982
[YU83]
Yu, CT, Chang CC, "On the design of a query processing strategy in a distributed database environment", *Proc. ACM SIGMOD Conference,* San Jose, 1983, 30–39
[YUE75]
Yue PC, Wong CK, "Storage cost consideration in secondary index selection", *International Journal of Computer and Information Sciences,* 4,4, 1975
[ZANI79]
Zaniolo C, "Design of relational views over network schemas", *Proc. ACM SIGMOD Conference,* 1979, 179–190
[ZLOO77]
Zloof MM, "Query-by example: a data base language", *IBM System Journal,* 16,4, 1977, 324–343

List of Authors

Don S. Batory
Dept. of Computer Science
The University of Texas at Austin
Austin, TX 78712
USA

Marco A. Casanova
Centro Cientifico de Brasilia
IBM do Brasil
Brasilia
Brasil

Jim Clifford
Graduate School of
Business Administration
New York University
90 Trinity Place
New York, NY 10006
USA

Dean Daniels
Carnegie-Mellon University
Pittsburgh, PA 15213
USA

Umeshwar Dayal
Computer Corporation of America
Four Cambridge Center
Cambridge, MA 02142
USA

Anthony L. Furtado
Departamento de Informatica
PUC/RJ
Rio de Janeiro
Brasil

Sakti P. Ghosh
IBM Research Laboratory
San Jose, CA 95193
USA

Laura M. Haas
IBM Research Laboratory
San Jose, CA 95193
USA

Matthias Jarke
Graduate School of
Business Administration
New York University
90 Trinity Place
New York, NY 10006
USA

Yahiko Kambayashi
Dept. of Computer Science and
Communication Engineering
Kyushu University
Hakozaki, Higashi, Fukuoka, 812
Japan

Won Kim
MCC – Microelectronics &
Computer Technology Corporation
9430 Research Blvd.
Austin, TX 78759
USA

Jürgen Koch
Fachbereich Informatik
Johann Wolfgang Goethe Universität
Dantestraße 9
D-6000 Frankfurt 1
West Germany

Bruce G. Lindsay
IBM Research Laboratory
San Jose, CA 95193
USA

Guy M. Lohman
IBM Research Laboratory
San Jose, CA 95193
USA

Raymond Lorie
IBM Research Laboratory
San Jose, CA 95193
USA

Salvatore T. March
University of Minnesota
Minneapolis, MN 55455
USA

Dan McNabb
IBM Research Laboratory
San Jose, CA 95193
USA

Andreas Meier
IBM Research Laboratory
San Jose, CA 95193
USA

Present Address for Meier:
Institut für Informatik
ETH Zürich
CH-Zürich
Switzerland

C. Mohan
IBM Research Laboratory
San Jose, CA 95193
USA

Gultekin Ozsoyoglu
Department of Computer
Engineering and Science
Case Western Reserve University
Cleveland, OH 44106
USA

Z. Meral Ozsoyoglu
Department of Computer
Engineering and Science
Case Western Reserve University
Cleveland, OH 44106
USA

Wil Plouffe
IBM Research Laboratory
San Jose, CA 95193
USA

David S. Reiner
Computer Corporation of America
Four Cambridge Center
Cambridge, MA 02142
USA

Arnon Rosenthal
Computer Corporation of America
Four Cambridge Center
Cambridge, MA 02142
USA

Daniel Sagalowicz
Framentec
Monaco

Joachim W. Schmidt
Fachbereich Informatik
Johann Wolfgang Goethe Universität
Dantestraße 9
D-6000 Frankfurt 1
West Germany

Patricia G. Selinger
IBM Research Laboratory
San Jose, CA 95193
USA

David Elliot Shaw
Dept. of Computer Science
Columbia University
New York, NY 10027
USA

Michael Ubell
Britton-Lee, Inc.
14600 Winchester Boulevard
Los Gatos, CA 95030
USA

Yannis Vassiliou
Graduate School of
Business Administration
New York University
90 Trinity Place
New York, NY 10006
USA

Kyu-Young Whang
IBM T. J. Watson Research Center
Yorktown Heights, NY 10598
USA

Gio Wiederhold
Stanford University
Computer Science &
Electrical Engineering
Margaret Jacks Hall
Stanford, CA 94305
USA

Paul F. Wilms
IBM Research Laboratory
San Jose, CA 95193
USA

C. T. Yu
Dept. of Electrical Engineering and
Computer Science
University of Illinois at Chicago
Chicago, Il 60680
USA

Subject Index

Relational Database Systems

Analysis and Comparison

Editors: **J.W. Schmidt, M.L. Brodie**

1983. XV, 618 pages. ISBN 3-540-12032-7

Contents: Introduction. - Features of Relational Database Systems. - Analysis of Relational Database Management Systems. - Feature Summaries and Comparisons. - References.

The book is the most comprehensive and detailed analysis of existing relational database management systems to date. It presents a generic characterization of an RDBMS (independently of specific RDBMSs) in terms of:

- relational database constituents
- relational functional capabilities
- definition, generation and administration facilities
- interfaces and DBMS architecture
- operational aspects

These features are then used as a common basis to analyze fourteen of the most important existing RDBMSs. The fourteen systems analyses are then compared, in a tabular format, with respect to the features, and system feature summaries are presented.

The book is introduced by a foreword written by Dr. E. F. Codd, the inventor of the relational approach to databases.

The book is intended to assist the reader in developing a detailed understanding of the Relational Data Model, Relational Database Management Systems, and the state-of-the-art in relational DBMS technology. It provides a comprehensive check list of features with which to evaluate RDBMSs or DBMSs in general.